SEVEN SEAS ENTERTAINMENT PRESENTS

HOW *NOT* TO SUMMON A VOLUME 2 DEMON LORD

story by **YUKIYA MURASAKI** art by **NAOTO FUKUDA**

TRANSLATION
Garrison Denim

ADAPTATION
Lora Gray

LETTERING AND RETOUCH
Charles Pritchett

COVER DESIGN
KC Fabellon

PROOFREADER
Stephanie Cohen

EDITOR
Shannon Fay

PRODUCTION ASSISTANT
CK Russell

PRODUCTION MANAGER
Lissa Pattillo

EDITOR-IN-CHIEF
Adam Arnold

PUBLISHER
Jason DeAngelis

HOW NOT TO SUMMON A DEMON LORD VOLUME 2
© Yukiya Murasaki 2016, © Naoto Fukuda 2016, © Takahiro Tsurusaki 2016
All rights reserved.
First published in Japan in 2016 by Kodansha Ltd., Tokyo.
Publication rights for this English edition arranged through Kodansha Ltd.,
Tokyo.

Seven Seas books may be purchased in bulk for promotional, educational, or
business use. Please contact your local bookseller or the Macmillan Corporate
and Premium Sales Department at 1-800-221-7945, extension 5442, or by
e-mail at MacmillanSpecialMarkets@macmillan.com.

Seven Seas and the Seven Seas logo are trademarks of
Seven Seas Entertainment, LLC. All rights reserved.

ISBN: 978-1-626928-65-7

Printed in Canada

First Printing: October 2018

10 9 8 7 6 5 4 3 2 1

FOLLOW US ONLINE: w

READING DIRECTIONS

This book reads from *right to left*, Japanese style.
If this is your first time reading manga,
reading from the top right panel on each
take it from there. If you get lost, just
numbered diagram here. It may seem ba
first, but you'll get the hang of it! Have f

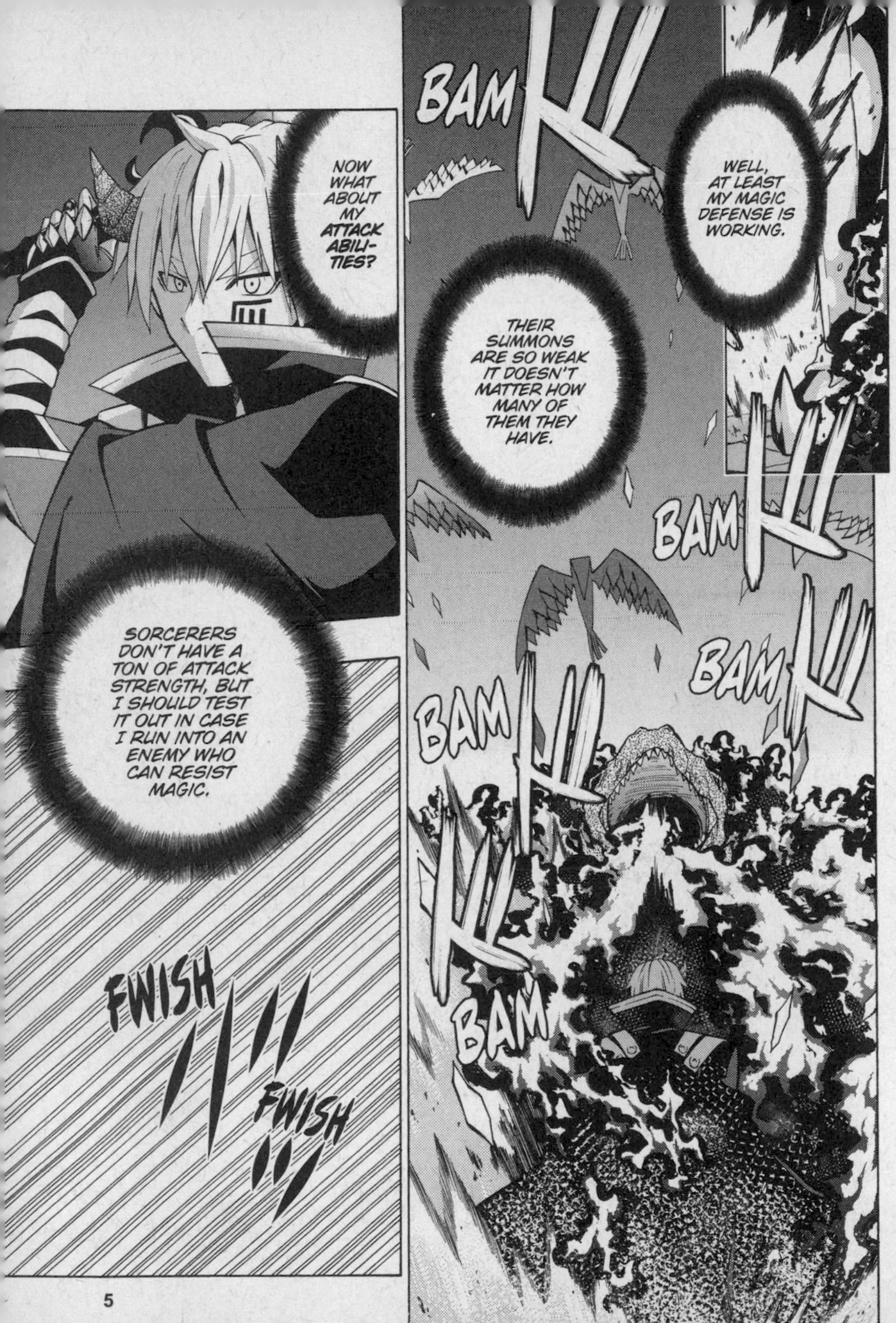
BAM
WELL, AT LEAST MY MAGIC DEFENSE IS WORKING.
THEIR SUMMONS ARE SO WEAK IT DOESN'T MATTER HOW MANY OF THEM THEY HAVE.
BAM
BAM
BAM
BAM
NOW WHAT ABOUT MY ATTACK ABILI-TIES?
SORCERERS DON'T HAVE A TON OF ATTACK STRENGTH, BUT I SHOULD TEST IT OUT IN CASE I RUN INTO AN ENEMY WHO CAN RESIST MAGIC.
FWISH
FWISH

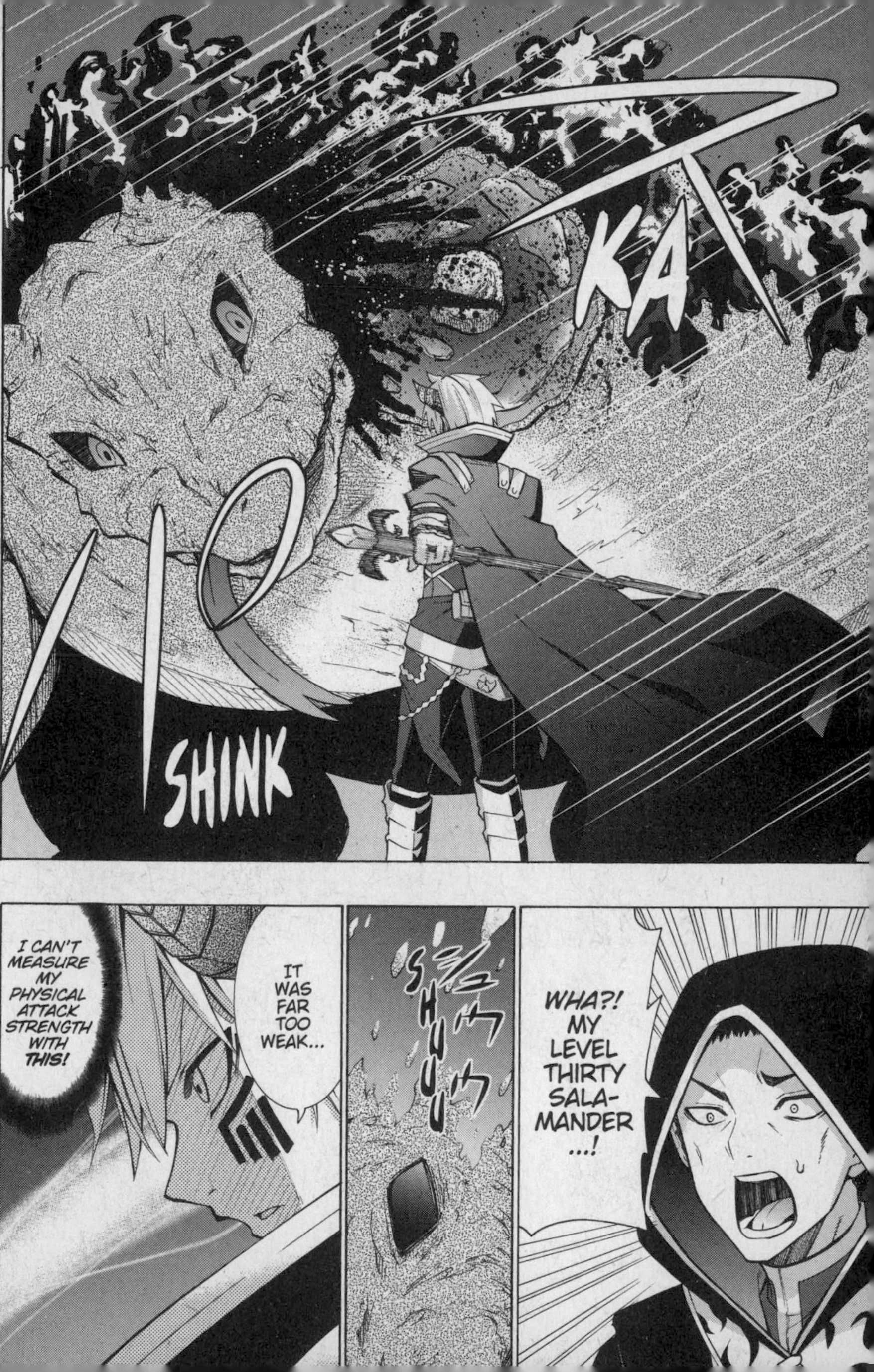
KA
SHINK
WHA?! MY LEVEL THIRTY SALAMANDER...!
SHUUU
IT WAS FAR TOO WEAK...
I CAN'T MEASURE MY PHYSICAL ATTACK STRENGTH WITH THIS!

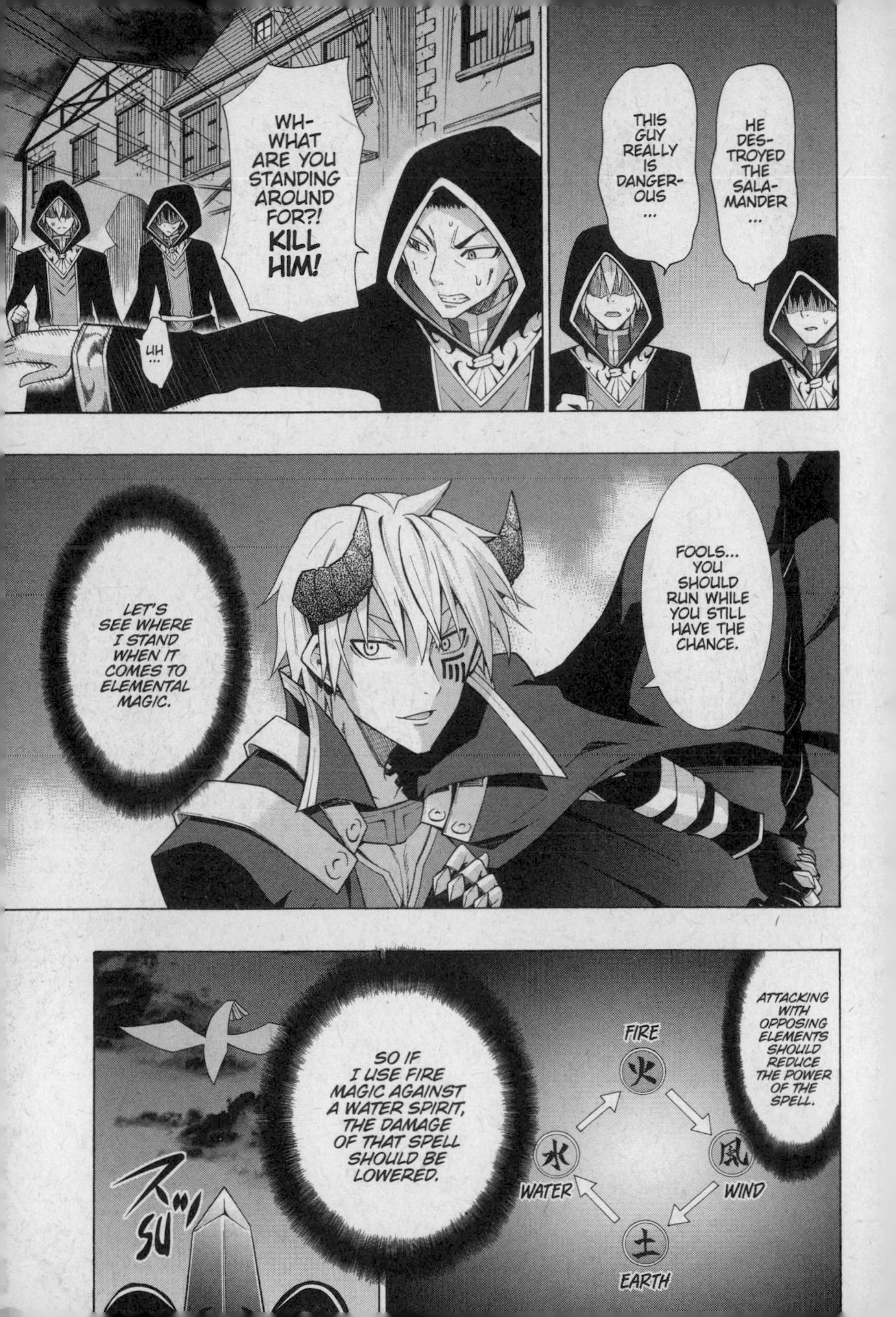
HE DESTROYED THE SALAMANDER...
THIS GUY REALLY IS DANGEROUS...
WH-WHAT ARE YOU STANDING AROUND FOR?! KILL HIM!
UH...
FOOLS... YOU SHOULD RUN WHILE YOU STILL HAVE THE CHANCE.
LET'S SEE WHERE I STAND WHEN IT COMES TO ELEMENTAL MAGIC.
ATTACKING WITH OPPOSING ELEMENTS SHOULD REDUCE THE POWER OF THE SPELL.
FIRE
火
風
WIND
土
EARTH
水
WATER
SO IF I USE FIRE MAGIC AGAINST A WATER SPIRIT, THE DAMAGE OF THAT SPELL SHOULD BE LOWERED.
スッ
SU

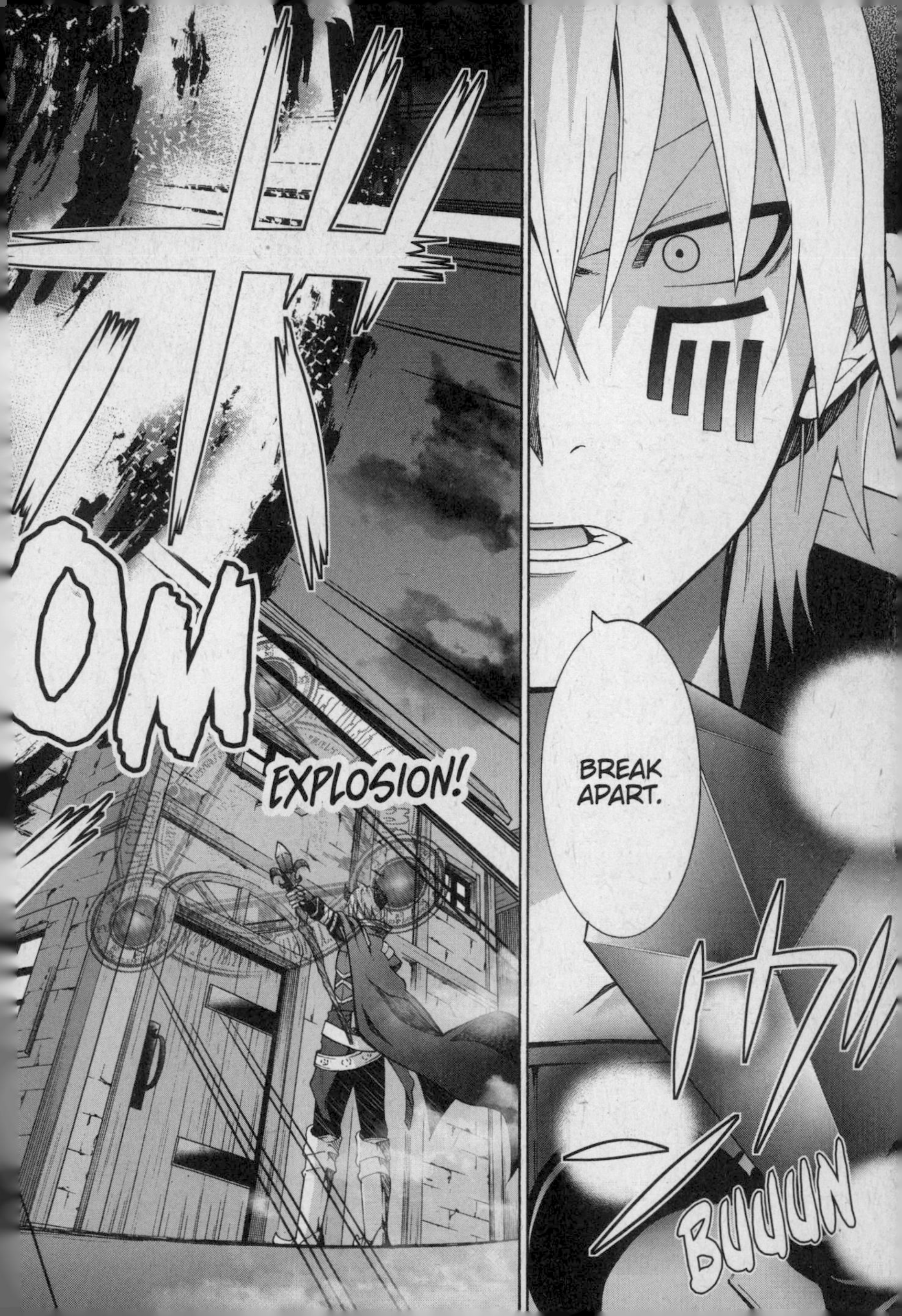
BREAK APART.
BUUUN
OM
EXPLOSION!

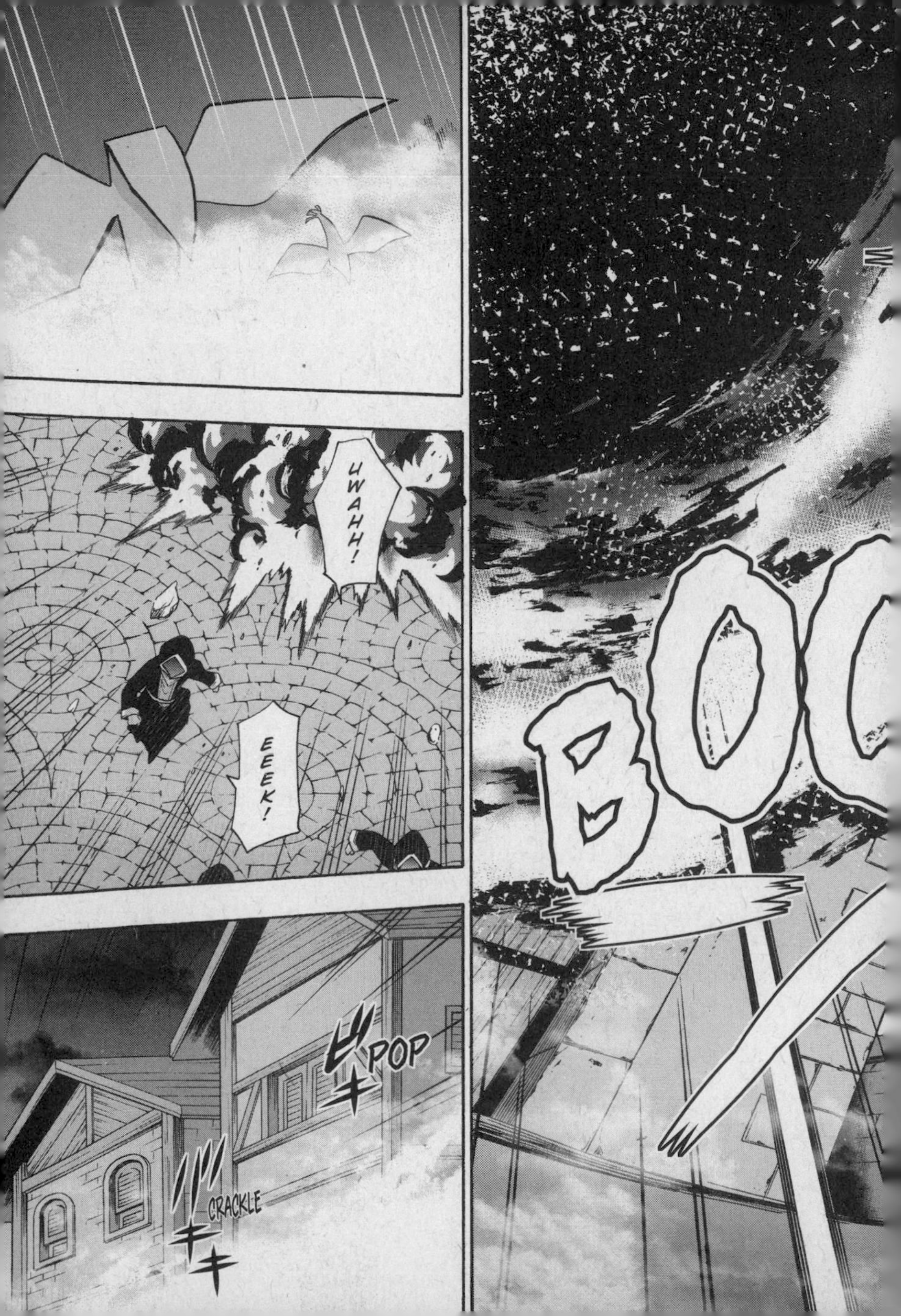
BOO
UWAHH!
EEEK!
POP
CRACKLE

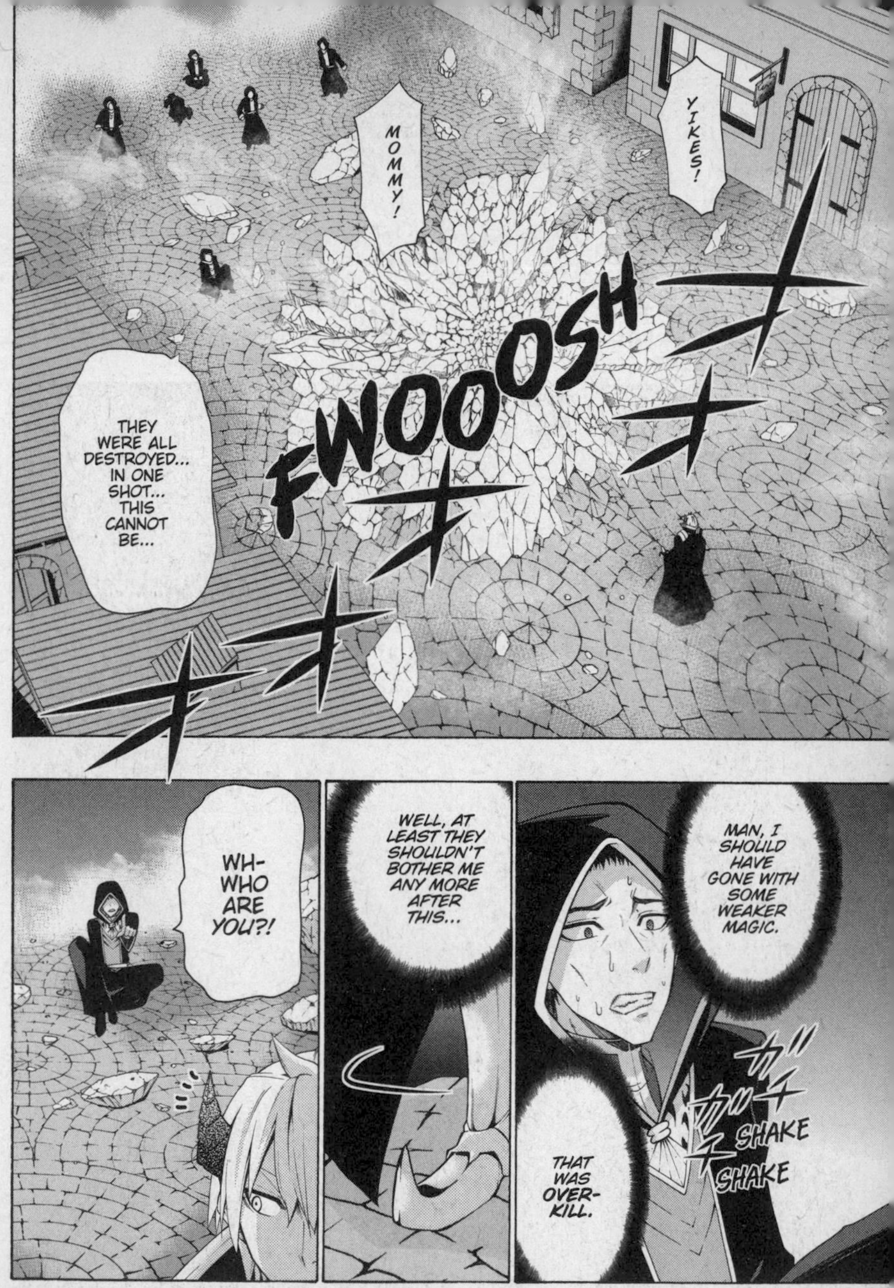
YIKES!
MOMMY!
FWOOOSH
THEY WERE ALL DESTROYED... IN ONE SHOT... THIS CANNOT BE...
MAN, I SHOULD HAVE GONE WITH SOME WEAKER MAGIC.
SHAKE SHAKE
THAT WAS OVER-KILL.
WELL, AT LEAST THEY SHOULDN'T BOTHER ME ANY MORE AFTER THIS...
WH-WHO ARE YOU?!

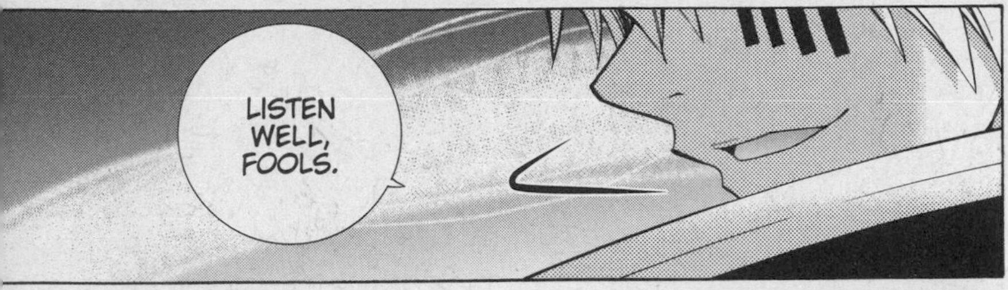
LISTEN WELL, FOOLS.
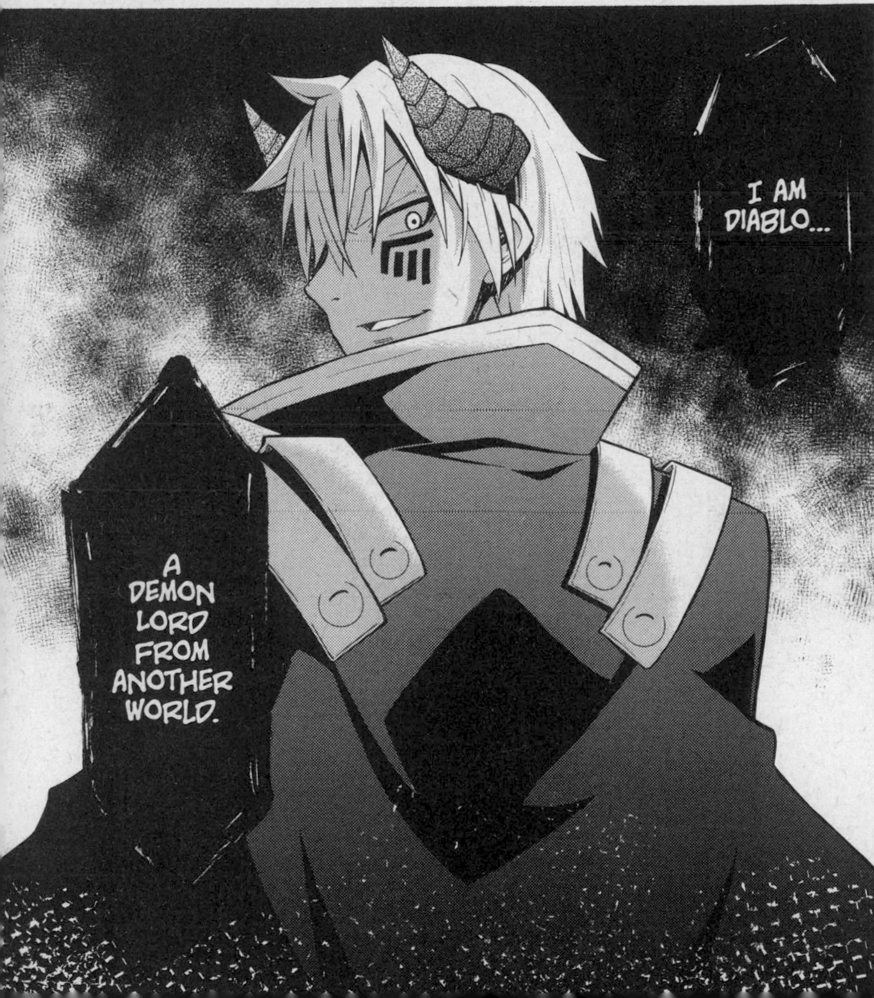
I AM DIABLO...
A DEMON LORD FROM ANOTHER WORLD.

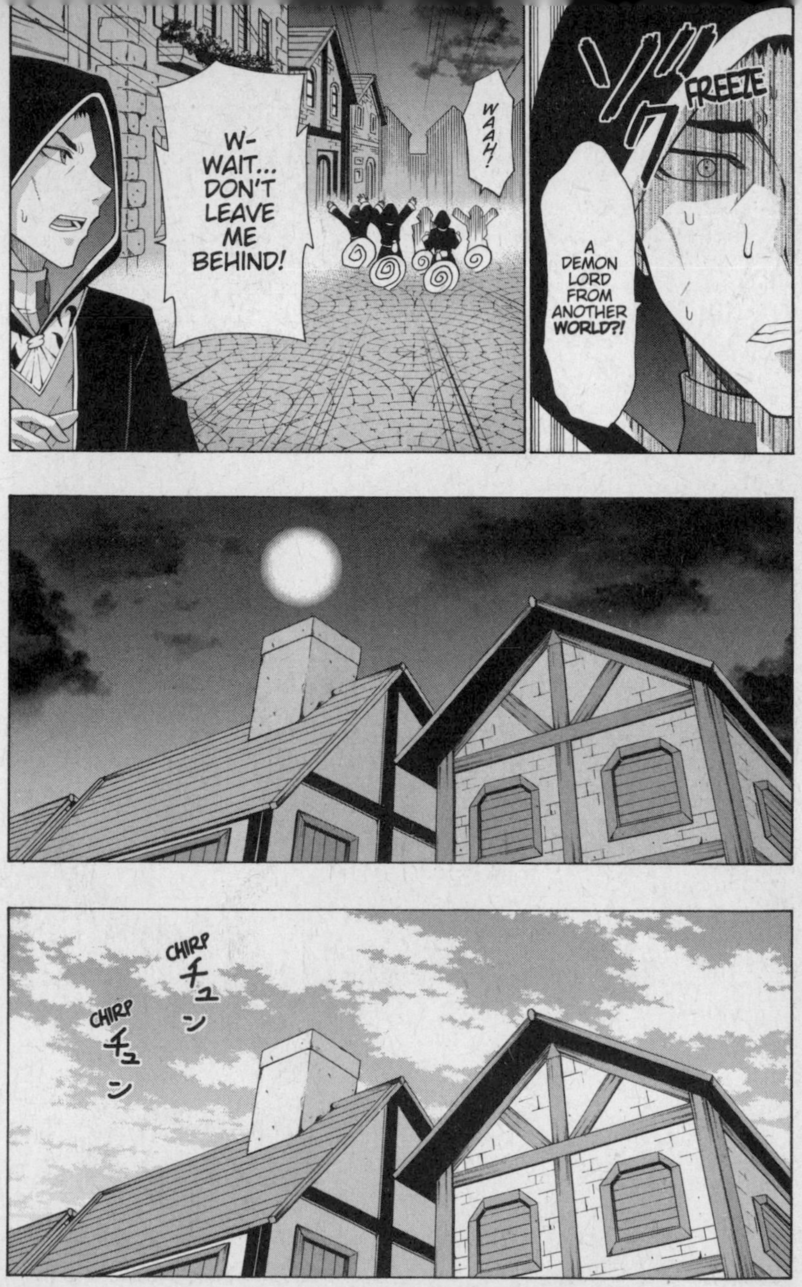
FREEZE
A DEMON LORD FROM ANOTHER WORLD?!
WAAH!
W-WAIT... DON'T LEAVE ME BEHIND!
CHIRP
チュン
CHIRP
チュン

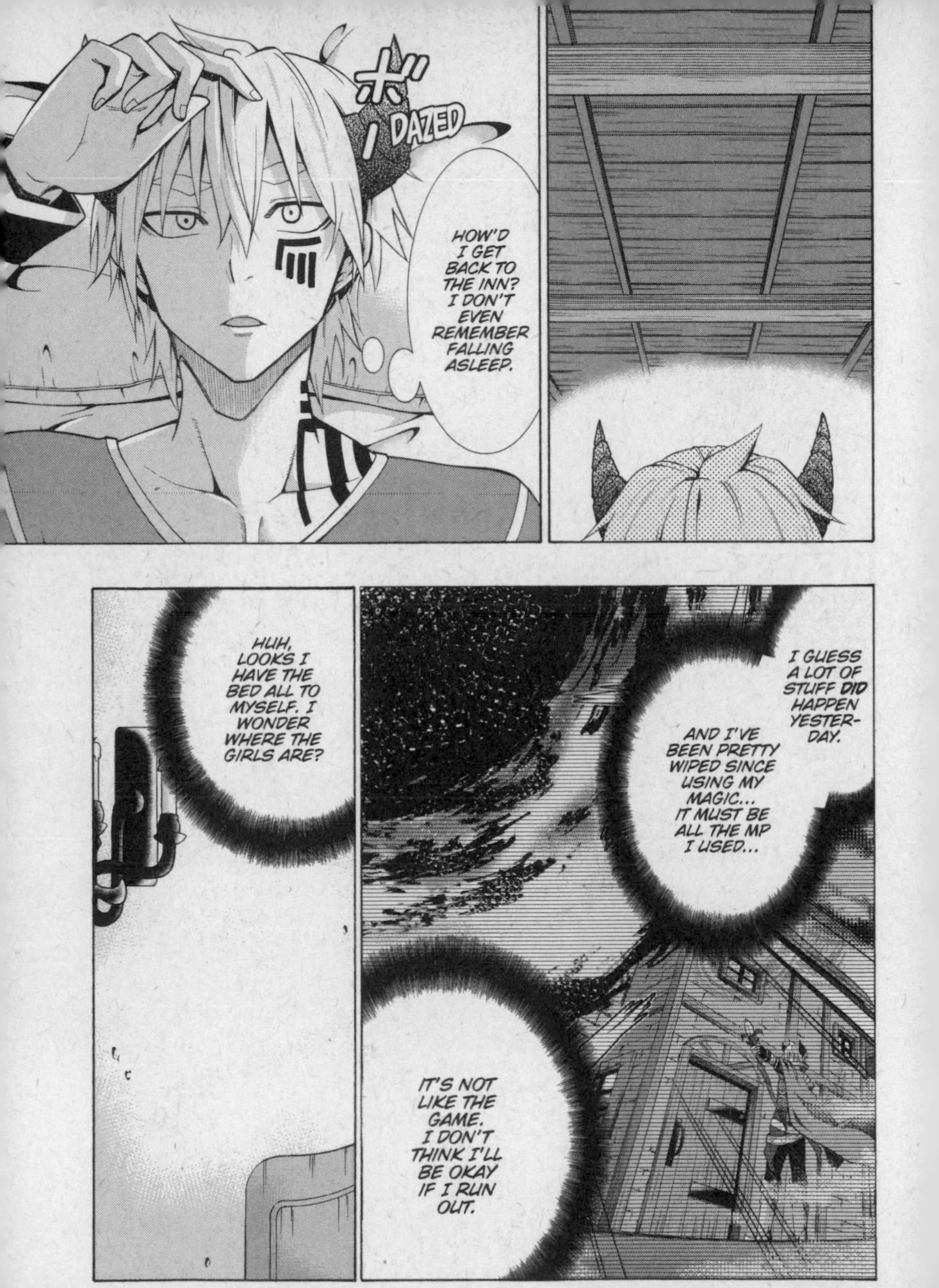
DAZED
HOW'D I GET BACK TO THE INN? I DON'T EVEN REMEMBER FALLING ASLEEP.
I GUESS A LOT OF STUFF DID HAPPEN YESTERDAY.
AND I'VE BEEN PRETTY WIPED SINCE USING MY MAGIC... IT MUST BE ALL THE MP I USED...
IT'S NOT LIKE THE GAME. I DON'T THINK I'LL BE OKAY IF I RUN OUT.
HUH, LOOKS I HAVE THE BED ALL TO MYSELF. I WONDER WHERE THE GIRLS ARE?

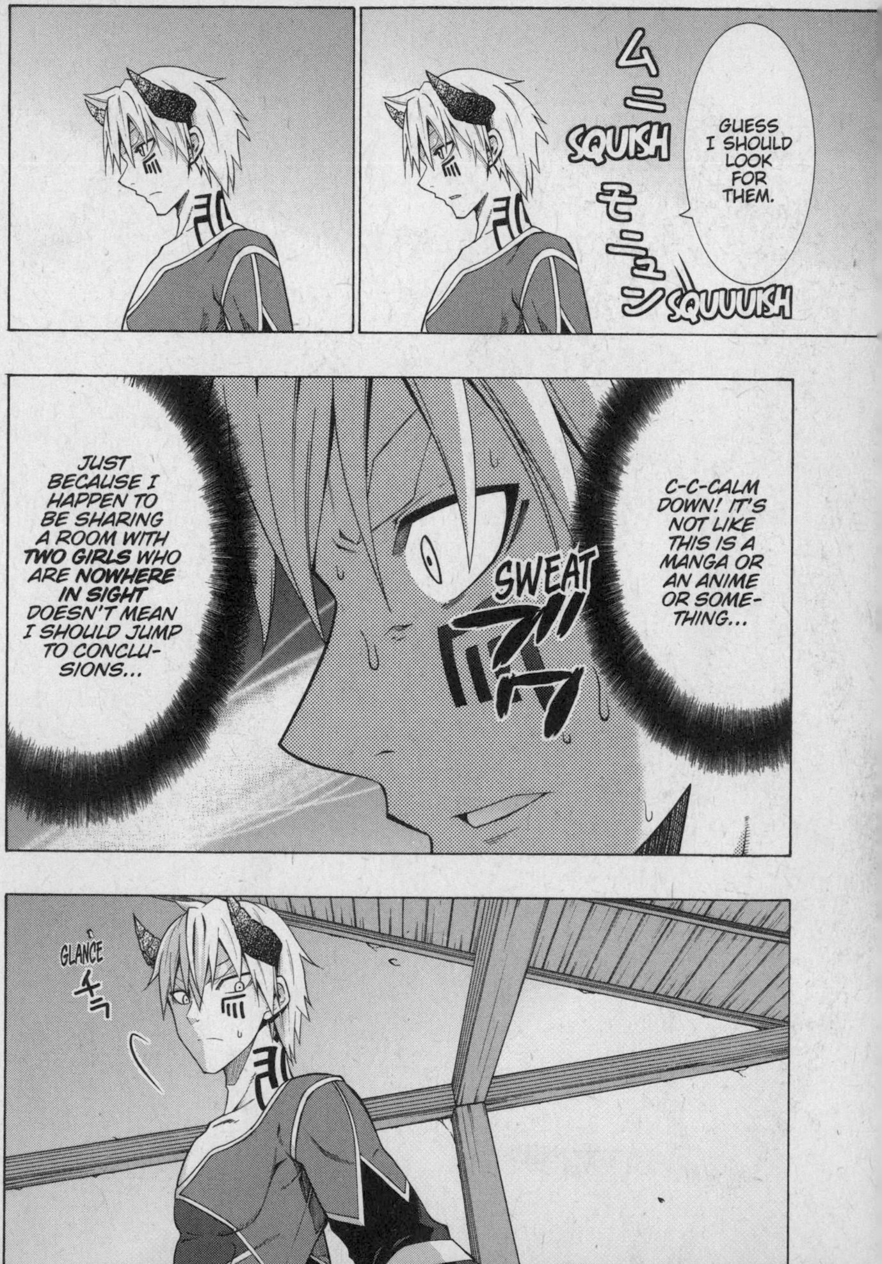
GUESS I SHOULD LOOK FOR THEM.
ムニ
SQUISH
モニュン
SQUUUISH
C-C-CALM DOWN! IT'S NOT LIKE THIS IS A MANGA OR AN ANIME OR SOME-THING...
SWEAT
JUST BECAUSE I HAPPEN TO BE SHARING A ROOM WITH TWO GIRLS WHO ARE NOWHERE IN SIGHT DOESN'T MEAN I SHOULD JUMP TO CONCLU-SIONS...
GLANCE

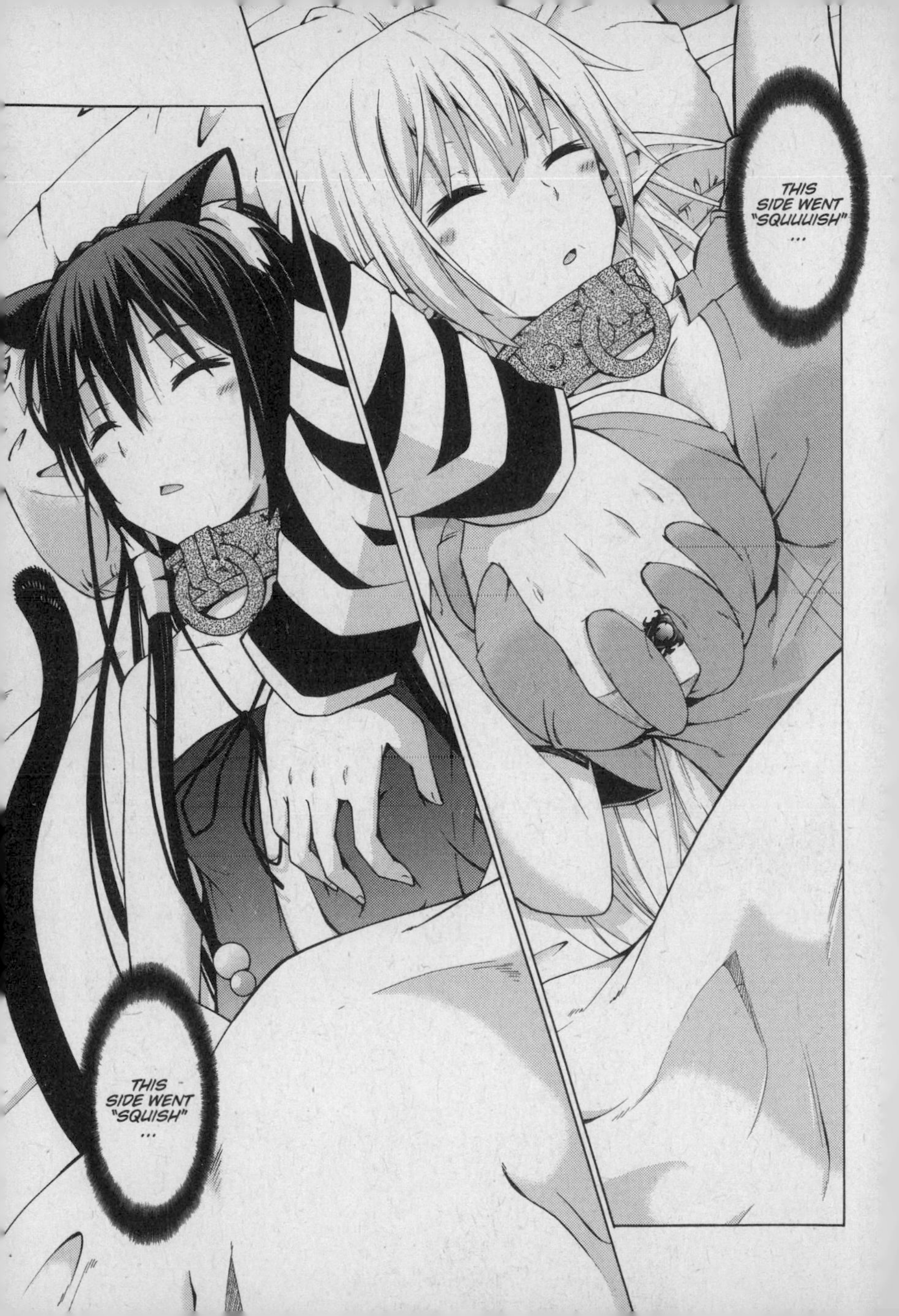
THIS SIDE WENT "SQUUUISH" ...
THIS SIDE WENT "SQUISH" ...

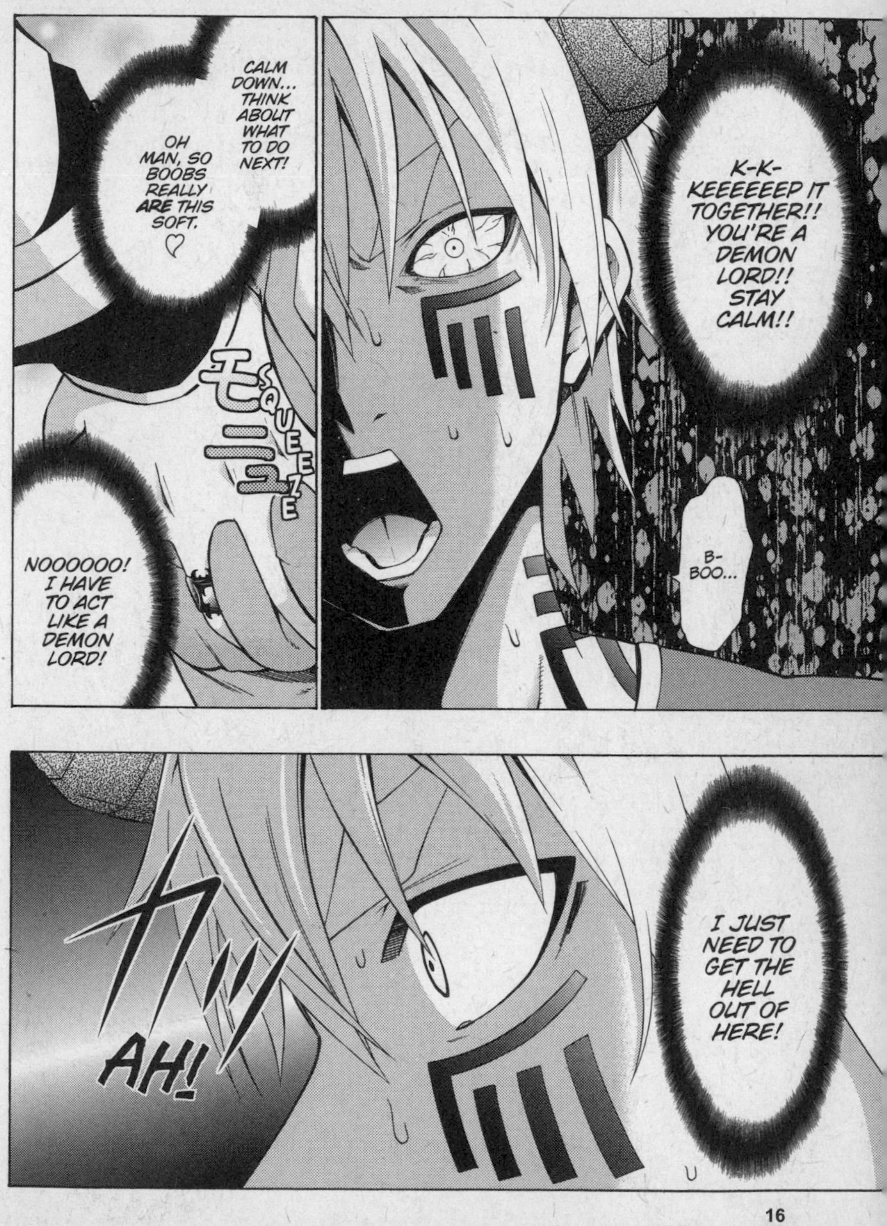
K-K-KEEEEEEP IT TOGETHER!! YOU'RE A DEMON LORD!! STAY CALM!!
B-BOO...
CALM DOWN... THINK ABOUT WHAT TO DO NEXT!
OH MAN, SO BOOBS REALLY ARE THIS SOFT. ♡
SQUEEZE
NOOOOOO! I HAVE TO ACT LIKE A DEMON LORD!
I JUST NEED TO GET THE HELL OUT OF HERE!
AH!

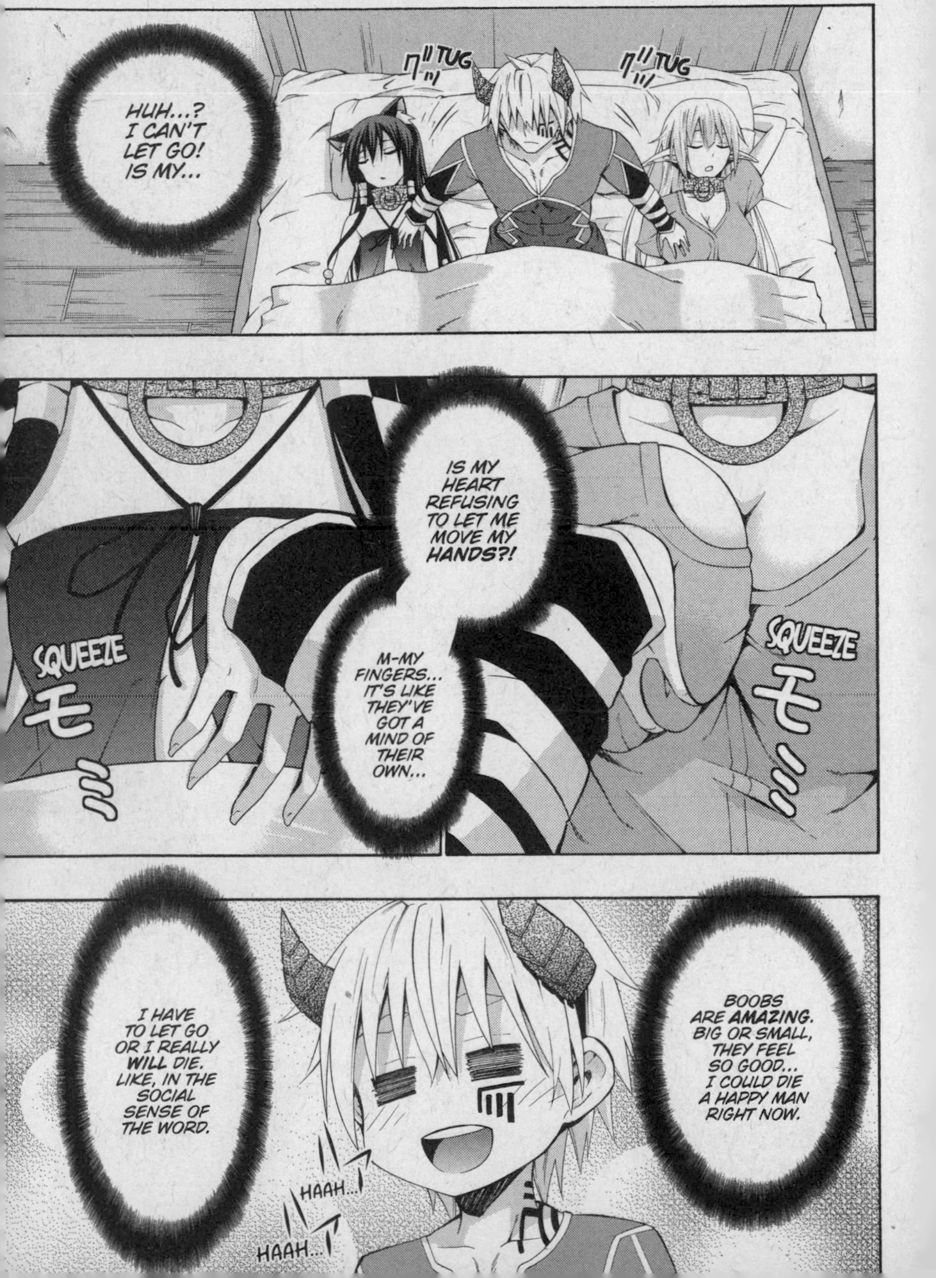
TUG
TUG
HUH...? I CAN'T LET GO! IS MY...
IS MY HEART REFUSING TO LET ME MOVE MY HANDS?!
SQUEEZE
M-MY FINGERS... IT'S LIKE THEY'VE GOT A MIND OF THEIR OWN...
SQUEEZE
BOOBS ARE AMAZING. BIG OR SMALL, THEY FEEL SO GOOD... I COULD DIE A HAPPY MAN RIGHT NOW.
I HAVE TO LET GO OR I REALLY WILL DIE. LIKE, IN THE SOCIAL SENSE OF THE WORD.
HAAH...
HAAH...

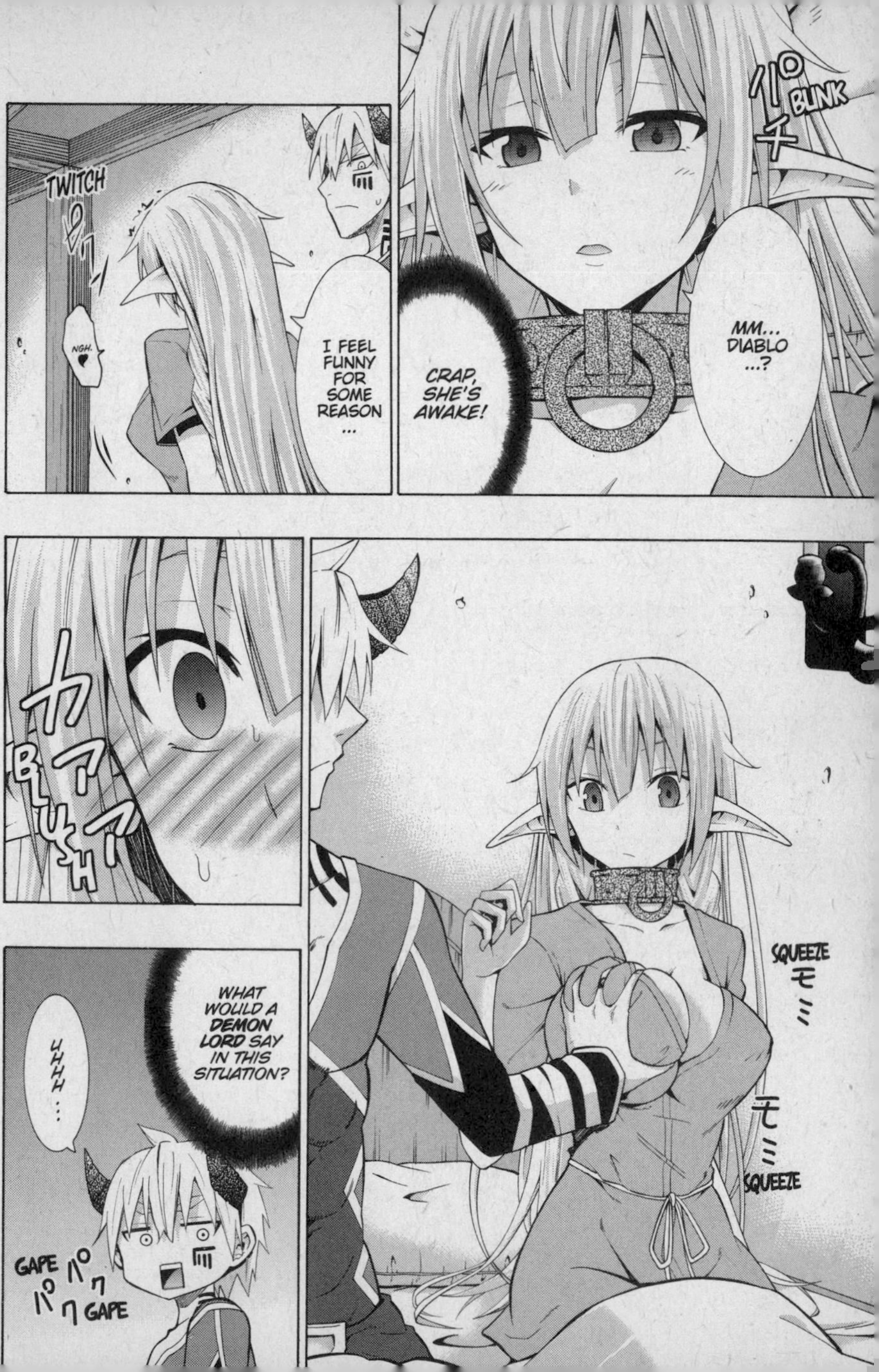
BLINK
MM... DIABLO ...?
CRAP, SHE'S AWAKE!
TWITCH
NGH.
I FEEL FUNNY FOR SOME REASON ...
SQUEEZE
SQUEEZE
BLUSH
WHAT WOULD A DEMON LORD SAY IN THIS SITUATION?
UHHH...
GAPE GAPE

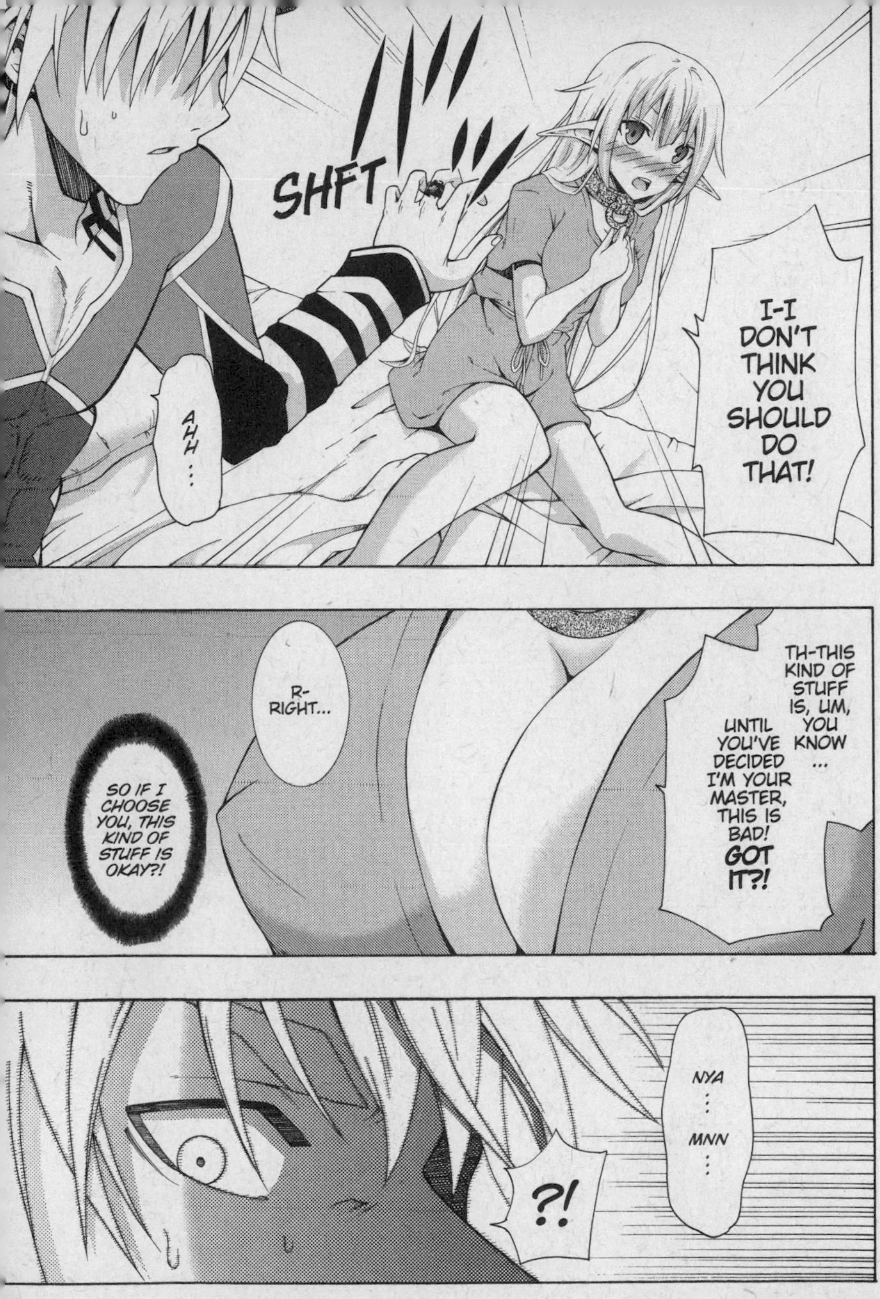
I-I DON'T THINK YOU SHOULD DO THAT!
SHFT
AHH...
TH-THIS KIND OF STUFF IS, UM, YOU KNOW...
UNTIL YOU'VE DECIDED I'M YOUR MASTER, THIS IS BAD! GOT IT?!
R-RIGHT...
SO IF I CHOOSE YOU, THIS KIND OF STUFF IS OKAY?!
NYA... MNN...
?!

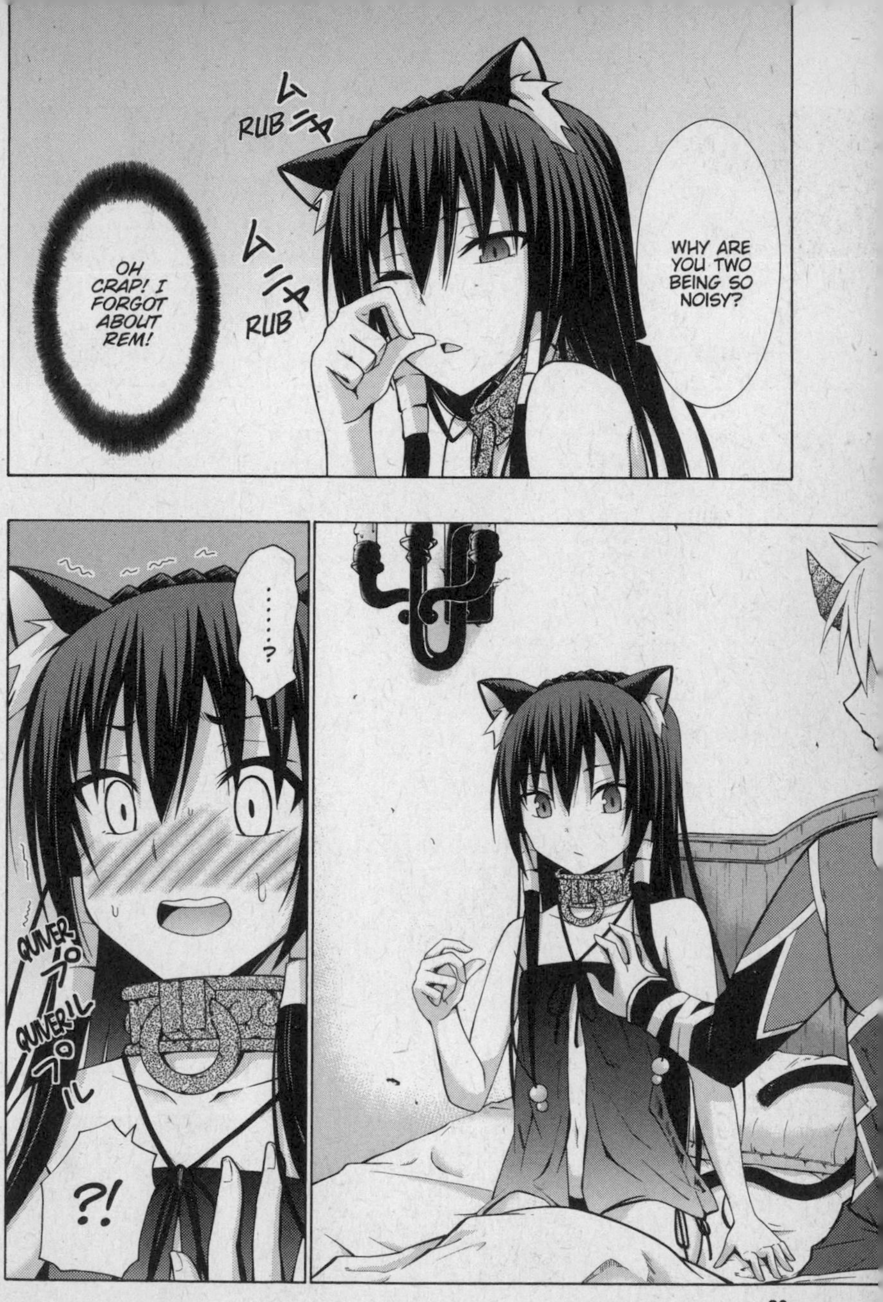
WHY ARE YOU TWO BEING SO NOISY?
ムニャ RUB
ムニャ RUB
OH CRAP! I FORGOT ABOUT REM!
......?
QUIVER プル
QUIVER プル
?!

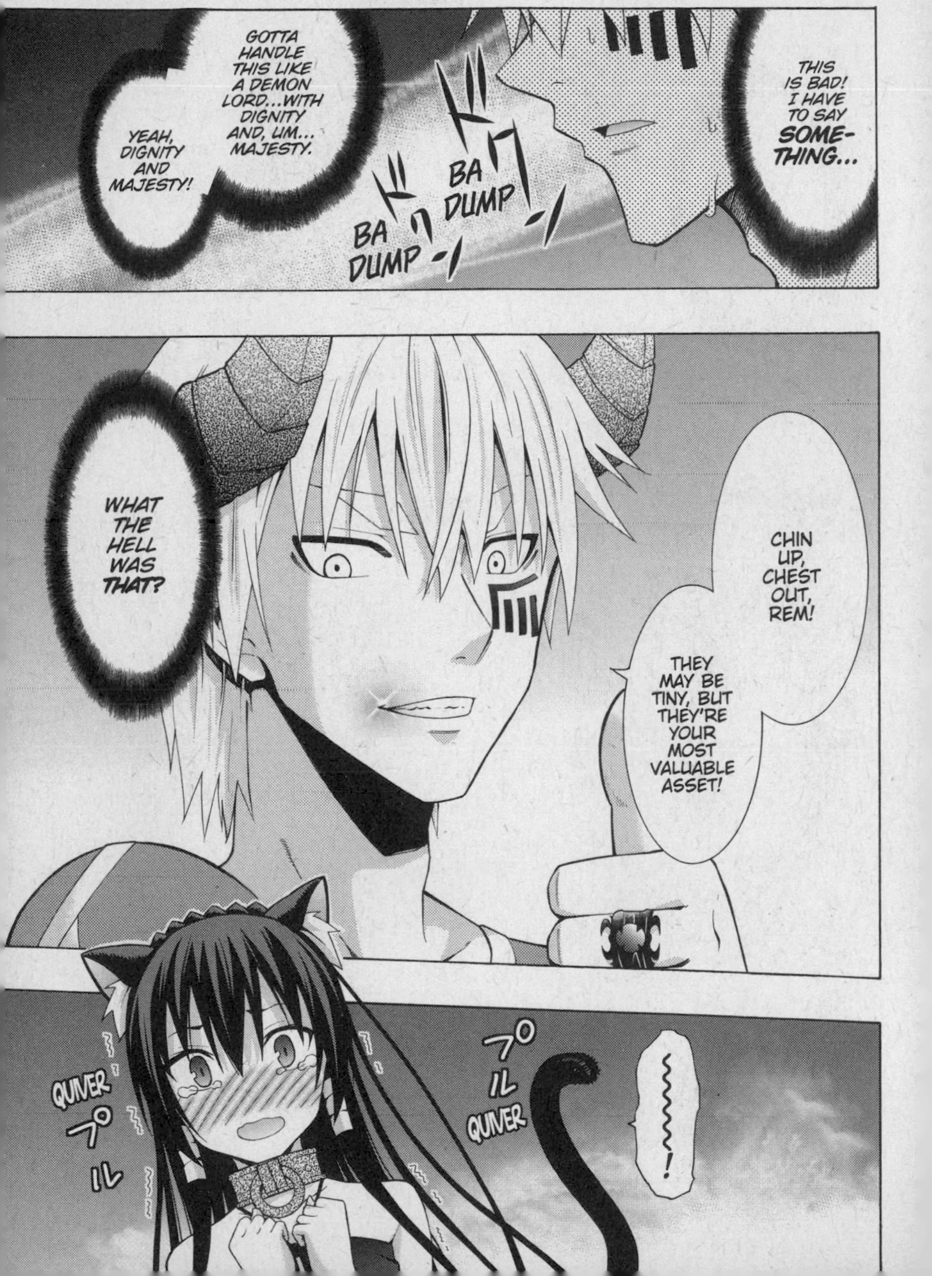
THIS IS BAD! I HAVE TO SAY SOMETHING...
BA DUMP
BA DUMP
GOTTA HANDLE THIS LIKE A DEMON LORD...WITH DIGNITY AND, UM... MAJESTY.
YEAH, DIGNITY AND MAJESTY!
CHIN UP, CHEST OUT, REM!
THEY MAY BE TINY, BUT THEY'RE YOUR MOST VALUABLE ASSET!
WHAT THE HELL WAS THAT?
...!
プル
QUIVER
プル
QUIVER

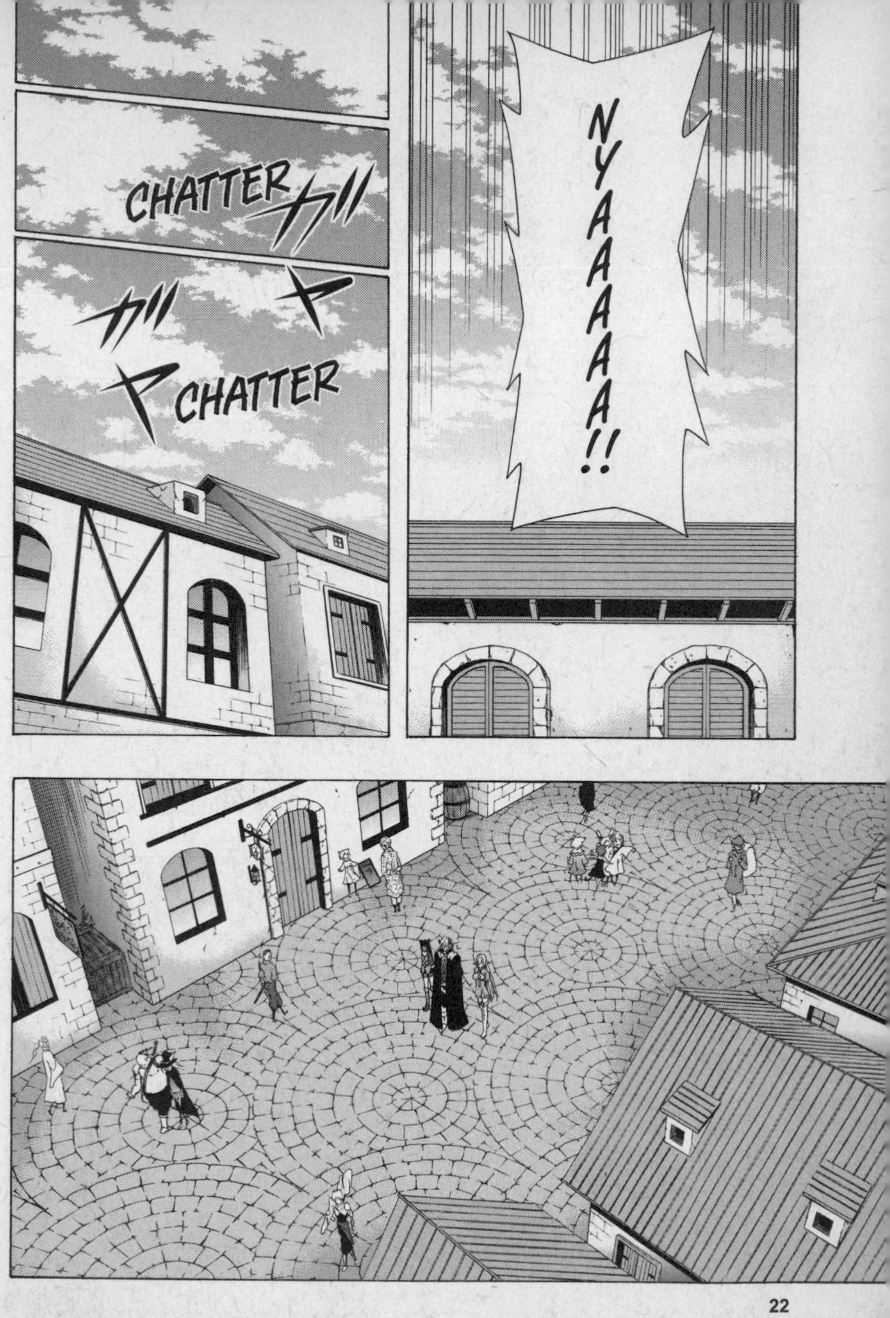
NYAAAAAA!!
CHATTER
CHATTER

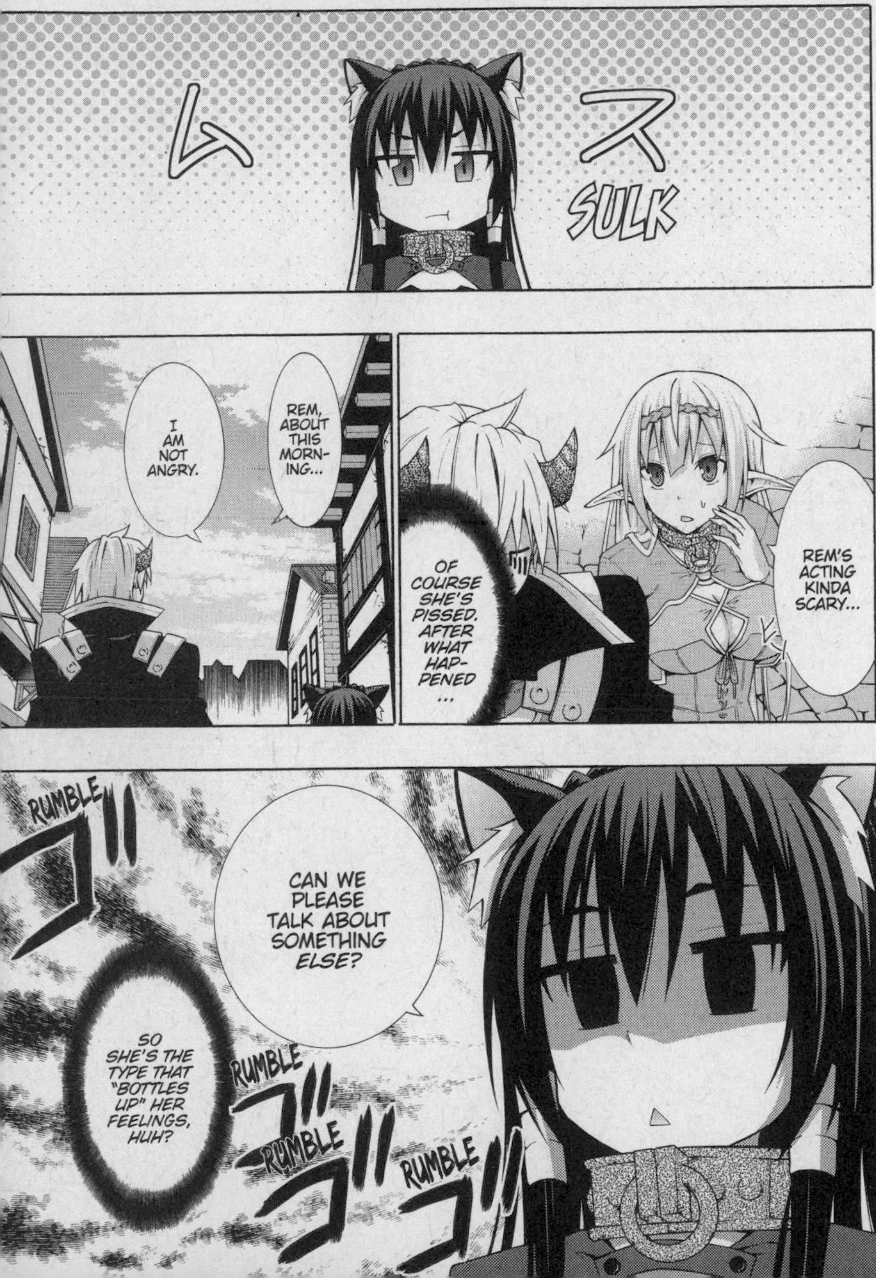
ムス
SULK
REM'S ACTING KINDA SCARY...
OF COURSE SHE'S PISSED. AFTER WHAT HAP-PENED...
REM, ABOUT THIS MORN-ING...
I AM NOT ANGRY.
RUMBLE
CAN WE PLEASE TALK ABOUT SOMETHING ELSE?
SO SHE'S THE TYPE THAT "BOTTLES UP" HER FEELINGS, HUH?
RUMBLE
RUMBLE
RUMBLE

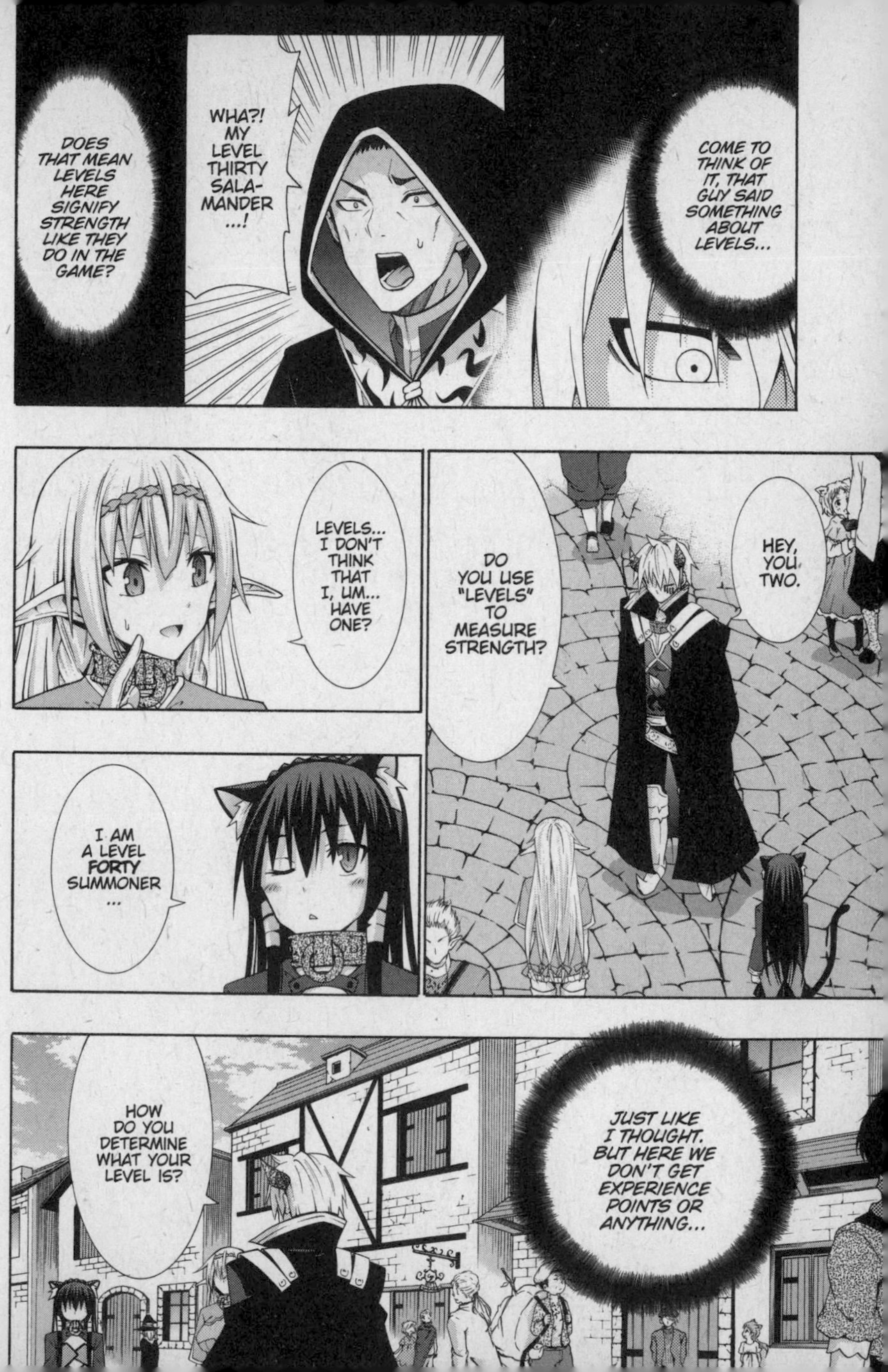
COME TO THINK OF IT, THAT GUY SAID SOMETHING ABOUT LEVELS...
WHA?! MY LEVEL THIRTY SALA-MANDER ...!
DOES THAT MEAN LEVELS HERE SIGNIFY STRENGTH LIKE THEY DO IN THE GAME?
HEY, YOU TWO.
DO YOU USE "LEVELS" TO MEASURE STRENGTH?
LEVELS... I DON'T THINK THAT I, UM... HAVE ONE?
I AM A LEVEL FORTY SUMMONER ...
JUST LIKE I THOUGHT. BUT HERE WE DON'T GET EXPERIENCE POINTS OR ANYTHING...
HOW DO YOU DETERMINE WHAT YOUR LEVEL IS?

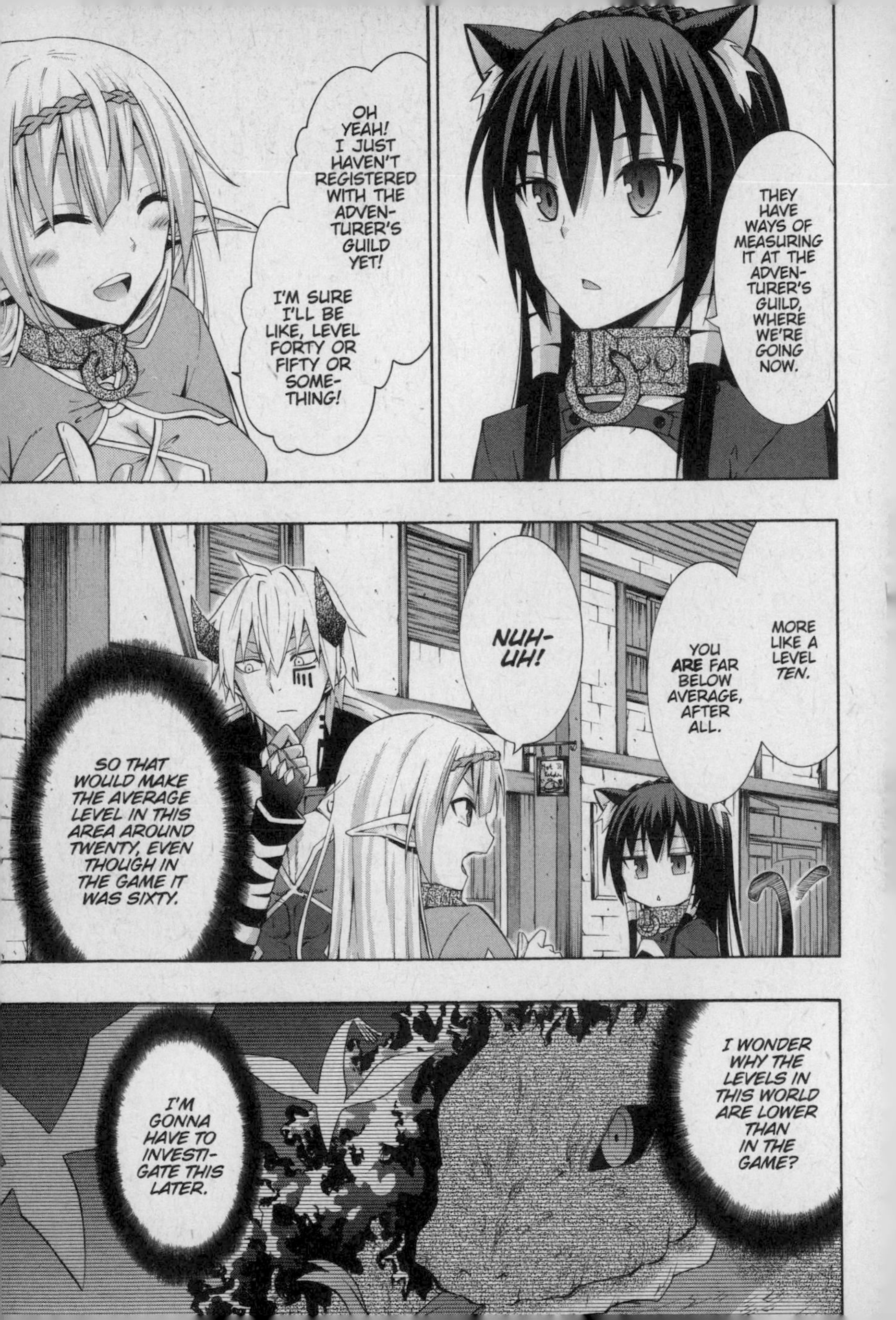
THEY HAVE WAYS OF MEASURING IT AT THE ADVENTURER'S GUILD, WHERE WE'RE GOING NOW.
OH YEAH! I JUST HAVEN'T REGISTERED WITH THE ADVENTURER'S GUILD YET!
I'M SURE I'LL BE LIKE, LEVEL FORTY OR FIFTY OR SOMETHING!
MORE LIKE A LEVEL TEN.
YOU ARE FAR BELOW AVERAGE, AFTER ALL.
NUH-UH!
SO THAT WOULD MAKE THE AVERAGE LEVEL IN THIS AREA AROUND TWENTY, EVEN THOUGH IN THE GAME IT WAS SIXTY.
I WONDER WHY THE LEVELS IN THIS WORLD ARE LOWER THAN IN THE GAME?
I'M GONNA HAVE TO INVESTIGATE THIS LATER.

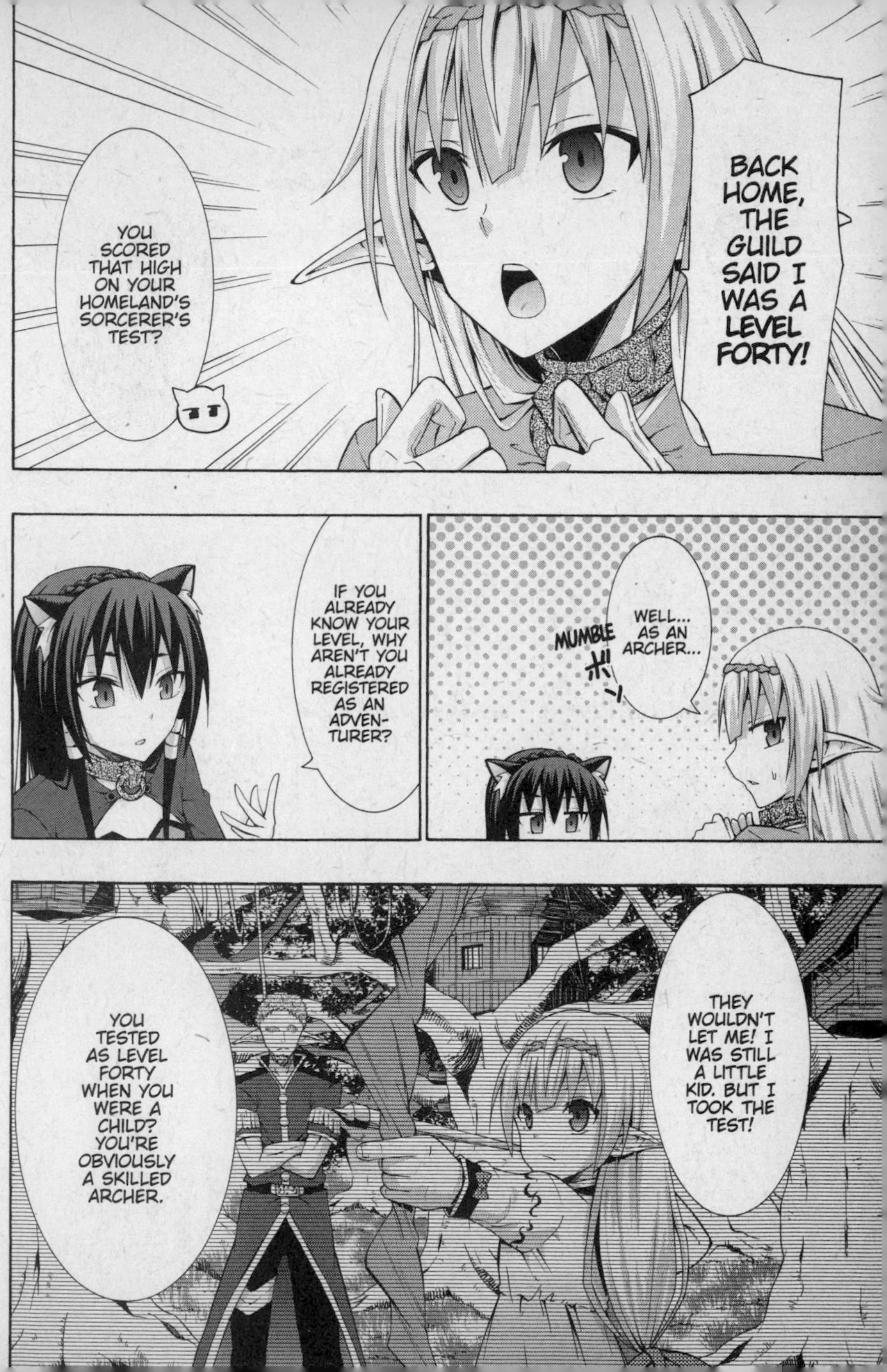
BACK HOME, THE GUILD SAID I WAS A LEVEL FORTY!
YOU SCORED THAT HIGH ON YOUR HOMELAND'S SORCERER'S TEST?
WELL... AS AN ARCHER...
MUMBLE
IF YOU ALREADY KNOW YOUR LEVEL, WHY AREN'T YOU ALREADY REGISTERED AS AN ADVEN-TURER?
THEY WOULDN'T LET ME! I WAS STILL A LITTLE KID. BUT I TOOK THE TEST!
YOU TESTED AS LEVEL FORTY WHEN YOU WERE A CHILD? YOU'RE OBVIOUSLY A SKILLED ARCHER.

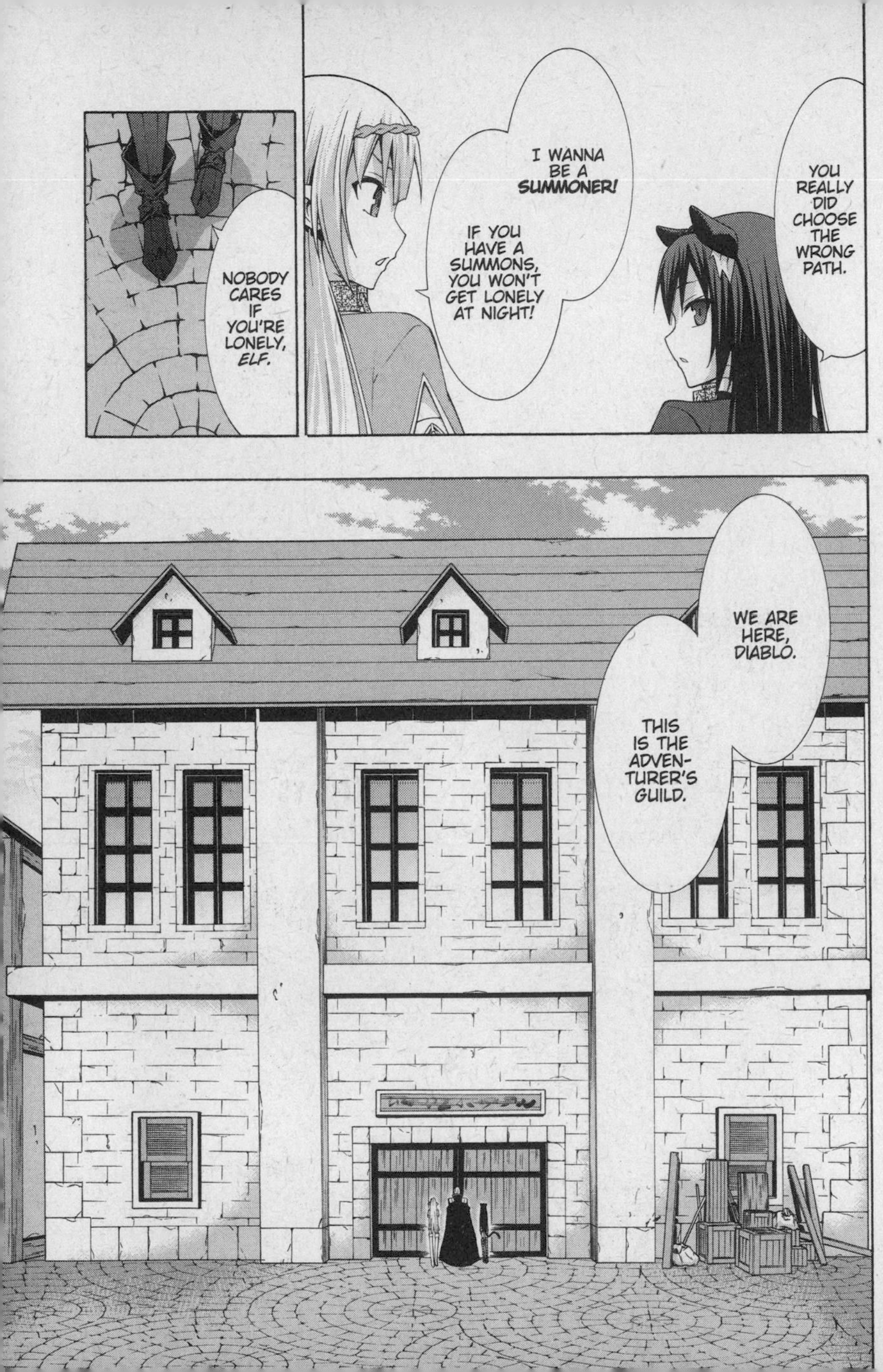
YOU REALLY DID CHOOSE THE WRONG PATH.
I WANNA BE A SUMMONER!
IF YOU HAVE A SUMMONS, YOU WON'T GET LONELY AT NIGHT!
NOBODY CARES IF YOU'RE LONELY, *ELF*.
WE ARE HERE, DIABLO.
THIS IS THE ADVEN-TURER'S GUILD.

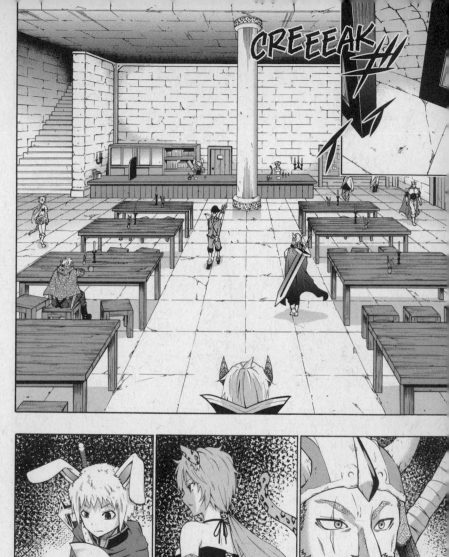

CREEEAK

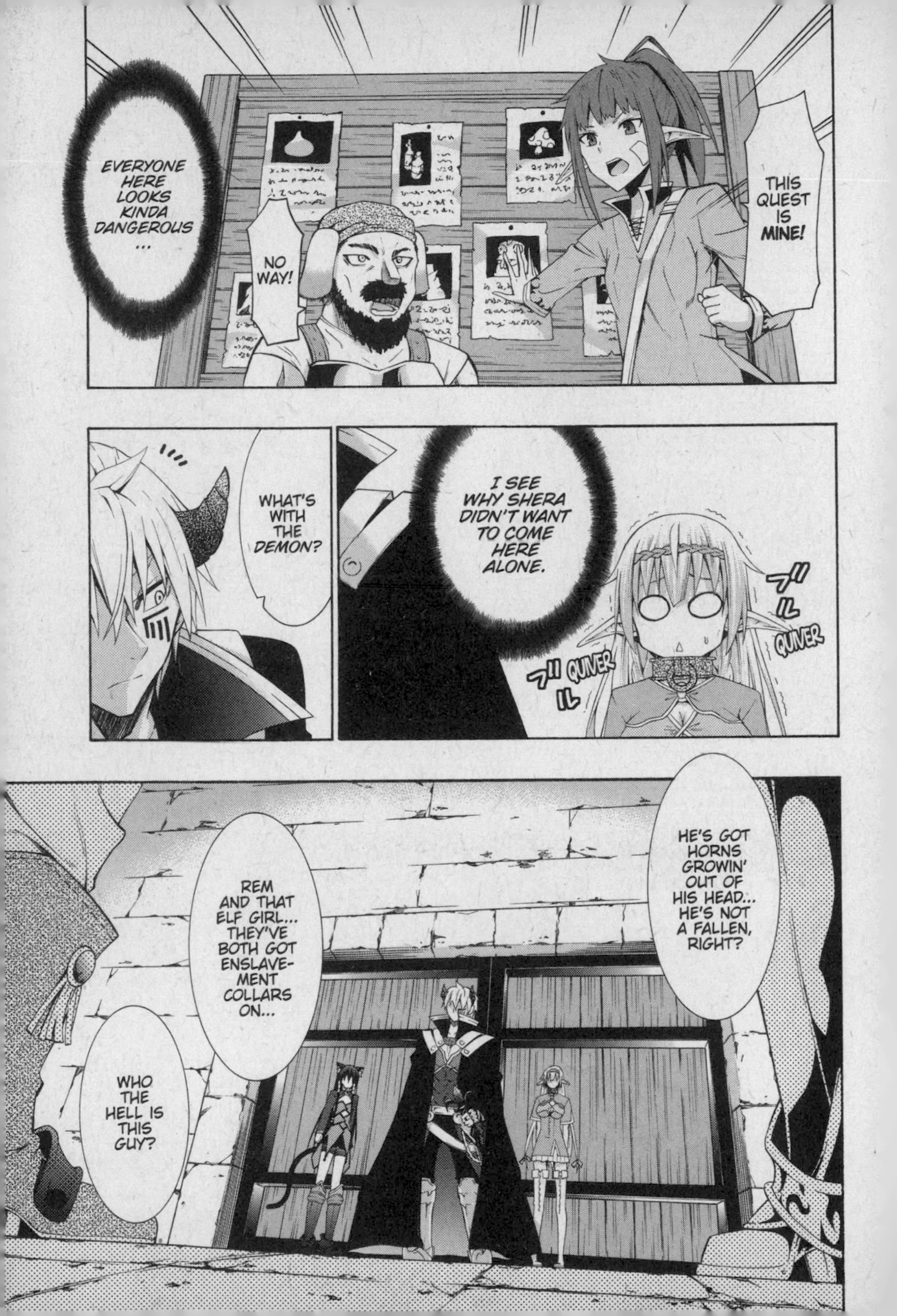
THIS QUEST IS MINE!
NO WAY!
EVERYONE HERE LOOKS KINDA DANGEROUS...
I SEE WHY SHERA DIDN'T WANT TO COME HERE ALONE.
QUIVER
QUIVER
WHAT'S WITH THE DEMON?
HE'S GOT HORNS GROWIN' OUT OF HIS HEAD... HE'S NOT A FALLEN, RIGHT?
REM AND THAT ELF GIRL... THEY'VE BOTH GOT ENSLAVEMENT COLLARS ON...
WHO THE HELL IS THIS GUY?

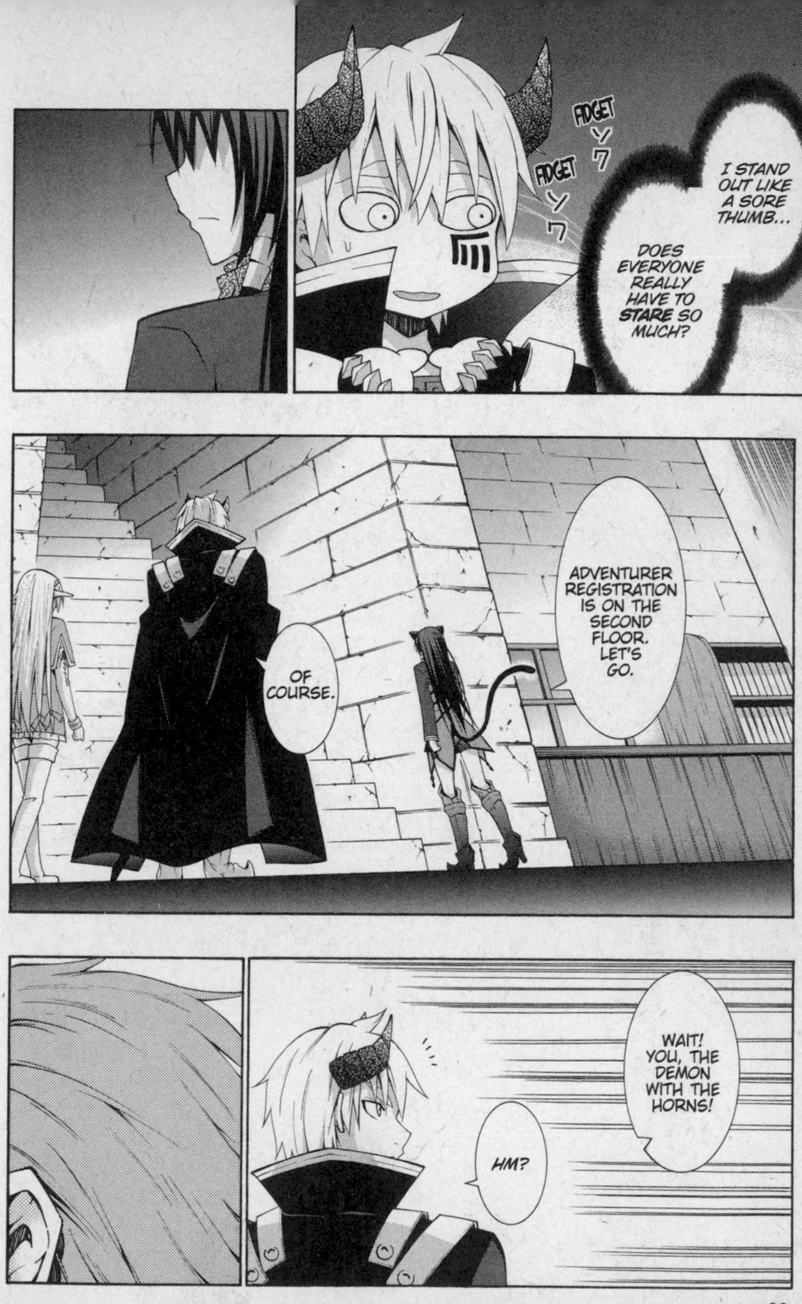
FIDGET ソワ
FIDGET ソワ
I STAND OUT LIKE A SORE THUMB...
DOES EVERYONE REALLY HAVE TO STARE SO MUCH?
ADVENTURER REGISTRATION IS ON THE SECOND FLOOR. LET'S GO.
OF COURSE.
WAIT! YOU, THE DEMON WITH THE HORNS!
HM?

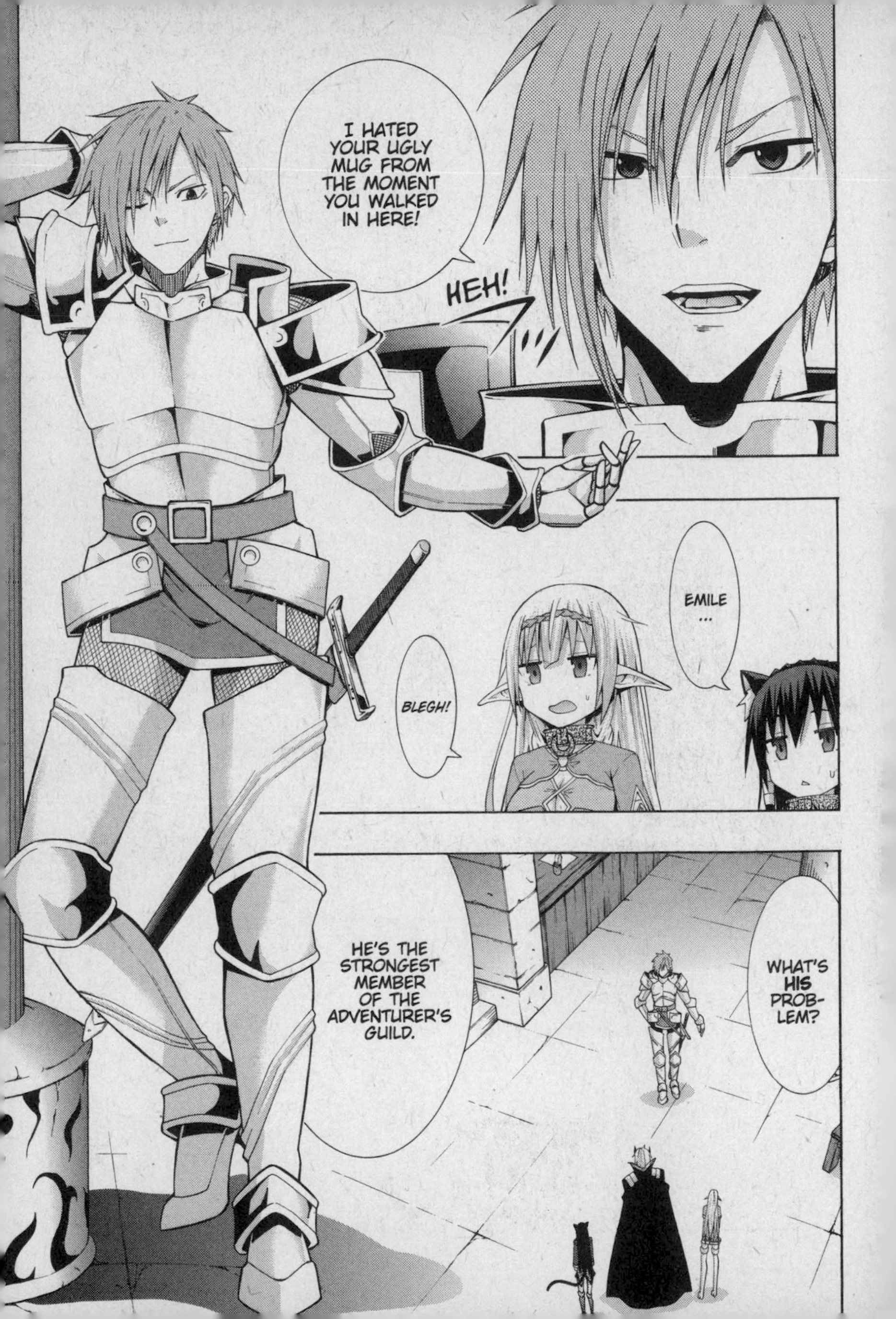
I HATED YOUR UGLY MUG FROM THE MOMENT YOU WALKED IN HERE!
HEH!
EMILE ...
BLEGH!
WHAT'S HIS PROBLEM?
HE'S THE STRONGEST MEMBER OF THE ADVENTURER'S GUILD.

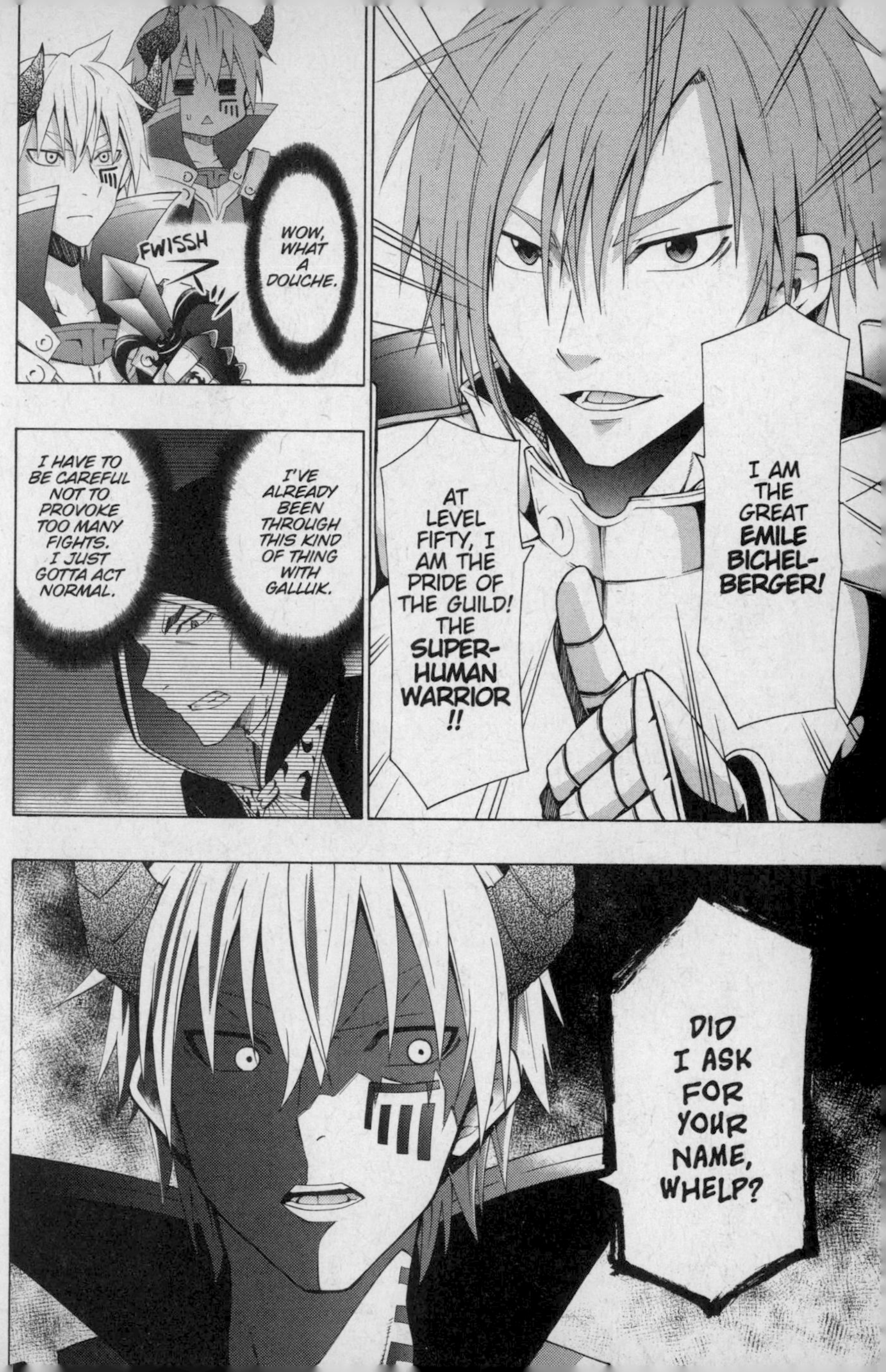
I AM THE GREAT EMILE BICHEL-BERGER!
AT LEVEL FIFTY, I AM THE PRIDE OF THE GUILD! THE SUPER-HUMAN WARRIOR!!
WOW, WHAT A DOUCHE.
FWISSH
I'VE ALREADY BEEN THROUGH THIS KIND OF THING WITH GALLUK.
I HAVE TO BE CAREFUL NOT TO PROVOKE TOO MANY FIGHTS. I JUST GOTTA ACT NORMAL.
DID I ASK FOR YOUR NAME, WHELP?

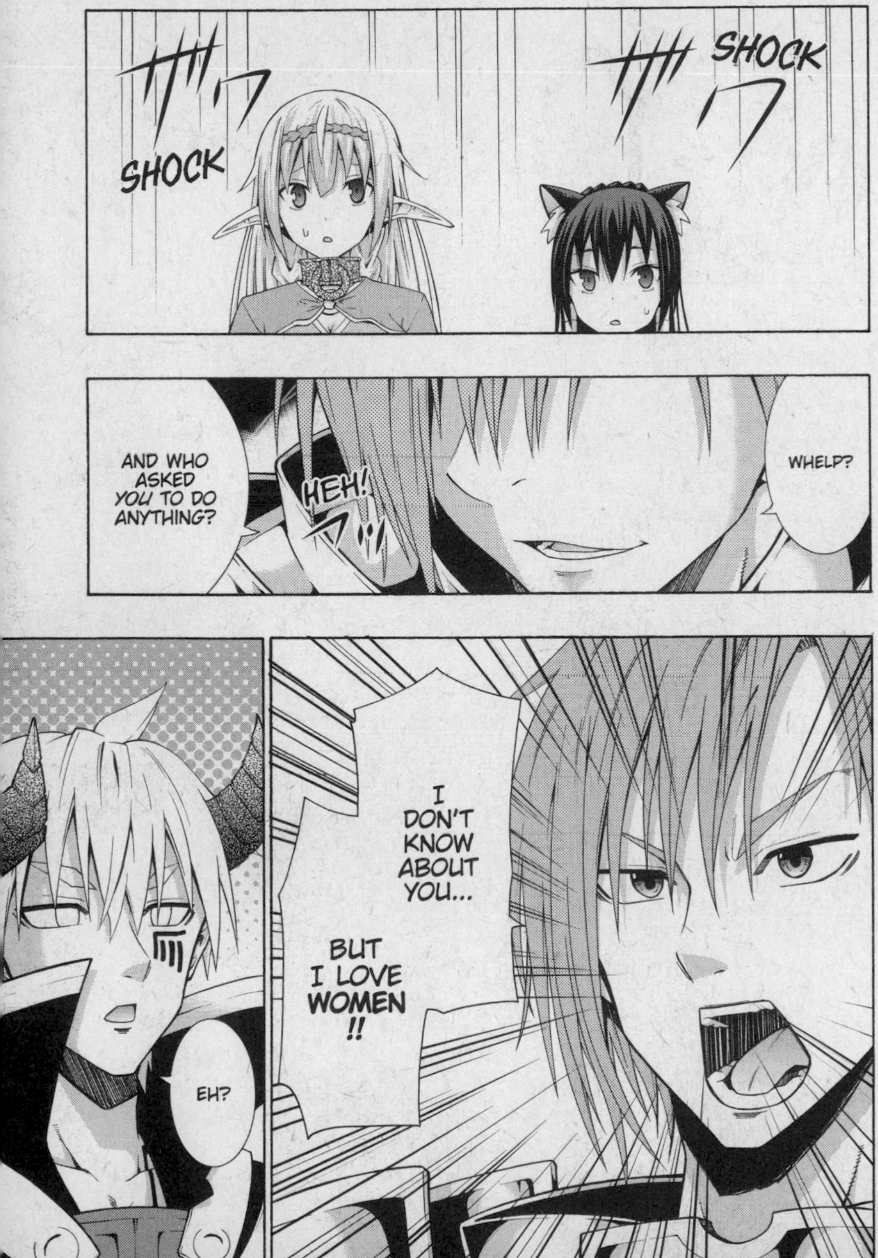
SHOCK
SHOCK
WHELP?
HEH!
AND WHO ASKED YOU TO DO ANYTHING?
I DON'T KNOW ABOUT YOU...
BUT I LOVE WOMEN!!
EH?

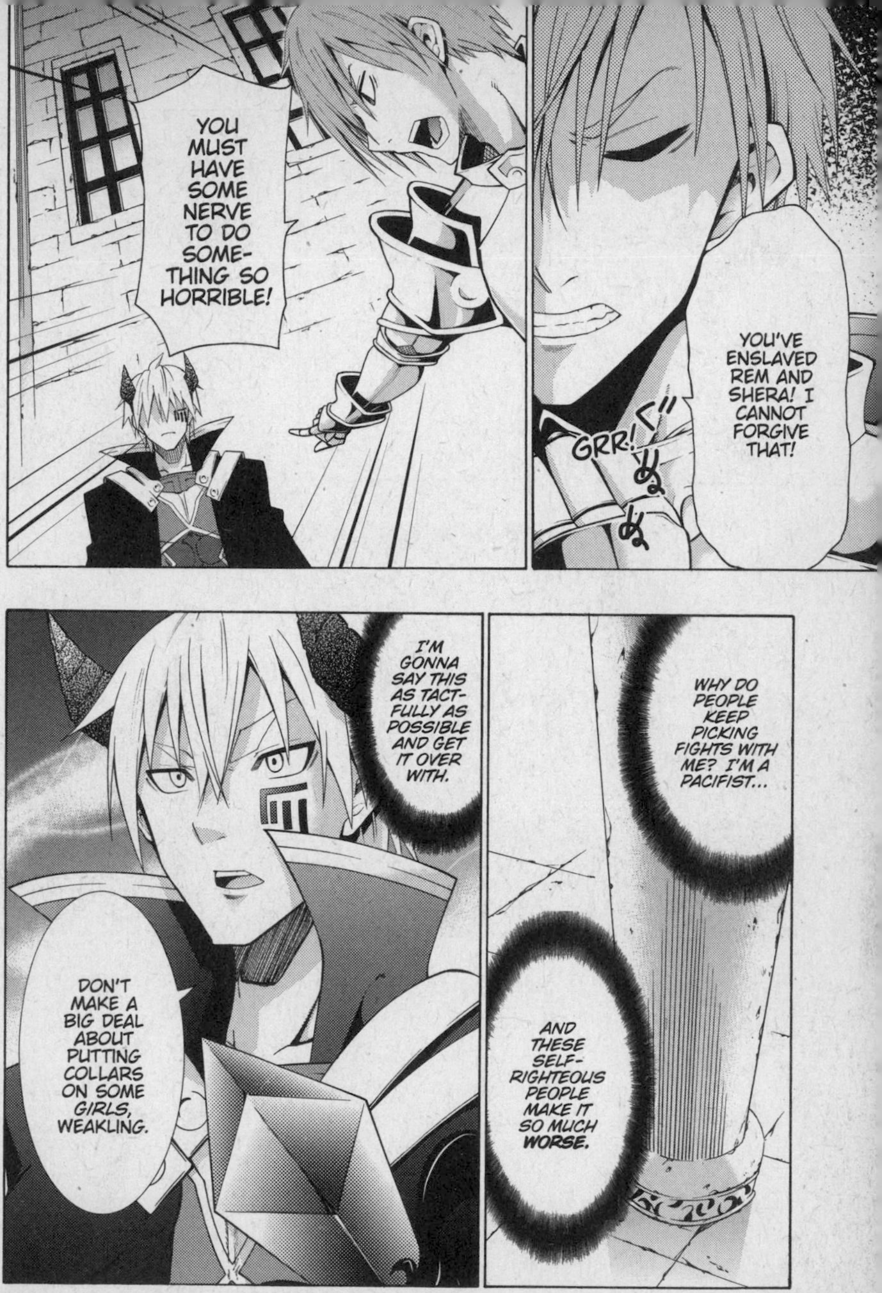
GRR!
ぐぬぬ
YOU'VE ENSLAVED REM AND SHERA! I CANNOT FORGIVE THAT!
YOU MUST HAVE SOME NERVE TO DO SOME-THING SO HORRIBLE!
WHY DO PEOPLE KEEP PICKING FIGHTS WITH ME? I'M A PACIFIST...
AND THESE SELF-RIGHTEOUS PEOPLE MAKE IT SO MUCH WORSE.
I'M GONNA SAY THIS AS TACT-FULLY AS POSSIBLE AND GET IT OVER WITH.
DON'T MAKE A BIG DEAL ABOUT PUTTING COLLARS ON SOME GIRLS, WEAKLING.

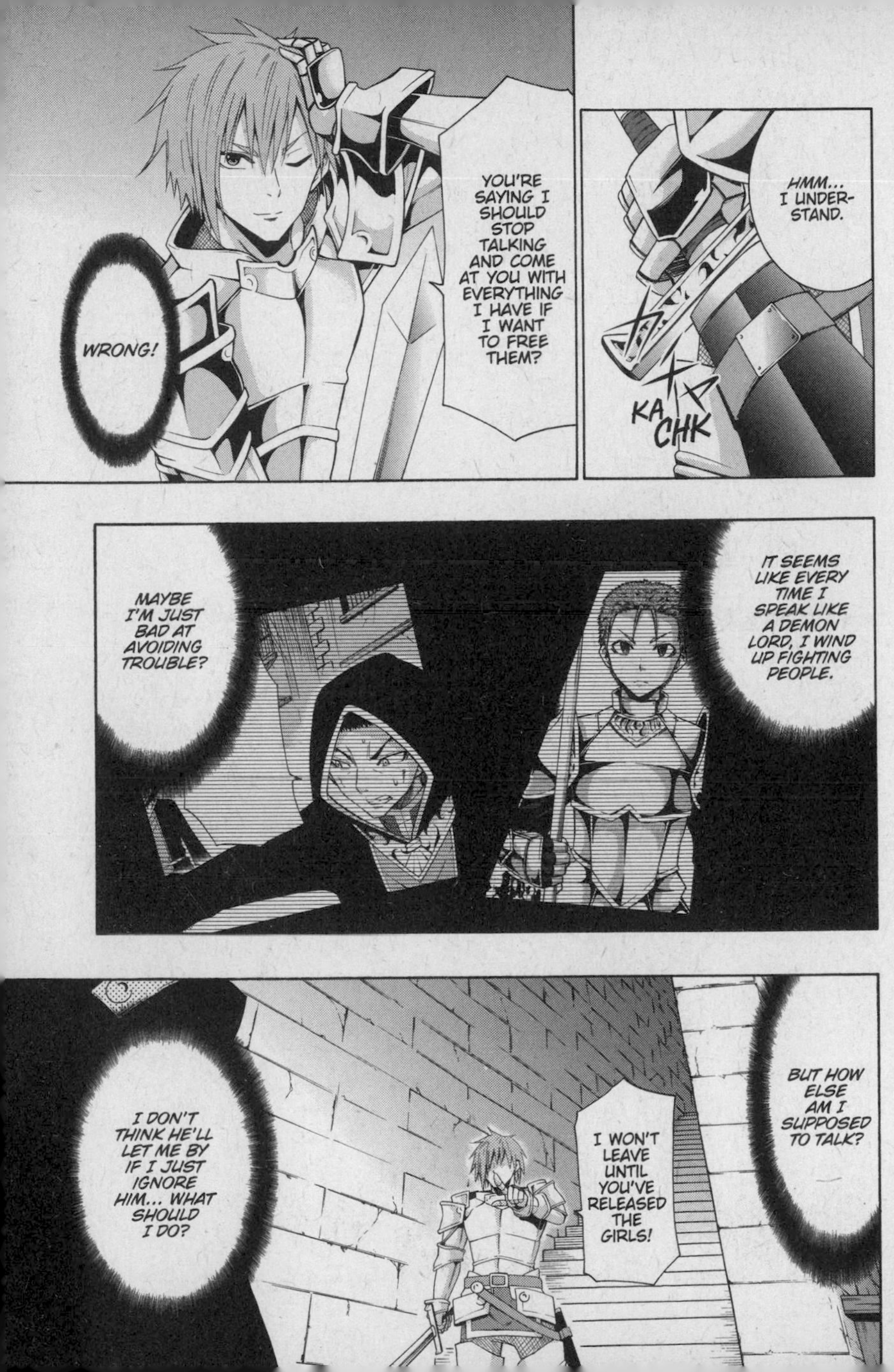
HMM... I UNDER-STAND.
KA CHK
YOU'RE SAYING I SHOULD STOP TALKING AND COME AT YOU WITH EVERYTHING I HAVE IF I WANT TO FREE THEM?
WRONG!
IT SEEMS LIKE EVERY TIME I SPEAK LIKE A DEMON LORD, I WIND UP FIGHTING PEOPLE.
MAYBE I'M JUST BAD AT AVOIDING TROUBLE?
BUT HOW ELSE AM I SUPPOSED TO TALK?
I WON'T LEAVE UNTIL YOU'VE RELEASED THE GIRLS!
I DON'T THINK HE'LL LET ME BY IF I JUST IGNORE HIM... WHAT SHOULD I DO?

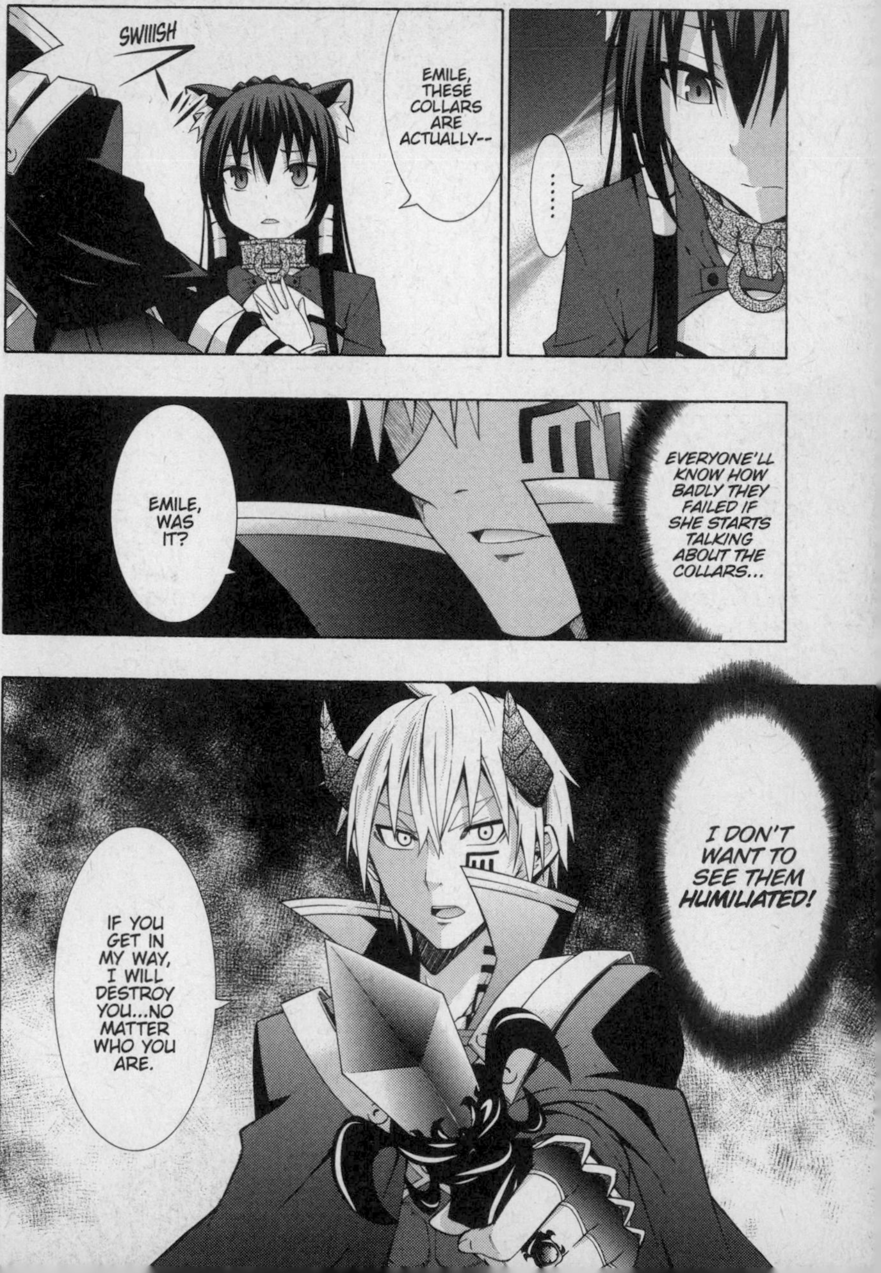
......
SWIIISH
EMILE, THESE COLLARS ARE ACTUALLY--
EVERYONE'LL KNOW HOW BADLY THEY FAILED IF SHE STARTS TALKING ABOUT THE COLLARS...
EMILE, WAS IT?
I DON'T WANT TO SEE THEM HUMILIATED!
IF YOU GET IN MY WAY, I WILL DESTROY YOU...NO MATTER WHO YOU ARE.

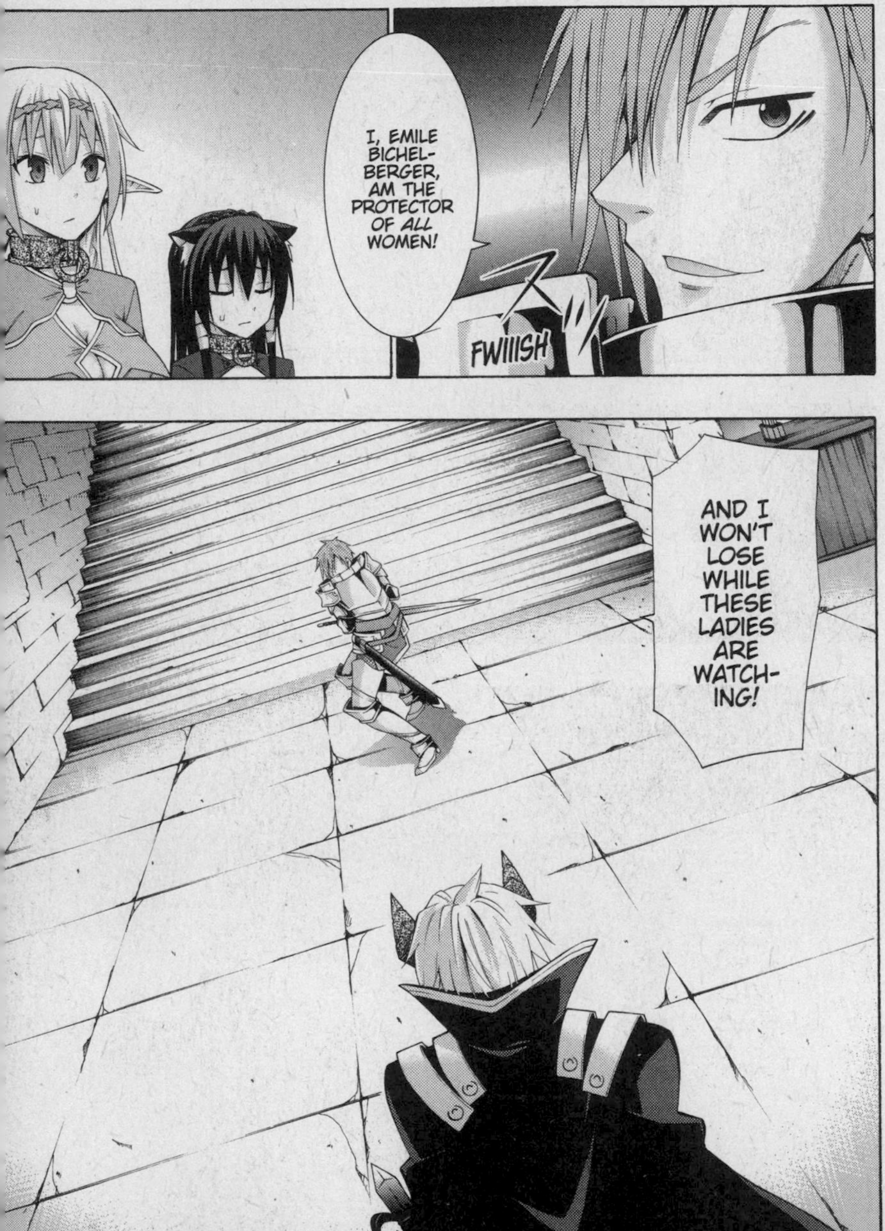
I, EMILE BICHEL-BERGER, AM THE PROTECTOR OF *ALL* WOMEN!
FWIIISH
AND I WON'T LOSE WHILE THESE LADIES ARE WATCH-ING!

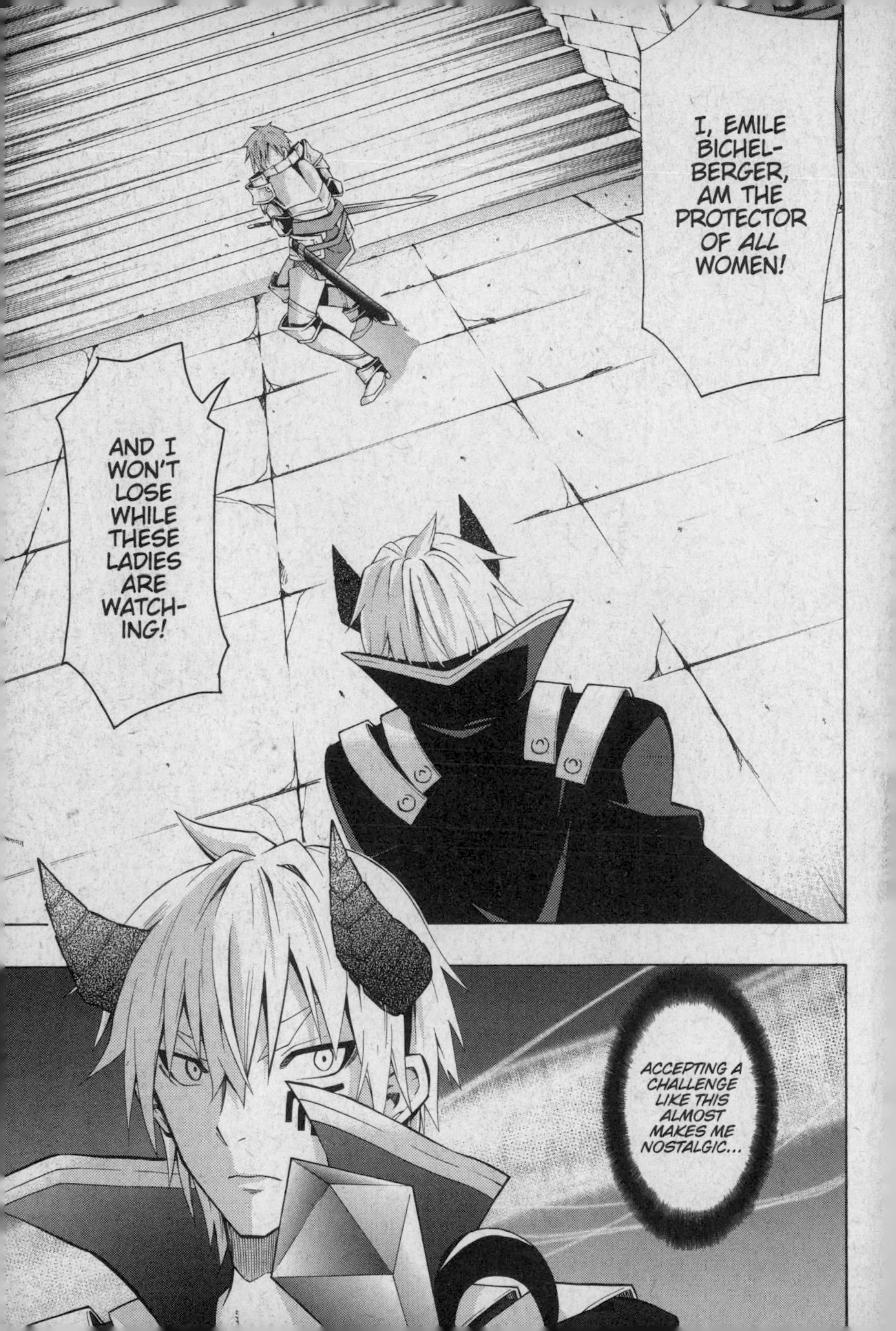
I, EMILE BICHEL-BERGER, AM THE PROTECTOR OF ALL WOMEN!
AND I WON'T LOSE WHILE THESE LADIES ARE WATCH-ING!
ACCEPTING A CHALLENGE LIKE THIS ALMOST MAKES ME NOSTALGIC...

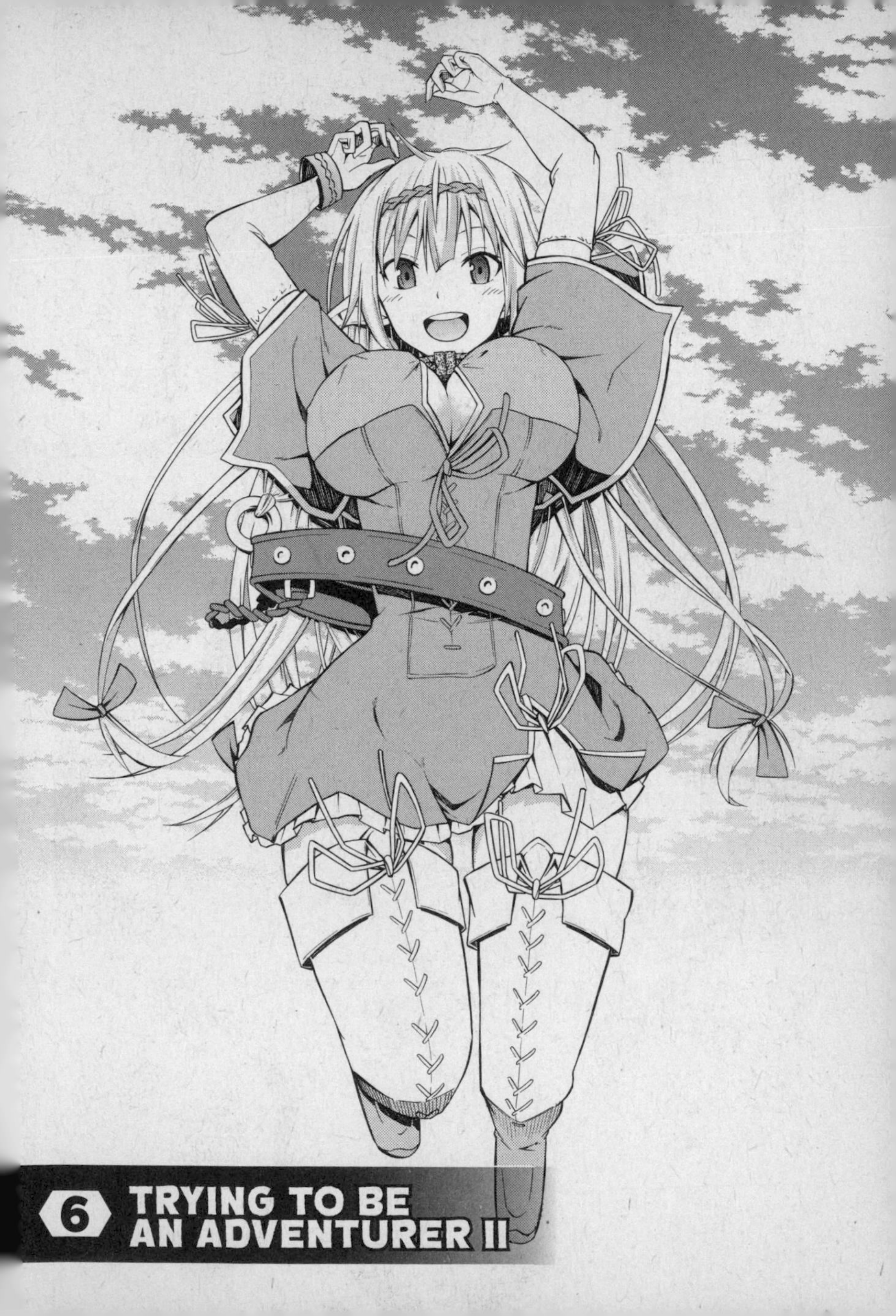

6 TRYING TO BE AN ADVENTURER II

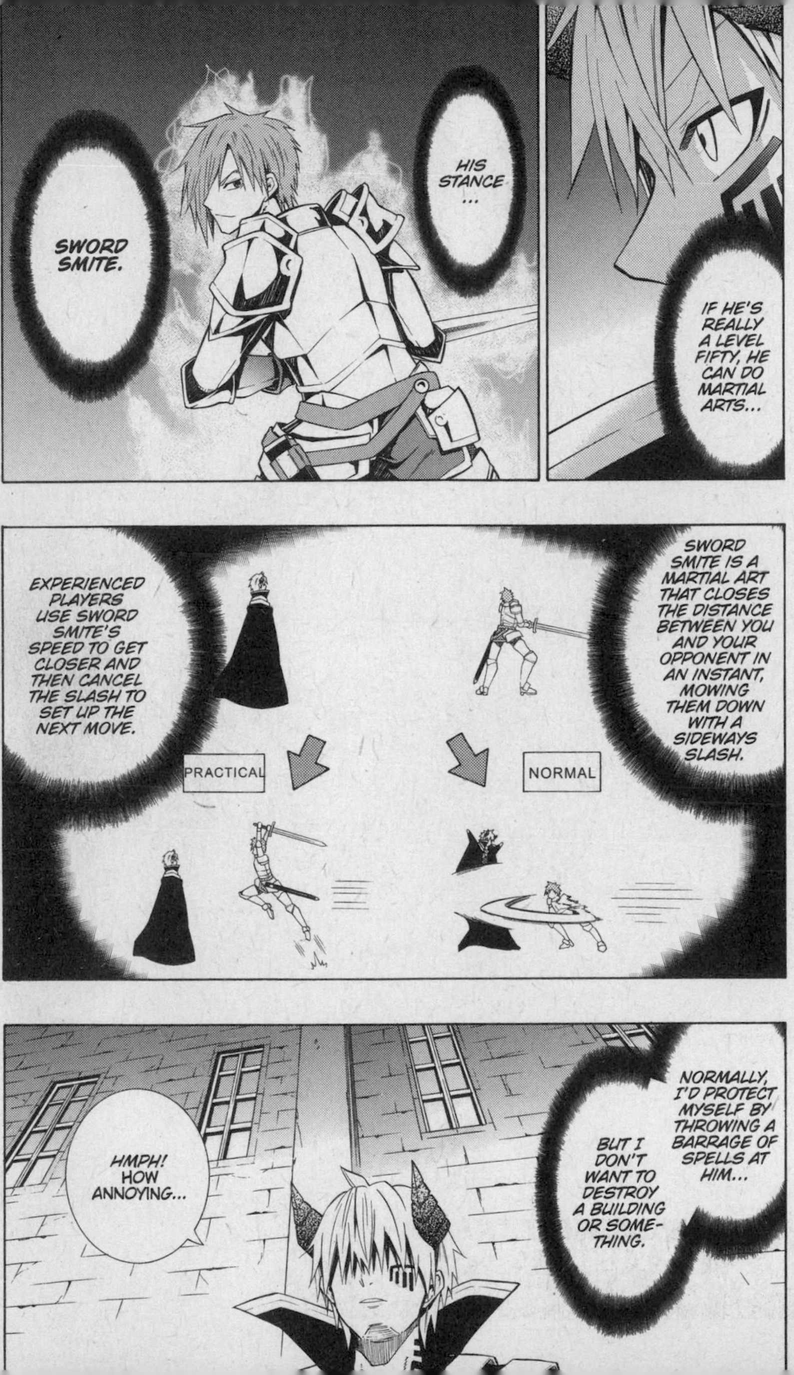
IF HE'S REALLY A LEVEL FIFTY, HE CAN DO MARTIAL ARTS...
HIS STANCE...
SWORD SMITE.
SWORD SMITE IS A MARTIAL ART THAT CLOSES THE DISTANCE BETWEEN YOU AND YOUR OPPONENT IN AN INSTANT, MOWING THEM DOWN WITH A SIDEWAYS SLASH.
NORMAL
PRACTICAL
EXPERIENCED PLAYERS USE SWORD SMITE'S SPEED TO GET CLOSER AND THEN CANCEL THE SLASH TO SET UP THE NEXT MOVE.
NORMALLY, I'D PROTECT MYSELF BY THROWING A BARRAGE OF SPELLS AT HIM...
BUT I DON'T WANT TO DESTROY A BUILDING OR SOME-THING.
HMPH! HOW ANNOYING...

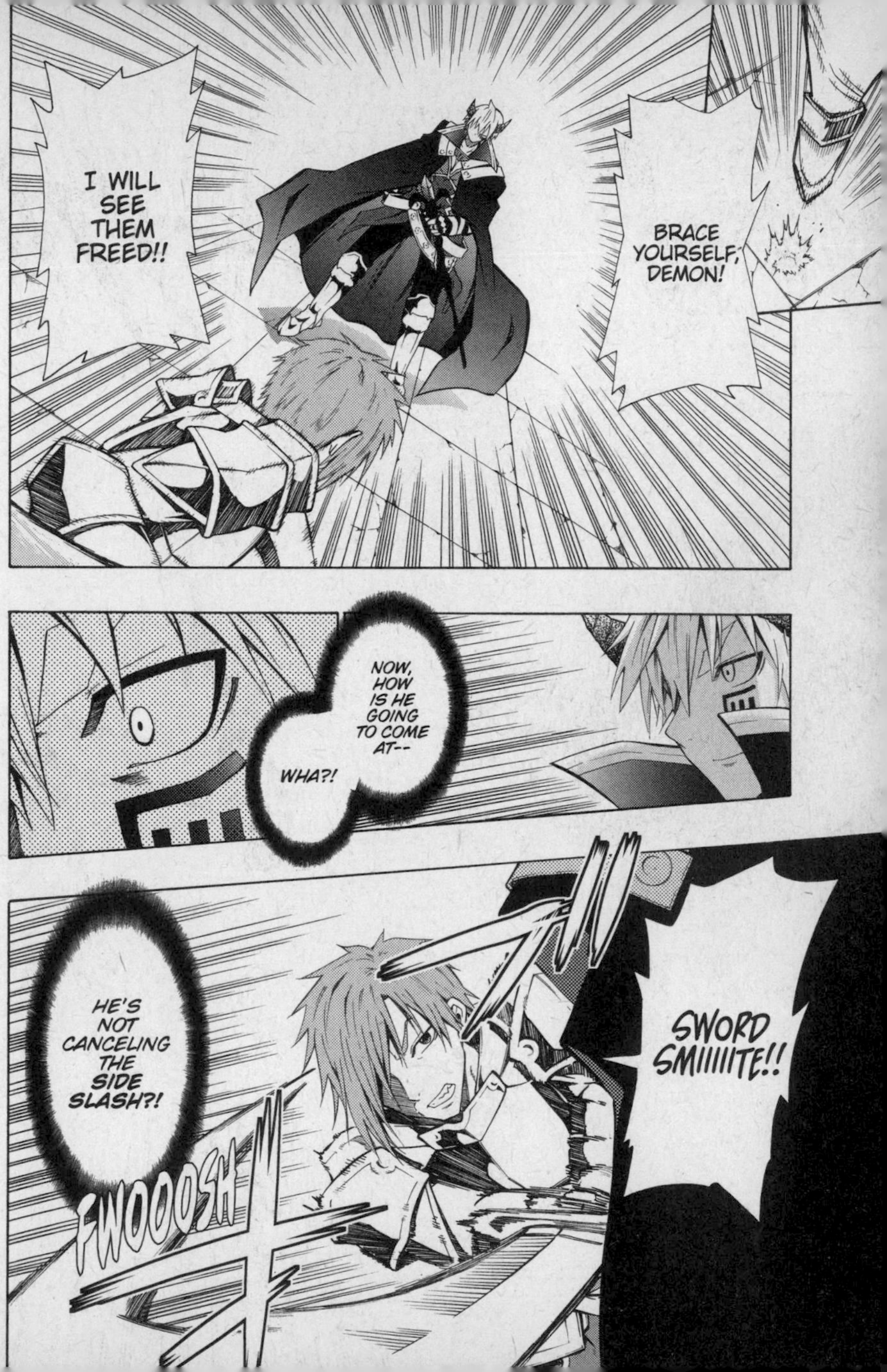

BRACE YOURSELF, DEMON!
I WILL SEE THEM FREED!!
NOW, HOW IS HE GOING TO COME AT--
WHA?!
SWORD SMIIIIITE!!
HE'S NOT CANCELING THE SIDE SLASH?!
FWOOOSH

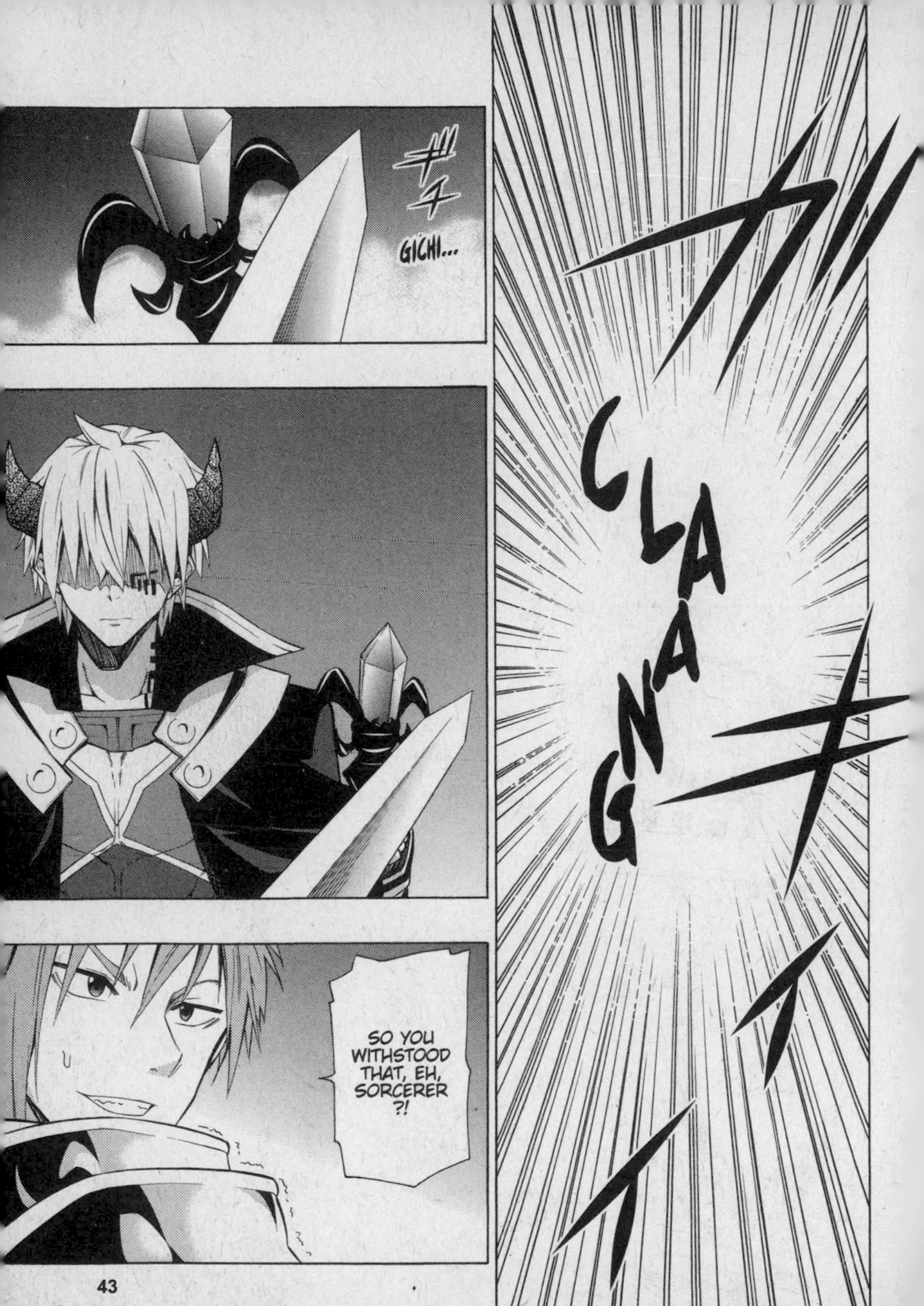
CLAANG
GICHI...
SO YOU WITHSTOOD THAT, EH, SORCERER?!

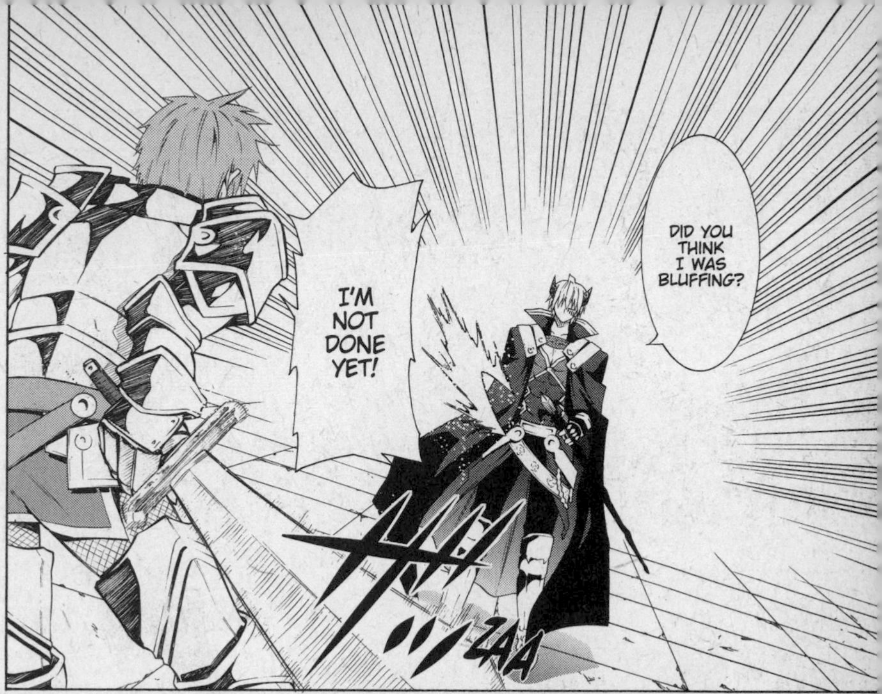
DID YOU THINK I WAS BLUFFING?
I'M NOT DONE YET!
ZAA

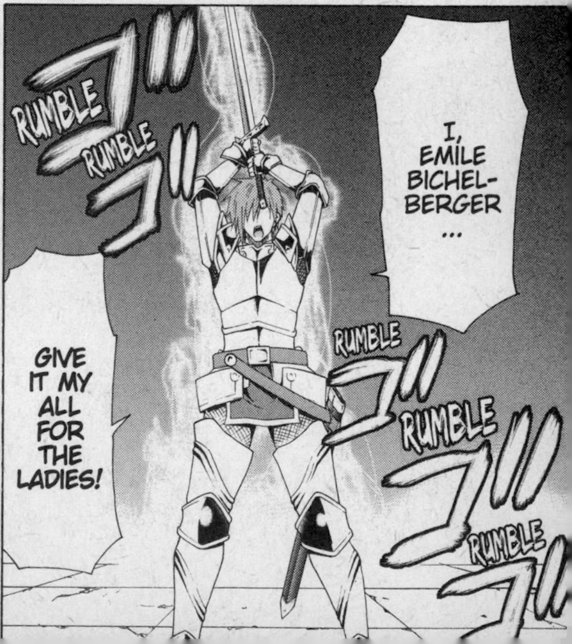
RUMBLE
RUMBLE
I, EMILE BICHEL-BERGER...
GIVE IT MY ALL FOR THE LADIES!
RUMBLE
RUMBLE
RUMBLE

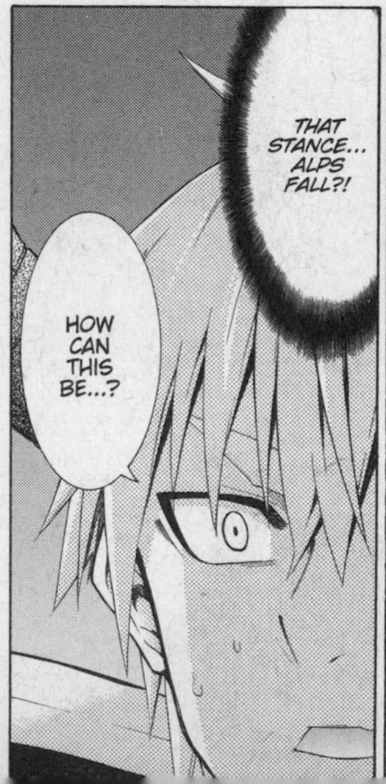
THAT STANCE... ALPS FALL?!
HOW CAN THIS BE...?

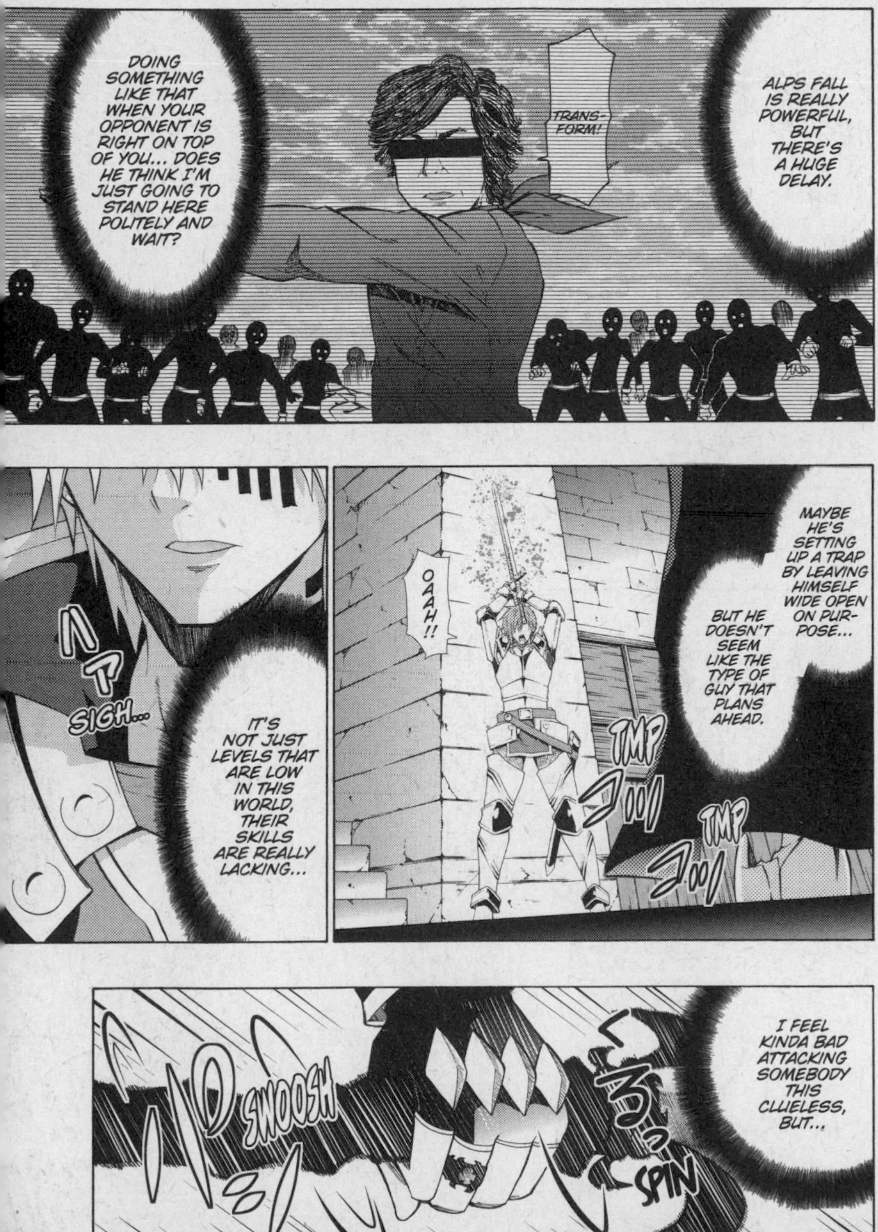
ALPS FALL IS REALLY POWERFUL, BUT THERE'S A HUGE DELAY.
TRANS-FORM!
DOING SOMETHING LIKE THAT WHEN YOUR OPPONENT IS RIGHT ON TOP OF YOU... DOES HE THINK I'M JUST GOING TO STAND HERE POLITELY AND WAIT?
MAYBE HE'S SETTING UP A TRAP BY LEAVING HIMSELF WIDE OPEN ON PURPOSE...
BUT HE DOESN'T SEEM LIKE THE TYPE OF GUY THAT PLANS AHEAD.
OAAH!!
TMP
TMP
SIGH...
IT'S NOT JUST LEVELS THAT ARE LOW IN THIS WORLD, THEIR SKILLS ARE REALLY LACKING...
I FEEL KINDA BAD ATTACKING SOMEBODY THIS CLUELESS, BUT...
SPIN
SWOOSH

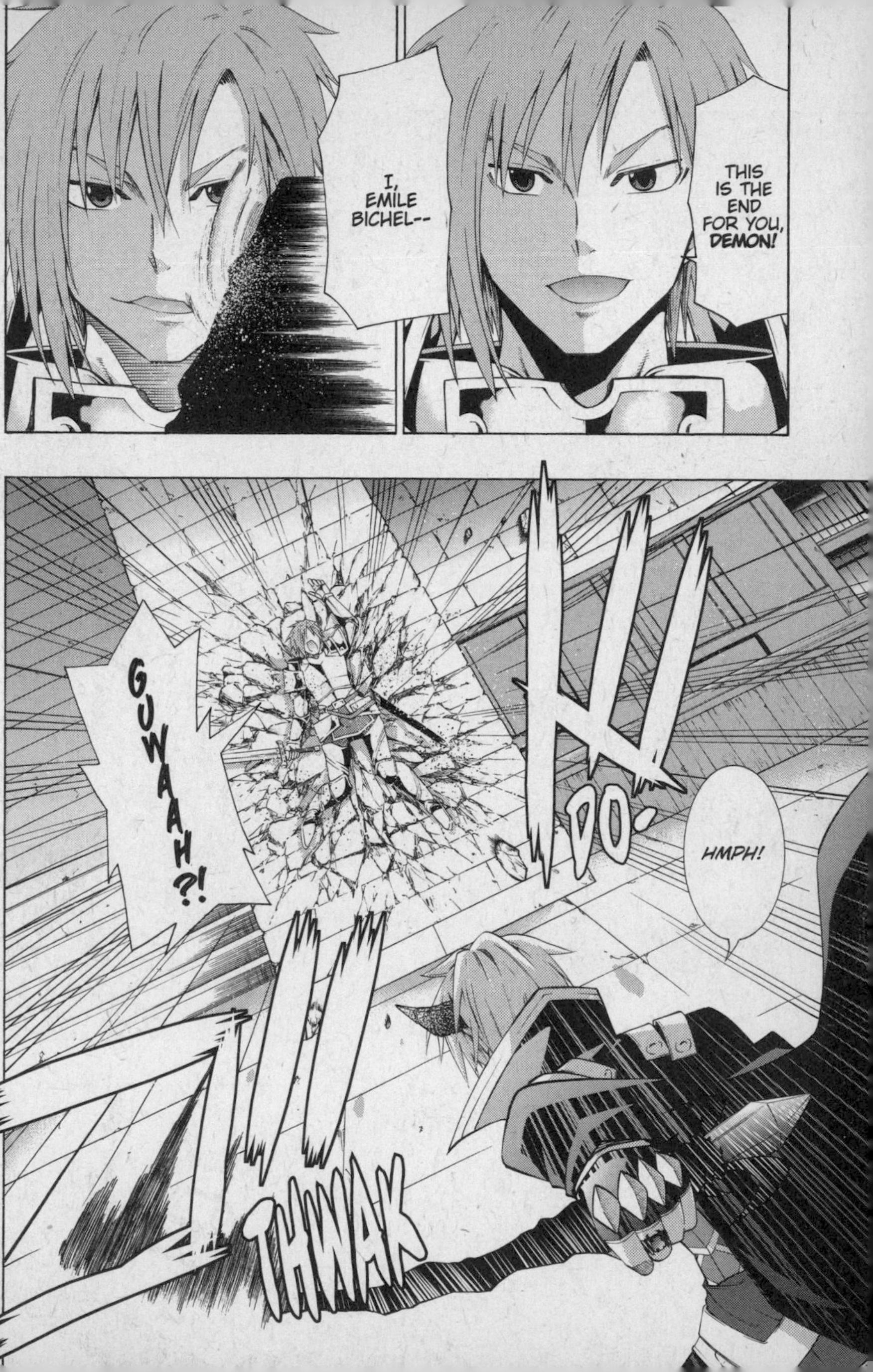
THIS IS THE END FOR YOU, DEMON!
I, EMILE BICHEL--
DO
HMPH!
GUWAAH?!
THWAK

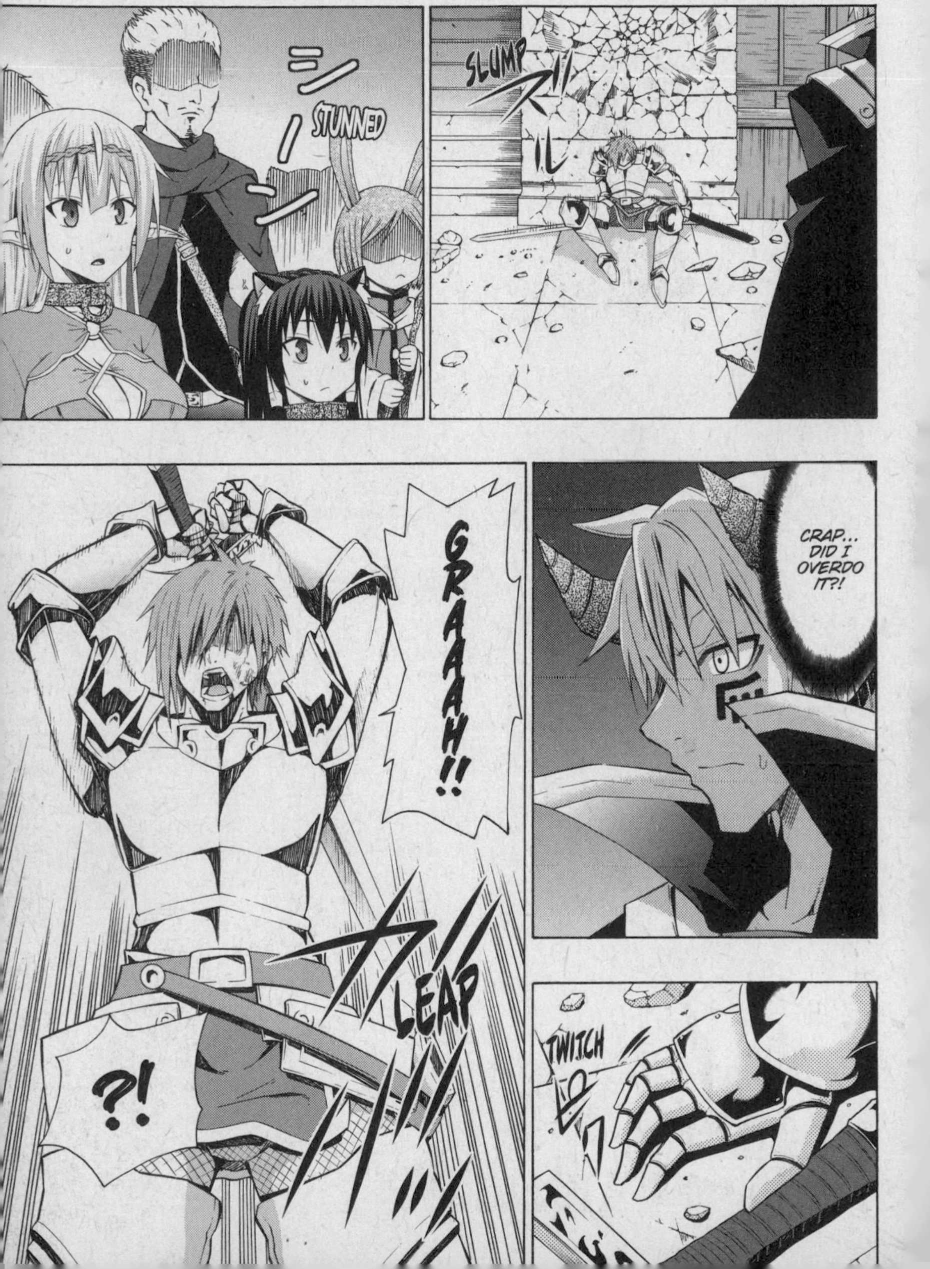
SLUMP
STUNNED
CRAP... DID I OVERDO IT?!
TWITCH
GRAAAAH!!
LEAP
?!

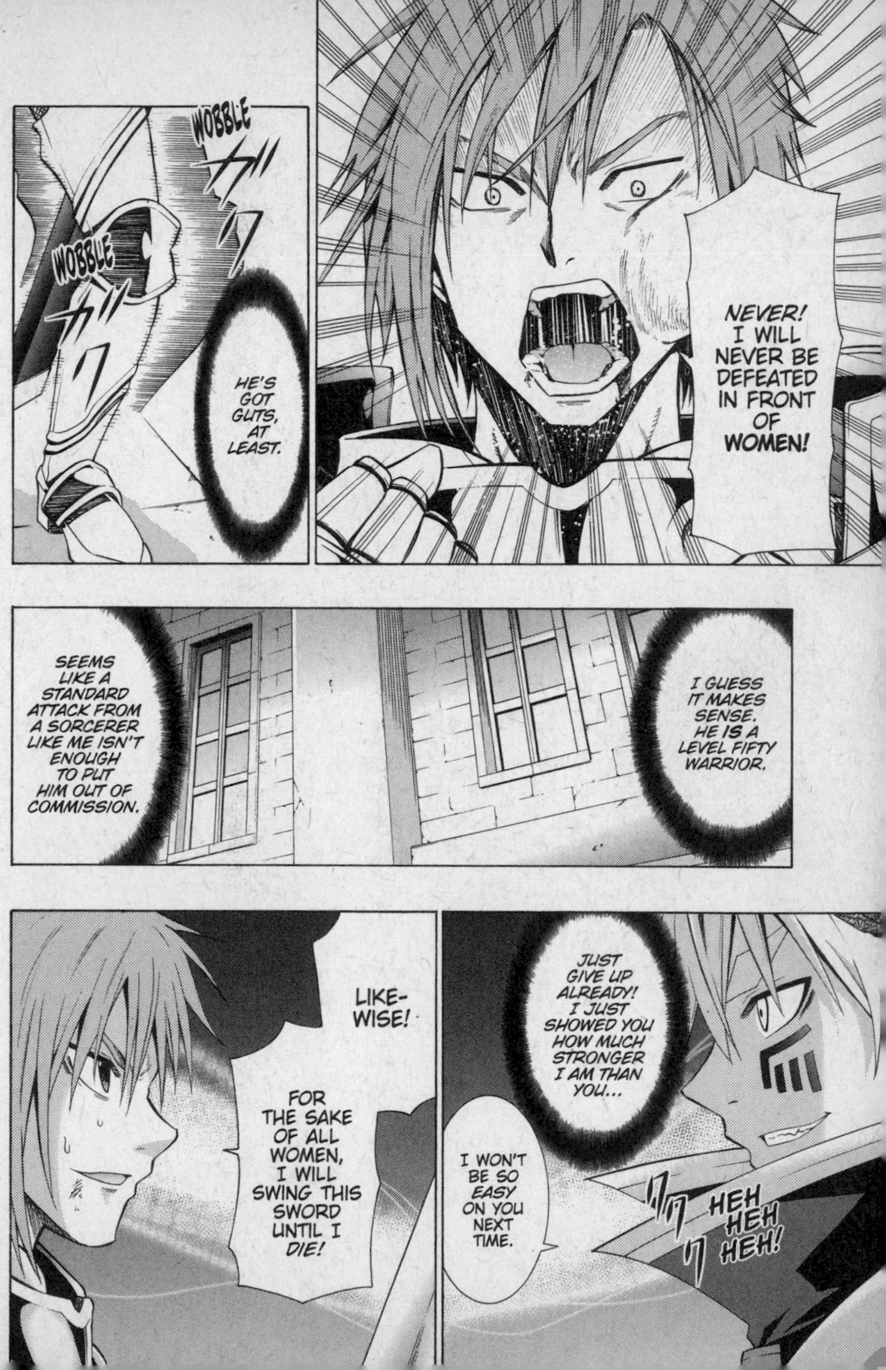
NEVER! I WILL NEVER BE DEFEATED IN FRONT OF WOMEN!
WOBBLE
WOBBLE
HE'S GOT GUTS, AT LEAST.
I GUESS IT MAKES SENSE. HE IS A LEVEL FIFTY WARRIOR.
SEEMS LIKE A STANDARD ATTACK FROM A SORCERER LIKE ME ISN'T ENOUGH TO PUT HIM OUT OF COMMISSION.
JUST GIVE UP ALREADY! I JUST SHOWED YOU HOW MUCH STRONGER I AM THAN YOU...
I WON'T BE SO EASY ON YOU NEXT TIME.
HEH HEH HEH!
LIKE-WISE!
FOR THE SAKE OF ALL WOMEN, I WILL SWING THIS SWORD UNTIL I DIE!

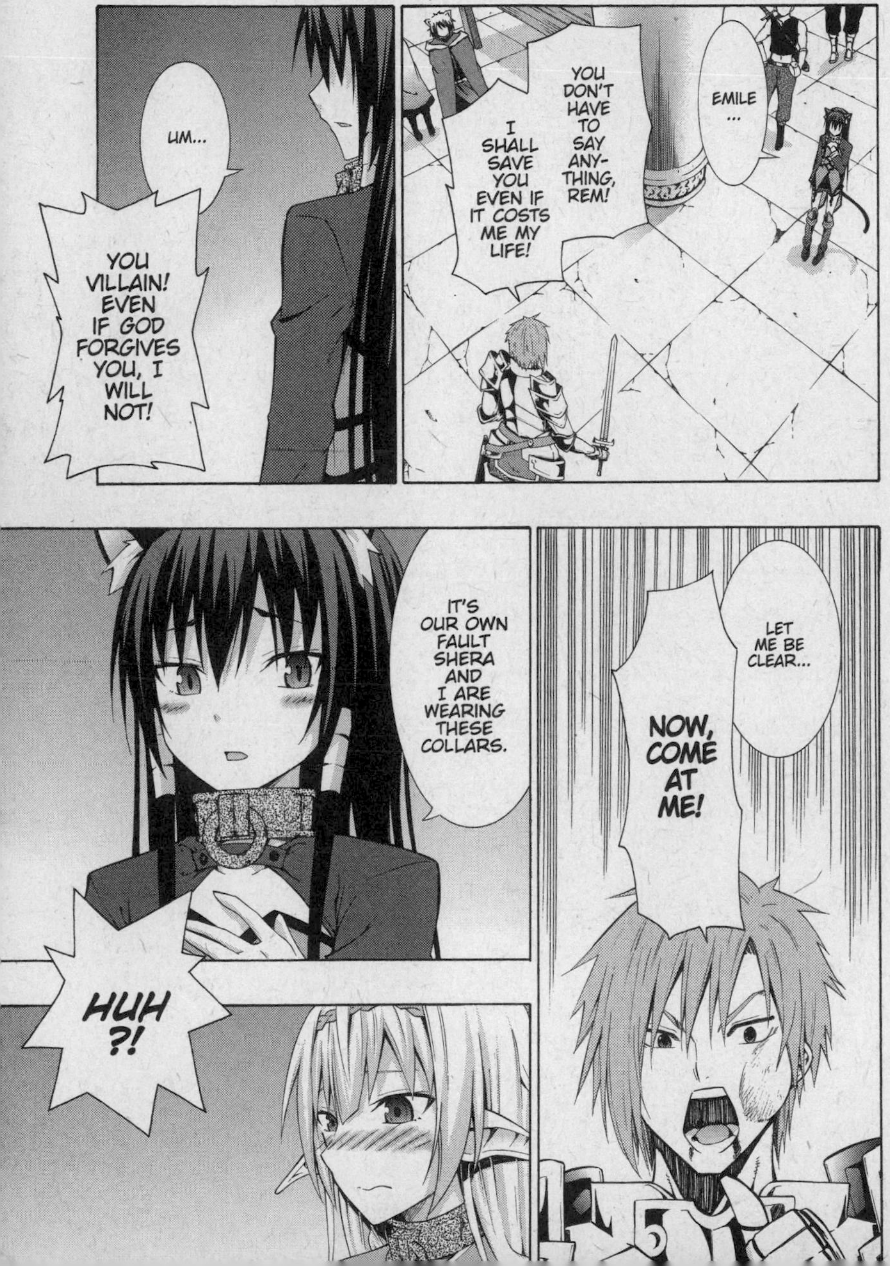
EMILE ...
YOU DON'T HAVE TO SAY ANY-THING, REM!
I SHALL SAVE YOU EVEN IF IT COSTS ME MY LIFE!
UM...
YOU VILLAIN! EVEN IF GOD FORGIVES YOU, I WILL NOT!
LET ME BE CLEAR...
NOW, COME AT ME!
IT'S OUR OWN FAULT SHERA AND I ARE WEARING THESE COLLARS.
HUH ?!

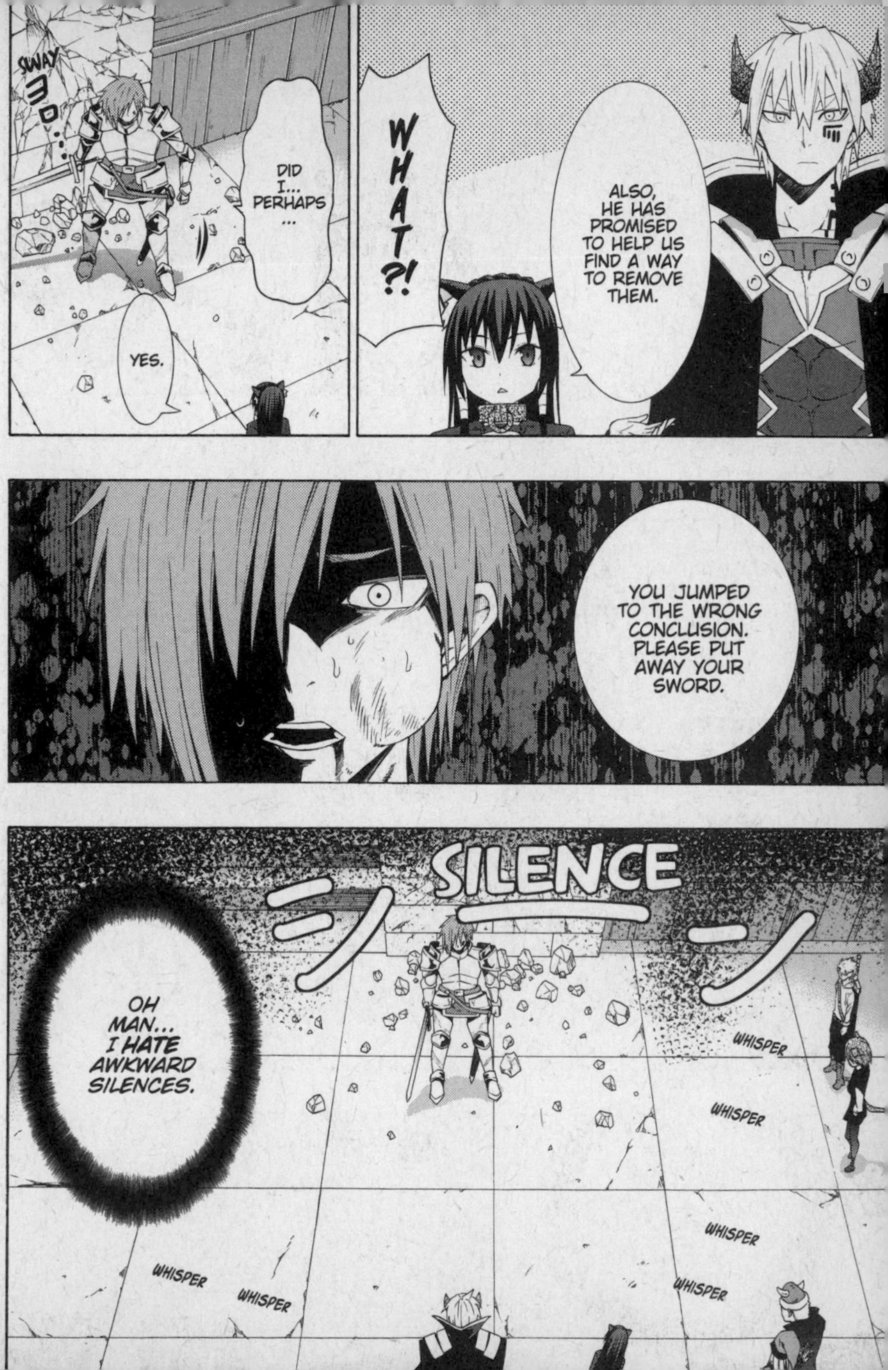
ALSO, HE HAS PROMISED TO HELP US FIND A WAY TO REMOVE THEM.
WHAT?!
SWAY
DID I... PERHAPS ...
YES.
YOU JUMPED TO THE WRONG CONCLUSION. PLEASE PUT AWAY YOUR SWORD.
SILENCE
OH MAN... I HATE AWKWARD SILENCES.
WHISPER
WHISPER
WHISPER
WHISPER
WHISPER
WHISPER

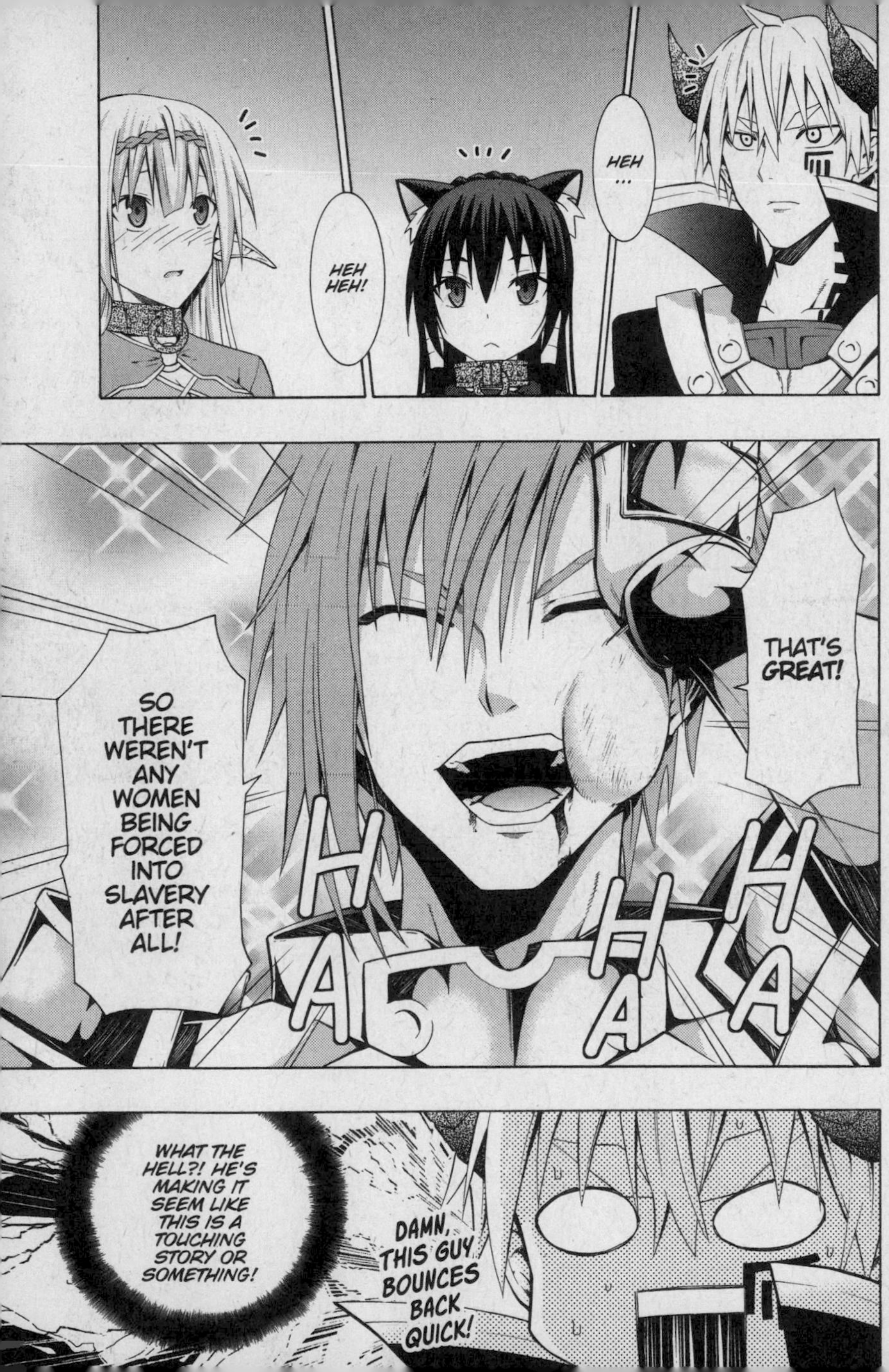
HEH ...
HEH HEH!
THAT'S GREAT!
SO THERE WEREN'T ANY WOMEN BEING FORCED INTO SLAVERY AFTER ALL!
HA HA HA HA
DAMN, THIS GUY BOUNCES BACK QUICK!
WHAT THE HELL?! HE'S MAKING IT SEEM LIKE THIS IS A TOUCHING STORY OR SOMETHING!

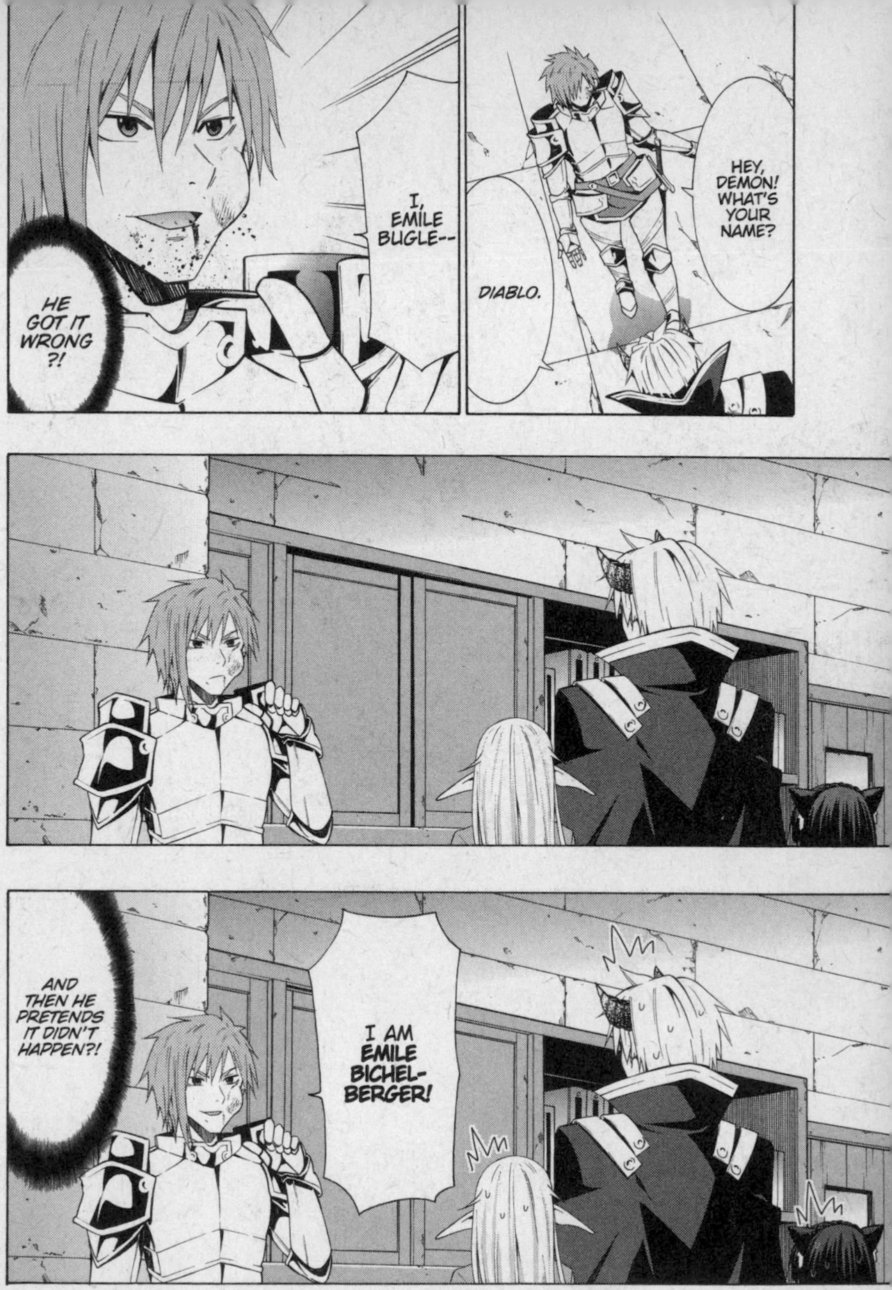
HEY, DEMON! WHAT'S YOUR NAME?
DIABLO.
I, EMILE BUGLE--
HE GOT IT WRONG?!
I AM EMILE BICHEL-BERGER!
AND THEN HE PRETENDS IT DIDN'T HAPPEN?!

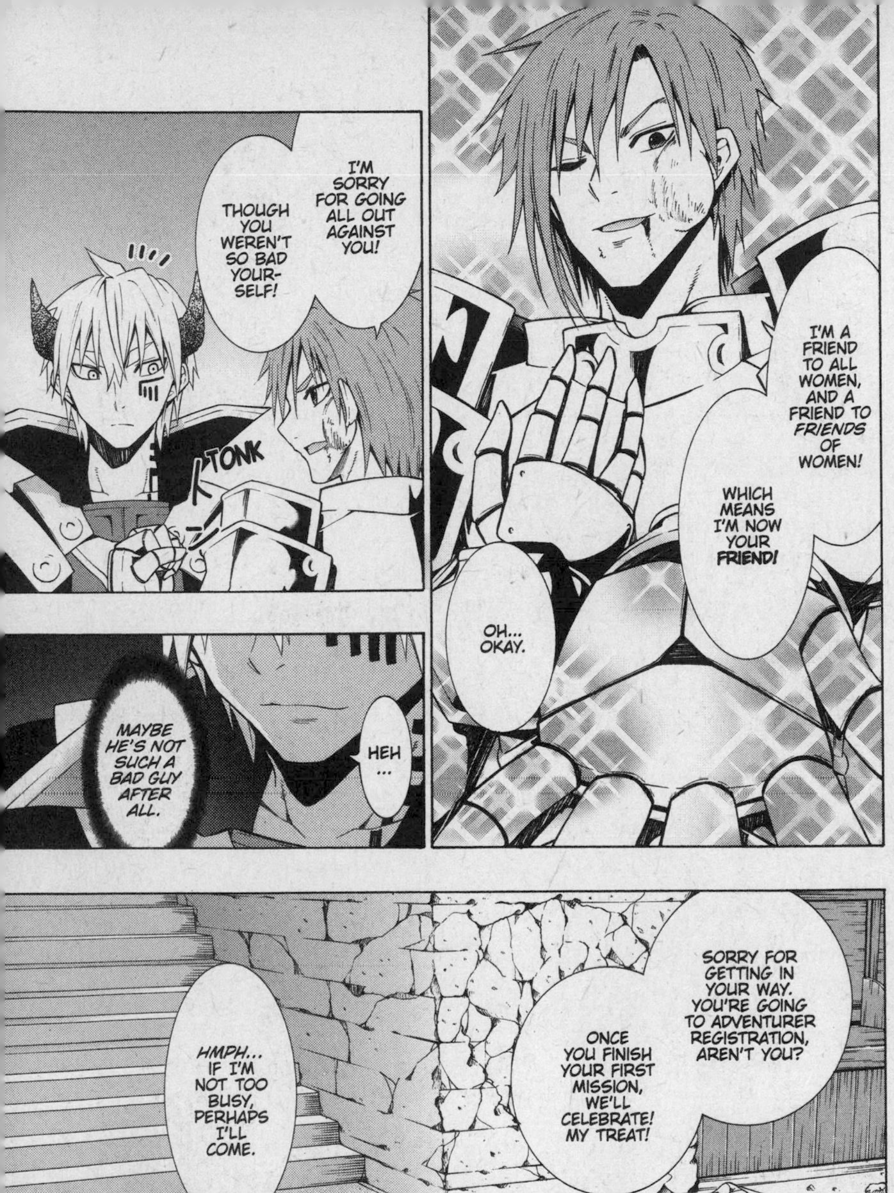
I'M SORRY FOR GOING ALL OUT AGAINST YOU!
THOUGH YOU WEREN'T SO BAD YOUR-SELF!
TONK
HEH ...
MAYBE HE'S NOT SUCH A BAD GUY AFTER ALL.
I'M A FRIEND TO ALL WOMEN, AND A FRIEND TO *FRIENDS* OF WOMEN!
WHICH MEANS I'M NOW YOUR **FRIEND!**
OH... OKAY.
SORRY FOR GETTING IN YOUR WAY. YOU'RE GOING TO ADVENTURER REGISTRATION, AREN'T YOU?
ONCE YOU FINISH YOUR FIRST MISSION, WE'LL CELEBRATE! MY TREAT!
HMPH... IF I'M NOT TOO BUSY, PERHAPS I'LL COME.

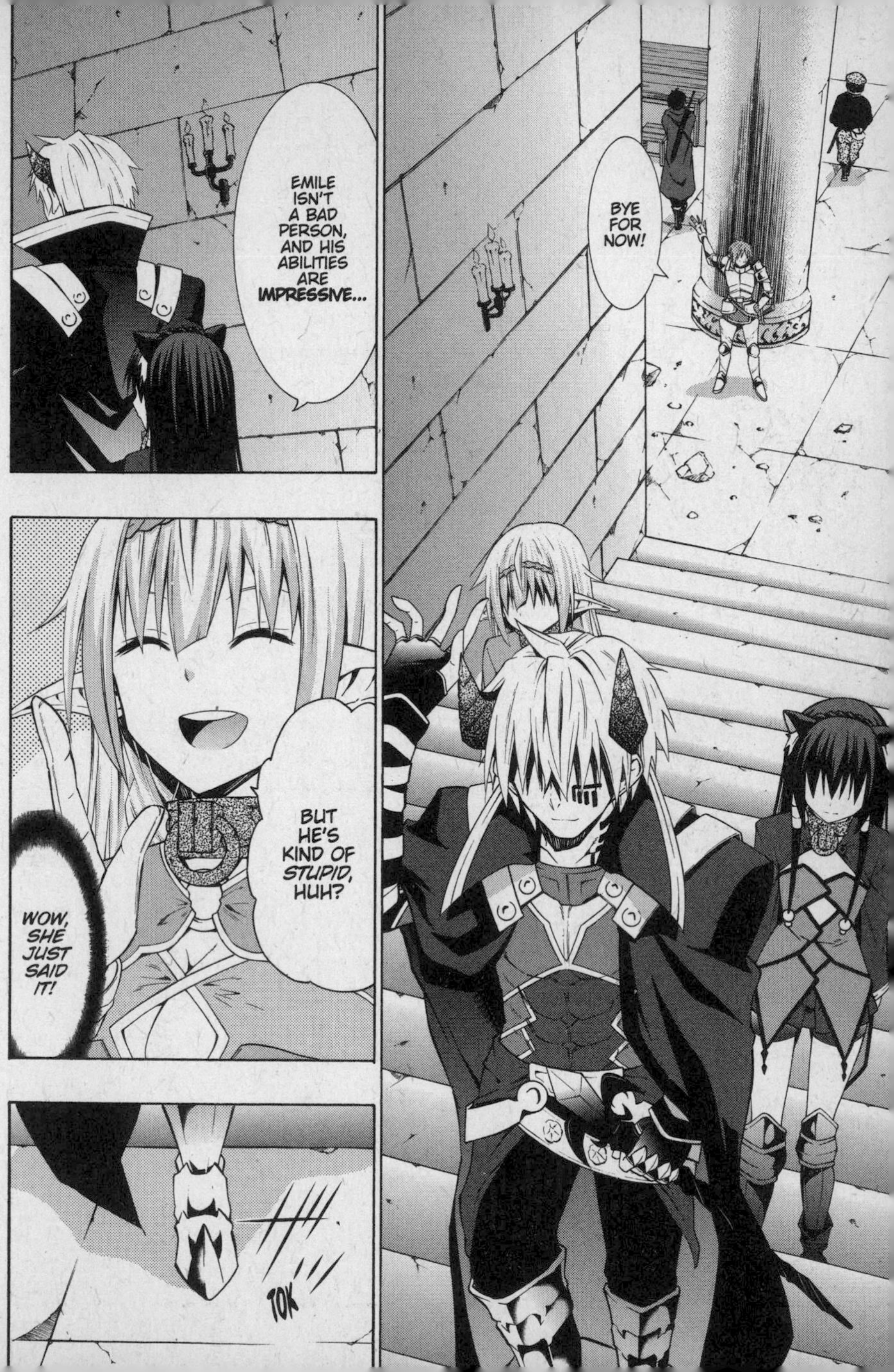
BYE FOR NOW!
EMILE ISN'T A BAD PERSON, AND HIS ABILITIES ARE IMPRESSIVE...
BUT HE'S KIND OF STUPID, HUH?
WOW, SHE JUST SAID IT!
TOK

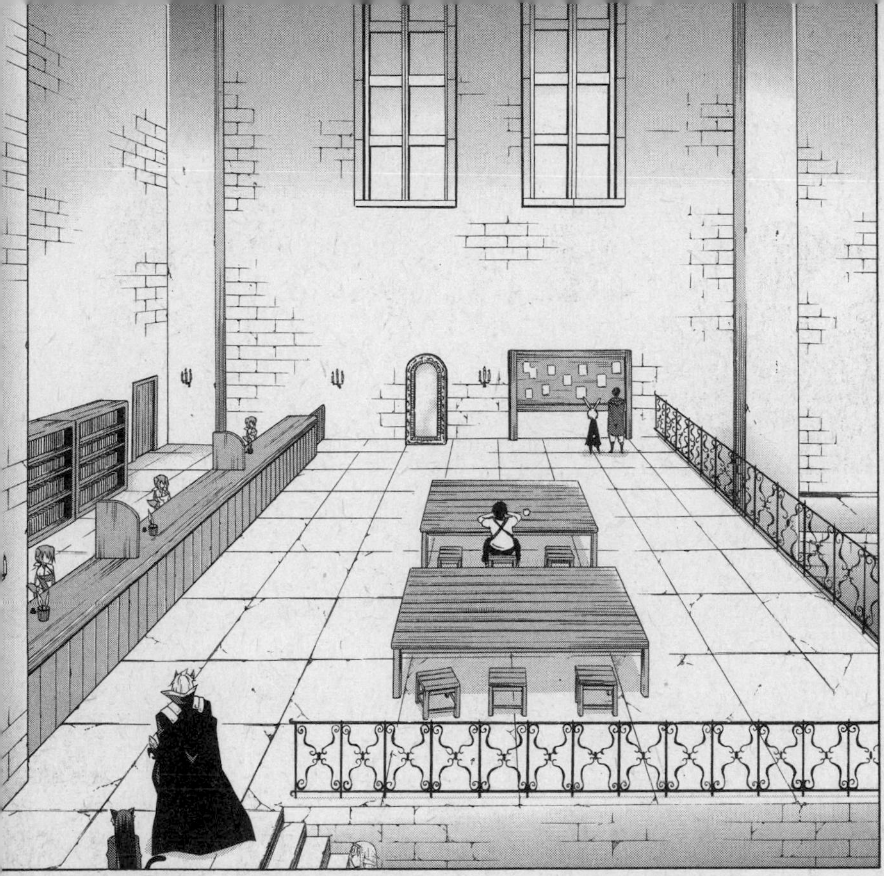

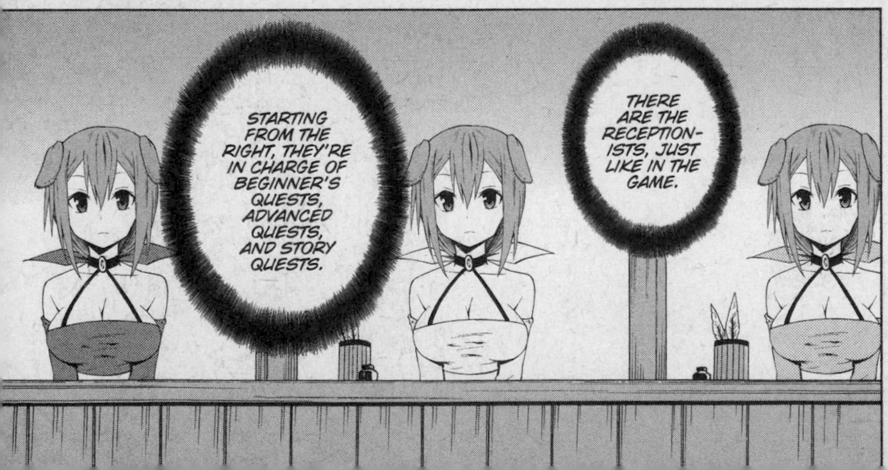
THERE ARE THE RECEPTIONISTS, JUST LIKE IN THE GAME.
STARTING FROM THE RIGHT, THEY'RE IN CHARGE OF BEGINNER'S QUESTS, ADVANCED QUESTS, AND STORY QUESTS.

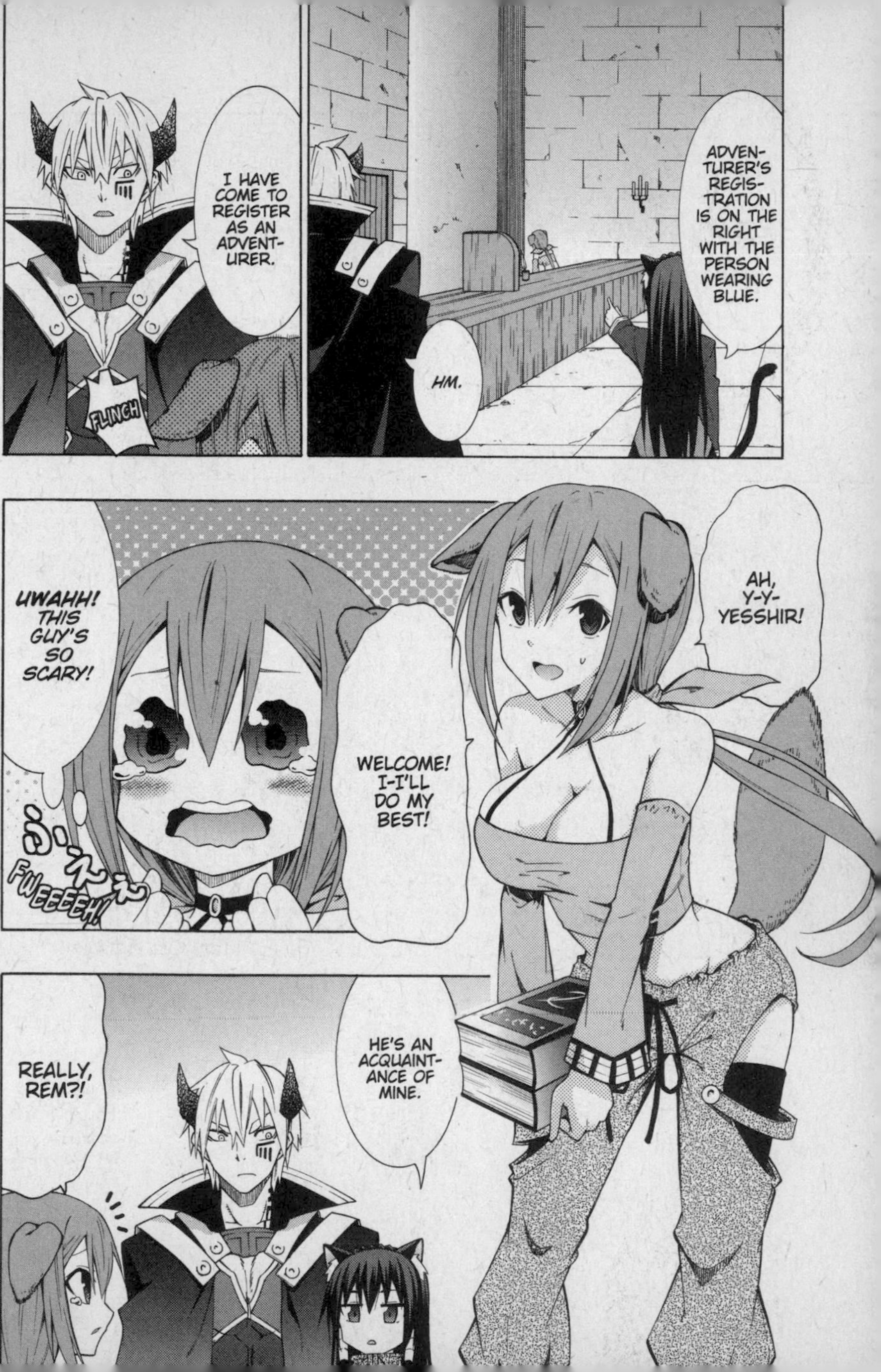
ADVENTURER'S REGISTRATION IS ON THE RIGHT WITH THE PERSON WEARING BLUE.
HM.
I HAVE COME TO REGISTER AS AN ADVENTURER.
FLINCH
AH, Y-Y-YESSHIR!
WELCOME! I-I'LL DO MY BEST!
UWAHH! THIS GUY'S SO SCARY!
FWEEEEH!
HE'S AN ACQUAINTANCE OF MINE.
REALLY, REM?!

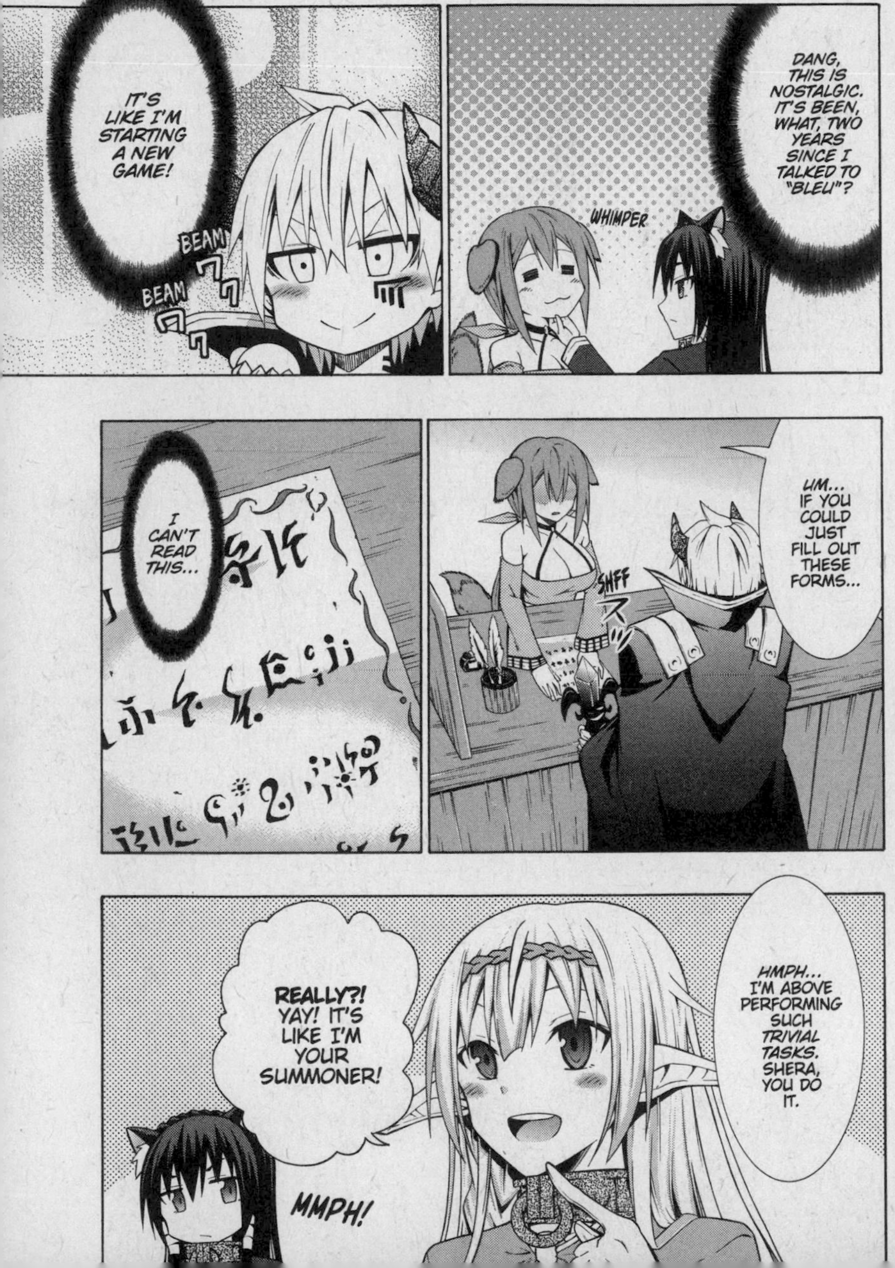
DANG, THIS IS NOSTALGIC. IT'S BEEN, WHAT, TWO YEARS SINCE I TALKED TO "BLEU"?
WHIMPER
IT'S LIKE I'M STARTING A NEW GAME!
BEAM
BEAM
UM... IF YOU COULD JUST FILL OUT THESE FORMS...
SHFF
I CAN'T READ THIS...
HMPH... I'M ABOVE PERFORMING SUCH TRIVIAL TASKS. SHERA, YOU DO IT.
REALLY?! YAY! IT'S LIKE I'M YOUR SUMMONER!
MMPH!

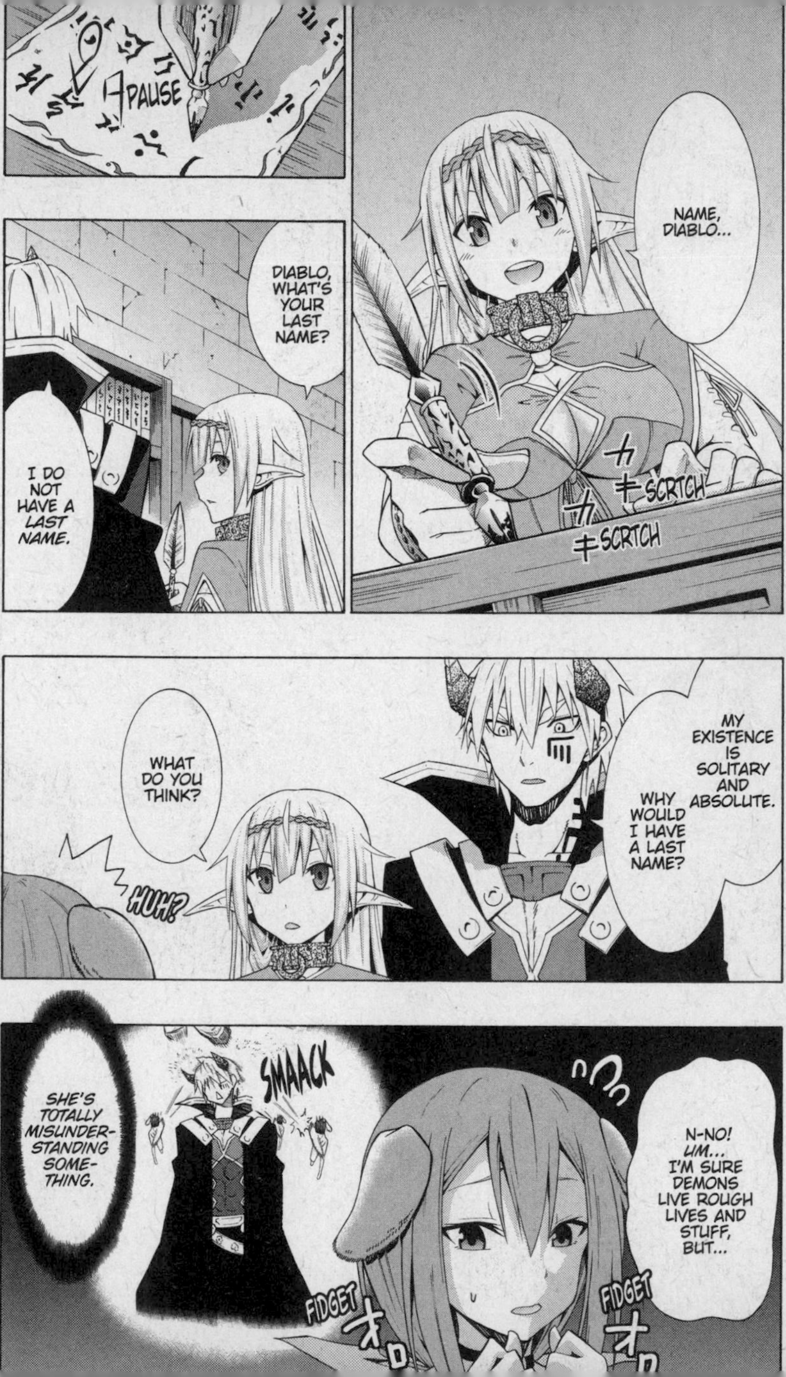
NAME, DIABLO...
SCRTCH
SCRTCH
PAUSE
DIABLO, WHAT'S YOUR LAST NAME?
I DO NOT HAVE A LAST NAME.
MY EXISTENCE IS SOLITARY AND ABSOLUTE.
WHY WOULD I HAVE A LAST NAME?
WHAT DO YOU THINK?
HUH?
N-NO! UM... I'M SURE DEMONS LIVE ROUGH LIVES AND STUFF, BUT...
FIDGET
FIDGET
SMAACK
SHE'S TOTALLY MISUNDER-STANDING SOME-THING.

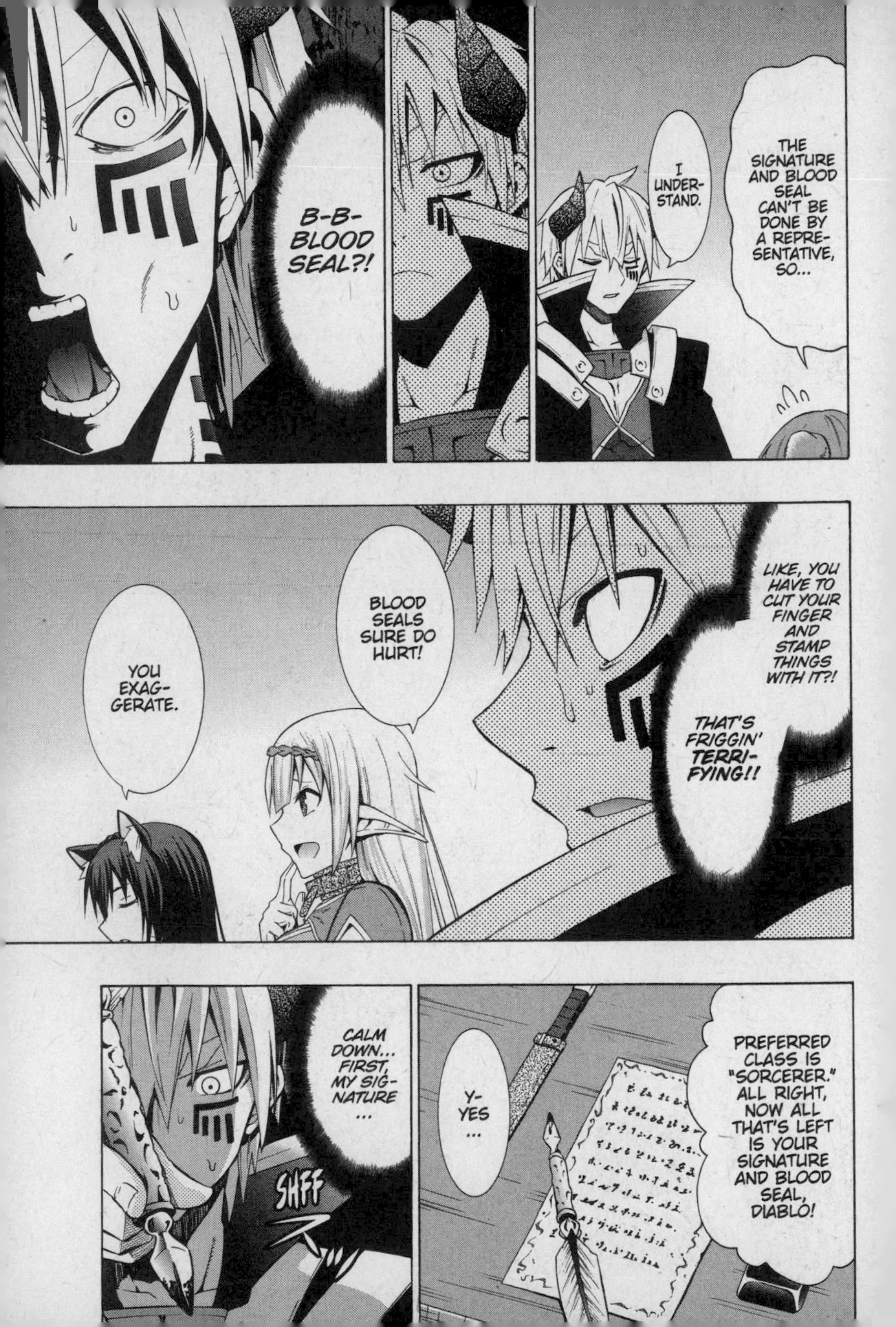
THE SIGNATURE AND BLOOD SEAL CAN'T BE DONE BY A REPRESENTATIVE, SO...
I UNDERSTAND.
B-B-BLOOD SEAL?!
LIKE, YOU HAVE TO CUT YOUR FINGER AND STAMP THINGS WITH IT?!
THAT'S FRIGGIN' TERRIFYING!!
BLOOD SEALS SURE DO HURT!
YOU EXAGGERATE.
PREFERRED CLASS IS "SORCERER." ALL RIGHT, NOW ALL THAT'S LEFT IS YOUR SIGNATURE AND BLOOD SEAL, DIABLO!
Y-YES...
CALM DOWN... FIRST, MY SIGNATURE...
SHFF

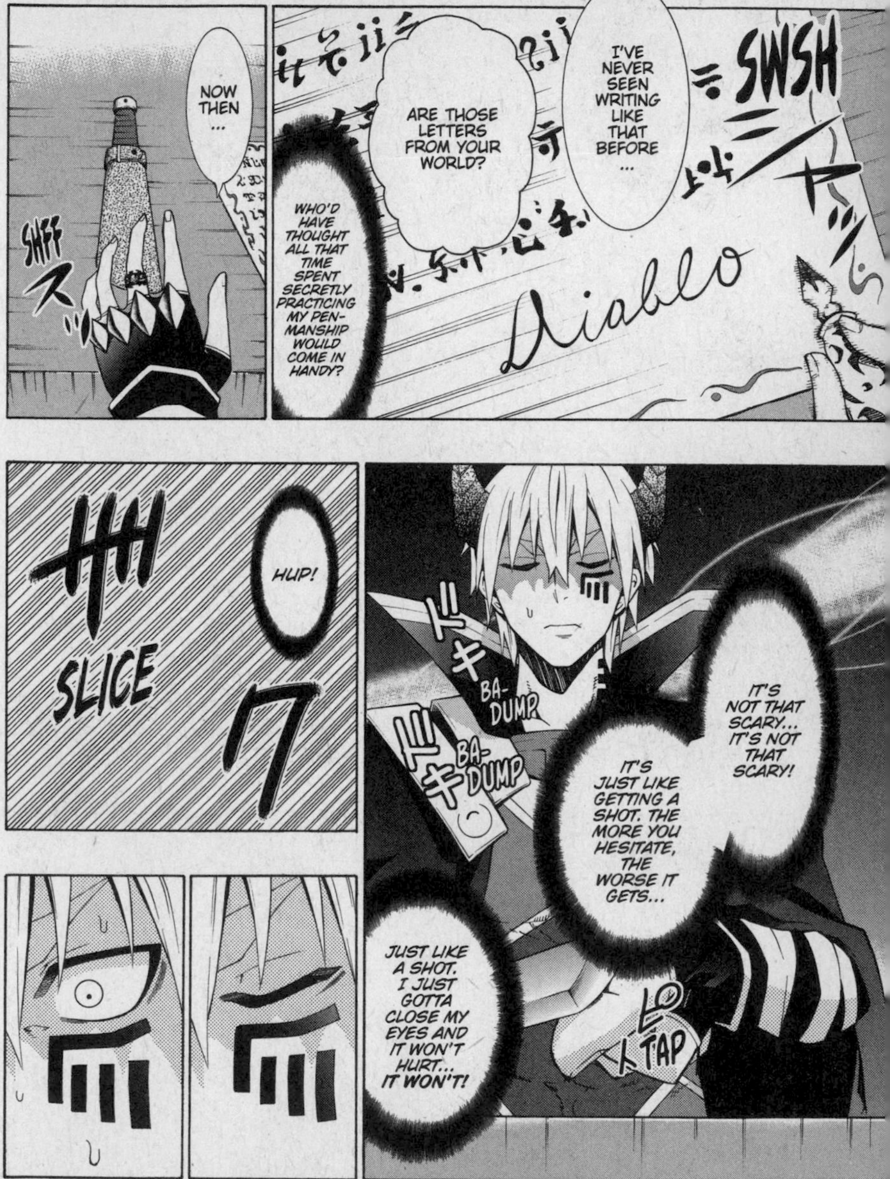
SWSH
I'VE NEVER SEEN WRITING LIKE THAT BEFORE...
ARE THOSE LETTERS FROM YOUR WORLD?
WHO'D HAVE THOUGHT ALL THAT TIME SPENT SECRETLY PRACTICING MY PEN-MANSHIP WOULD COME IN HANDY?
Diablo
NOW THEN...
SHFF
BA-DUMP
BA-DUMP
IT'S NOT THAT SCARY... IT'S NOT THAT SCARY!
IT'S JUST LIKE GETTING A SHOT. THE MORE YOU HESITATE, THE WORSE IT GETS...
JUST LIKE A SHOT. I JUST GOTTA CLOSE MY EYES AND IT WON'T HURT... IT WON'T!
TAP
HUP!
SLICE

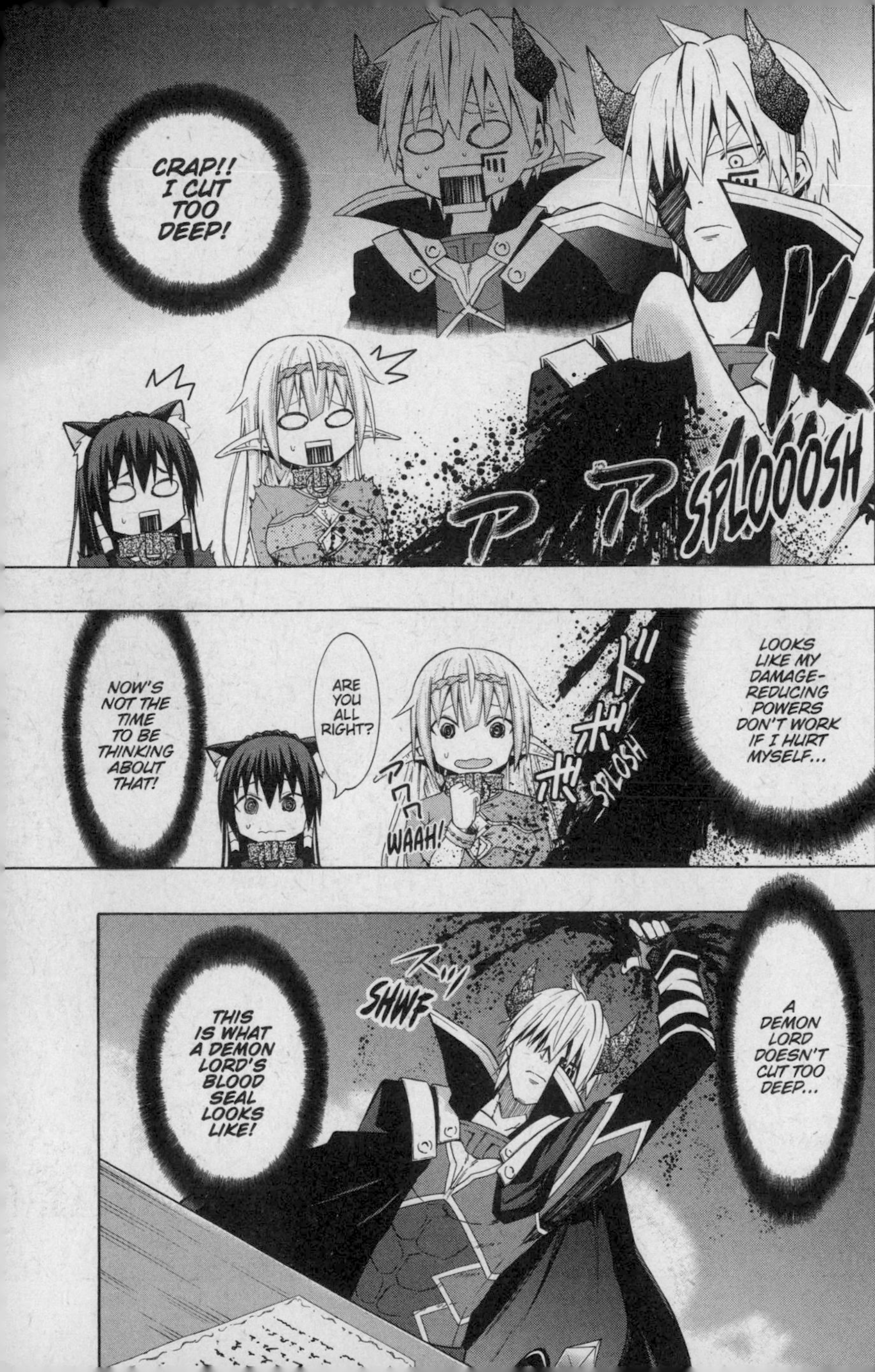
SPLOOOSH
CRAP!! I CUT TOO DEEP!
LOOKS LIKE MY DAMAGE-REDUCING POWERS DON'T WORK IF I HURT MYSELF...
SPLOSH
WAAH!
ARE YOU ALL RIGHT?
NOW'S NOT THE TIME TO BE THINKING ABOUT THAT!
A DEMON LORD DOESN'T CUT TOO DEEP...
SHWF
THIS IS WHAT A DEMON LORD'S BLOOD SEAL LOOKS LIKE!

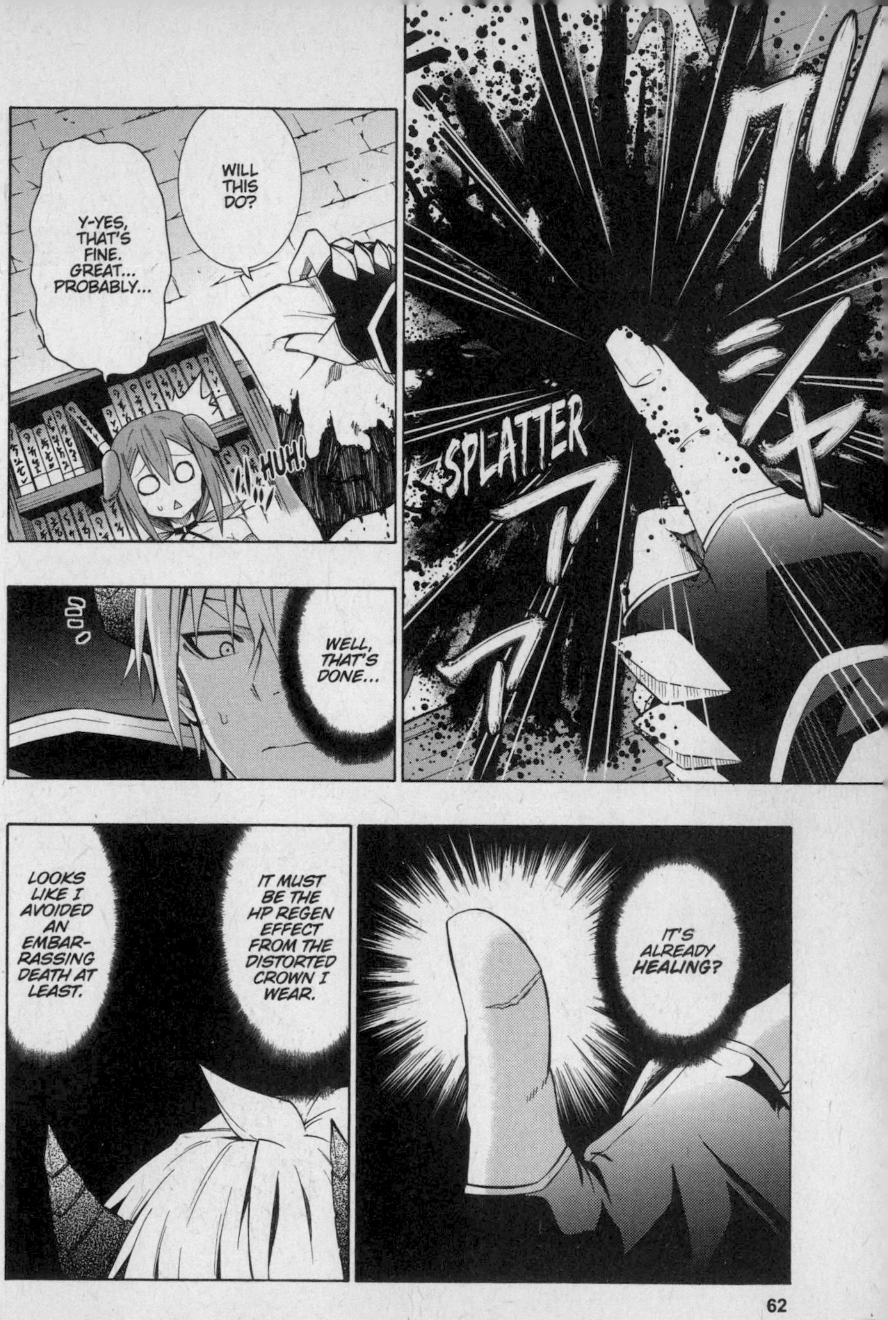
SPLATTER
WILL THIS DO?
Y-YES, THAT'S FINE. GREAT... PROBABLY...
HUH!
WELL, THAT'S DONE...
IT'S ALREADY HEALING?
IT MUST BE THE HP REGEN EFFECT FROM THE DISTORTED CROWN I WEAR.
LOOKS LIKE I AVOIDED AN EMBARRASSING DEATH AT LEAST.

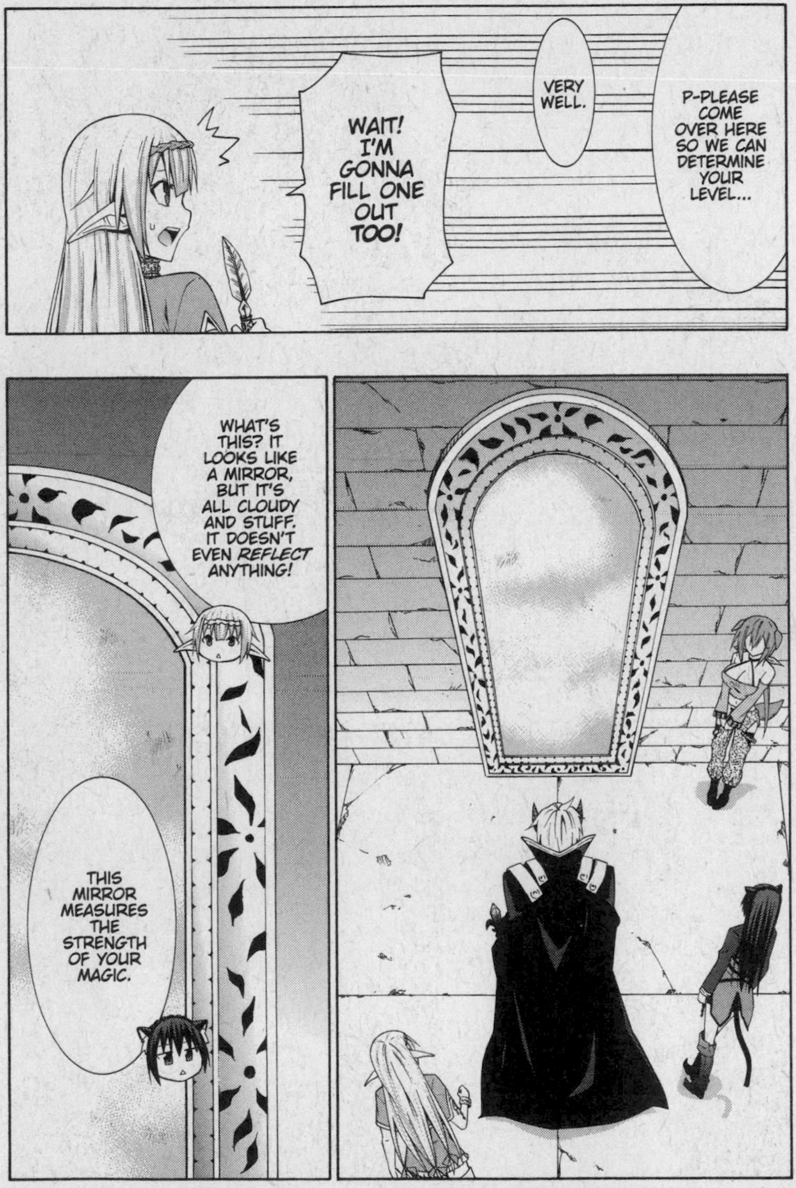
P-PLEASE COME OVER HERE SO WE CAN DETERMINE YOUR LEVEL...
VERY WELL.
WAIT! I'M GONNA FILL ONE OUT TOO!
WHAT'S THIS? IT LOOKS LIKE A MIRROR, BUT IT'S ALL CLOUDY AND STUFF. IT DOESN'T EVEN *REFLECT* ANYTHING!
THIS MIRROR MEASURES THE STRENGTH OF YOUR MAGIC.

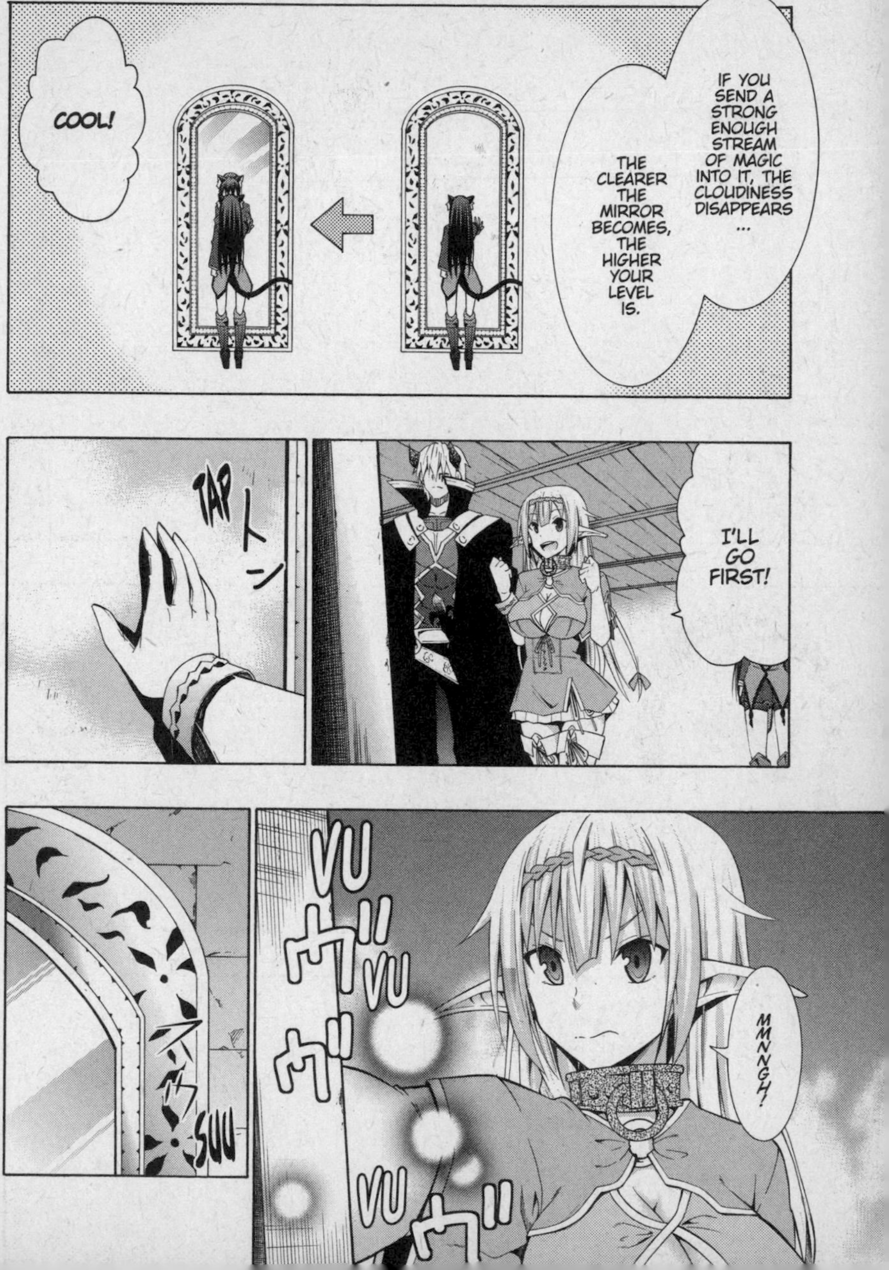
IF YOU SEND A STRONG ENOUGH STREAM OF MAGIC INTO IT, THE CLOUDINESS DISAPPEARS...
THE CLEARER THE MIRROR BECOMES, THE HIGHER YOUR LEVEL IS.
COOL!
I'LL GO FIRST!
TAP トン
MMNNGH!
VU ヴ VU ヴ VU ヴ
SUU スー

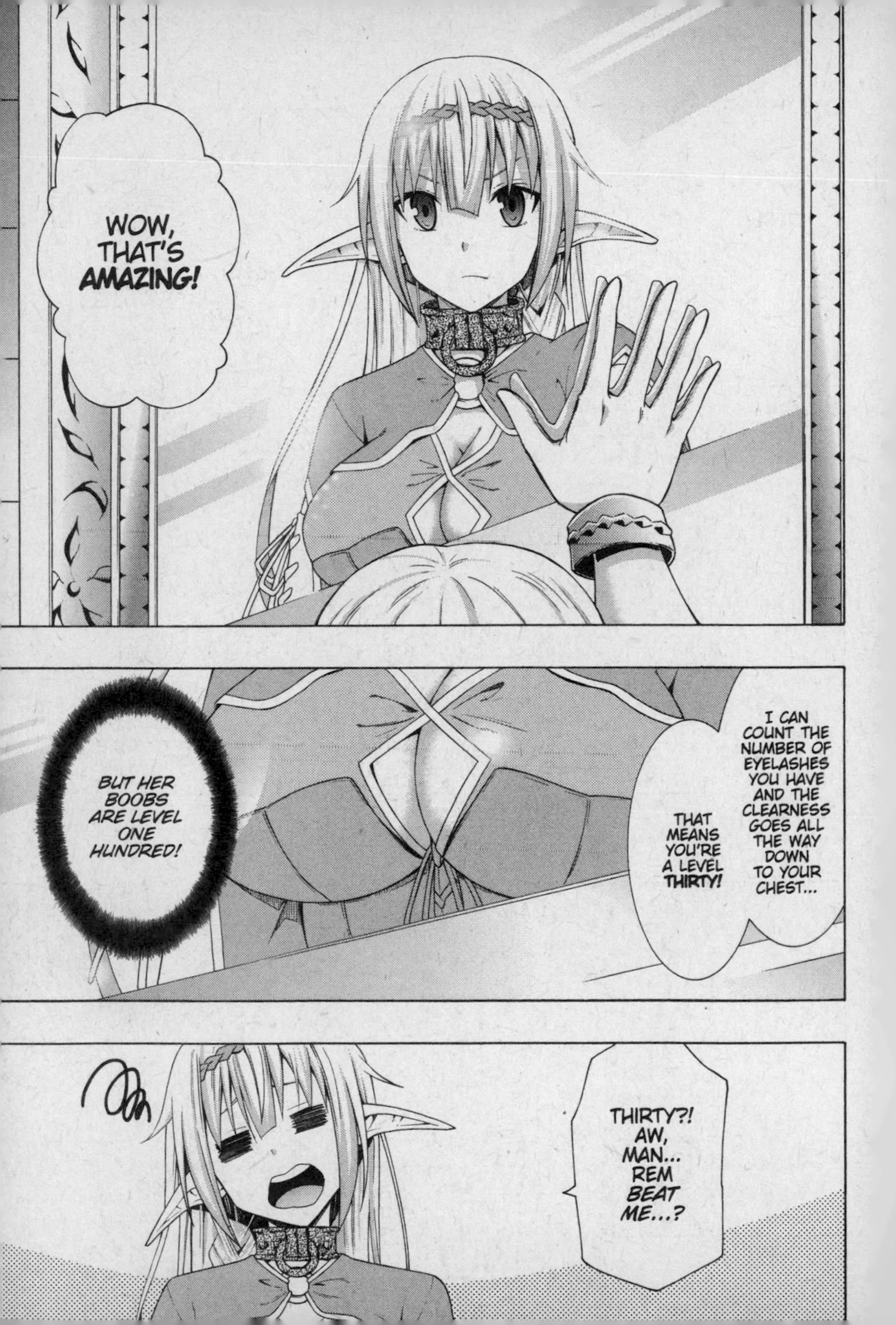
WOW, THAT'S AMAZING!
I CAN COUNT THE NUMBER OF EYELASHES YOU HAVE AND THE CLEARNESS GOES ALL THE WAY DOWN TO YOUR CHEST...
THAT MEANS YOU'RE A LEVEL THIRTY!
BUT HER BOOBS ARE LEVEL ONE HUNDRED!
THIRTY?! AW, MAN... REM BEAT ME...?

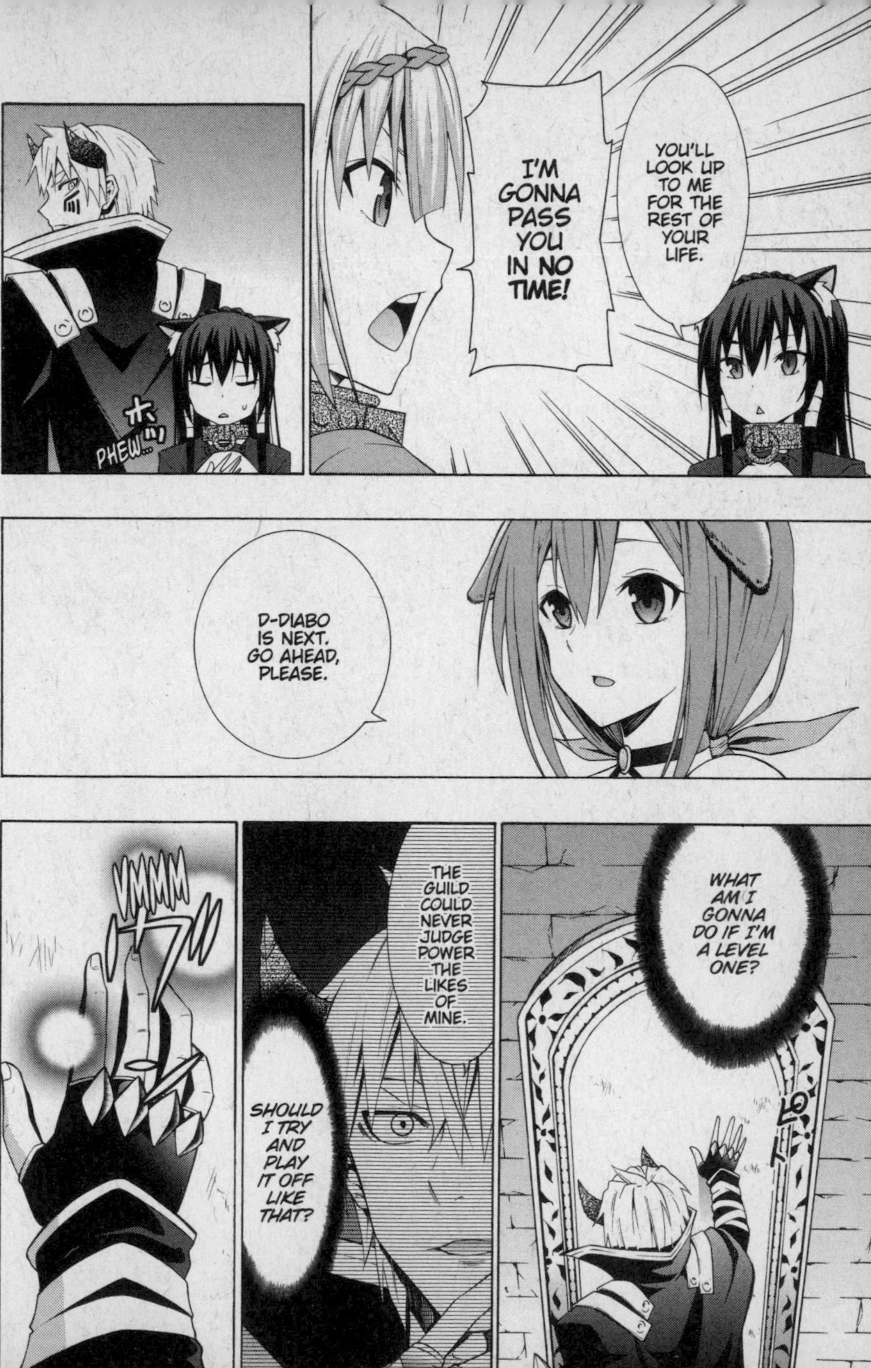
YOU'LL LOOK UP TO ME FOR THE REST OF YOUR LIFE.
I'M GONNA PASS YOU IN NO TIME!
PHEW...
D-DIABO IS NEXT. GO AHEAD, PLEASE.
WHAT AM I GONNA DO IF I'M A LEVEL ONE?
THE GUILD COULD NEVER JUDGE POWER THE LIKES OF MINE.
SHOULD I TRY AND PLAY IT OFF LIKE THAT?
VMMM

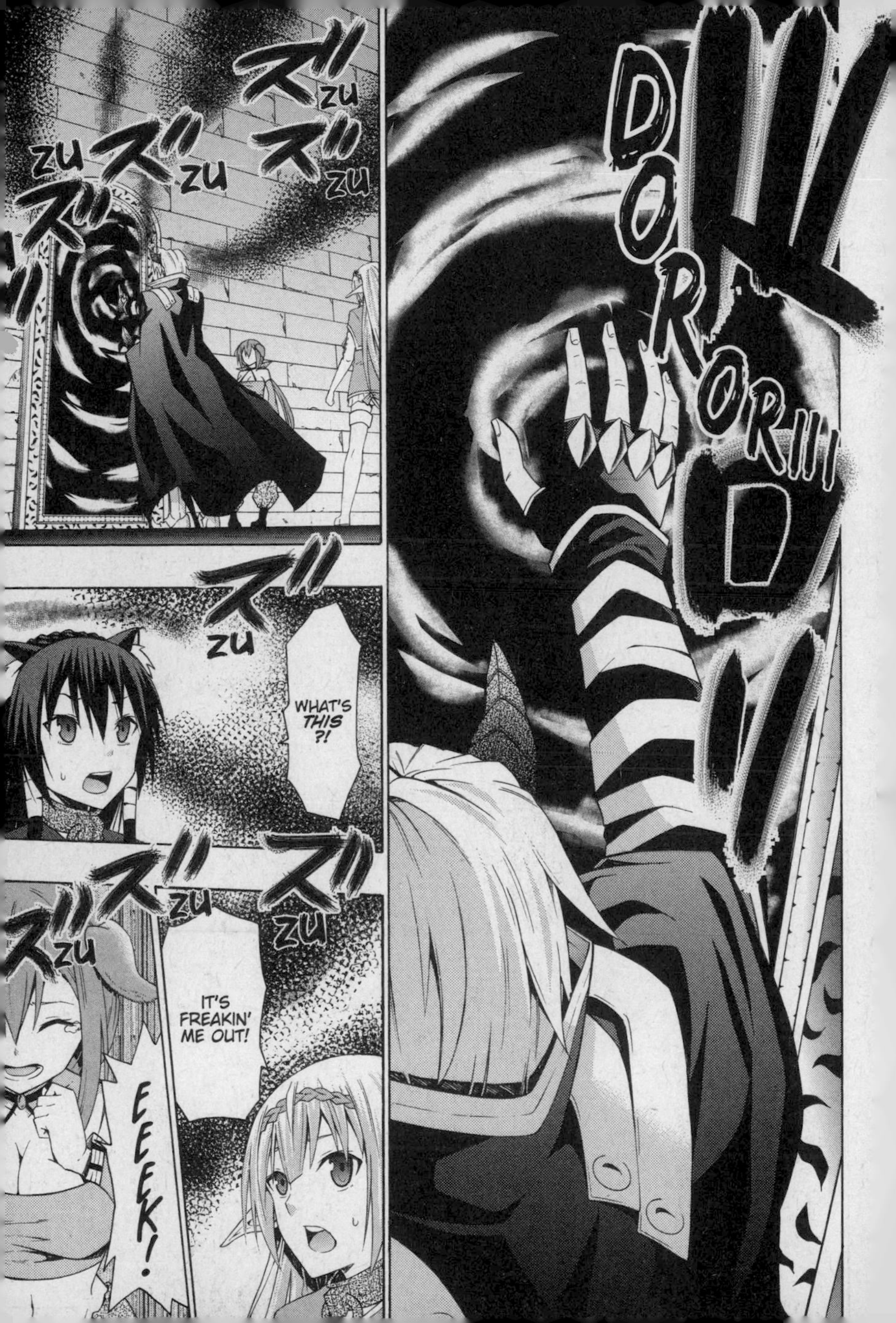
DORORIII
zu
zu
zu
zu
zu
WHAT'S *THIS* ?!
zu
zu
zu
IT'S FREAKIN' ME OUT!
EEEK!

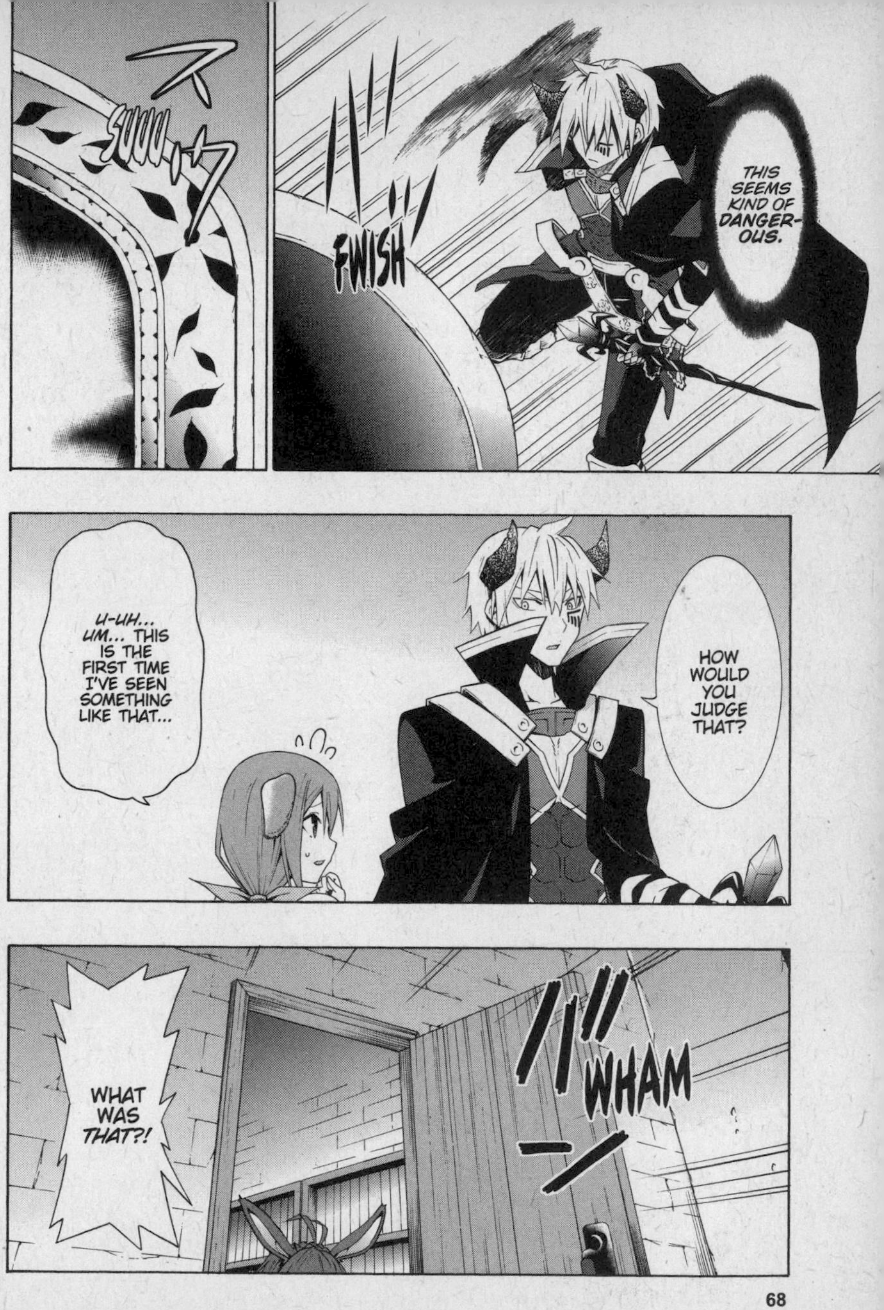
FWISH
THIS SEEMS KIND OF DANGER-OUS.
SUUUU
HOW WOULD YOU JUDGE THAT?
U-UH... UM... THIS IS THE FIRST TIME I'VE SEEN SOMETHING LIKE THAT...
WHAM
WHAT WAS THAT?!

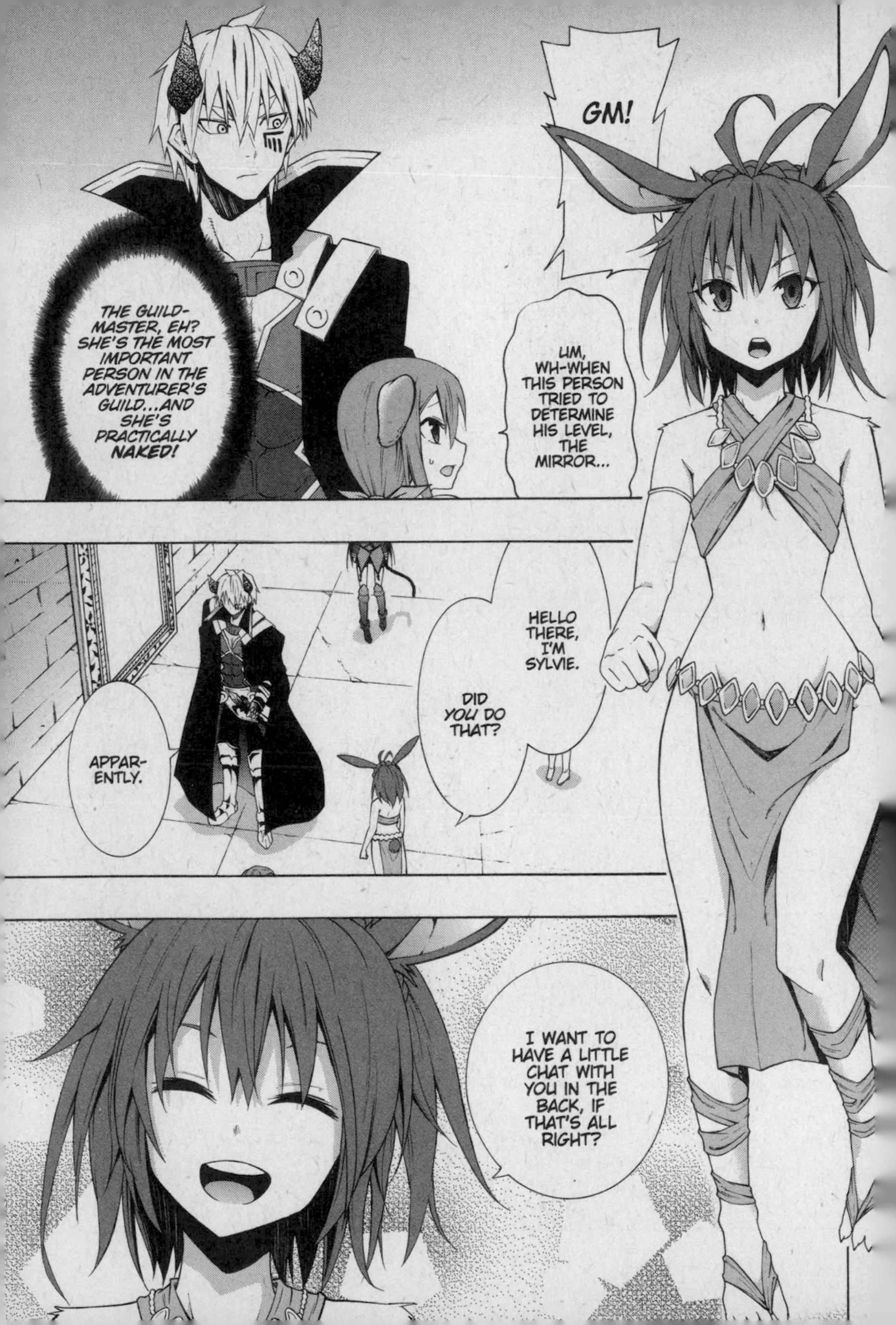
GM!
UM, WH-WHEN THIS PERSON TRIED TO DETERMINE HIS LEVEL, THE MIRROR...
THE GUILD-MASTER, EH? SHE'S THE MOST IMPORTANT PERSON IN THE ADVENTURER'S GUILD...AND SHE'S PRACTICALLY NAKED!
HELLO THERE, I'M SYLVIE.
DID YOU DO THAT?
APPAR-ENTLY.
I WANT TO HAVE A LITTLE CHAT WITH YOU IN THE BACK, IF THAT'S ALL RIGHT?

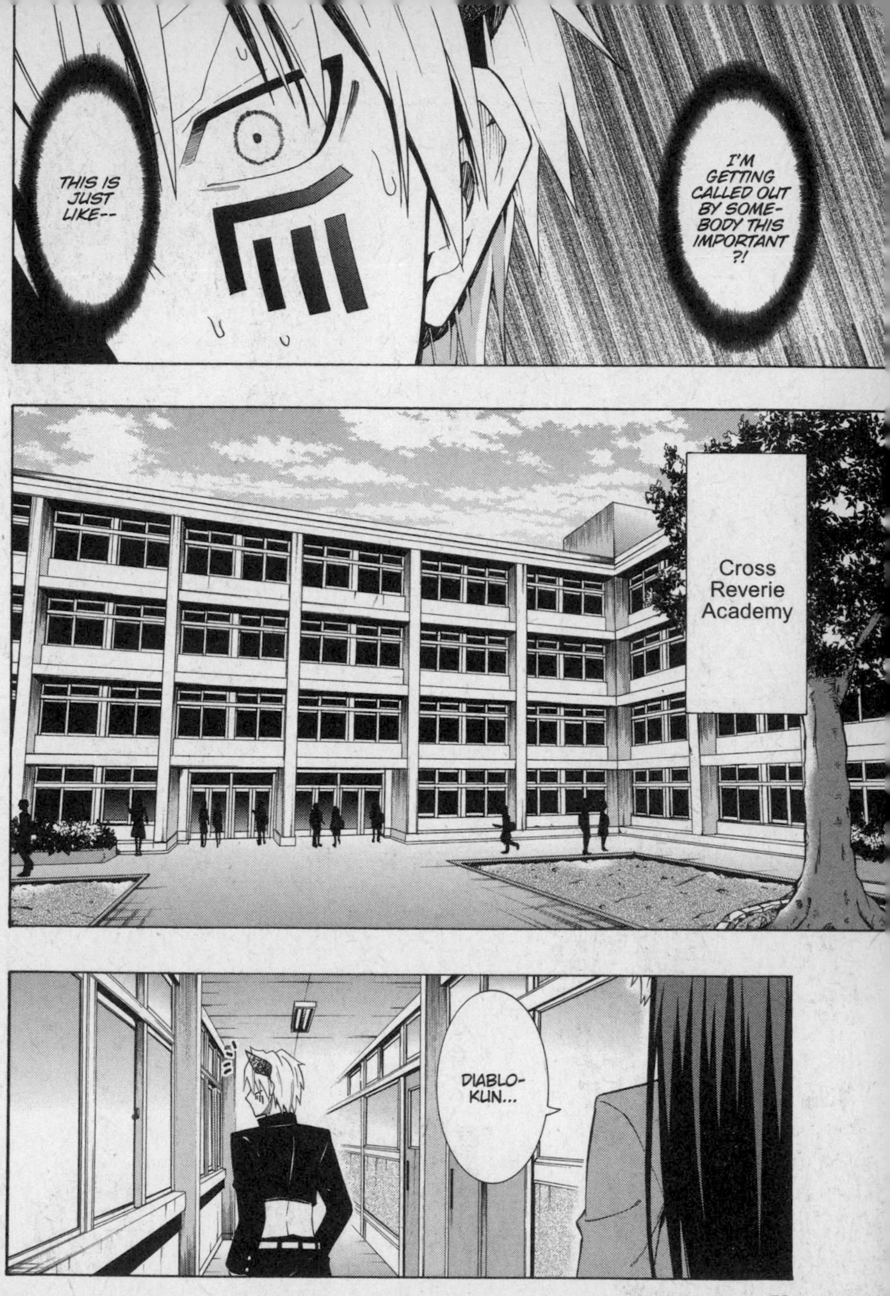
I'M GETTING CALLED OUT BY SOME-BODY THIS IMPORTANT ?!
THIS IS JUST LIKE--
Cross Reverie Academy
DIABLO-KUN...

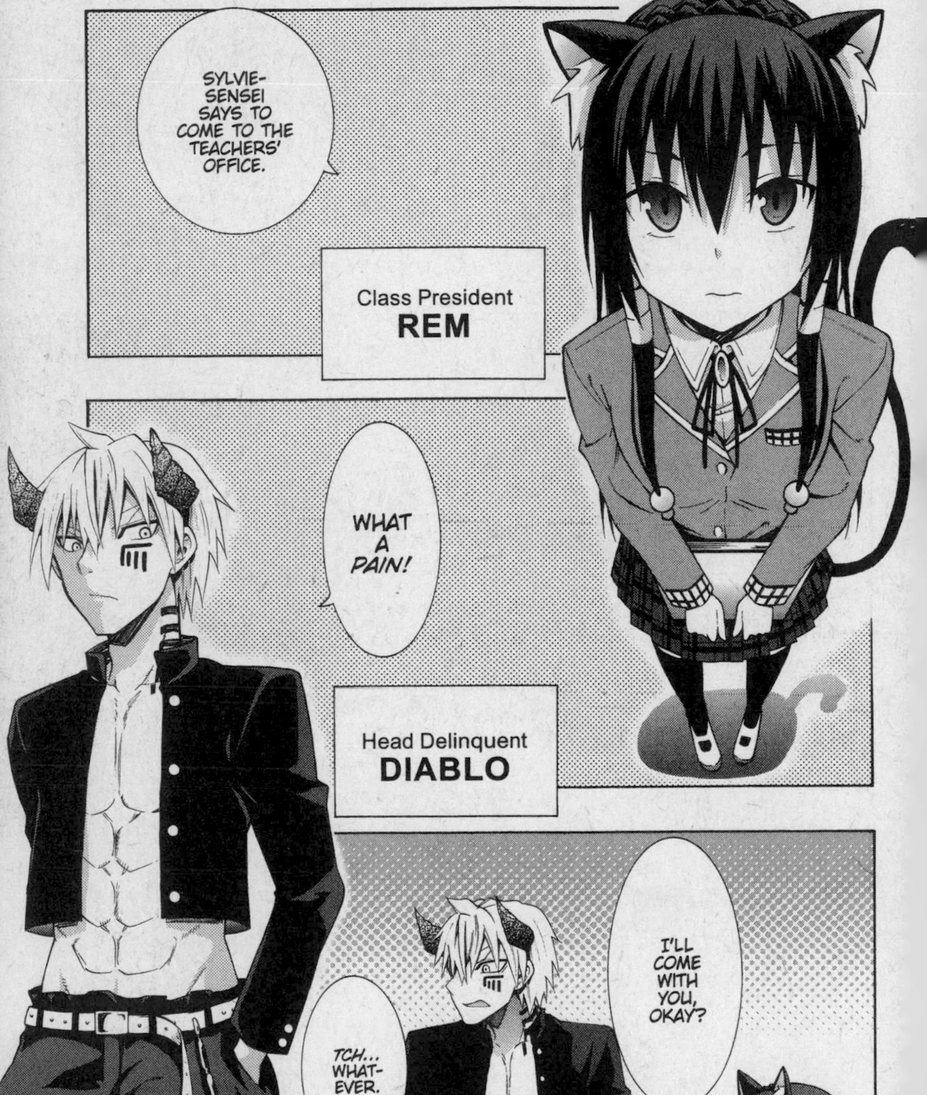
SYLVIE-SENSEI SAYS TO COME TO THE TEACHERS' OFFICE.
Class President REM
WHAT A PAIN!
Head Delinquent DIABLO
I'LL COME WITH YOU, OKAY?
TCH... WHATEVER.

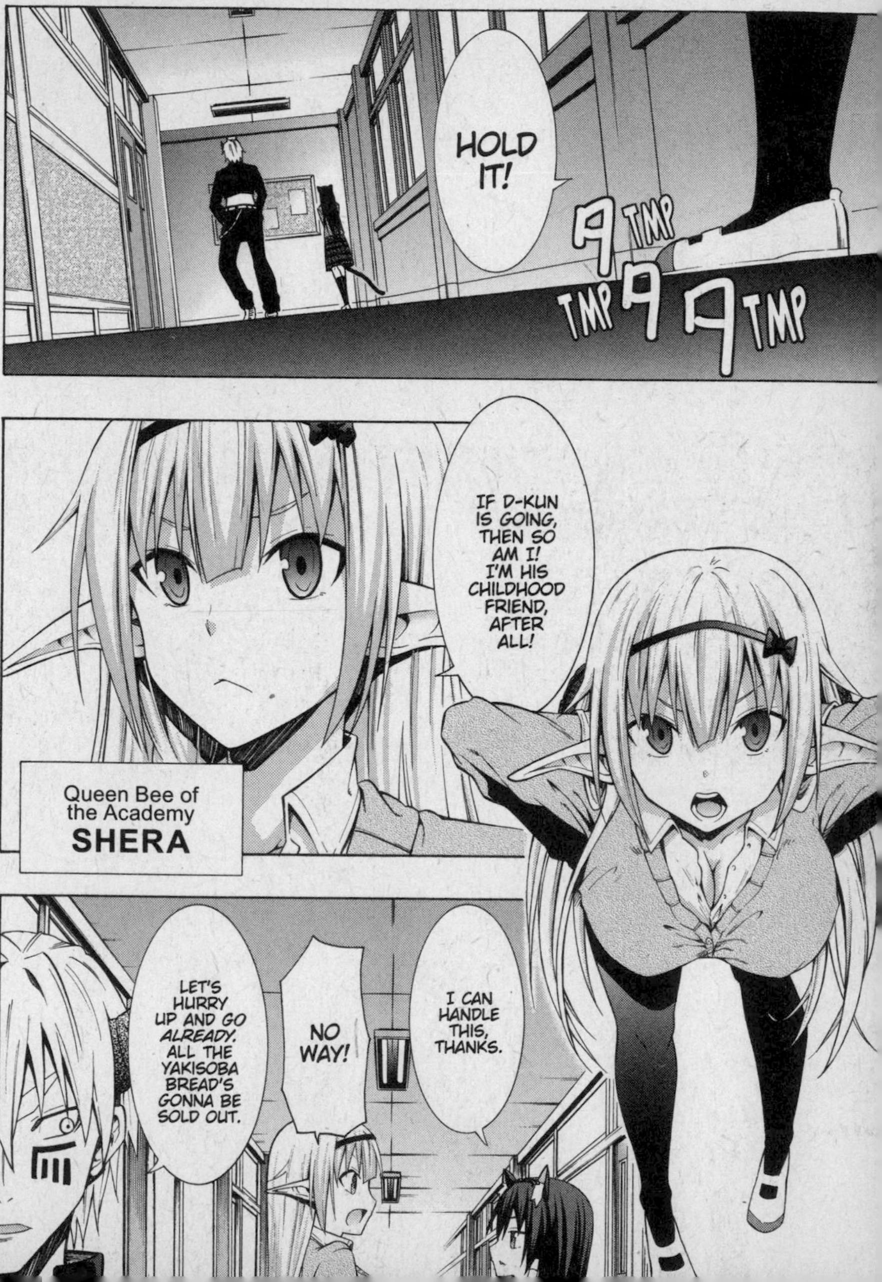
HOLD IT!
TMP TMP TMP TMP
IF D-KUN IS GOING, THEN SO AM I! I'M HIS CHILDHOOD FRIEND, AFTER ALL!
Queen Bee of the Academy
SHERA
I CAN HANDLE THIS, THANKS.
NO WAY!
LET'S HURRY UP AND GO ALREADY. ALL THE YAKISOBA BREAD'S GONNA BE SOLD OUT.

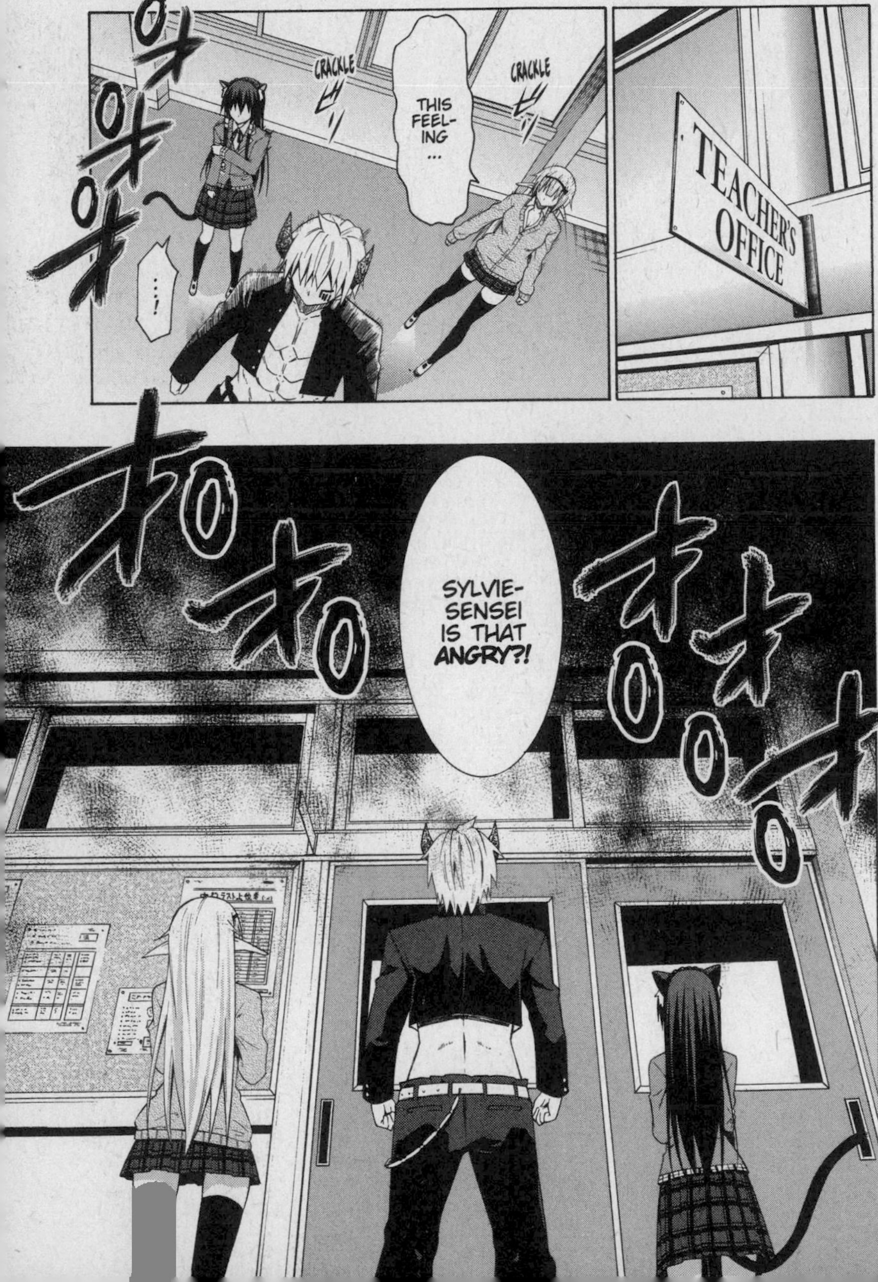
TEACHER'S OFFICE
CRACKLE
THIS FEEL-ING ...
CRACKLE
...!
SYLVIE-SENSEI IS THAT ANGRY?!

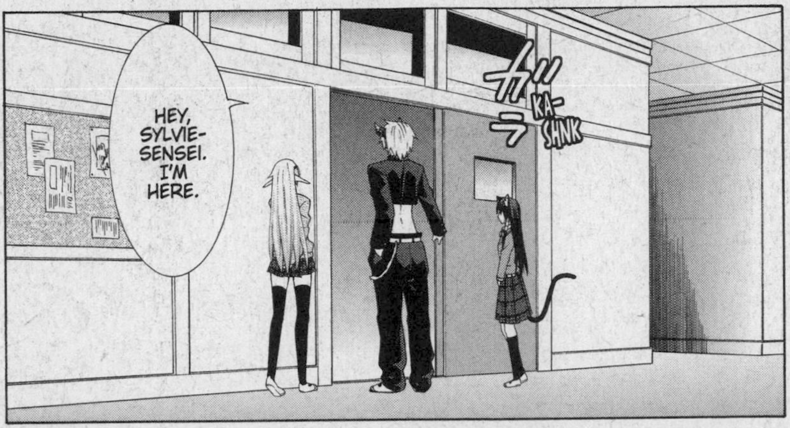
KA-SHNK
HEY, SYLVIE-SENSEI. I'M HERE.

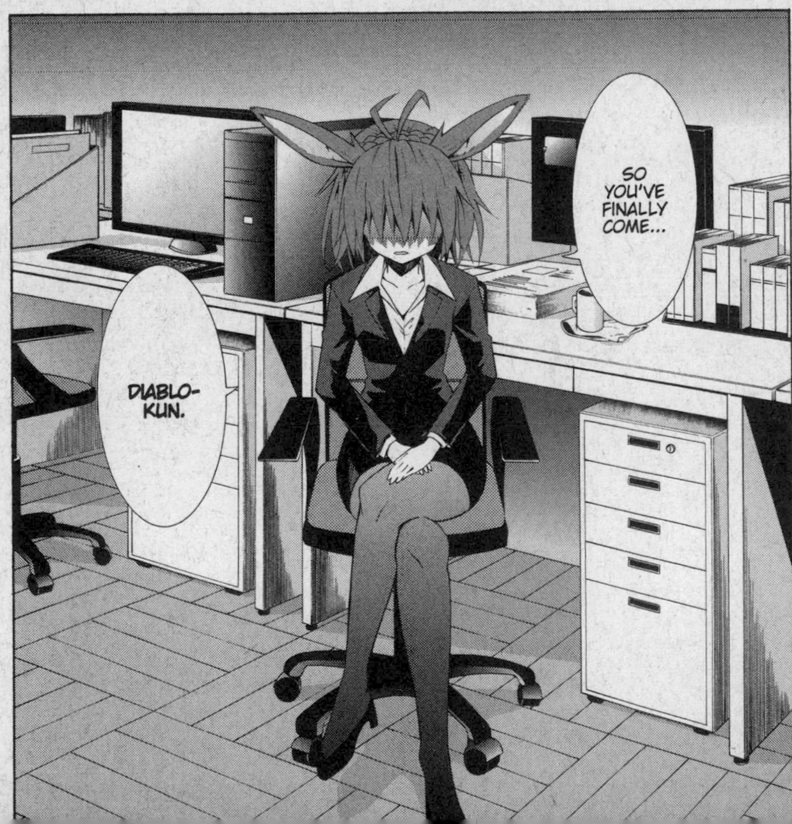
SO YOU'VE FINALLY COME...
DIABLO-KUN.

7 TRYING TO BE AN ADVENTURER III

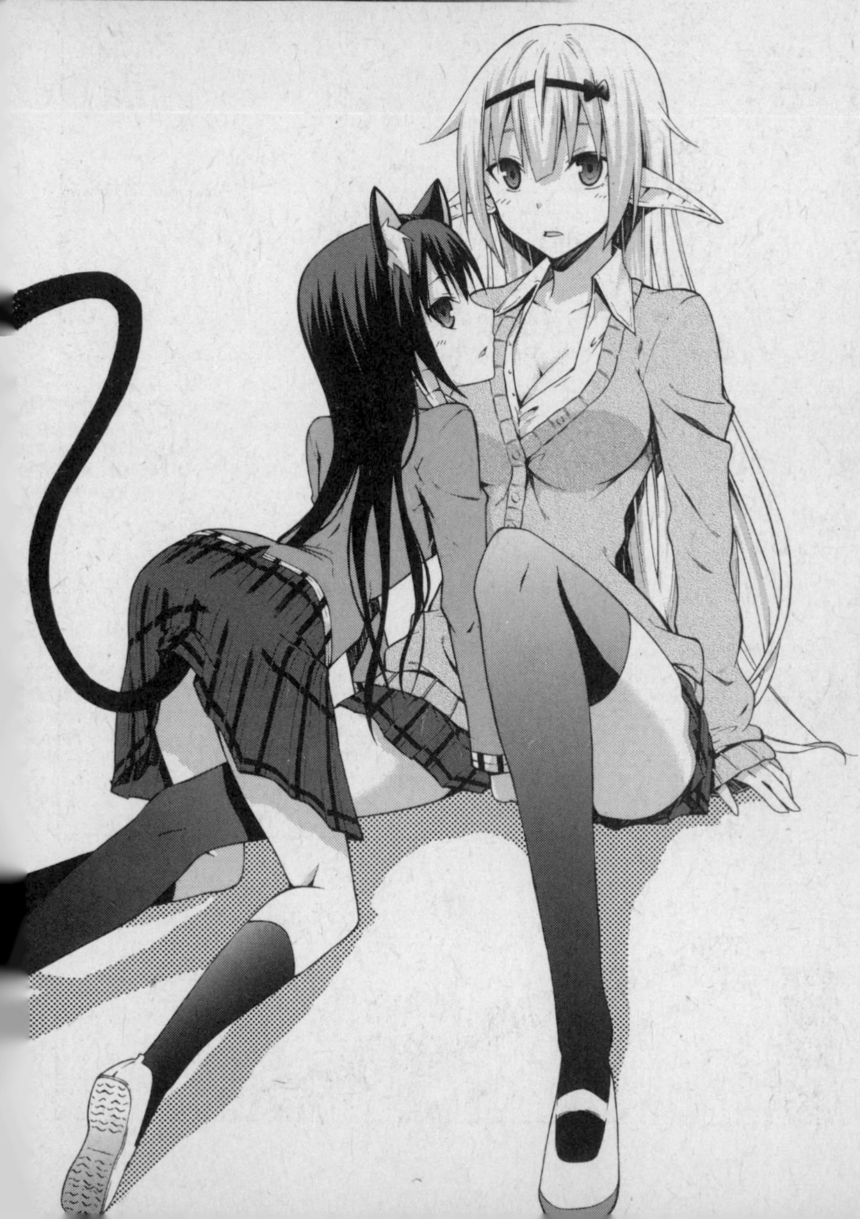

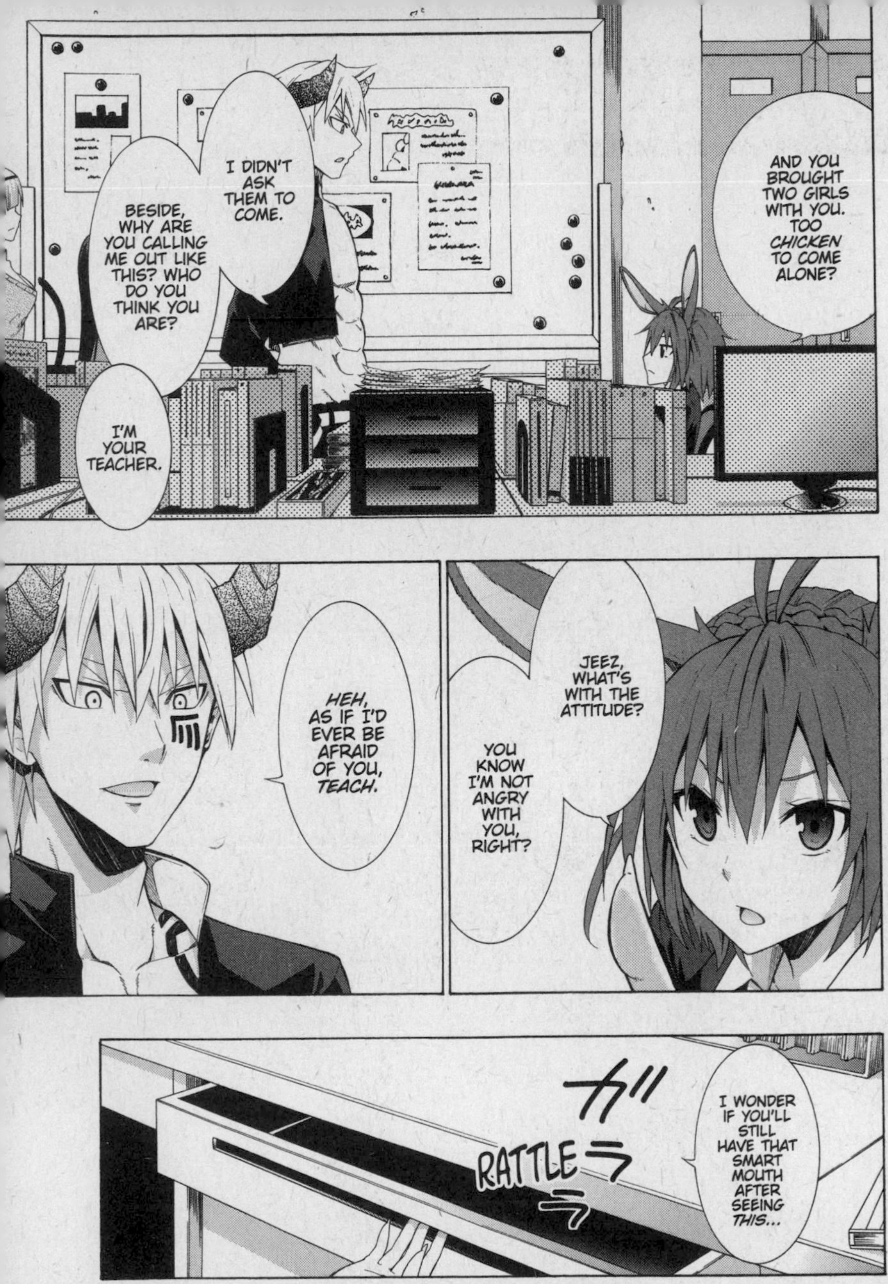
AND YOU BROUGHT TWO GIRLS WITH YOU. TOO *CHICKEN* TO COME ALONE?
I DIDN'T ASK THEM TO COME.
BESIDE, WHY ARE YOU CALLING ME OUT LIKE THIS? WHO DO YOU THINK YOU ARE?
I'M YOUR TEACHER.
JEEZ, WHAT'S WITH THE ATTITUDE?
YOU KNOW I'M NOT ANGRY WITH YOU, RIGHT?
HEH, AS IF I'D EVER BE AFRAID OF YOU, *TEACH*.
I WONDER IF YOU'LL STILL HAVE THAT SMART MOUTH AFTER SEEING *THIS*...
ガッ
RATTLE ラ ラ

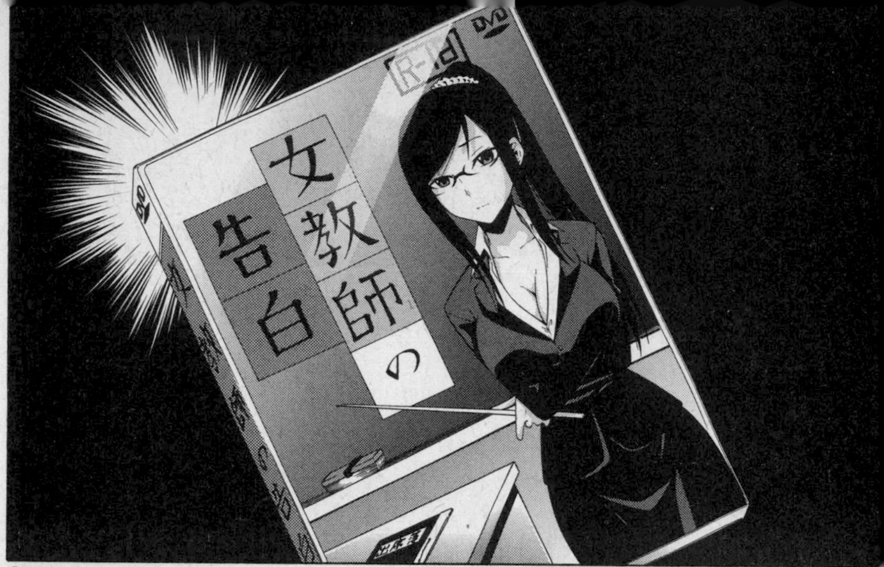
DVD
R-18
女教師の告白
Book: A Teacher's Confession

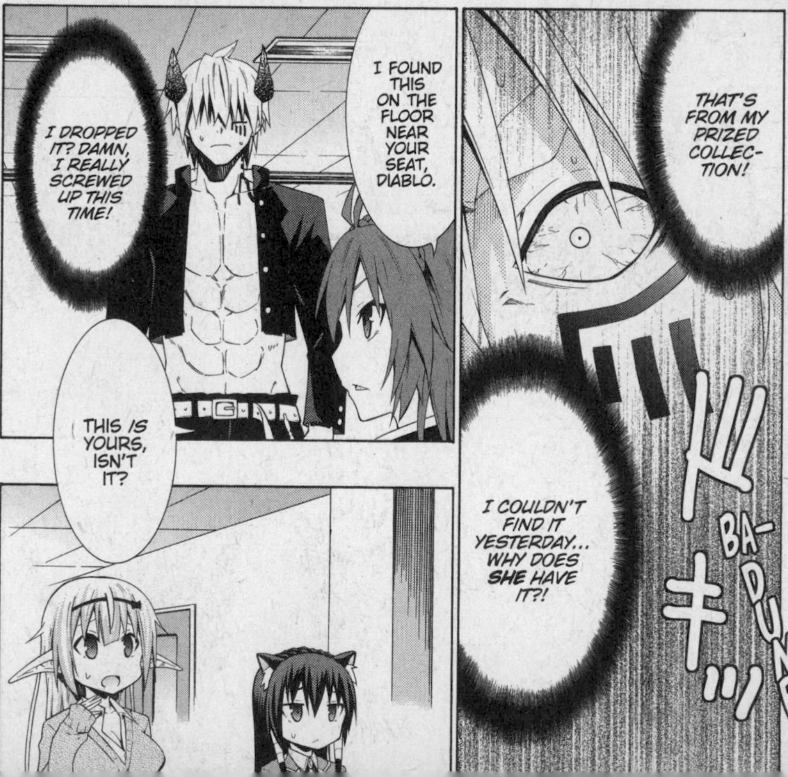
I FOUND THIS ON THE FLOOR NEAR YOUR SEAT, DIABLO.
I DROPPED IT? DAMN, I REALLY SCREWED UP THIS TIME!
THIS *IS* YOURS, ISN'T IT?
THAT'S FROM MY PRIZED COLLECTION!
I COULDN'T FIND IT YESTERDAY... WHY DOES **SHE** HAVE IT?!
BA-DUMP

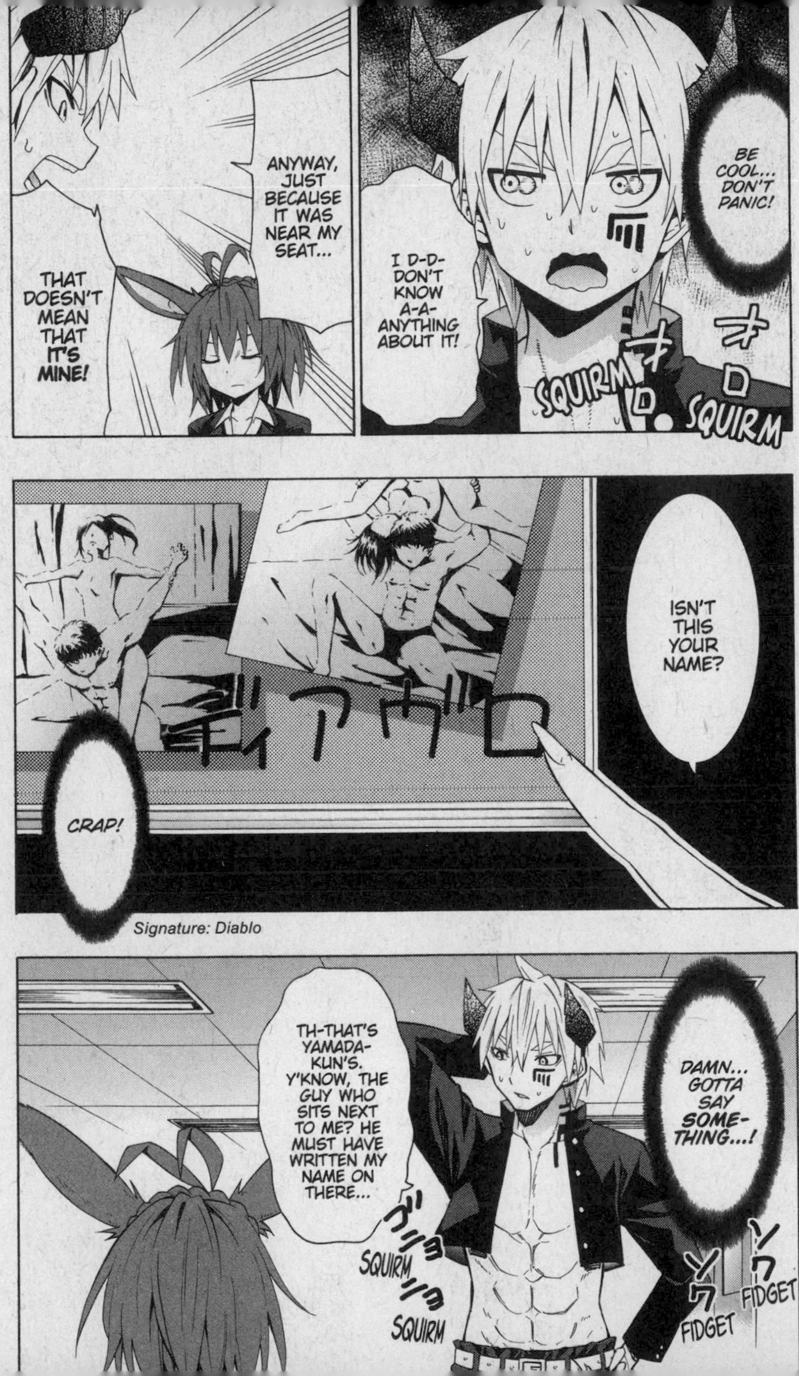
BE COOL... DON'T PANIC!
I D-D-DON'T KNOW A-A-ANYTHING ABOUT IT!
SQUIRM
SQUIRM
ANYWAY, JUST BECAUSE IT WAS NEAR MY SEAT...
THAT DOESN'T MEAN THAT IT'S MINE!
ISN'T THIS YOUR NAME?
ディアボロ
CRAP!
DAMN... GOTTA SAY SOME-THING...!
TH-THAT'S YAMADA-KUN'S. Y'KNOW, THE GUY WHO SITS NEXT TO ME? HE MUST HAVE WRITTEN MY NAME ON THERE...
FIDGET
FIDGET
SQUIRM
SQUIRM

Signature: Diablo

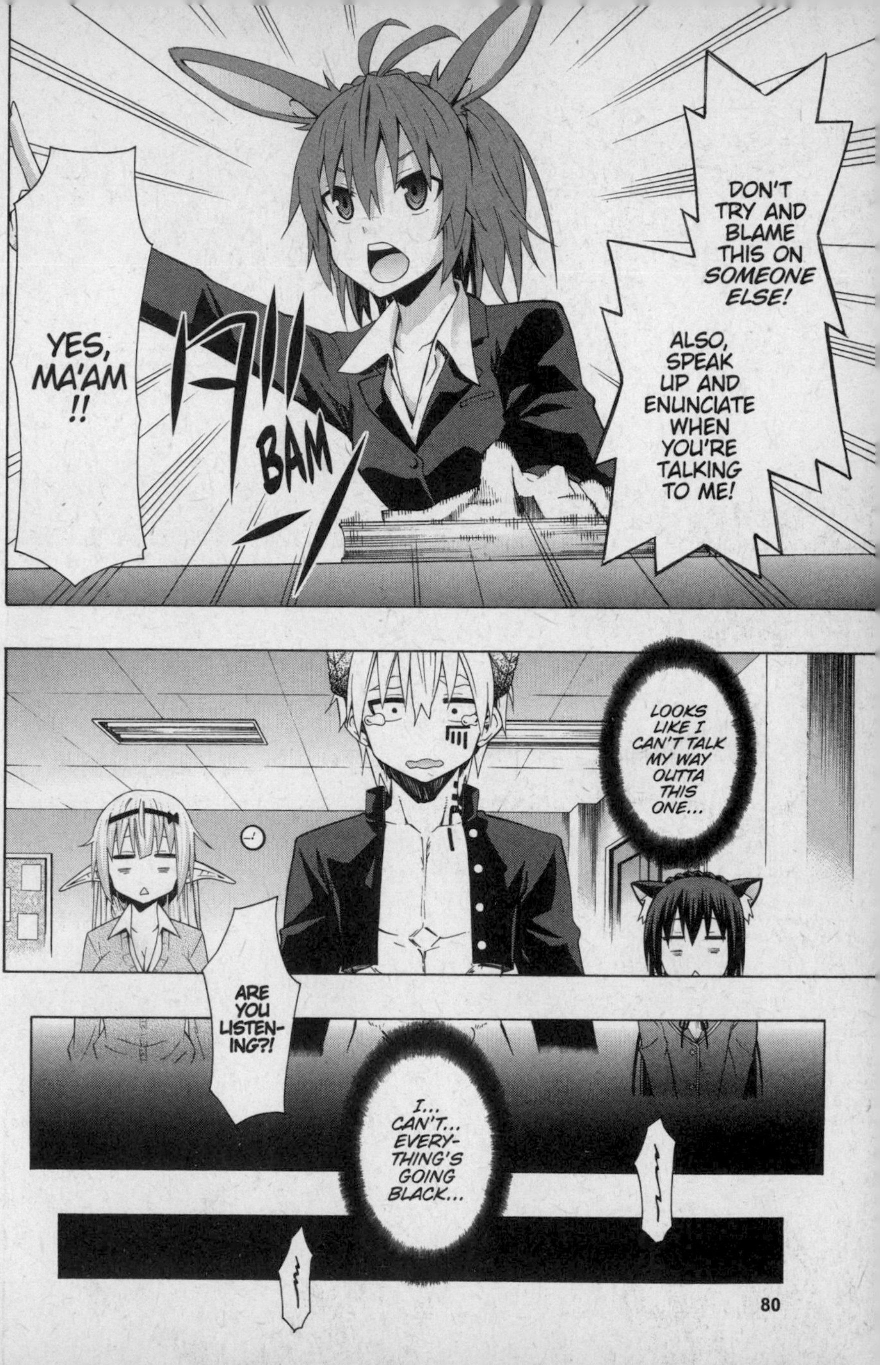
DON'T TRY AND BLAME THIS ON SOMEONE ELSE!
ALSO, SPEAK UP AND ENUNCIATE WHEN YOU'RE TALKING TO ME!
BAM
YES, MA'AM!!
LOOKS LIKE I CAN'T TALK MY WAY OUTTA THIS ONE...
ARE YOU LISTENING?!
I... CAN'T... EVERYTHING'S GOING BLACK...

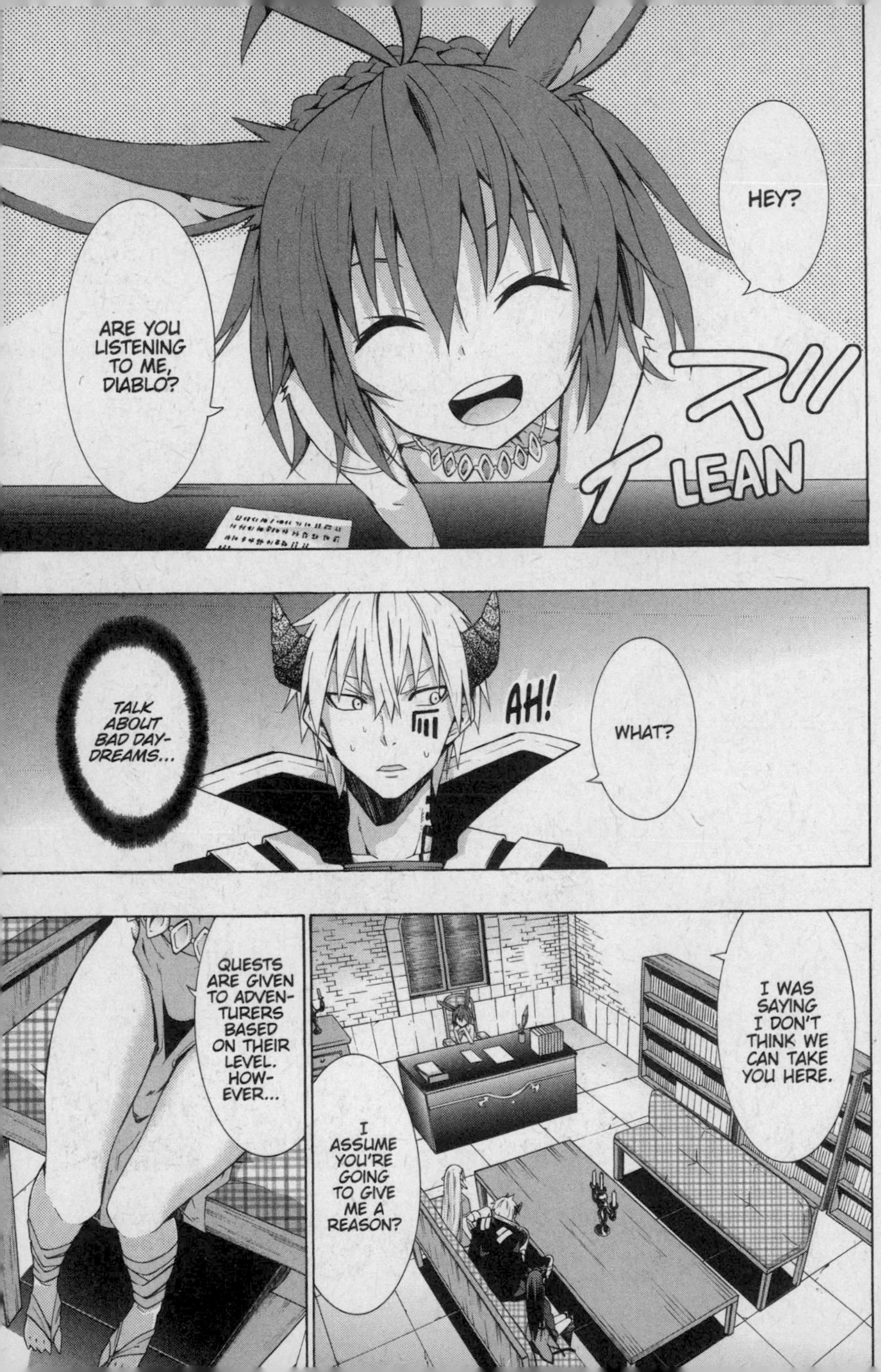
HEY?
ARE YOU LISTENING TO ME, DIABLO?
LEAN
WHAT?
AH!
TALK ABOUT BAD DAY-DREAMS...
I WAS SAYING I DON'T THINK WE CAN TAKE YOU HERE.
I ASSUME YOU'RE GOING TO GIVE ME A REASON?
QUESTS ARE GIVEN TO ADVEN-TURERS BASED ON THEIR LEVEL. HOW-EVER...

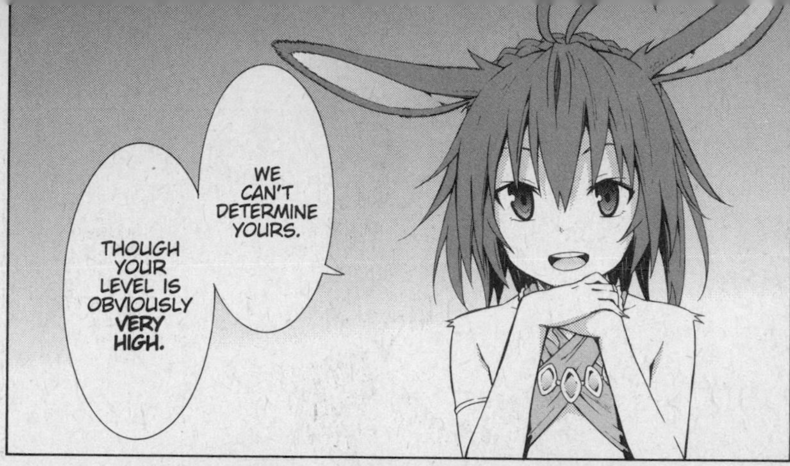
WE CAN'T DETERMINE YOURS.
THOUGH YOUR LEVEL IS OBVIOUSLY VERY HIGH.

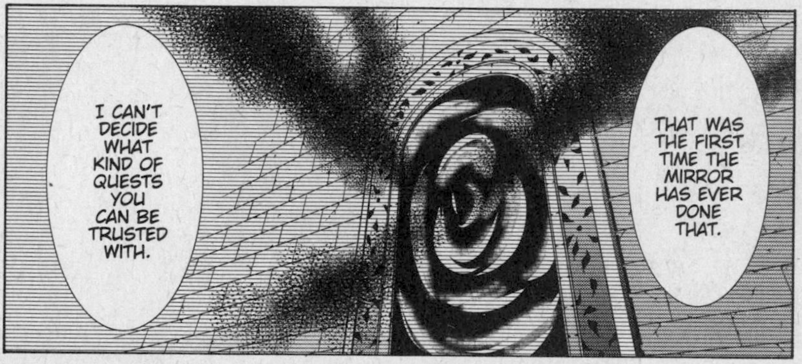
THAT WAS THE FIRST TIME THE MIRROR HAS EVER DONE THAT.
I CAN'T DECIDE WHAT KIND OF QUESTS YOU CAN BE TRUSTED WITH.

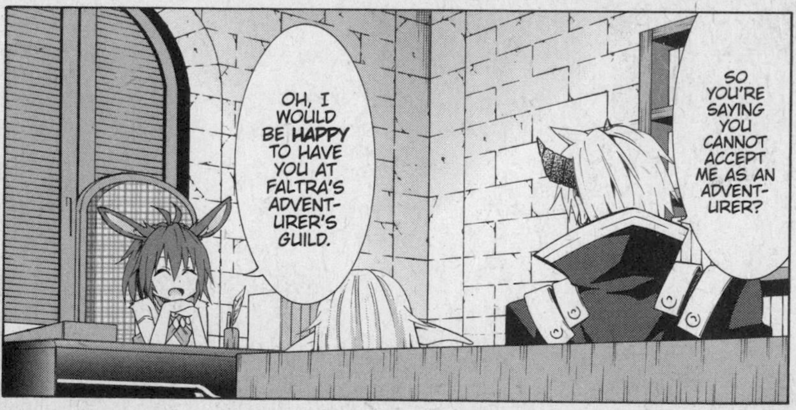
SO YOU'RE SAYING YOU CANNOT ACCEPT ME AS AN ADVENT-URER?
OH, I WOULD BE HAPPY TO HAVE YOU AT FALTRA'S ADVENT-URER'S GUILD.

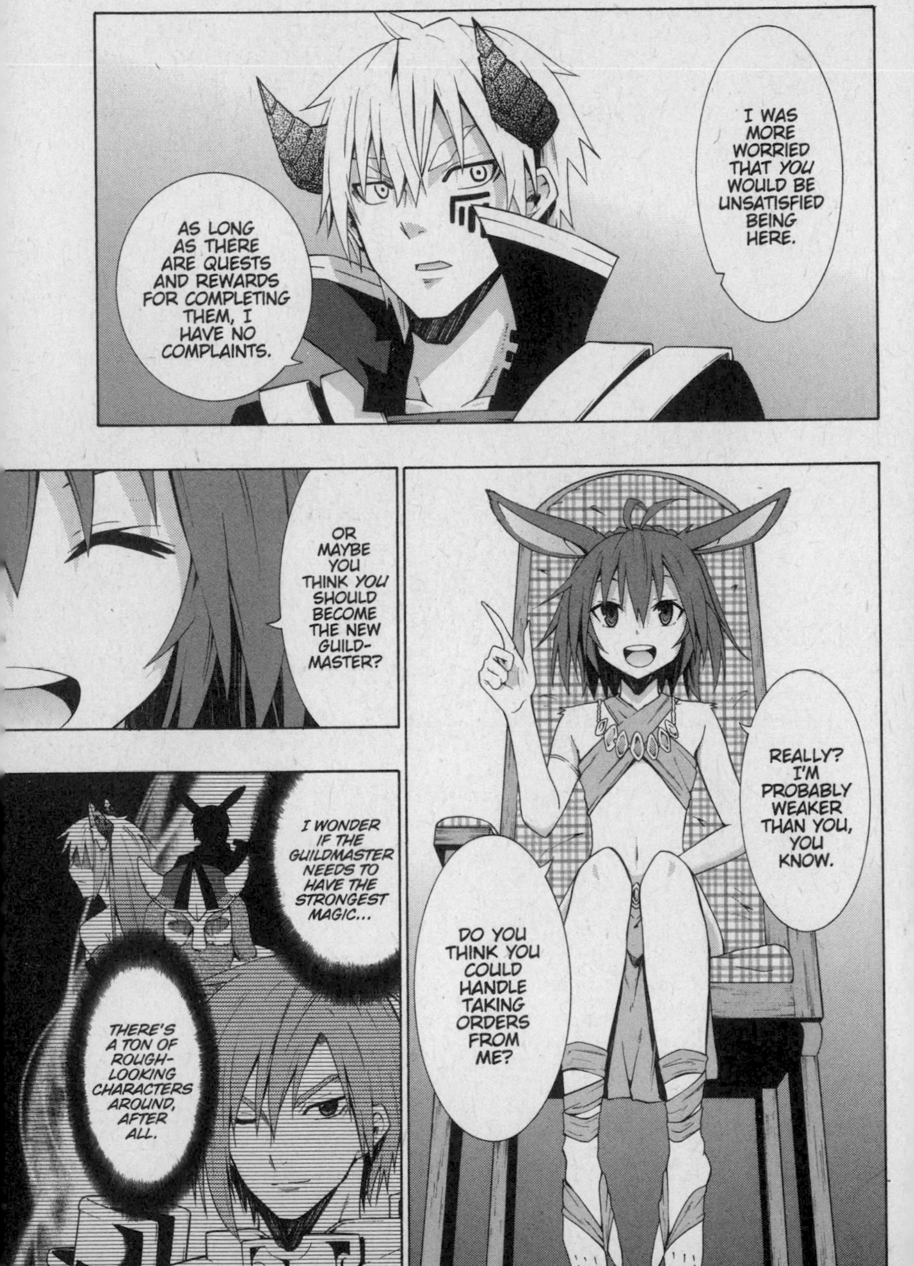

AS LONG AS THERE ARE QUESTS AND REWARDS FOR COMPLETING THEM, I HAVE NO COMPLAINTS.
I WAS MORE WORRIED THAT *YOU* WOULD BE UNSATISFIED BEING HERE.
OR MAYBE YOU THINK *YOU* SHOULD BECOME THE NEW GUILD-MASTER?
REALLY? I'M PROBABLY WEAKER THAN YOU, YOU KNOW.
DO YOU THINK YOU COULD HANDLE TAKING ORDERS FROM ME?
I WONDER IF THE GUILDMASTER NEEDS TO HAVE THE STRONGEST MAGIC...
THERE'S A TON OF ROUGH-LOOKING CHARACTERS AROUND, AFTER ALL.

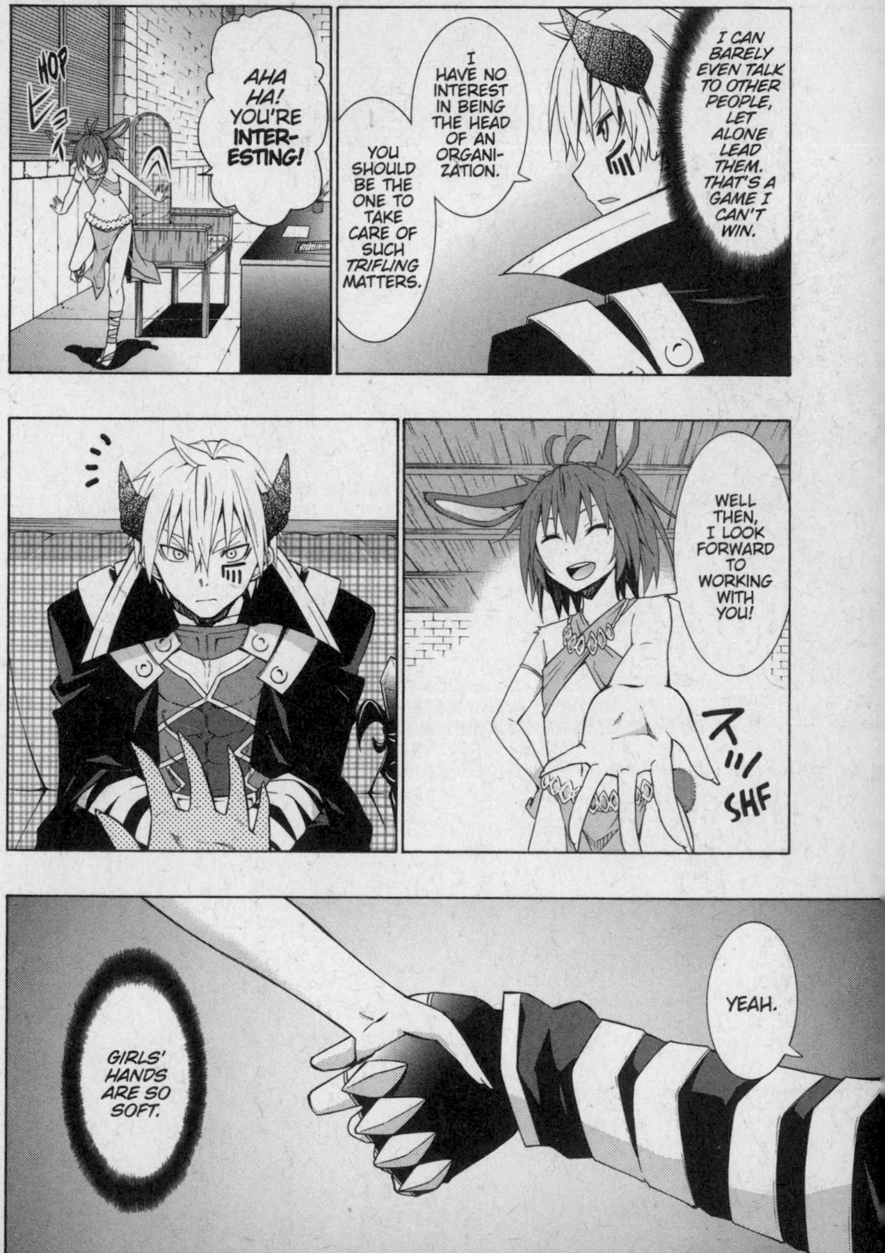
I CAN BARELY EVEN TALK TO OTHER PEOPLE, LET ALONE LEAD THEM. THAT'S A GAME I CAN'T WIN.
I HAVE NO INTEREST IN BEING THE HEAD OF AN ORGANIZATION.
YOU SHOULD BE THE ONE TO TAKE CARE OF SUCH TRIFLING MATTERS.
AHA HA! YOU'RE INTERESTING!
HOP
WELL THEN, I LOOK FORWARD TO WORKING WITH YOU!
SHF
YEAH.
GIRLS' HANDS ARE SO SOFT.

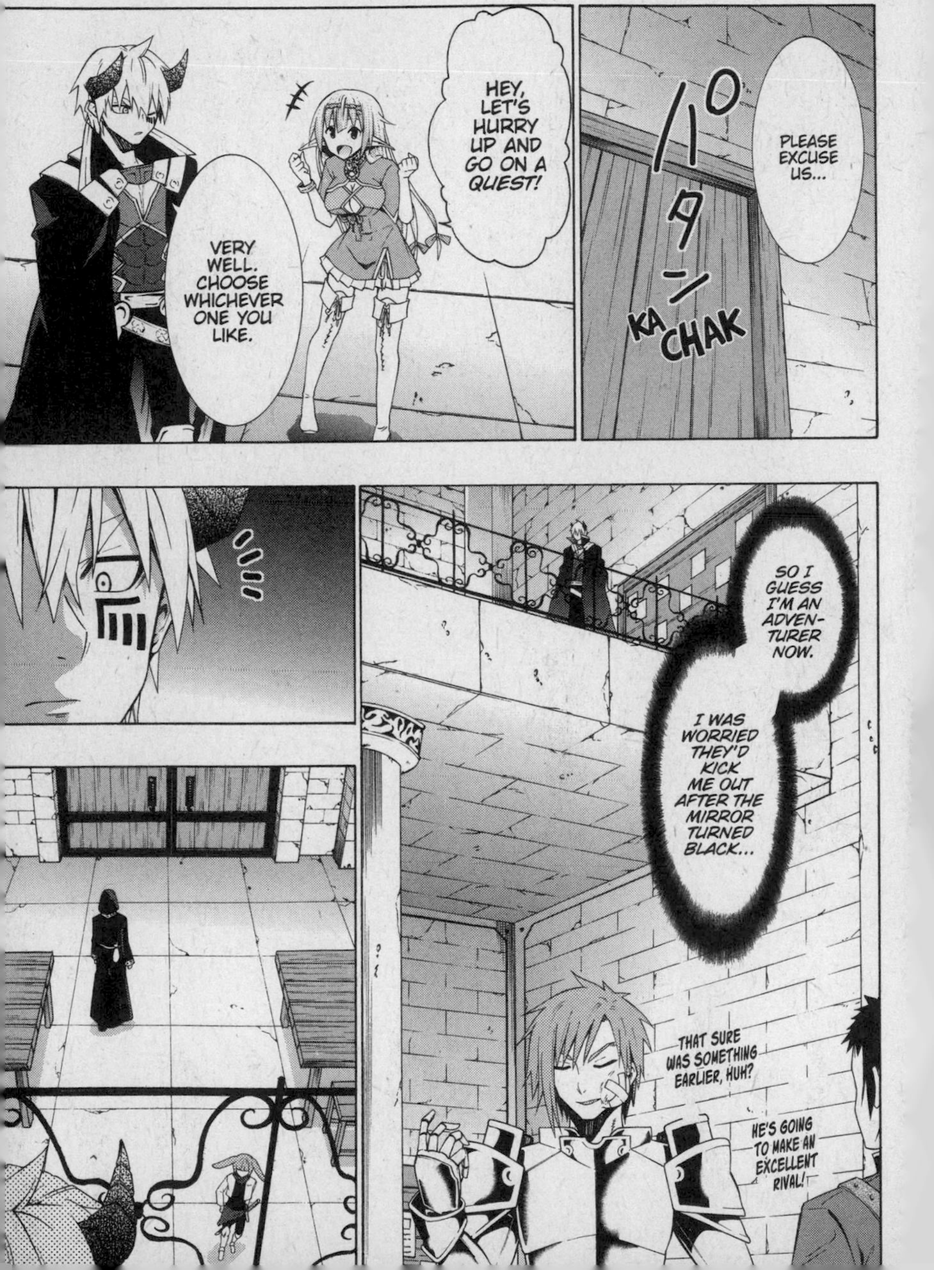
PLEASE EXCUSE US...
パタン
KA CHAK
HEY, LET'S HURRY UP AND GO ON A QUEST!
VERY WELL. CHOOSE WHICHEVER ONE YOU LIKE.
SO I GUESS I'M AN ADVEN-TURER NOW.
I WAS WORRIED THEY'D KICK ME OUT AFTER THE MIRROR TURNED BLACK...
THAT SURE WAS SOMETHING EARLIER, HUH?
HE'S GOING TO MAKE AN EXCELLENT RIVAL!

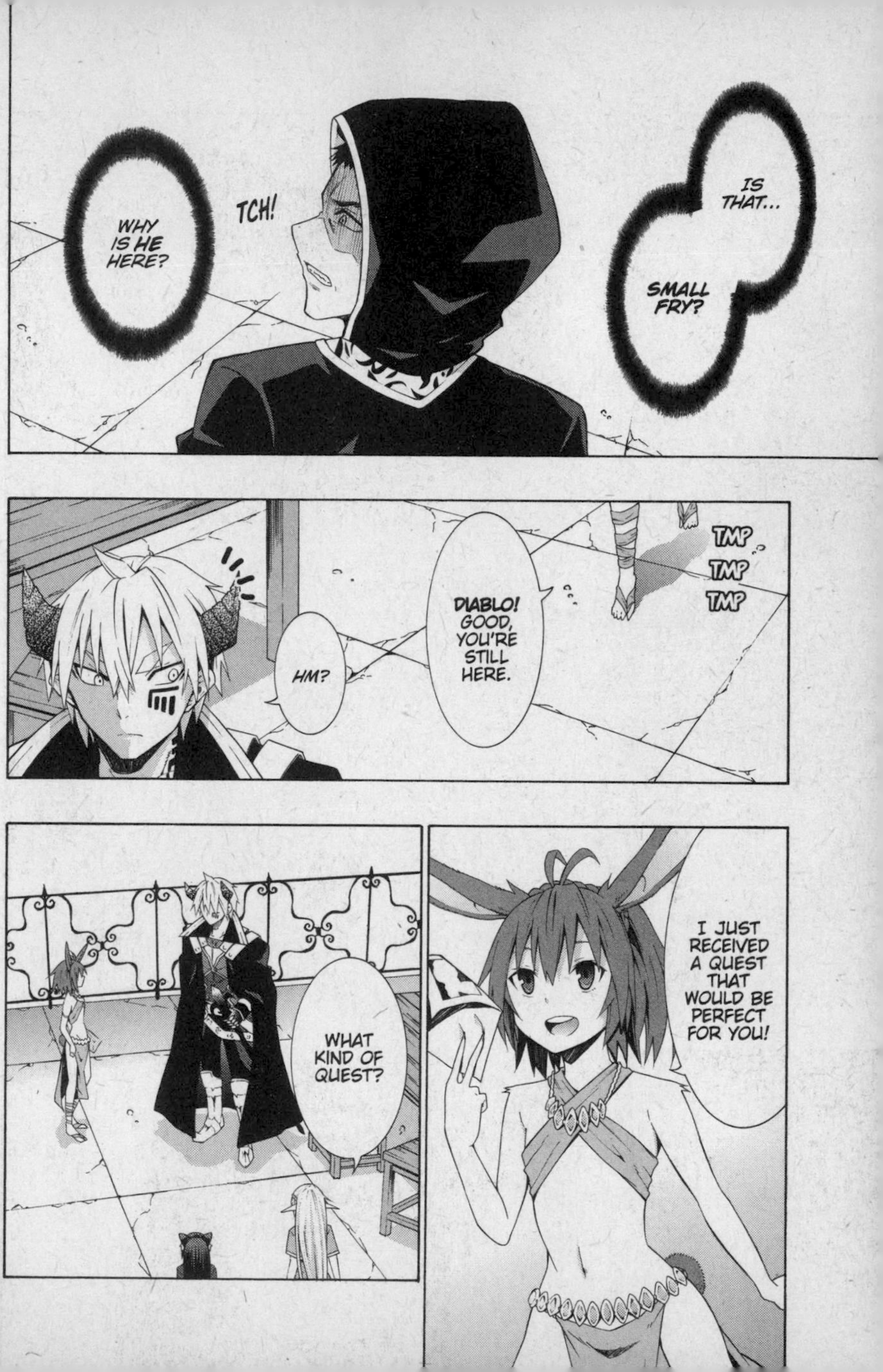
IS THAT...
SMALL FRY?
TCH!
WHY IS HE HERE?
TMP TMP TMP
DIABLO! GOOD, YOU'RE STILL HERE.
HM?
I JUST RECEIVED A QUEST THAT WOULD BE PERFECT FOR YOU!
WHAT KIND OF QUEST?

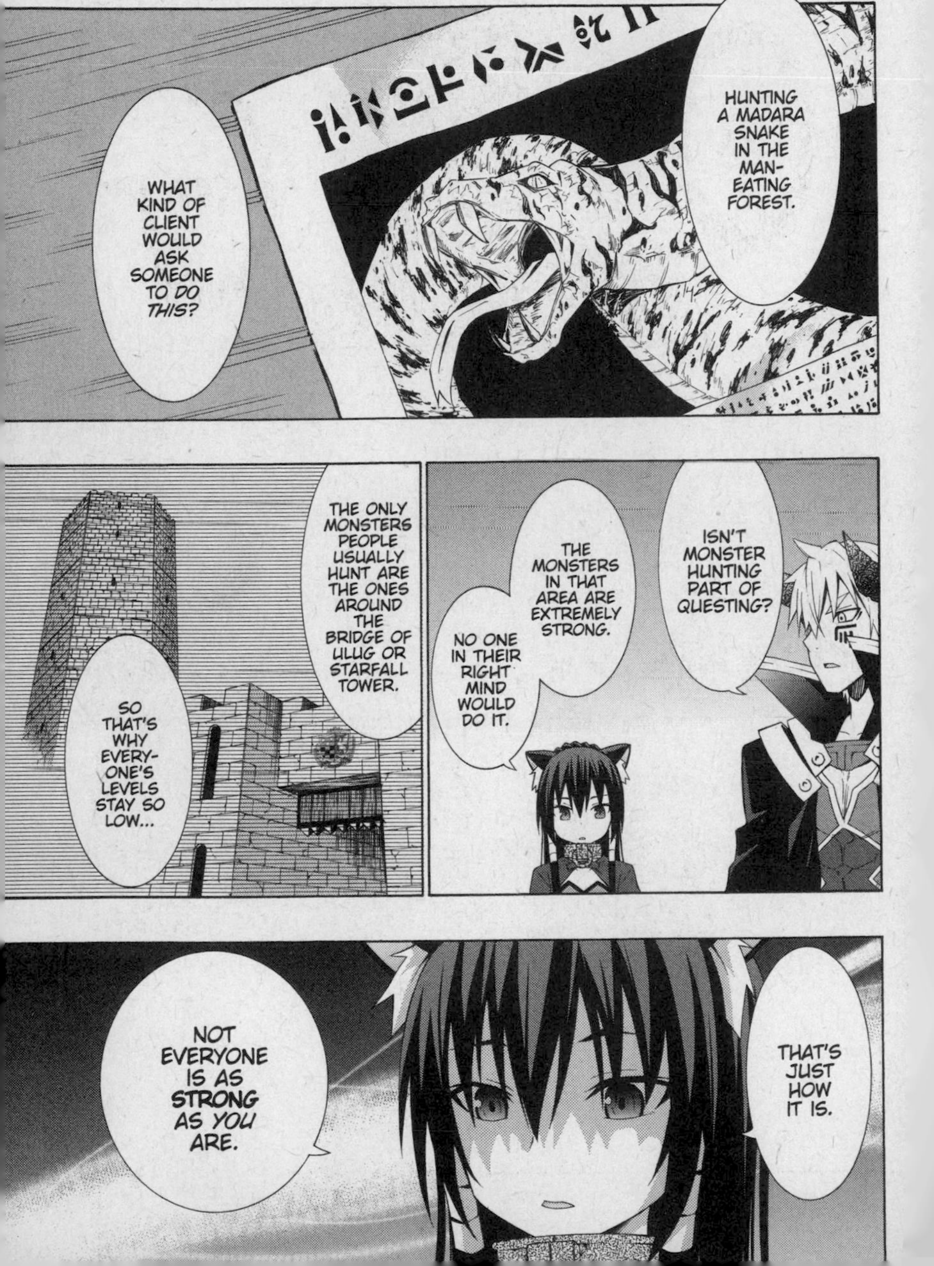
HUNTING A MADARA SNAKE IN THE MAN-EATING FOREST.
WHAT KIND OF CLIENT WOULD ASK SOMEONE TO DO *THIS?*
ISN'T MONSTER HUNTING PART OF QUESTING?
THE MONSTERS IN THAT AREA ARE EXTREMELY STRONG.
NO ONE IN THEIR RIGHT MIND WOULD DO IT.
THE ONLY MONSTERS PEOPLE USUALLY HUNT ARE THE ONES AROUND THE BRIDGE OF ULUG OR STARFALL TOWER.
SO THAT'S WHY EVERY-ONE'S LEVELS STAY SO LOW...
THAT'S JUST HOW IT IS.
NOT EVERYONE IS AS **STRONG** AS *YOU* ARE.

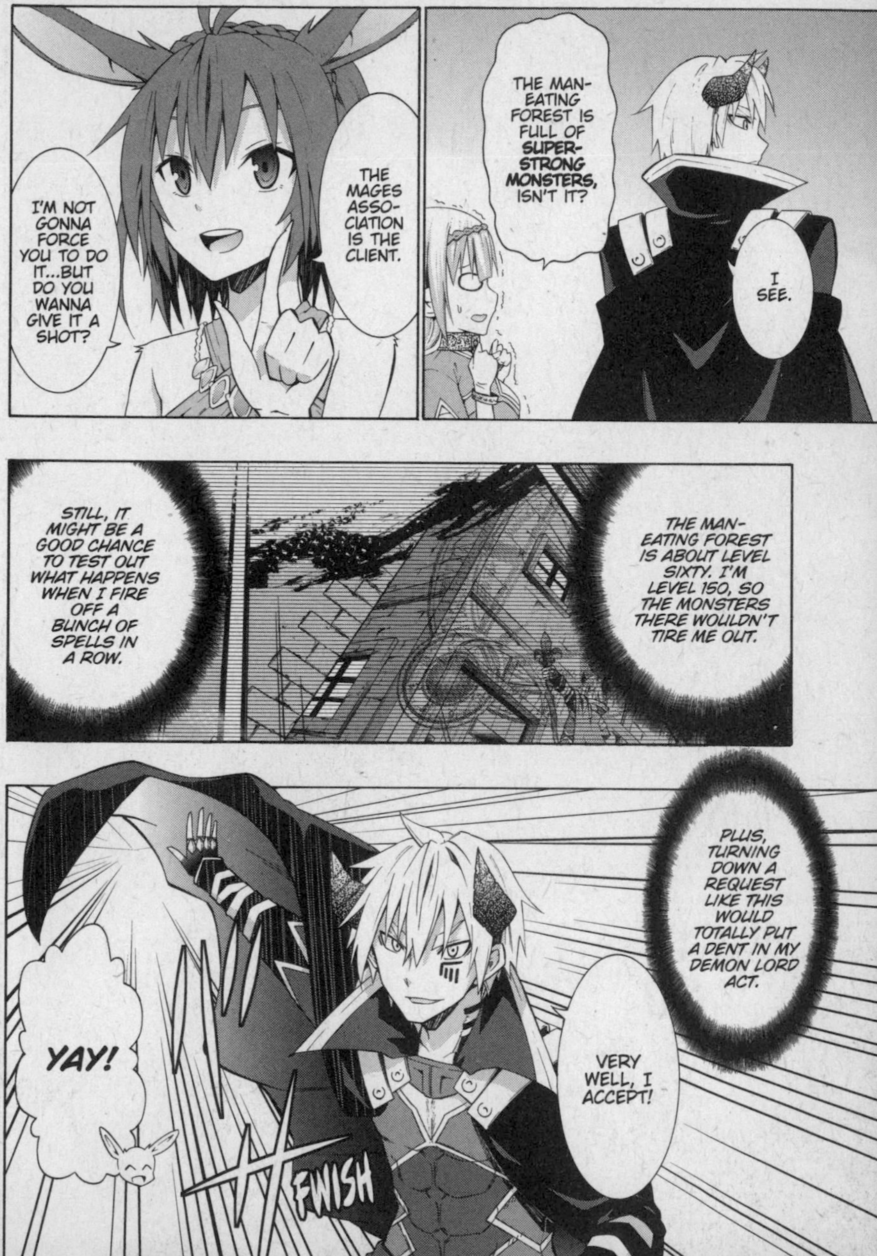
THE MAN-EATING FOREST IS FULL OF SUPER-STRONG MONSTERS, ISN'T IT?
I SEE.
THE MAGES ASSOCIATION IS THE CLIENT.
I'M NOT GONNA FORCE YOU TO DO IT...BUT DO YOU WANNA GIVE IT A SHOT?
THE MAN-EATING FOREST IS ABOUT LEVEL SIXTY. I'M LEVEL 150, SO THE MONSTERS THERE WOULDN'T TIRE ME OUT.
STILL, IT MIGHT BE A GOOD CHANCE TO TEST OUT WHAT HAPPENS WHEN I FIRE OFF A BUNCH OF SPELLS IN A ROW.
PLUS, TURNING DOWN A REQUEST LIKE THIS WOULD TOTALLY PUT A DENT IN MY DEMON LORD ACT.
VERY WELL, I ACCEPT!
FWISH
YAY!

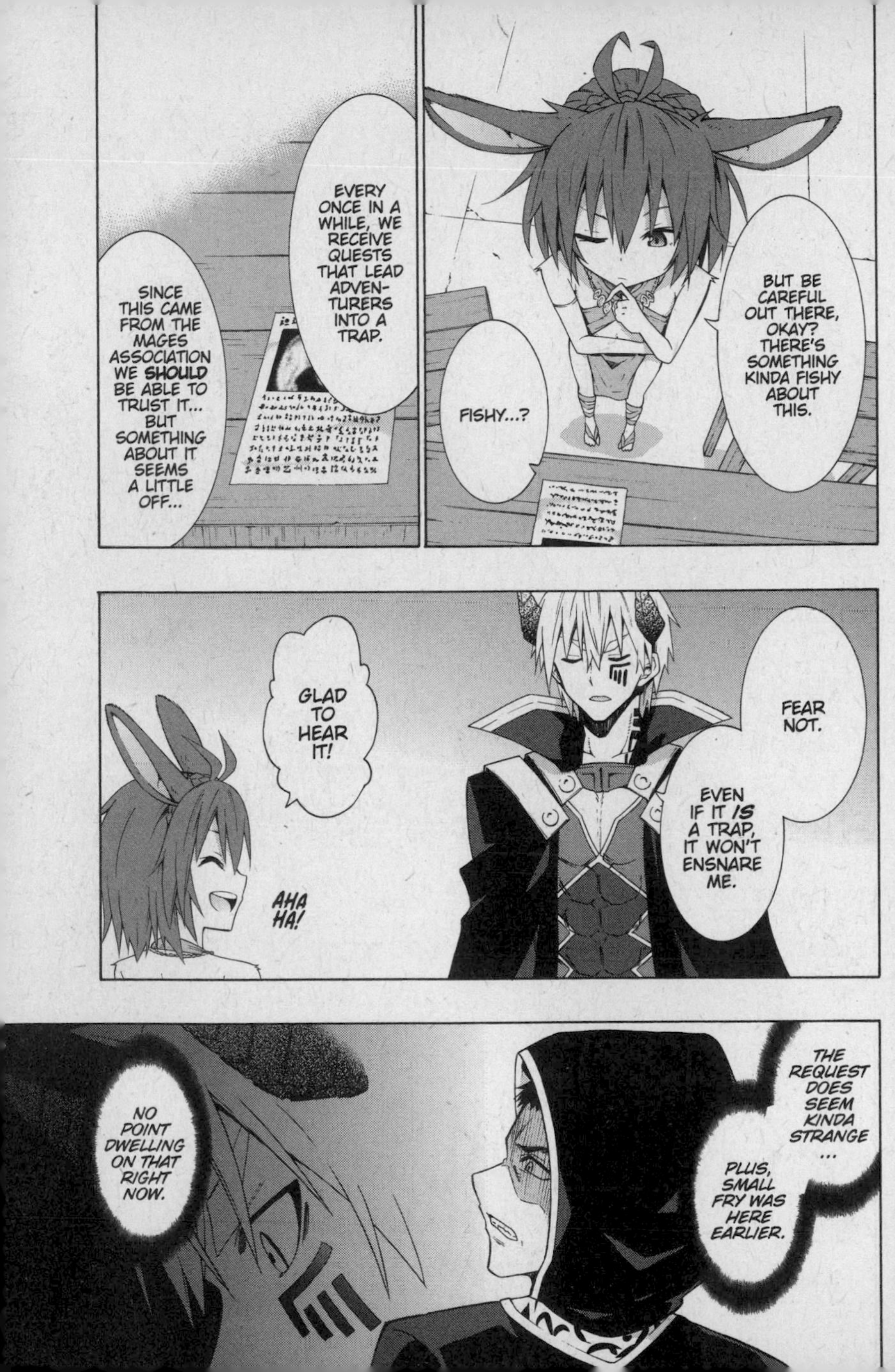
BUT BE CAREFUL OUT THERE, OKAY? THERE'S SOMETHING KINDA FISHY ABOUT THIS.
FISHY...?
EVERY ONCE IN A WHILE, WE RECEIVE QUESTS THAT LEAD ADVENTURERS INTO A TRAP.
SINCE THIS CAME FROM THE MAGES ASSOCIATION WE **SHOULD** BE ABLE TO TRUST IT... BUT SOMETHING ABOUT IT SEEMS A LITTLE OFF...
FEAR NOT.
EVEN IF IT *IS* A TRAP, IT WON'T ENSNARE ME.
GLAD TO HEAR IT!
AHA HA!
THE REQUEST DOES SEEM KINDA STRANGE...
PLUS, SMALL FRY WAS HERE EARLIER.
NO POINT DWELLING ON THAT RIGHT NOW.

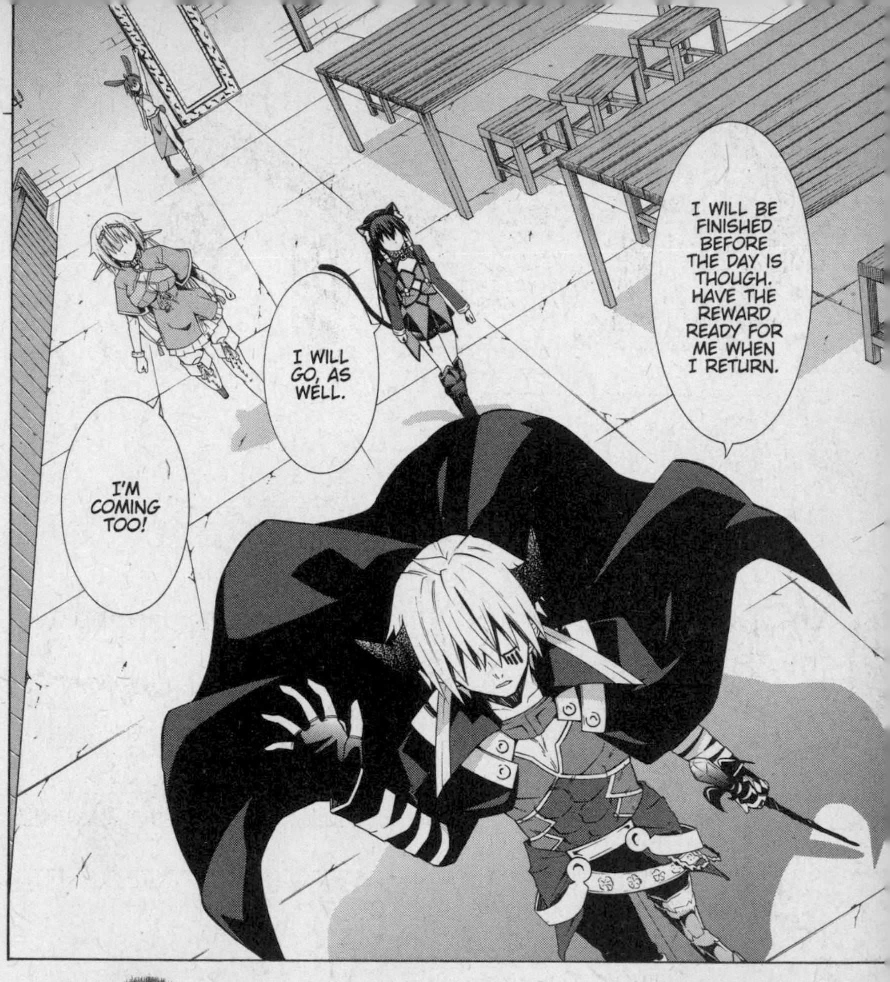
I WILL BE FINISHED BEFORE THE DAY IS THOUGH. HAVE THE REWARD READY FOR ME WHEN I RETURN.
I WILL GO, AS WELL.
I'M COMING TOO!

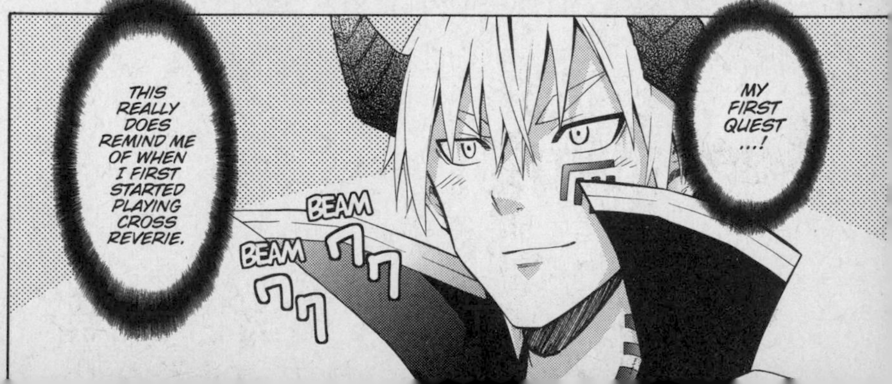
MY FIRST QUEST ...!
THIS REALLY DOES REMIND ME OF WHEN I FIRST STARTED PLAYING CROSS REVERIE.
BEAM
BEAM

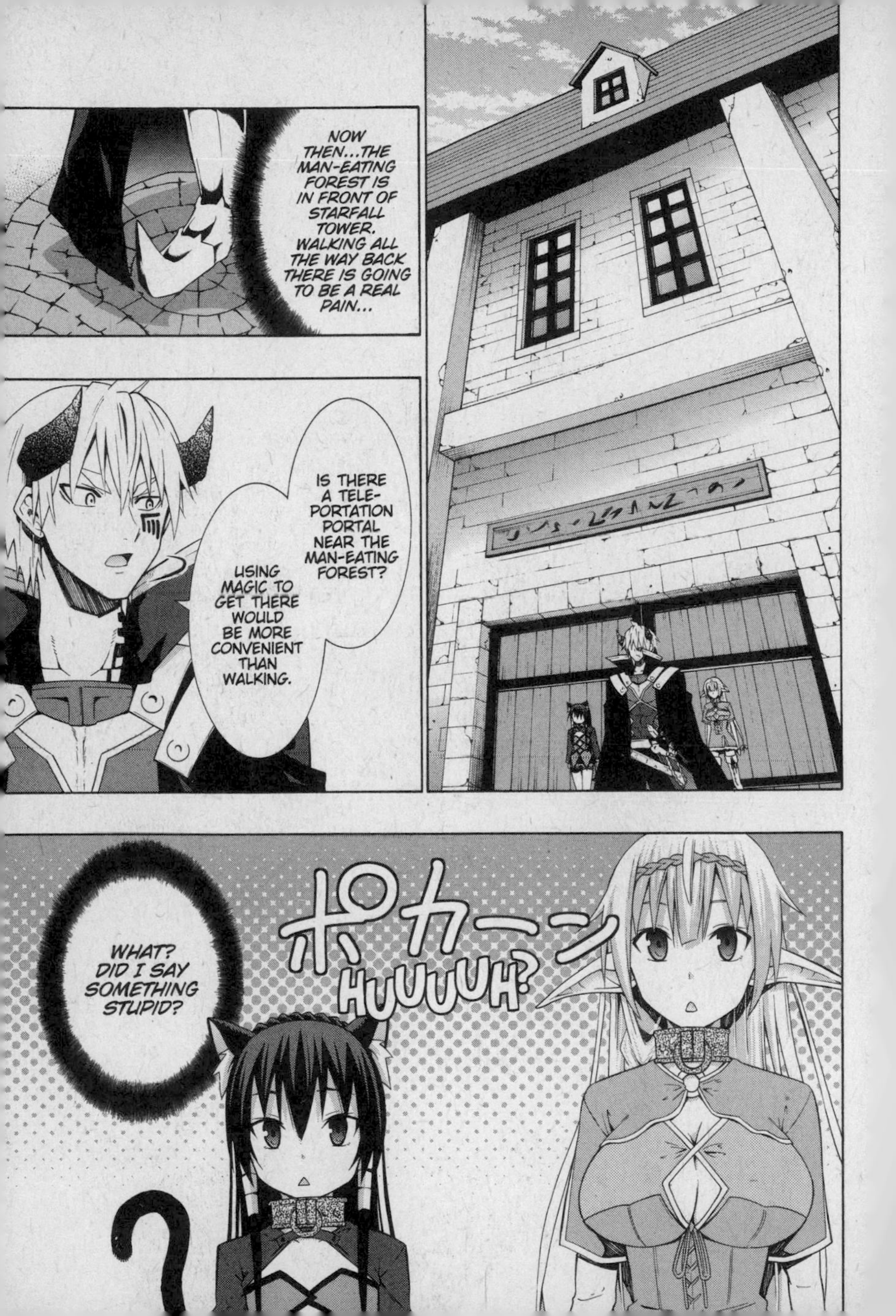
NOW THEN...THE MAN-EATING FOREST IS IN FRONT OF STARFALL TOWER. WALKING ALL THE WAY BACK THERE IS GOING TO BE A REAL PAIN...
IS THERE A TELE-PORTATION PORTAL NEAR THE MAN-EATING FOREST?
USING MAGIC TO GET THERE WOULD BE MORE CONVENIENT THAN WALKING.
ポカーン
HUUUUH?
WHAT? DID I SAY SOMETHING STUPID?

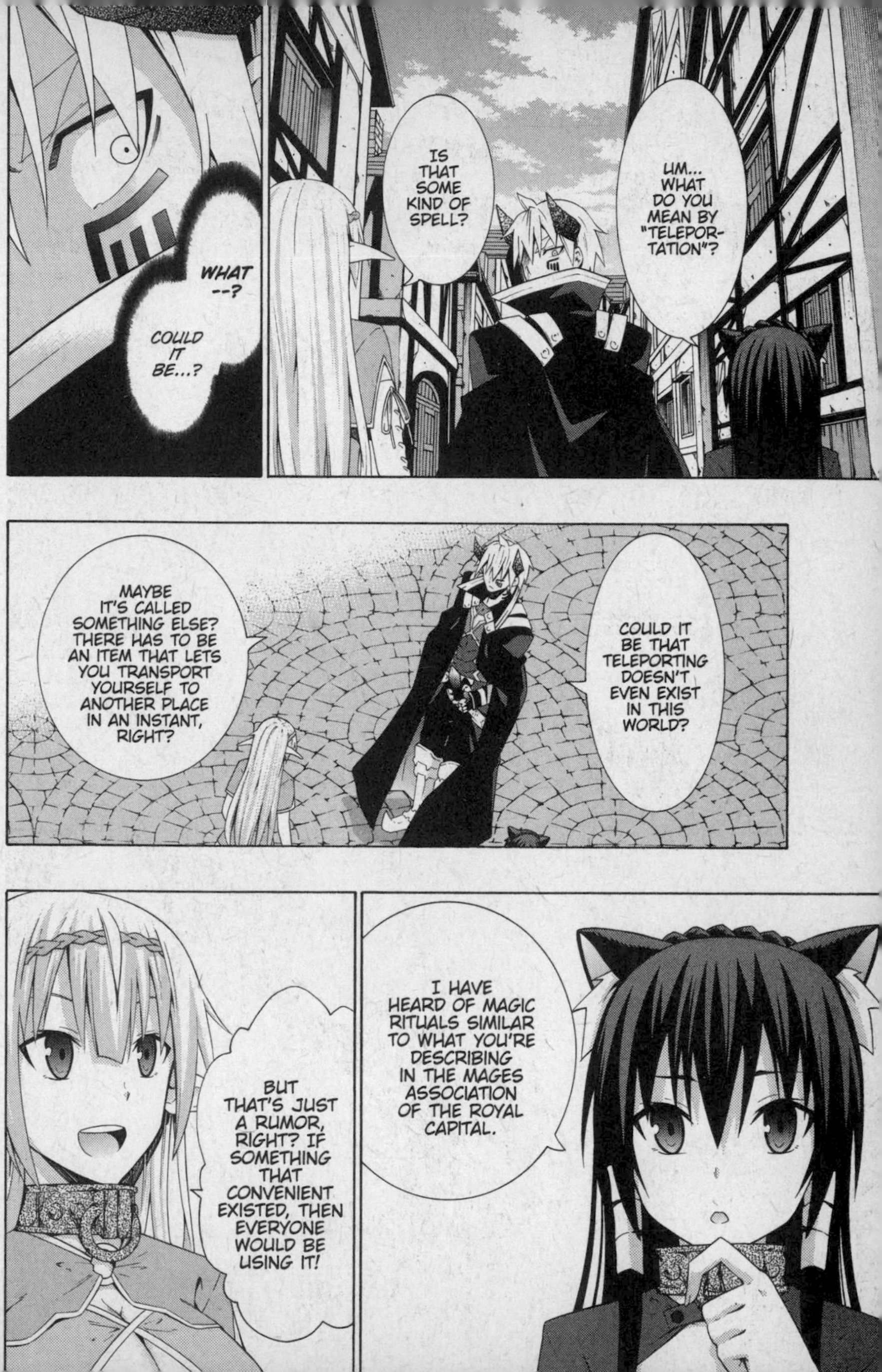
UM... WHAT DO YOU MEAN BY "TELEPORTATION"?
IS THAT SOME KIND OF SPELL?
WHAT --?
COULD IT BE...?
COULD IT BE THAT TELEPORTING DOESN'T EVEN EXIST IN THIS WORLD?
MAYBE IT'S CALLED SOMETHING ELSE? THERE HAS TO BE AN ITEM THAT LETS YOU TRANSPORT YOURSELF TO ANOTHER PLACE IN AN INSTANT, RIGHT?
I HAVE HEARD OF MAGIC RITUALS SIMILAR TO WHAT YOU'RE DESCRIBING IN THE MAGES ASSOCIATION OF THE ROYAL CAPITAL.
BUT THAT'S JUST A RUMOR, RIGHT? IF SOMETHING THAT CONVENIENT EXISTED, THEN EVERYONE WOULD BE USING IT!

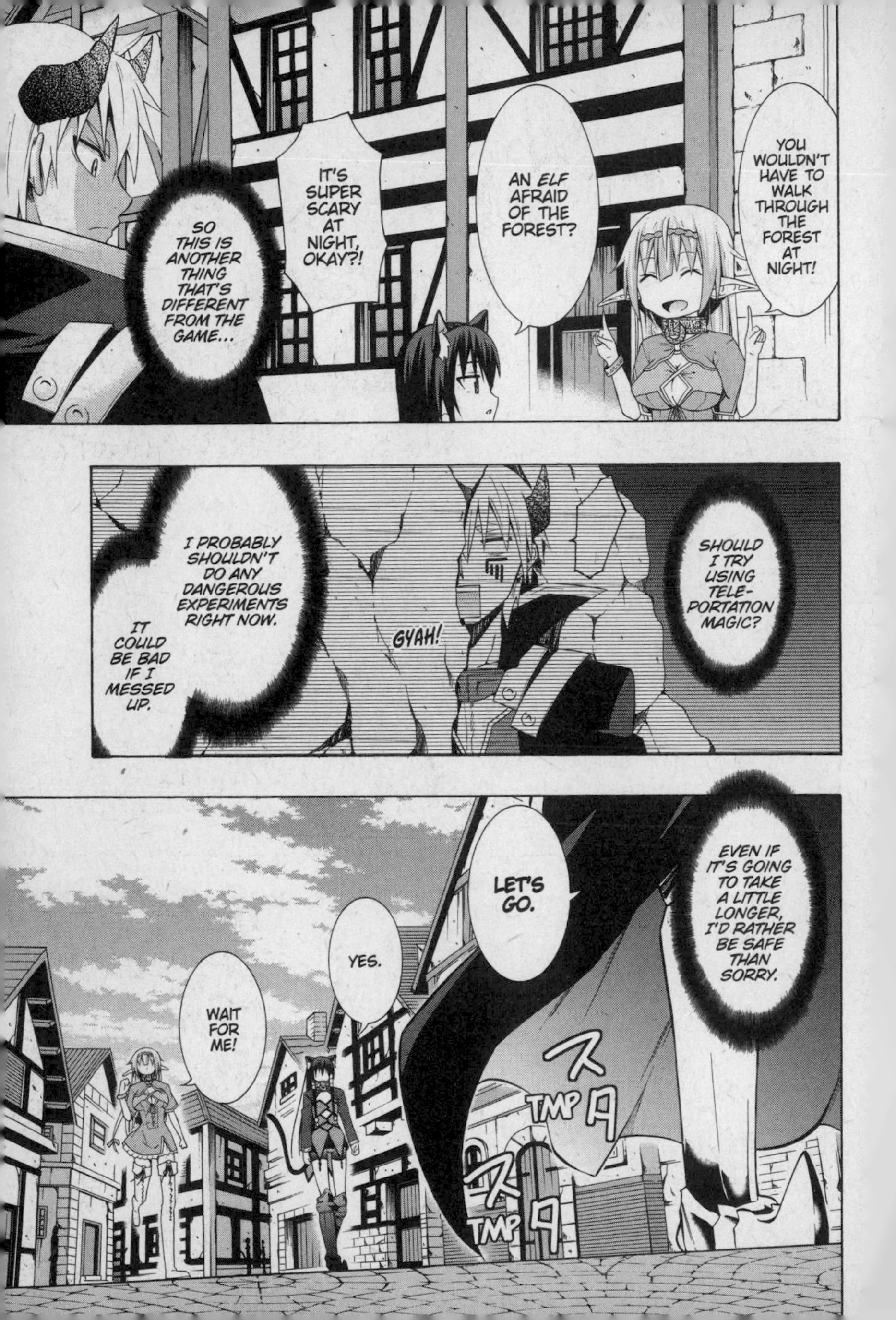
YOU WOULDN'T HAVE TO WALK THROUGH THE FOREST AT NIGHT!
AN *ELF* AFRAID OF THE FOREST?
IT'S SUPER SCARY AT NIGHT, OKAY?!
SO THIS IS ANOTHER THING THAT'S DIFFERENT FROM THE GAME...
SHOULD I TRY USING TELE-PORTATION MAGIC?
GYAH!
I PROBABLY SHOULDN'T DO ANY DANGEROUS EXPERIMENTS RIGHT NOW.
IT COULD BE BAD IF I MESSED UP.
EVEN IF IT'S GOING TO TAKE A LITTLE LONGER, I'D RATHER BE SAFE THAN SORRY.
LET'S GO.
TMP
TMP
YES.
WAIT FOR ME!

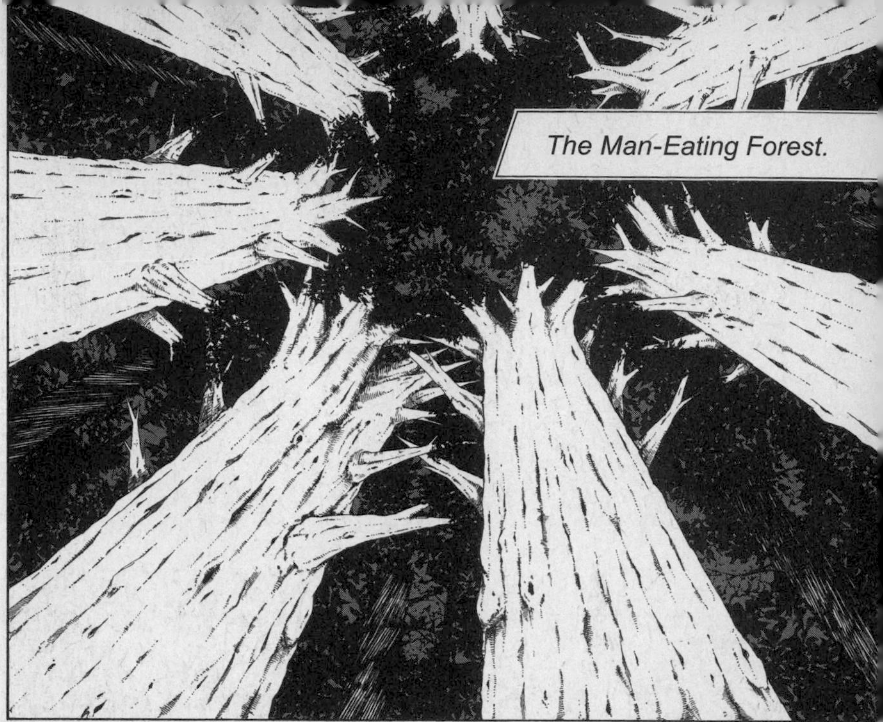
The Man-Eating Forest.

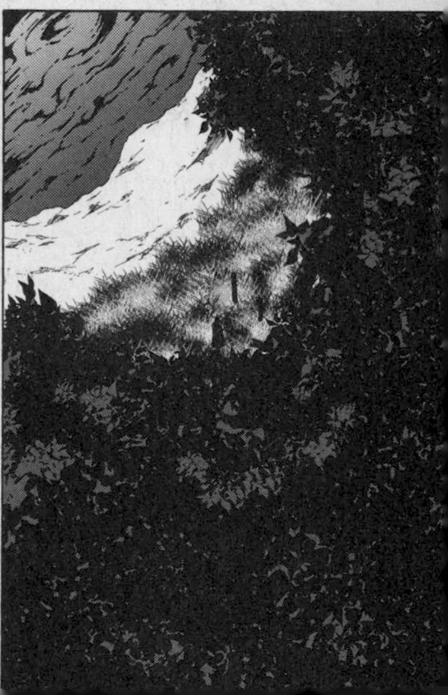

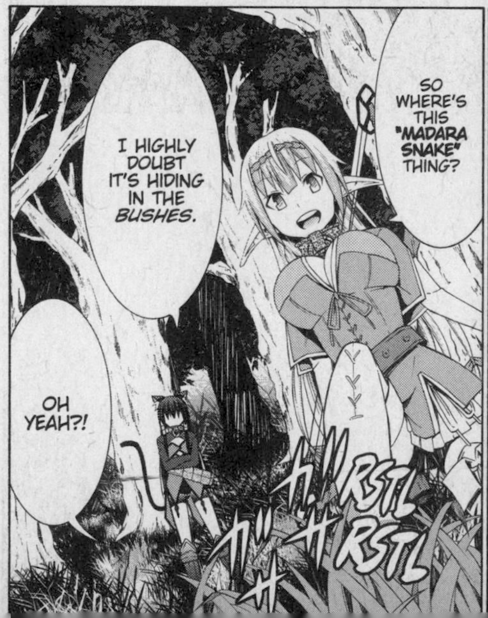
SO WHERE'S THIS "MADARA SNAKE" THING?
I HIGHLY DOUBT IT'S HIDING IN THE *BUSHES*.
OH YEAH?!
RSTL
RSTL

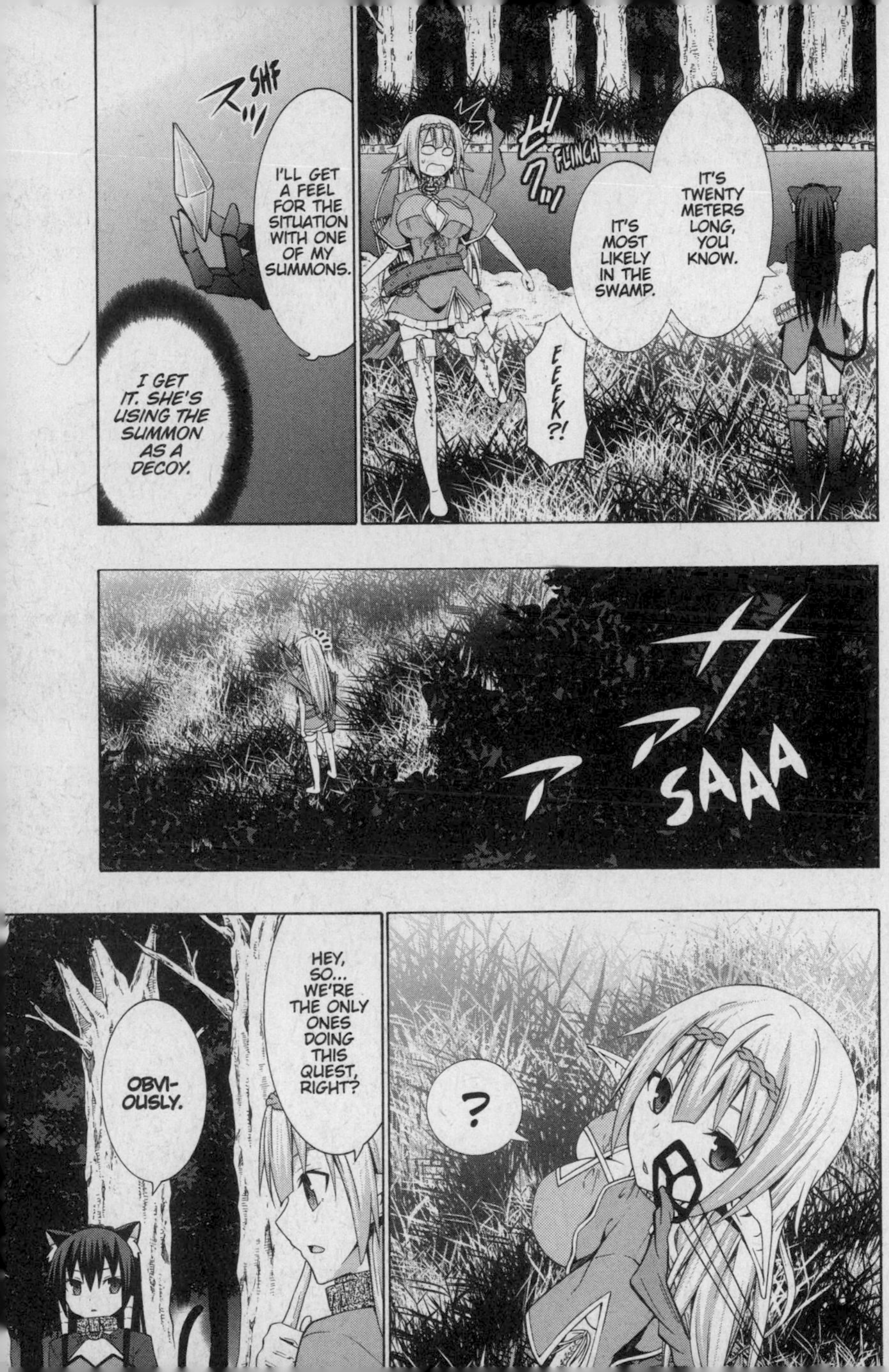
IT'S TWENTY METERS LONG, YOU KNOW.
IT'S MOST LIKELY IN THE SWAMP.
FLINCH
EEEK?!
SHF
I'LL GET A FEEL FOR THE SITUATION WITH ONE OF MY SUMMONS.
I GET IT. SHE'S USING THE SUMMON AS A DECOY.
SAAA
?
HEY, SO... WE'RE THE ONLY ONES DOING THIS QUEST, RIGHT?
OBVI-OUSLY.

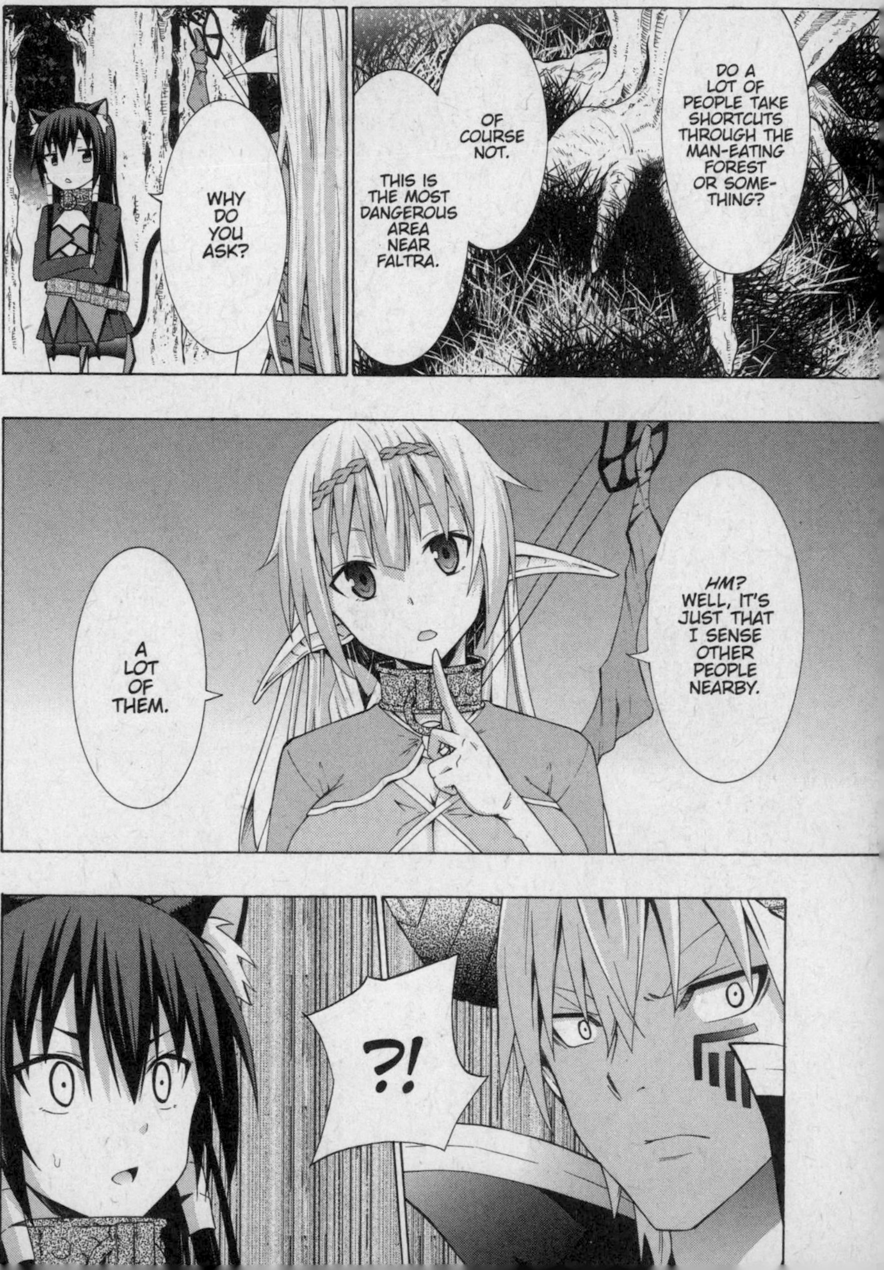
DO A LOT OF PEOPLE TAKE SHORTCUTS THROUGH THE MAN-EATING FOREST OR SOME-THING?
OF COURSE NOT.
THIS IS THE MOST DANGEROUS AREA NEAR FALTRA.
WHY DO YOU ASK?
HM? WELL, IT'S JUST THAT I SENSE OTHER PEOPLE NEARBY.
A LOT OF THEM.
?!

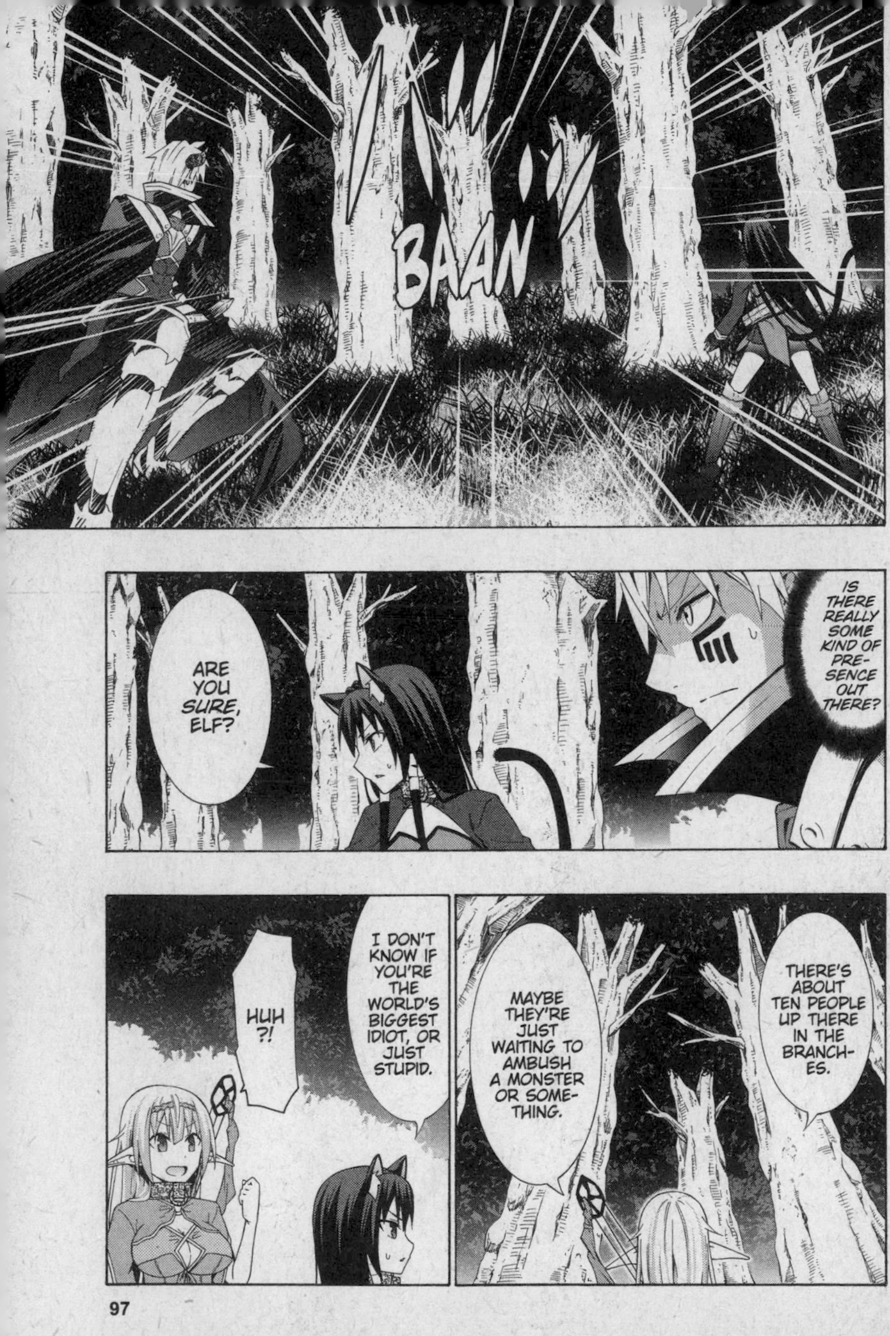
BAAN
IS THERE REALLY SOME KIND OF PRESENCE OUT THERE?
ARE YOU SURE, ELF?
THERE'S ABOUT TEN PEOPLE UP THERE IN THE BRANCHES.
MAYBE THEY'RE JUST WAITING TO AMBUSH A MONSTER OR SOMETHING.
I DON'T KNOW IF YOU'RE THE WORLD'S BIGGEST IDIOT, OR JUST STUPID.
HUH?!

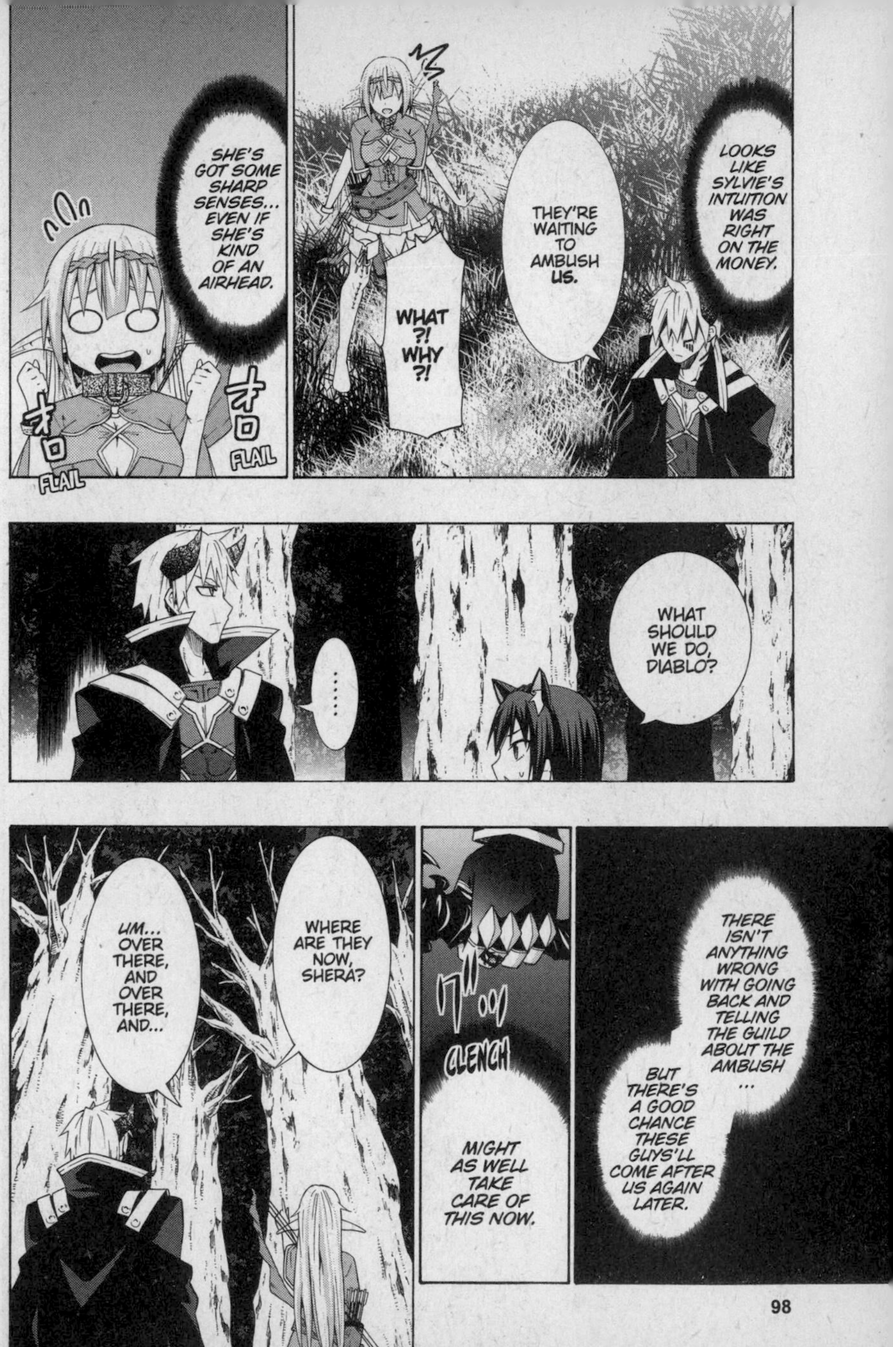
LOOKS LIKE SYLVIE'S INTUITION WAS RIGHT ON THE MONEY.
THEY'RE WAITING TO AMBUSH US.
WHAT?! WHY?!
SHE'S GOT SOME SHARP SENSES... EVEN IF SHE'S KIND OF AN AIRHEAD.
オロ
FLAIL
オロ
FLAIL
WHAT SHOULD WE DO, DIABLO?
......
THERE ISN'T ANYTHING WRONG WITH GOING BACK AND TELLING THE GUILD ABOUT THE AMBUSH...
BUT THERE'S A GOOD CHANCE THESE GUYS'LL COME AFTER US AGAIN LATER.
グッ
CLENCH
MIGHT AS WELL TAKE CARE OF THIS NOW.
WHERE ARE THEY NOW, SHERA?
UM... OVER THERE, AND OVER THERE, AND...

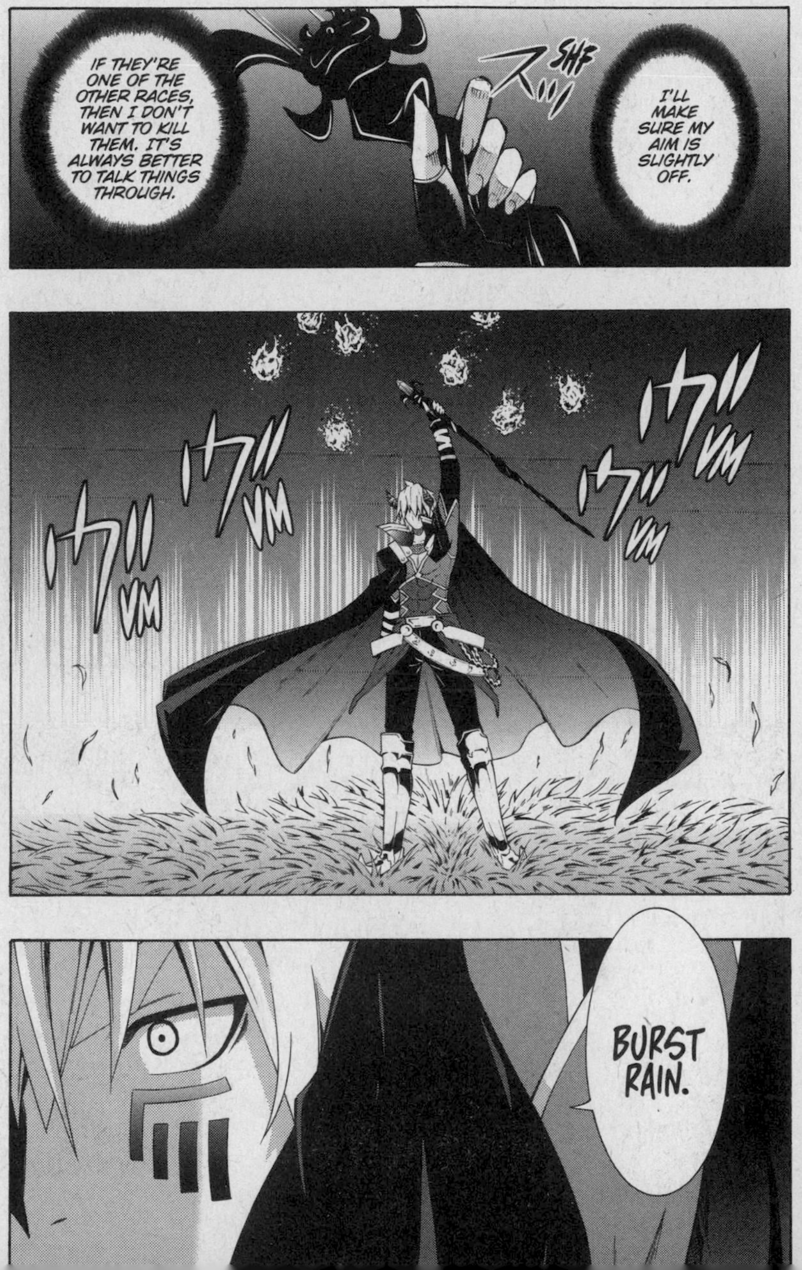
SHF
IF THEY'RE ONE OF THE OTHER RACES, THEN I DON'T WANT TO KILL THEM. IT'S ALWAYS BETTER TO TALK THINGS THROUGH.
I'LL MAKE SURE MY AIM IS SLIGHTLY OFF.
VM
VM
VM
VM
VM
BURST RAIN.

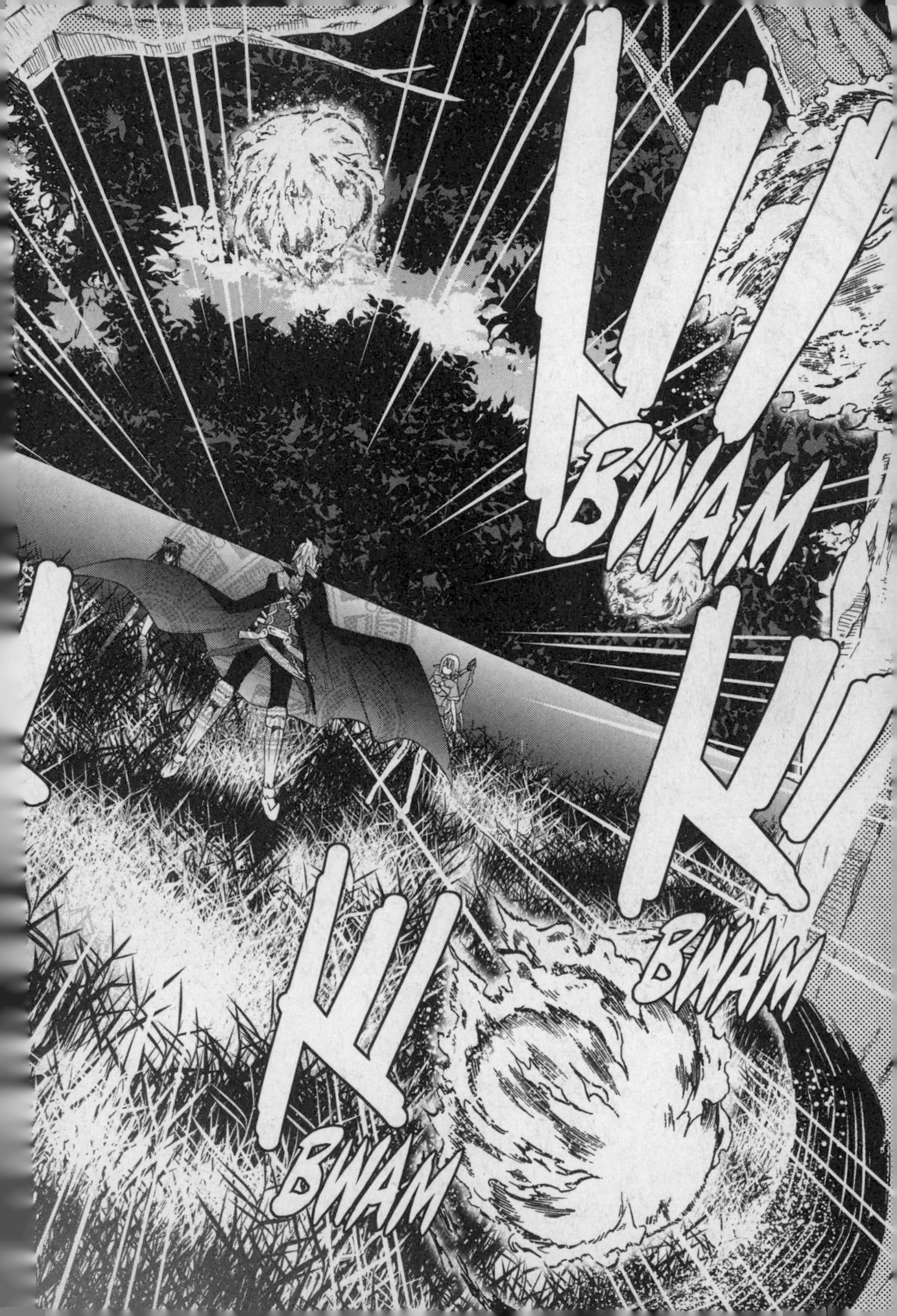
BWAM
BWAM
BWAM

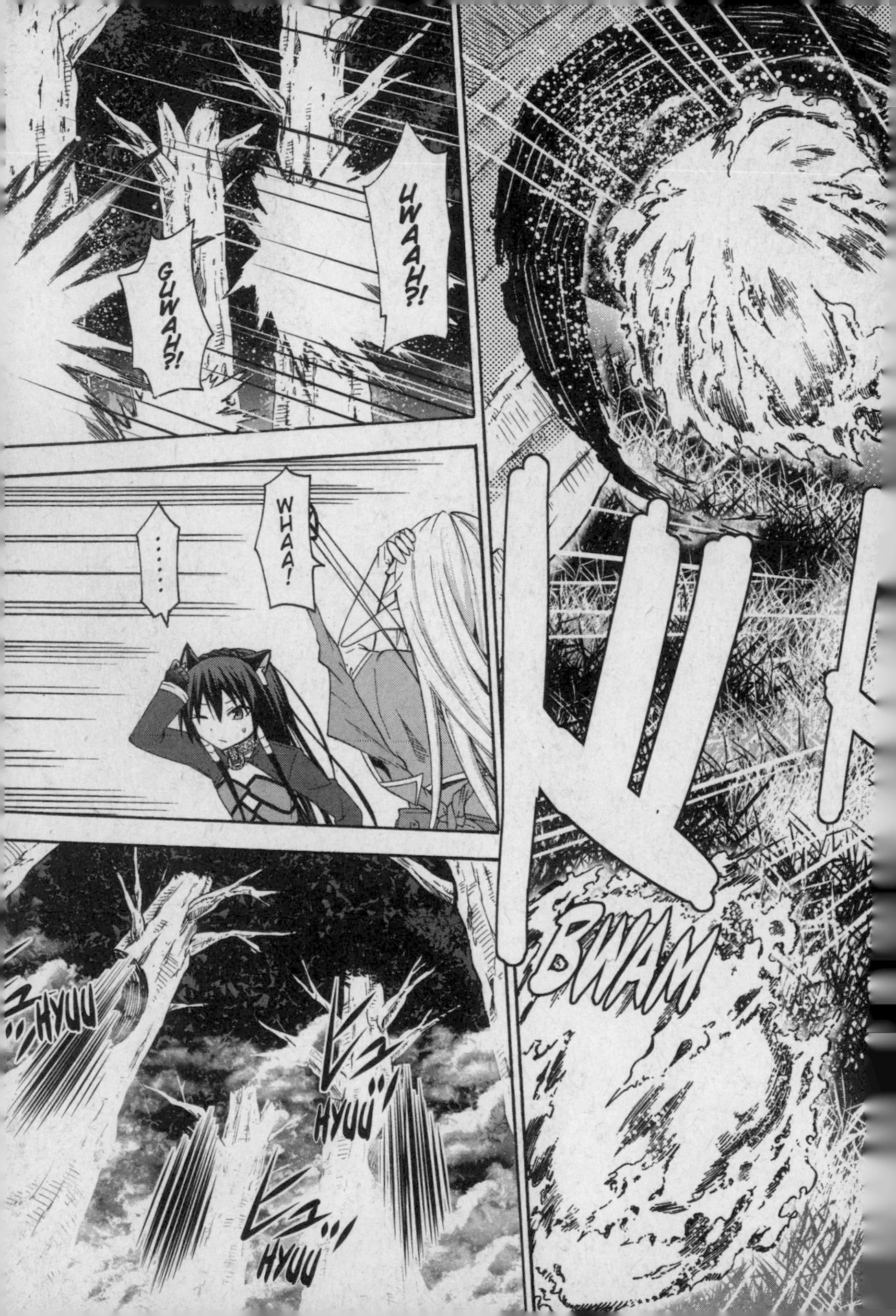
BWAM
UWAAH?!
GUWAH?!
WHAA!
......
HYUU
HYUU
HYUU

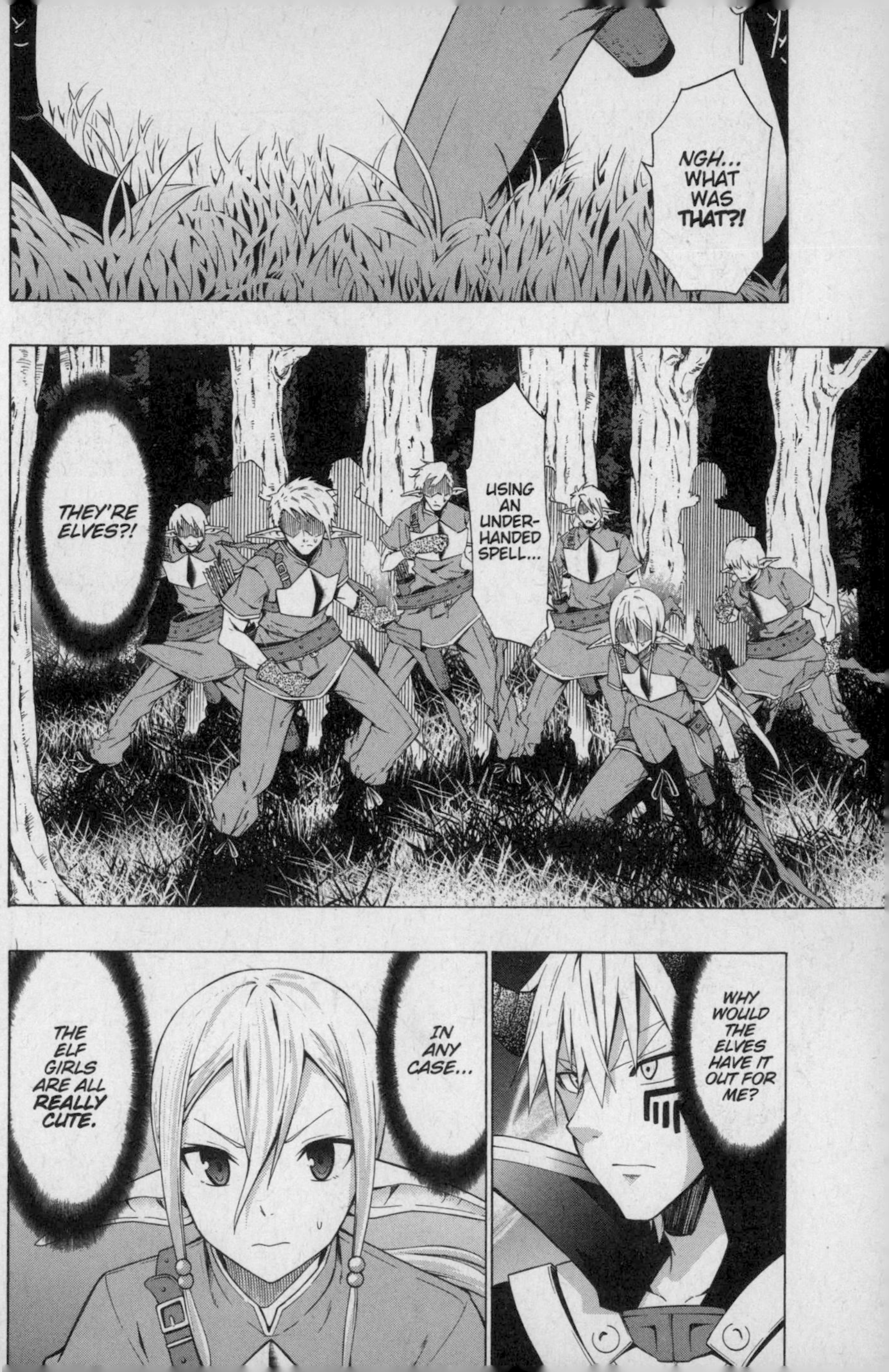
NGH... WHAT WAS THAT?!
USING AN UNDER-HANDED SPELL...
THEY'RE ELVES?!
WHY WOULD THE ELVES HAVE IT OUT FOR ME?
IN ANY CASE...
THE ELF GIRLS ARE ALL REALLY CUTE.

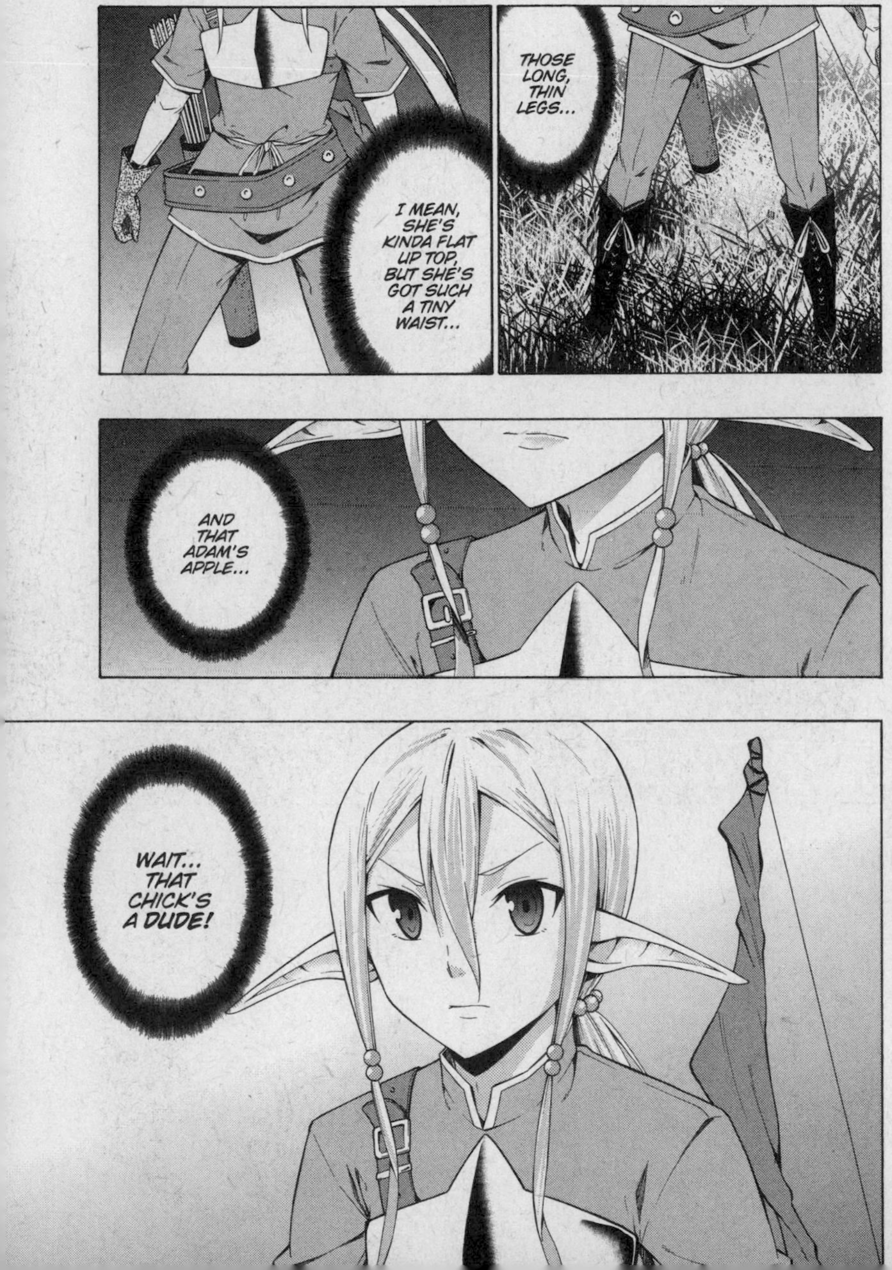
I MEAN, SHE'S KINDA FLAT UP TOP, BUT SHE'S GOT SUCH A TINY WAIST...
THOSE LONG, THIN LEGS...
AND THAT ADAM'S APPLE...
WAIT... THAT CHICK'S A DUDE!

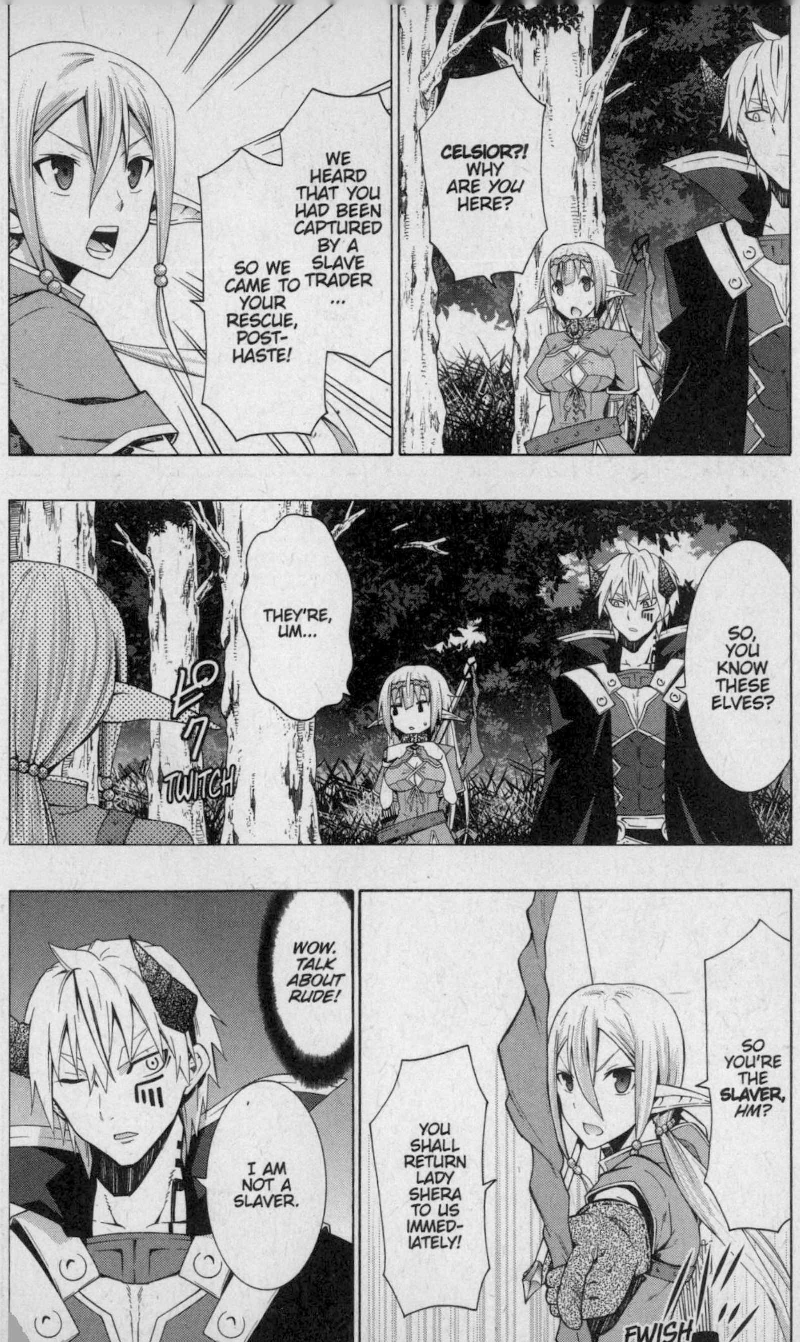
CELSIOR?! WHY ARE YOU HERE?
WE HEARD THAT YOU HAD BEEN CAPTURED BY A SLAVE TRADER ...
SO WE CAME TO YOUR RESCUE, POST-HASTE!
SO, YOU KNOW THESE ELVES?
THEY'RE, UM...
ピク
TWITCH
SO YOU'RE THE SLAVER, HM?
YOU SHALL RETURN LADY SHERA TO US IMMEDI-ATELY!
FWISH
WOW. TALK ABOUT RUDE!
I AM NOT A SLAVER.

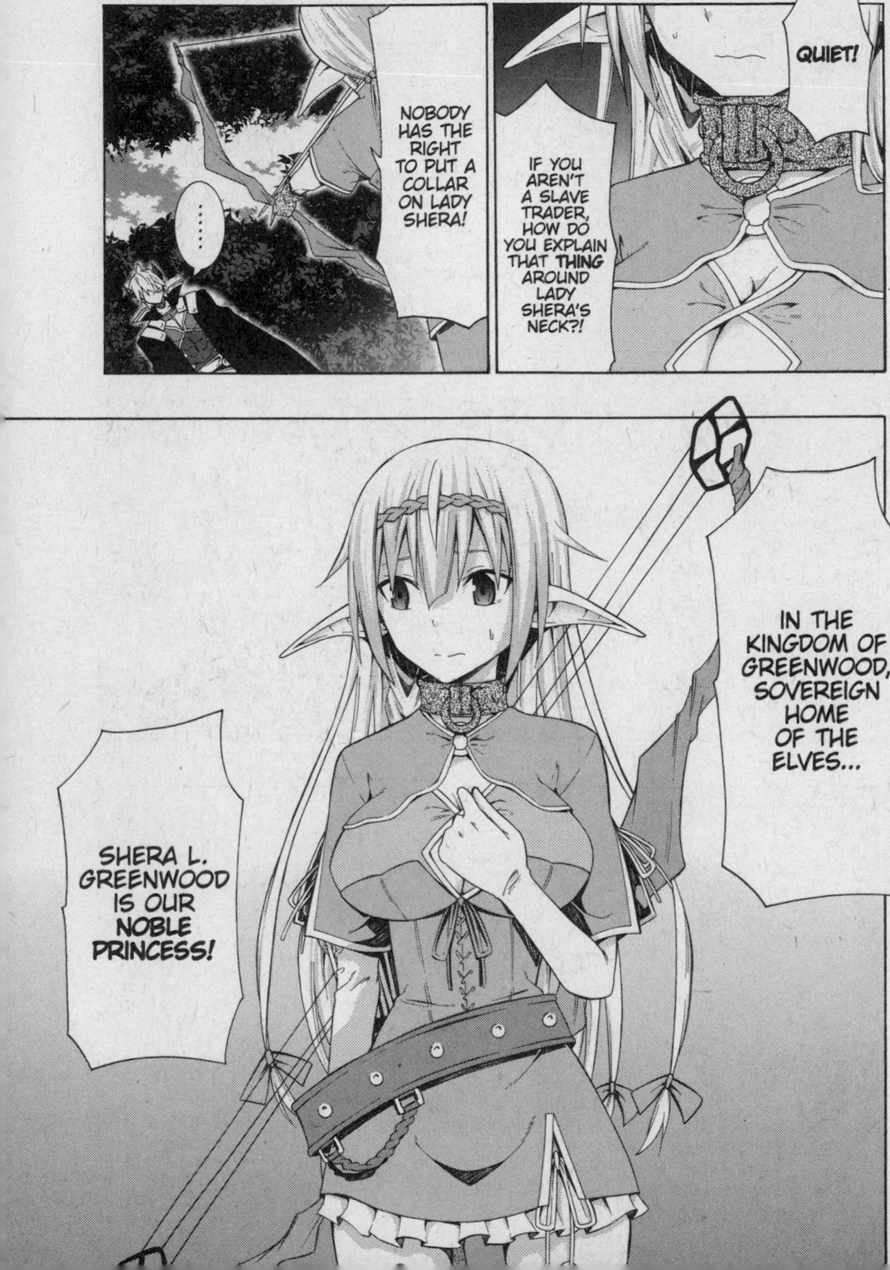
QUIET!
IF YOU AREN'T A SLAVE TRADER, HOW DO YOU EXPLAIN THAT THING AROUND LADY SHERA'S NECK?!
NOBODY HAS THE RIGHT TO PUT A COLLAR ON LADY SHERA!
......
IN THE KINGDOM OF GREENWOOD, SOVEREIGN HOME OF THE ELVES...
SHERA L. GREENWOOD IS OUR NOBLE PRINCESS!

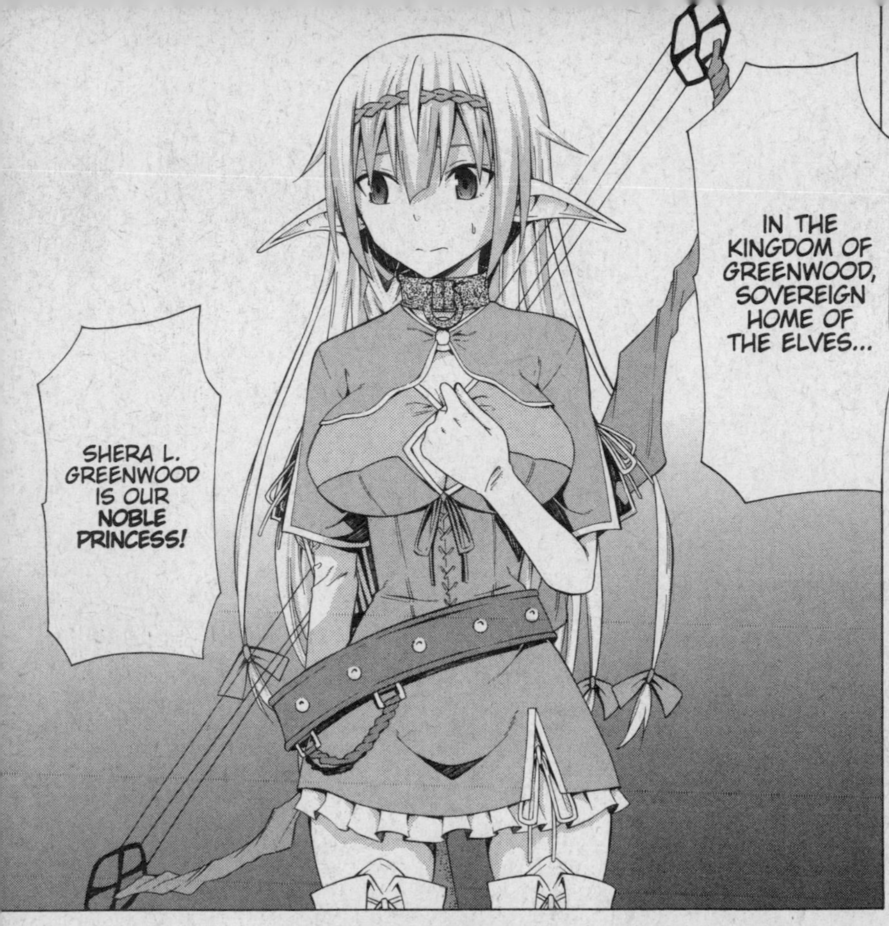
IN THE KINGDOM OF GREENWOOD, SOVEREIGN HOME OF THE ELVES...
SHERA L. GREENWOOD IS OUR NOBLE PRINCESS!

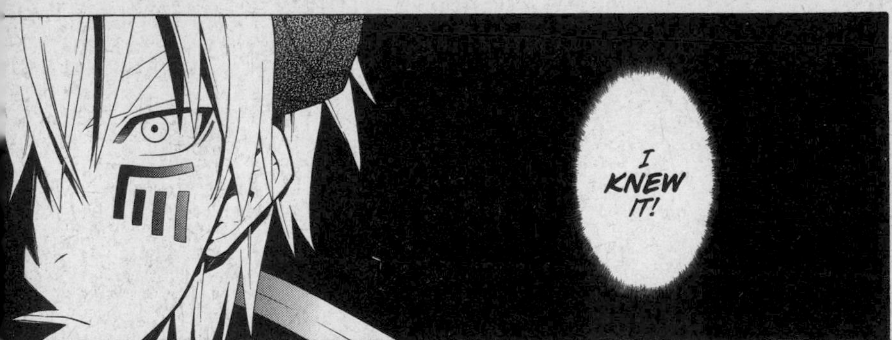
I KNEW IT!

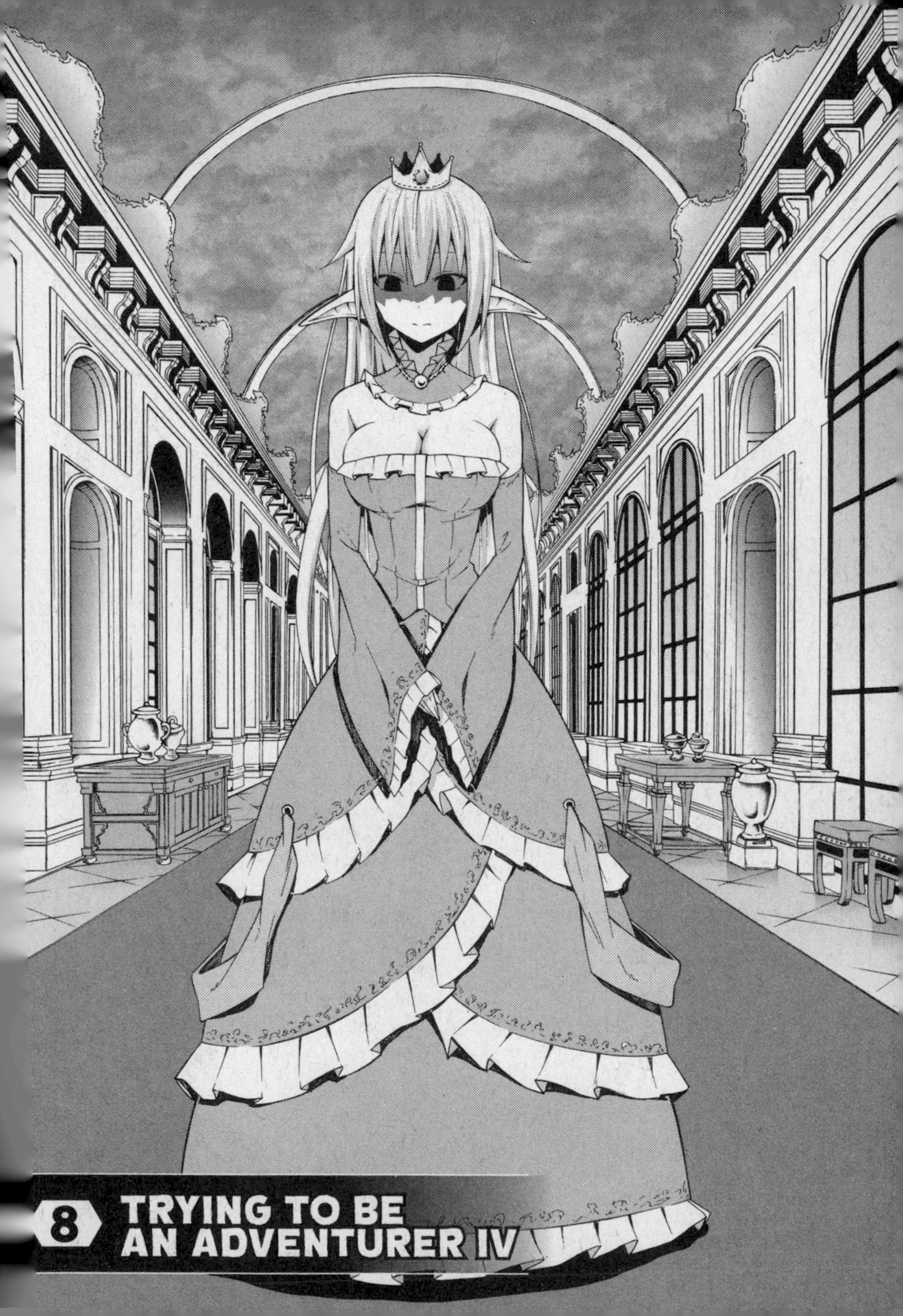
8
TRYING TO BE
AN ADVENTURER IV

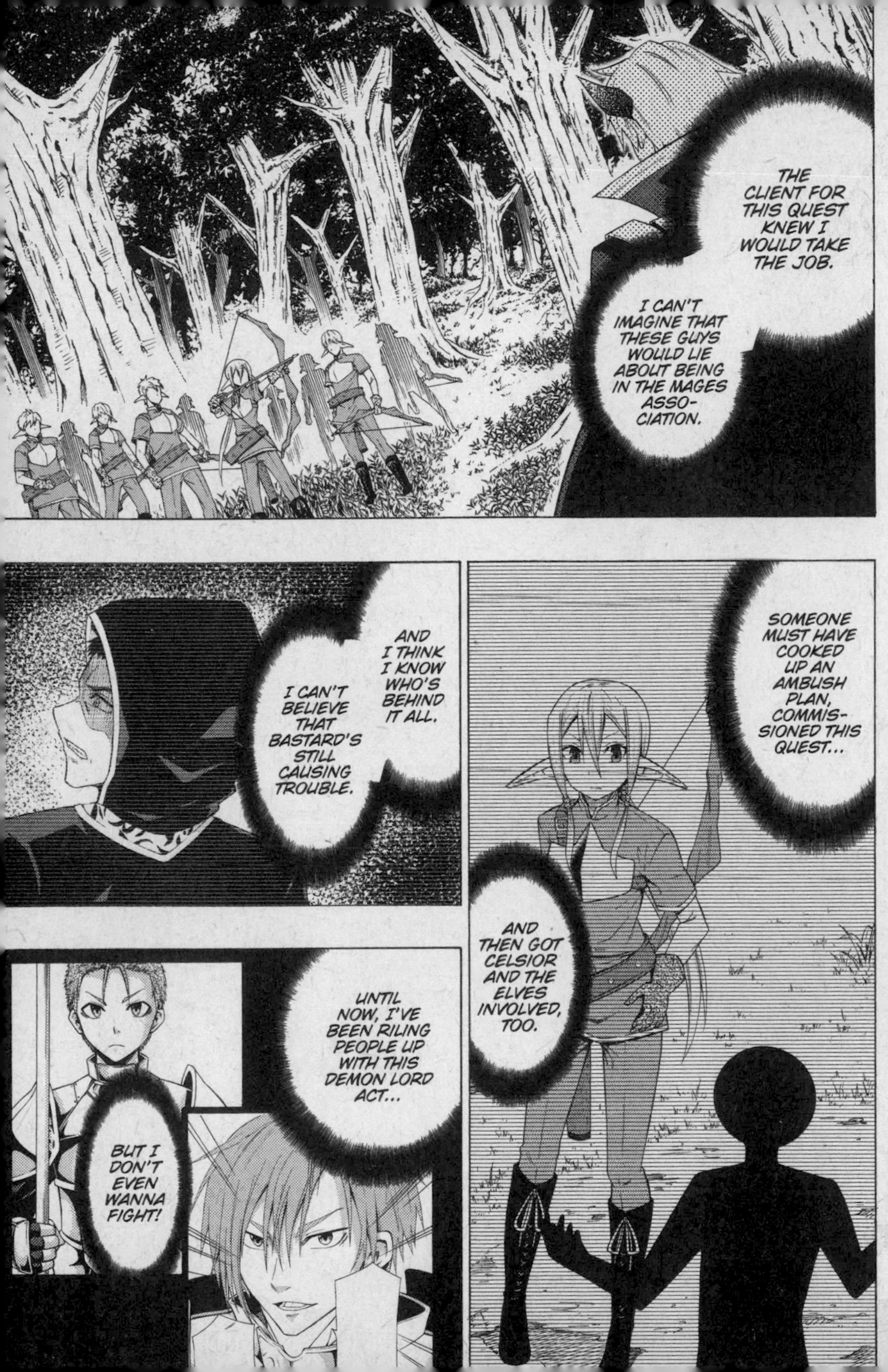
THE CLIENT FOR THIS QUEST KNEW I WOULD TAKE THE JOB.
I CAN'T IMAGINE THAT THESE GUYS WOULD LIE ABOUT BEING IN THE MAGES ASSO- CIATION.
SOMEONE MUST HAVE COOKED UP AN AMBUSH PLAN, COMMIS- SIONED THIS QUEST...
AND THEN GOT CELSIOR AND THE ELVES INVOLVED, TOO.
AND I THINK I KNOW WHO'S BEHIND IT ALL.
I CAN'T BELIEVE THAT BASTARD'S STILL CAUSING TROUBLE.
UNTIL NOW, I'VE BEEN RILING PEOPLE UP WITH THIS DEMON LORD ACT...
BUT I DON'T EVEN WANNA FIGHT!

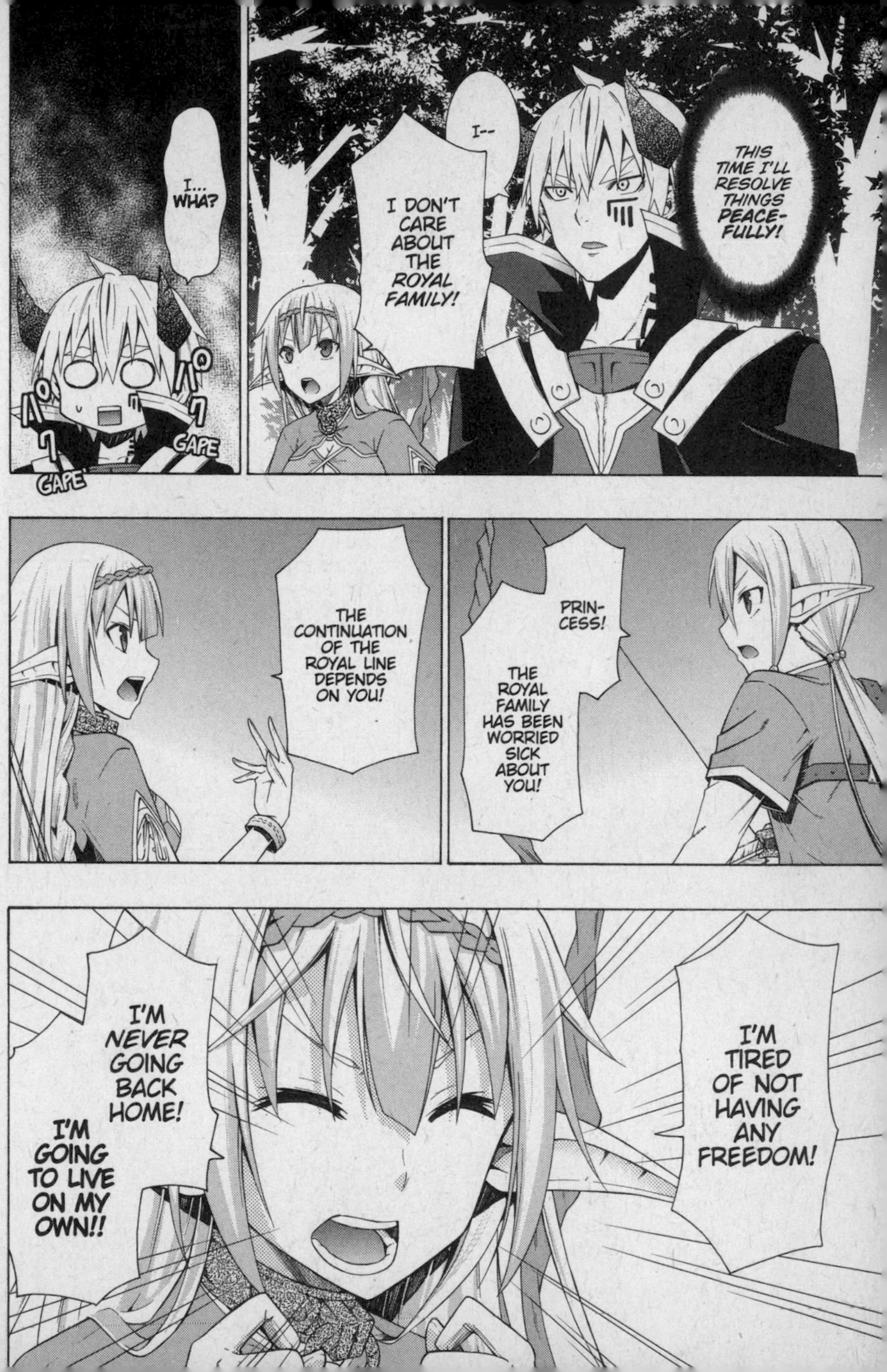
THIS TIME I'LL RESOLVE THINGS PEACEFULLY!
I--
I DON'T CARE ABOUT THE ROYAL FAMILY!
I... WHA?
GAPE
GAPE
PRINCESS!
THE ROYAL FAMILY HAS BEEN WORRIED SICK ABOUT YOU!
THE CONTINUATION OF THE ROYAL LINE DEPENDS ON YOU!
I'M TIRED OF NOT HAVING ANY FREEDOM!
I'M NEVER GOING BACK HOME!
I'M GOING TO LIVE ON MY OWN!!

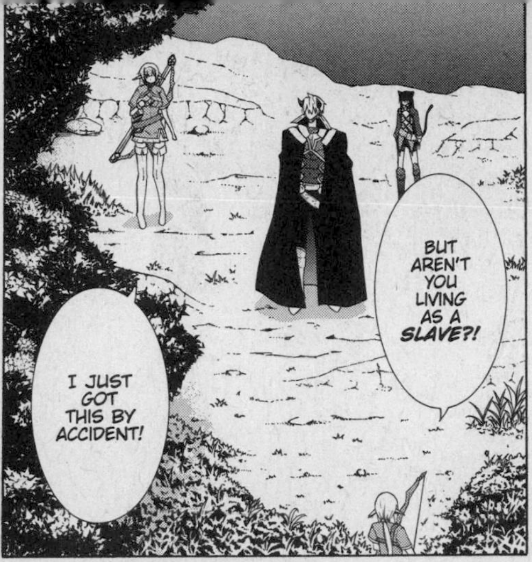
BUT AREN'T YOU LIVING AS A *SLAVE?!*
I JUST GOT THIS BY ACCIDENT!
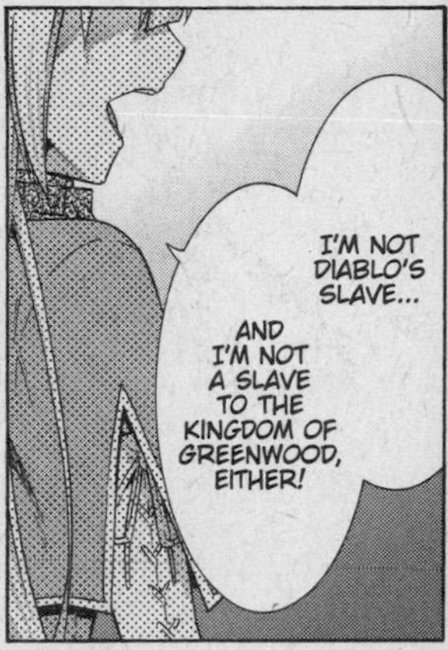
I'M NOT DIABLO'S SLAVE...
AND I'M NOT A SLAVE TO THE KINGDOM OF GREENWOOD, EITHER!
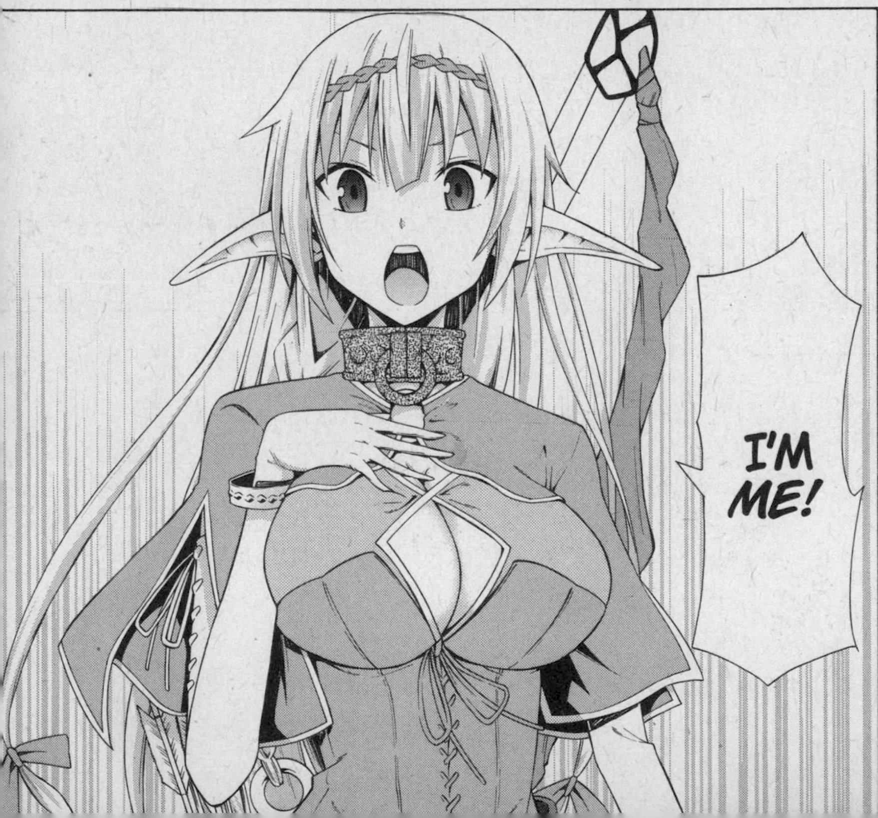
I'M *ME!*

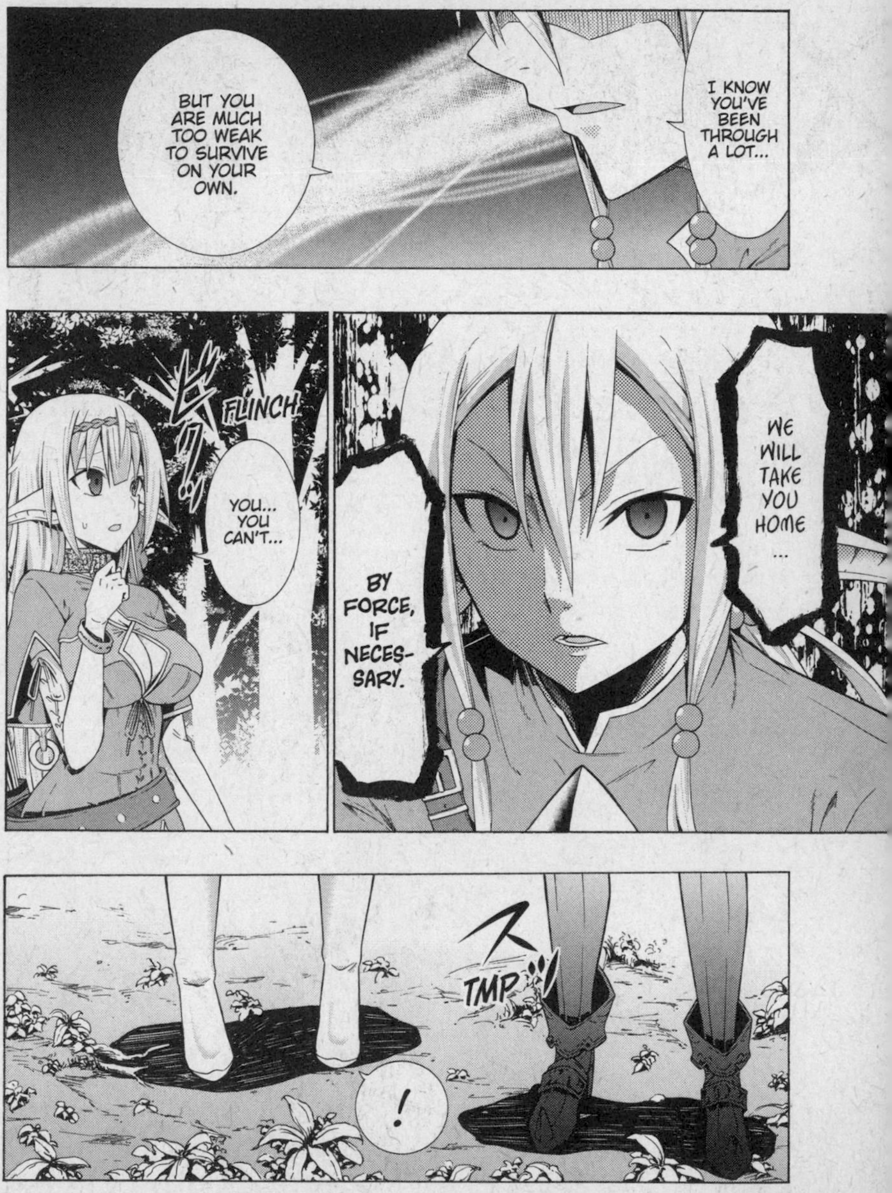
I KNOW YOU'VE BEEN THROUGH A LOT...
BUT YOU ARE MUCH TOO WEAK TO SURVIVE ON YOUR OWN.
WE WILL TAKE YOU HOME ...
BY FORCE, IF NECES-SARY.
FLINCH
YOU... YOU CAN'T...
TMP
!

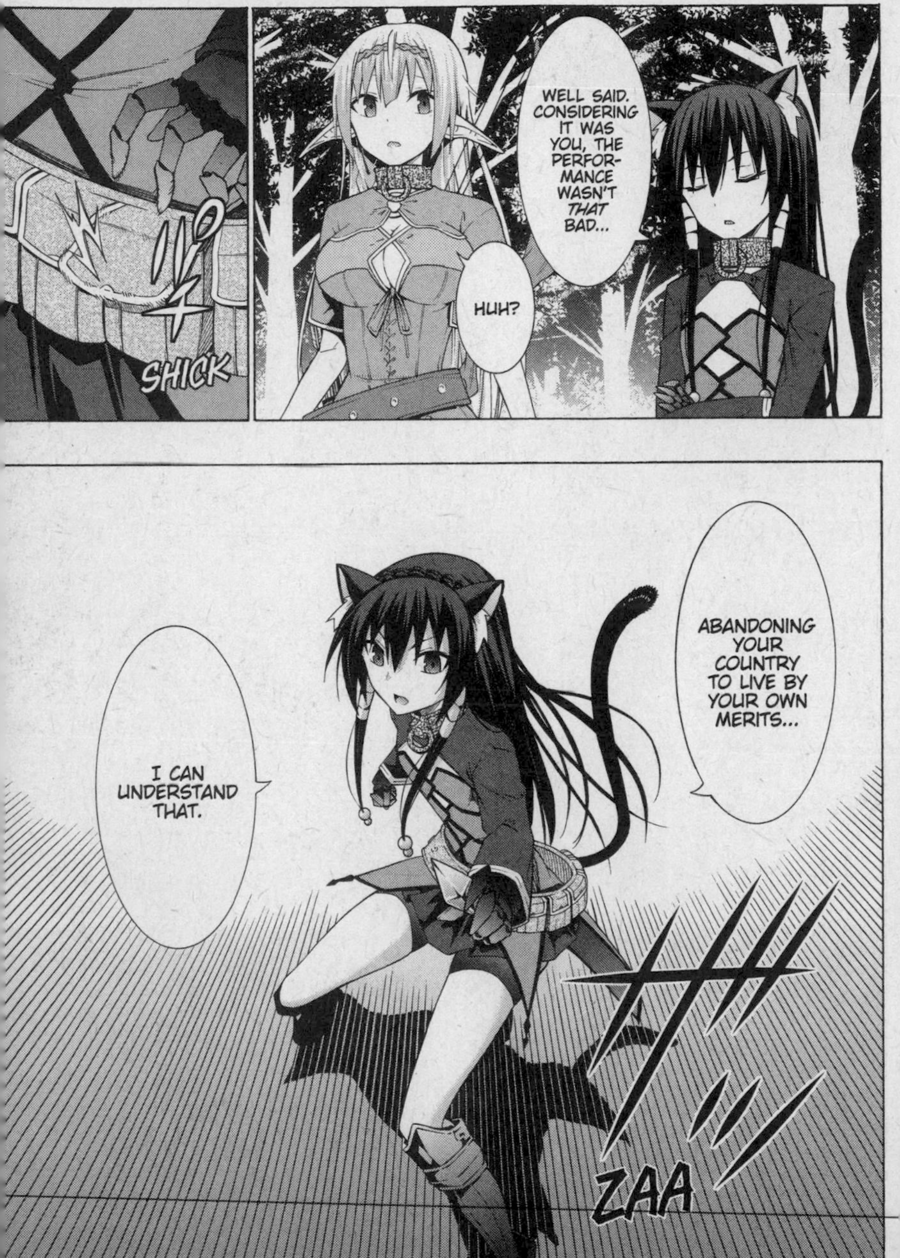
WELL SAID. CONSIDERING IT WAS YOU, THE PERFORMANCE WASN'T *THAT* BAD...
HUH?
SHICK
ABANDONING YOUR COUNTRY TO LIVE BY YOUR OWN MERITS...
I CAN UNDERSTAND THAT.
ZAA

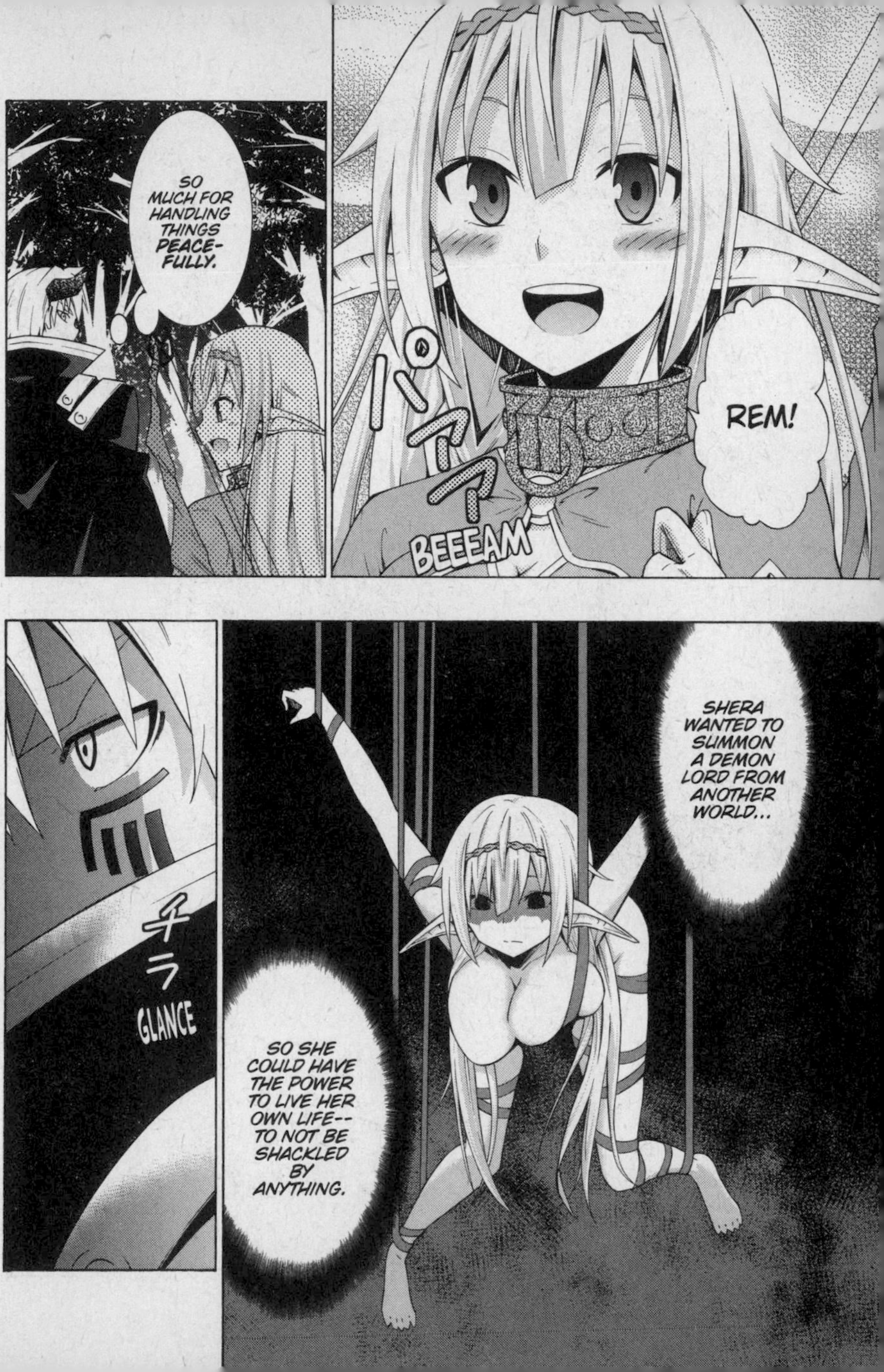
REM!
パァ
BEEEAM
SO MUCH FOR HANDLING THINGS PEACE-FULLY.
SHERA WANTED TO SUMMON A DEMON LORD FROM ANOTHER WORLD...
SO SHE COULD HAVE THE POWER TO LIVE HER OWN LIFE-- TO NOT BE SHACKLED BY ANYTHING.
チラ
GLANCE

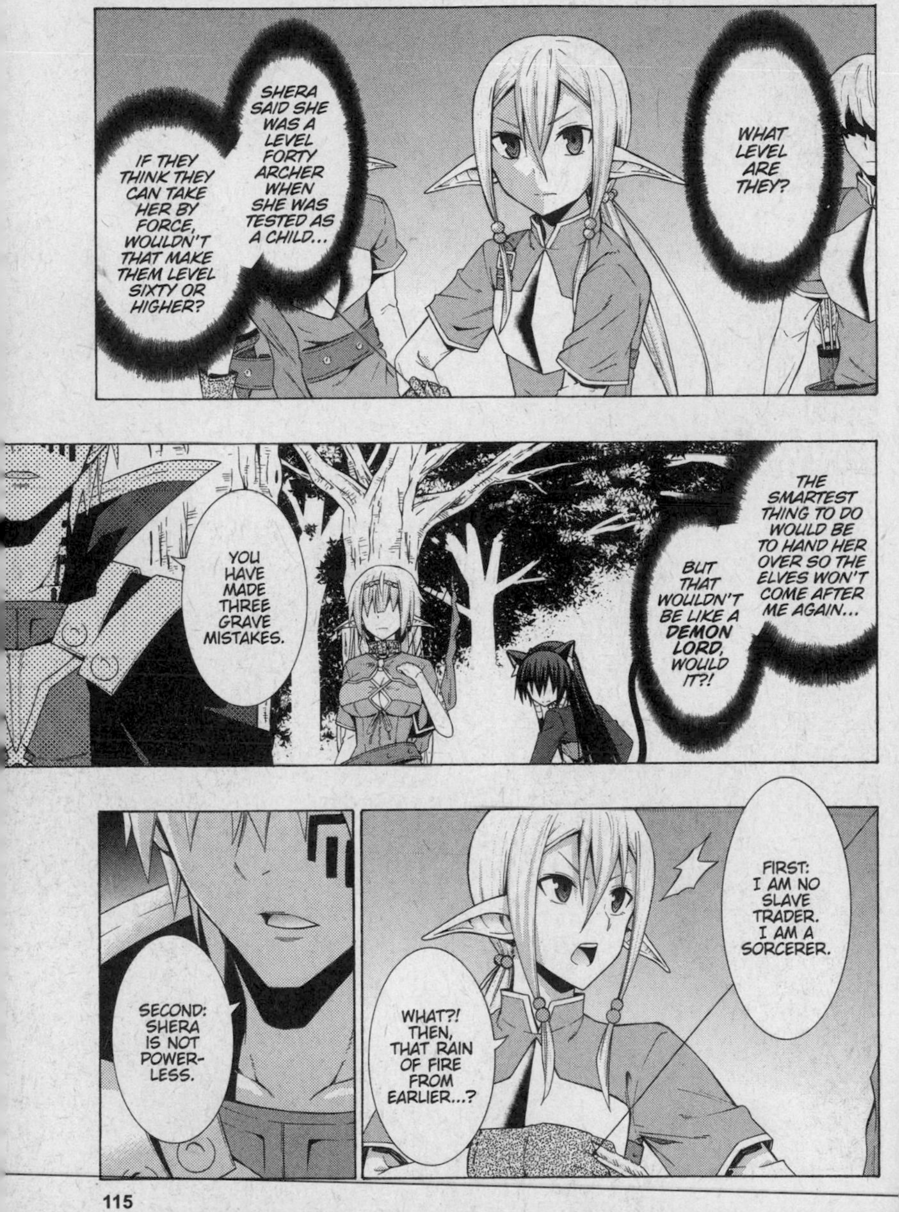
WHAT LEVEL ARE THEY?
SHERA SAID SHE WAS A LEVEL FORTY ARCHER WHEN SHE WAS TESTED AS A CHILD...
IF THEY THINK THEY CAN TAKE HER BY FORCE, WOULDN'T THAT MAKE THEM LEVEL SIXTY OR HIGHER?
THE SMARTEST THING TO DO WOULD BE TO HAND HER OVER SO THE ELVES WON'T COME AFTER ME AGAIN...
BUT THAT WOULDN'T BE LIKE A DEMON LORD, WOULD IT?!
YOU HAVE MADE THREE GRAVE MISTAKES.
FIRST: I AM NO SLAVE TRADER. I AM A SORCERER.
WHAT?! THEN, THAT RAIN OF FIRE FROM EARLIER...?
SECOND: SHERA IS NOT POWER-LESS.

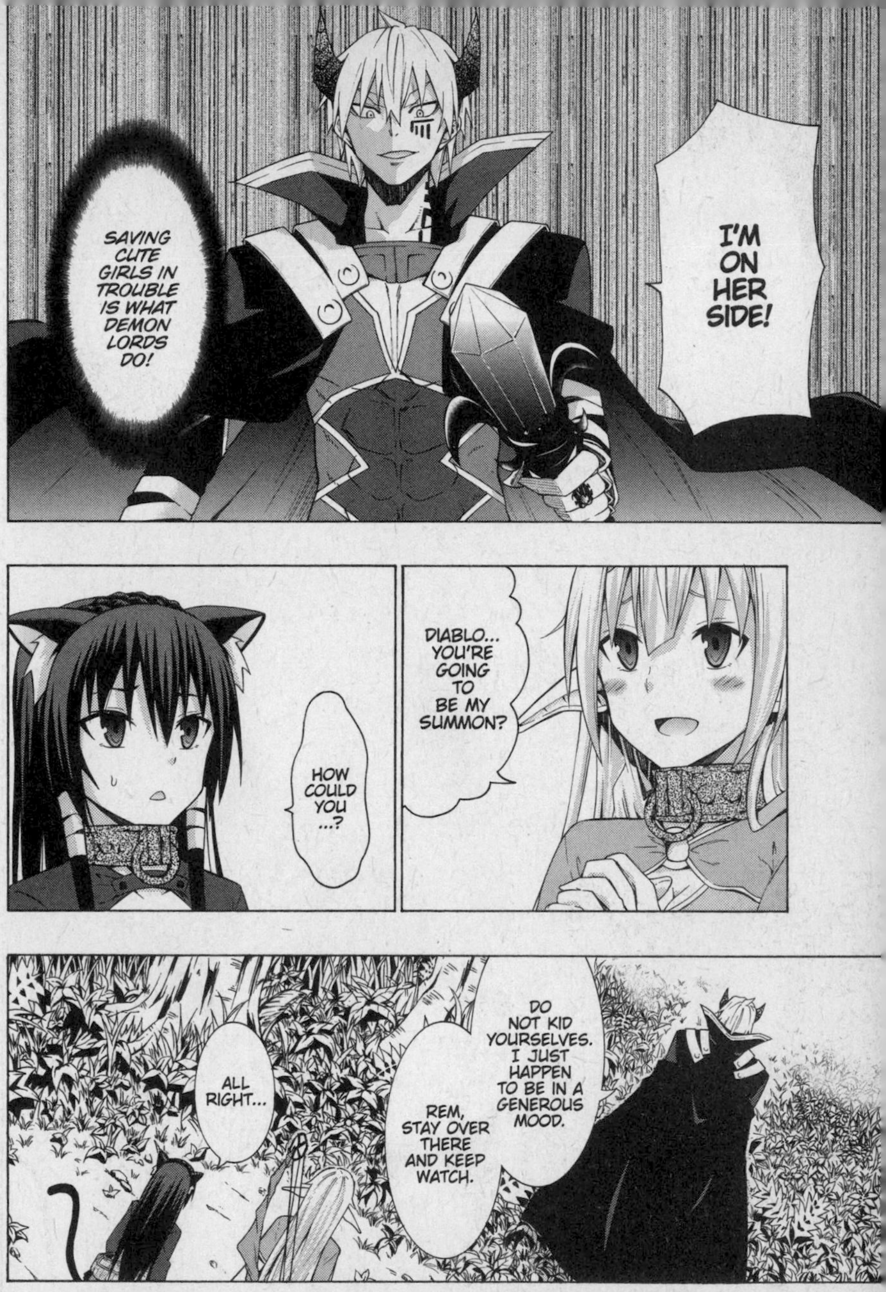
I'M ON HER SIDE!
SAVING CUTE GIRLS IN TROUBLE IS WHAT DEMON LORDS DO!
DIABLO... YOU'RE GOING TO BE MY SUMMON?
HOW COULD YOU ...?
DO NOT KID YOURSELVES. I JUST HAPPEN TO BE IN A GENEROUS MOOD.
REM, STAY OVER THERE AND KEEP WATCH.
ALL RIGHT...

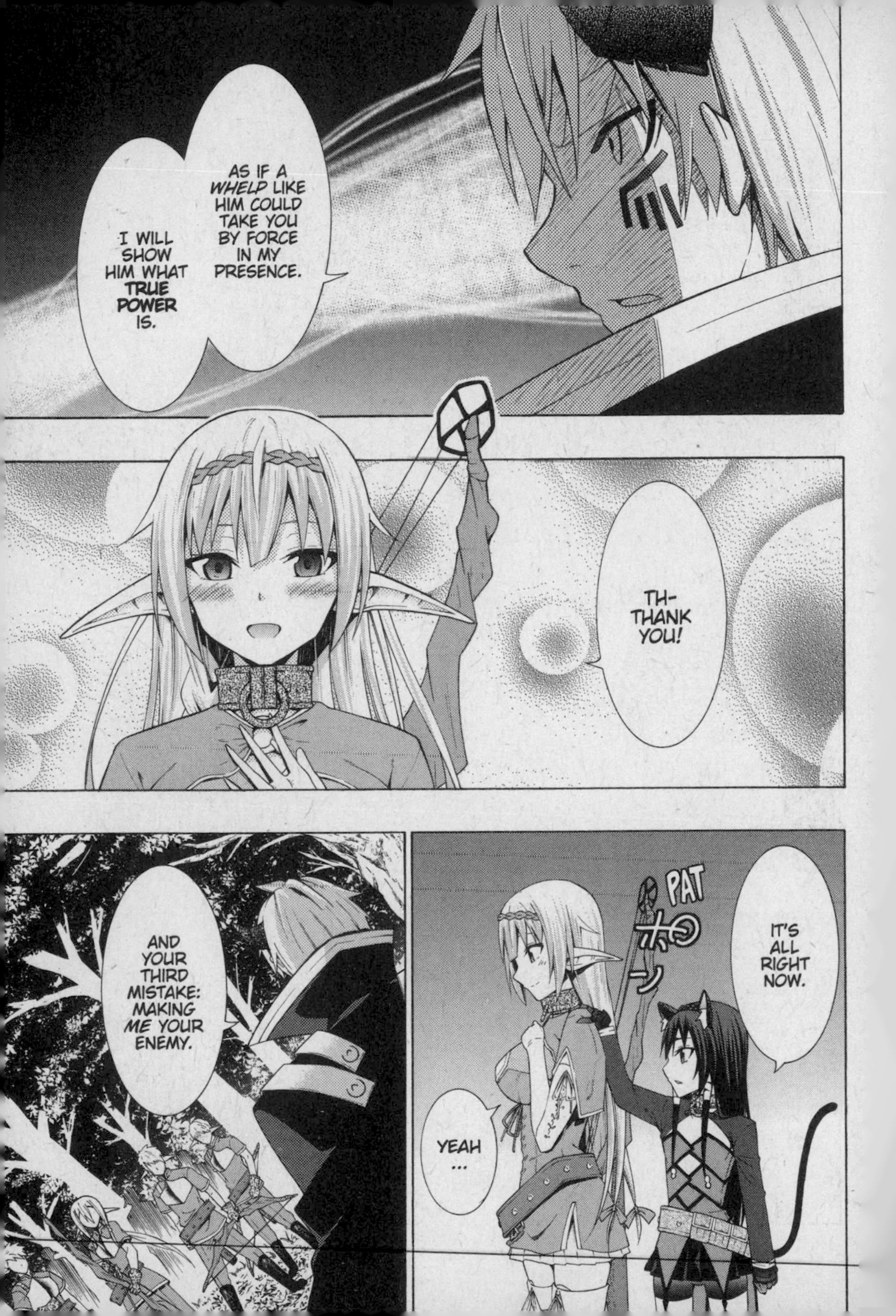
AS IF A WHELP LIKE HIM COULD TAKE YOU BY FORCE IN MY PRESENCE.
I WILL SHOW HIM WHAT TRUE POWER IS.
TH-THANK YOU!
IT'S ALL RIGHT NOW.
PAT
YEAH...
AND YOUR THIRD MISTAKE: MAKING ME YOUR ENEMY.

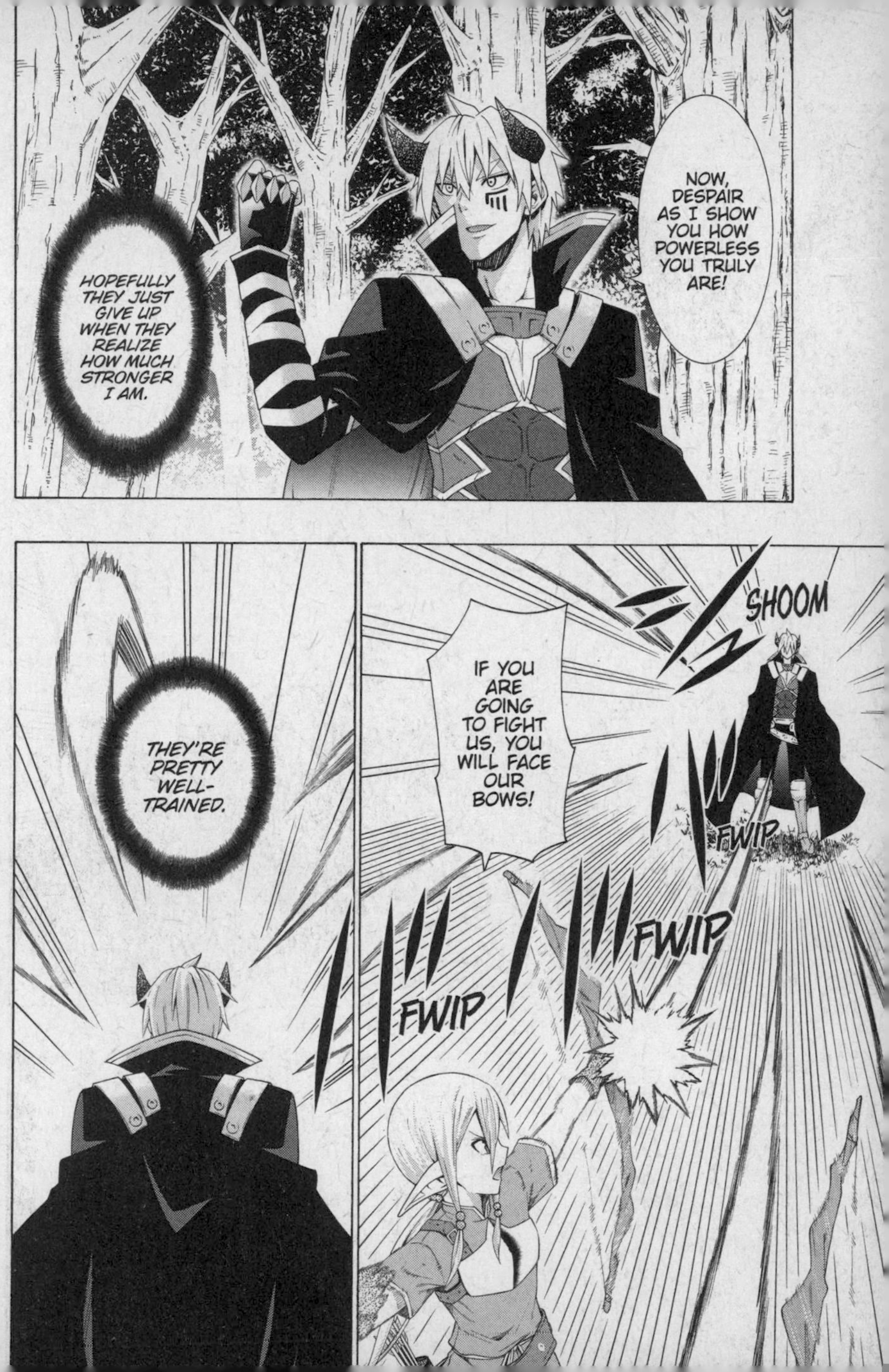
NOW, DESPAIR AS I SHOW YOU HOW POWERLESS YOU TRULY ARE!
HOPEFULLY THEY JUST GIVE UP WHEN THEY REALIZE HOW MUCH STRONGER I AM.
SHOOM
IF YOU ARE GOING TO FIGHT US, YOU WILL FACE OUR BOWS!
FWIP
FWIP
FWIP
THEY'RE PRETTY WELL-TRAINED.

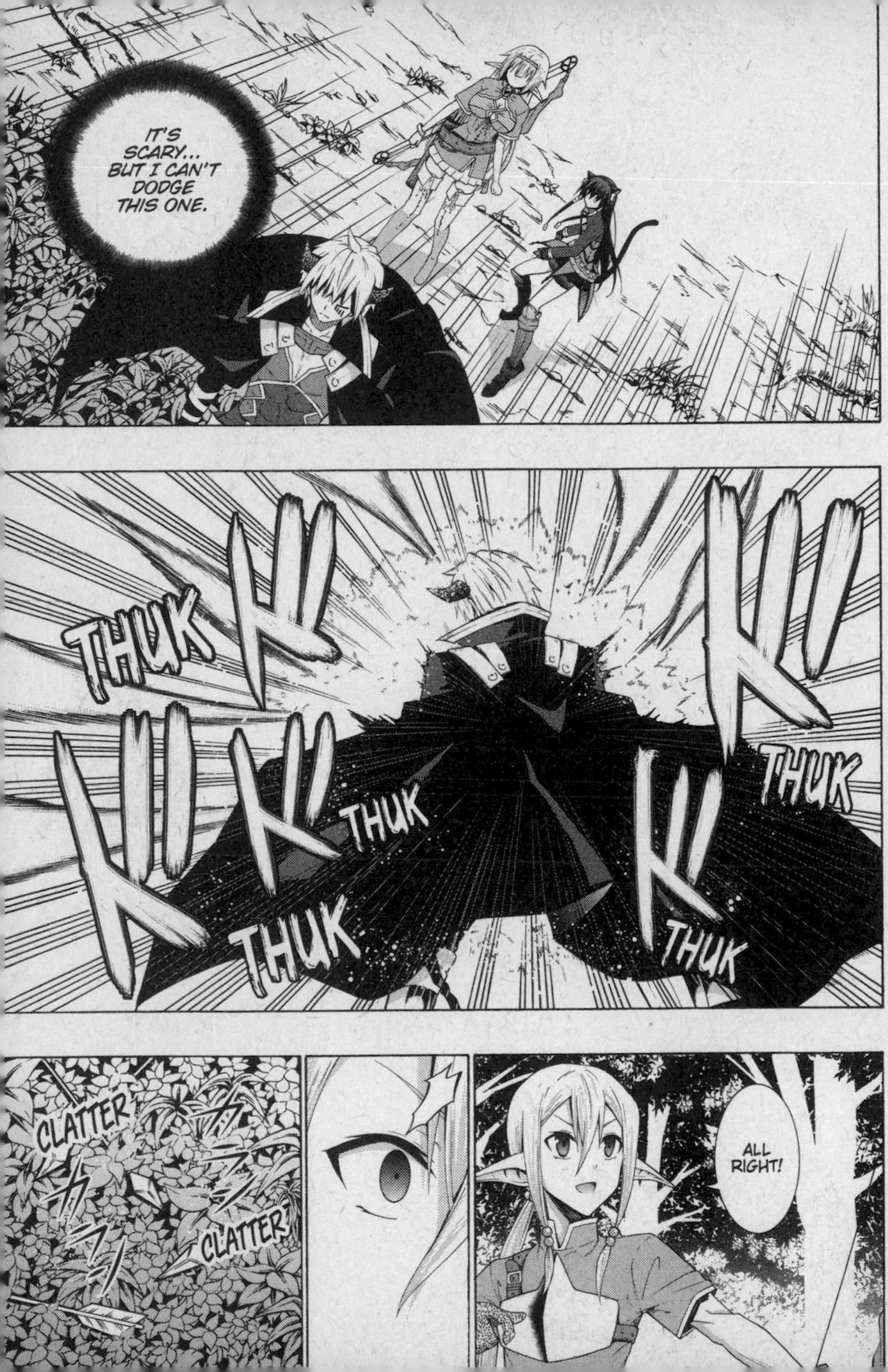
IT'S SCARY... BUT I CAN'T DODGE THIS ONE.
THUK
THUK
THUK
THUK
THUK
ALL RIGHT!
CLATTER
CLATTER

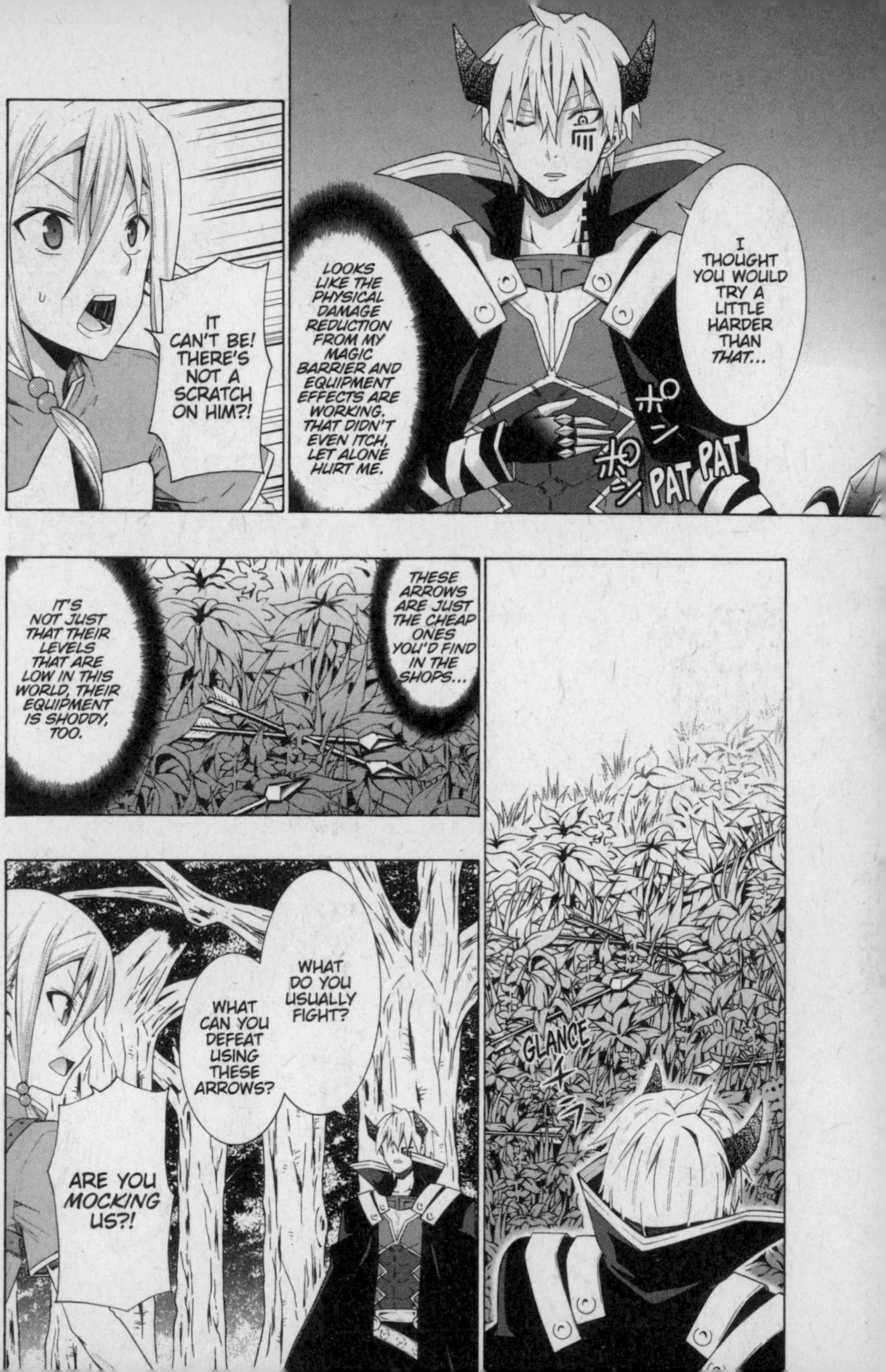
I THOUGHT YOU WOULD TRY A LITTLE HARDER THAN THAT...
ポン
ポン
PAT PAT
LOOKS LIKE THE PHYSICAL DAMAGE REDUCTION FROM MY MAGIC BARRIER AND EQUIPMENT EFFECTS ARE WORKING. THAT DIDN'T EVEN ITCH, LET ALONE HURT ME.
IT CAN'T BE! THERE'S NOT A SCRATCH ON HIM?!
GLANCE
チラ
THESE ARROWS ARE JUST THE CHEAP ONES YOU'D FIND IN THE SHOPS...
IT'S NOT JUST THAT THEIR LEVELS THAT ARE LOW IN THIS WORLD, THEIR EQUIPMENT IS SHODDY, TOO.
WHAT DO YOU USUALLY FIGHT?
WHAT CAN YOU DEFEAT USING THESE ARROWS?
ARE YOU MOCKING US?!

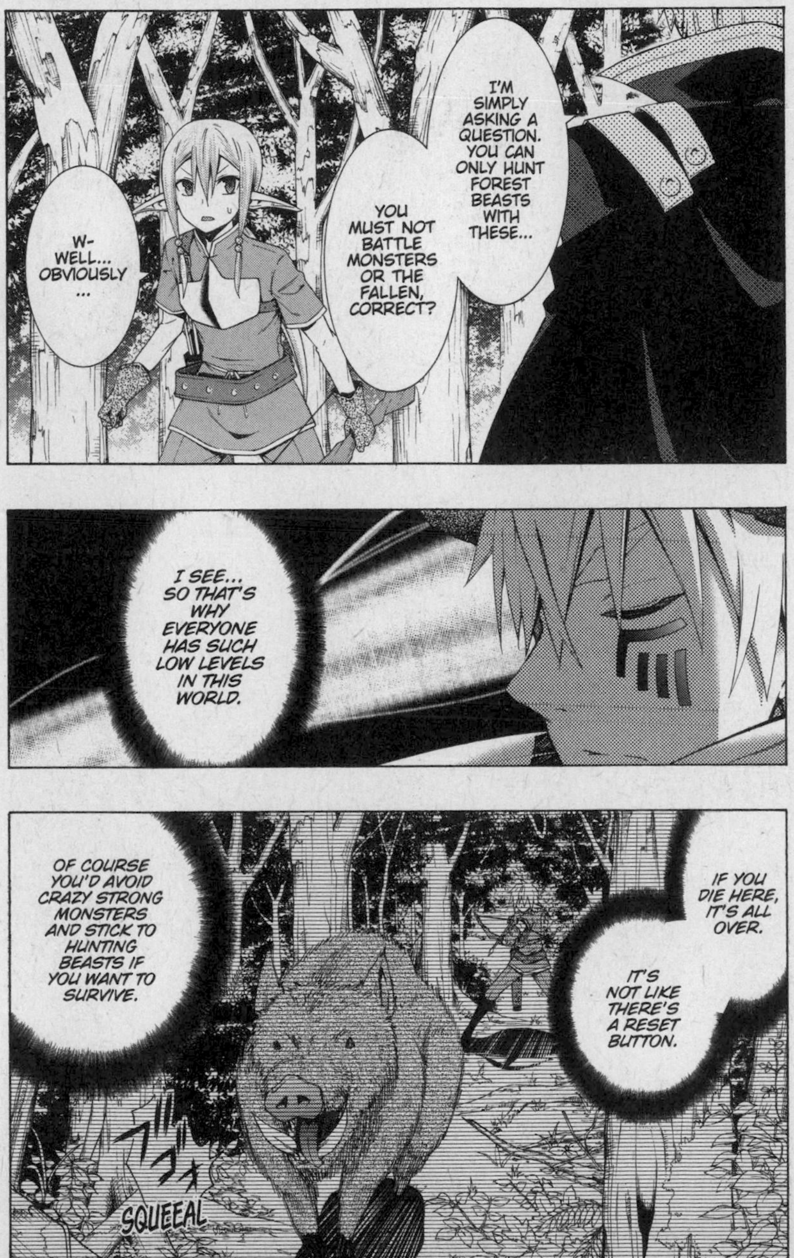
I'M SIMPLY ASKING A QUESTION. YOU CAN ONLY HUNT FOREST BEASTS WITH THESE...
YOU MUST NOT BATTLE MONSTERS OR THE FALLEN, CORRECT?
W-WELL... OBVIOUSLY...
I SEE... SO THAT'S WHY EVERYONE HAS SUCH LOW LEVELS IN THIS WORLD.
IF YOU DIE HERE, IT'S ALL OVER.
IT'S NOT LIKE THERE'S A RESET BUTTON.
OF COURSE YOU'D AVOID CRAZY STRONG MONSTERS AND STICK TO HUNTING BEASTS IF YOU WANT TO SURVIVE.
SQUEEAL

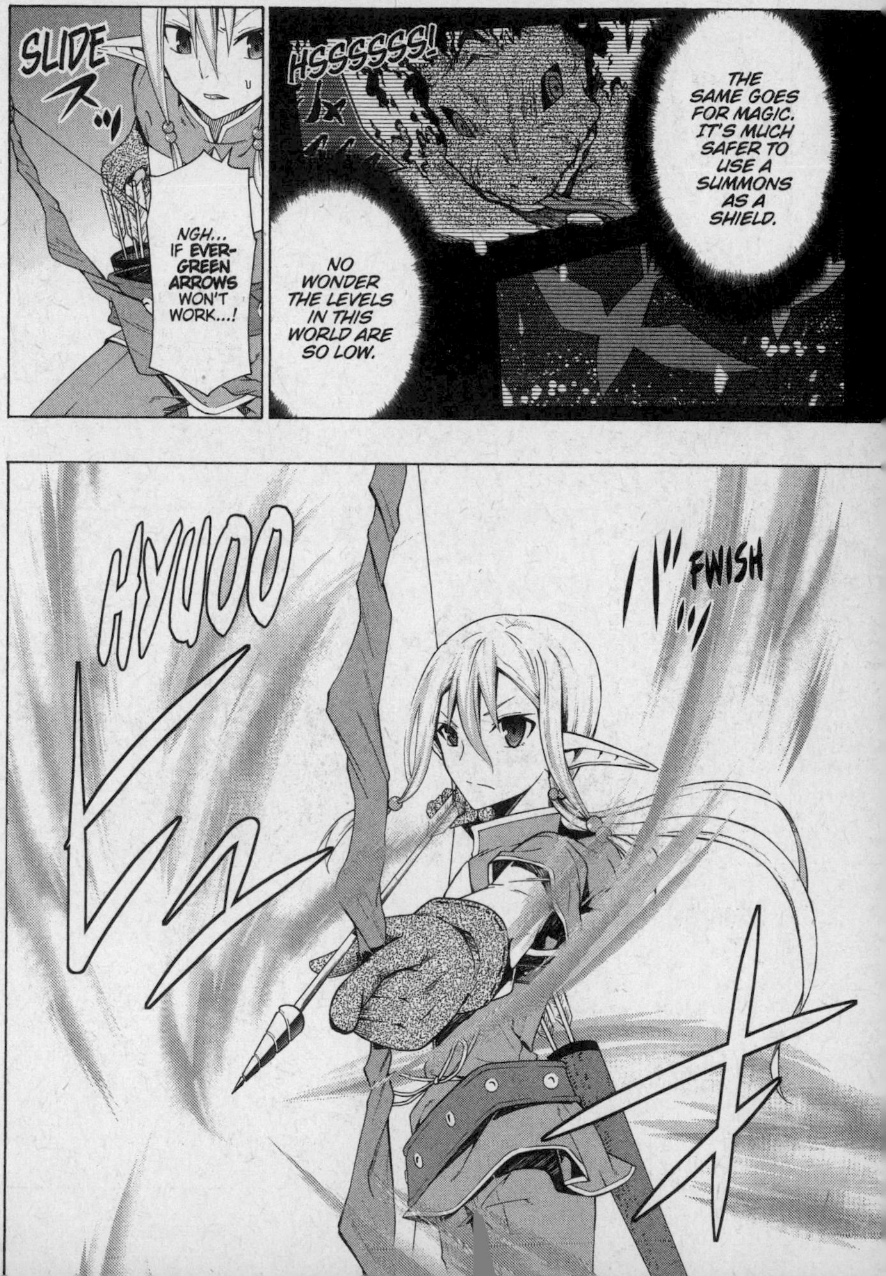
HSSSSSS!
THE SAME GOES FOR MAGIC. IT'S MUCH SAFER TO USE A SUMMONS AS A SHIELD.
NO WONDER THE LEVELS IN THIS WORLD ARE SO LOW.
SLIDE
NGH... IF EVER-GREEN ARROWS WON'T WORK...!
FWISH
HYUOO

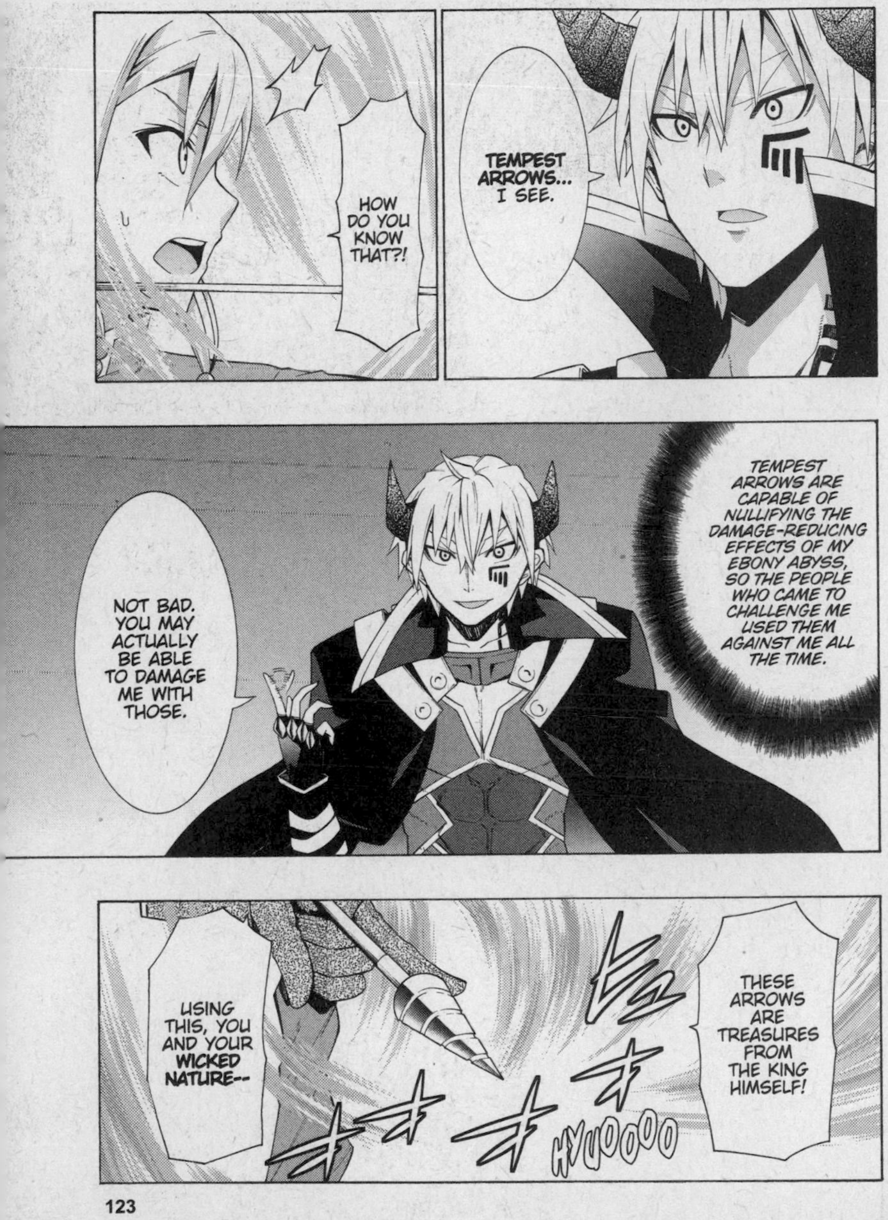
TEMPEST ARROWS... I SEE.
HOW DO YOU KNOW THAT?!
TEMPEST ARROWS ARE CAPABLE OF NULLIFYING THE DAMAGE-REDUCING EFFECTS OF MY EBONY ABYSS, SO THE PEOPLE WHO CAME TO CHALLENGE ME USED THEM AGAINST ME ALL THE TIME.
NOT BAD. YOU MAY ACTUALLY BE ABLE TO DAMAGE ME WITH THOSE.
THESE ARROWS ARE TREASURES FROM THE KING HIMSELF!
HYUOOOO
USING THIS, YOU AND YOUR WICKED NATURE--

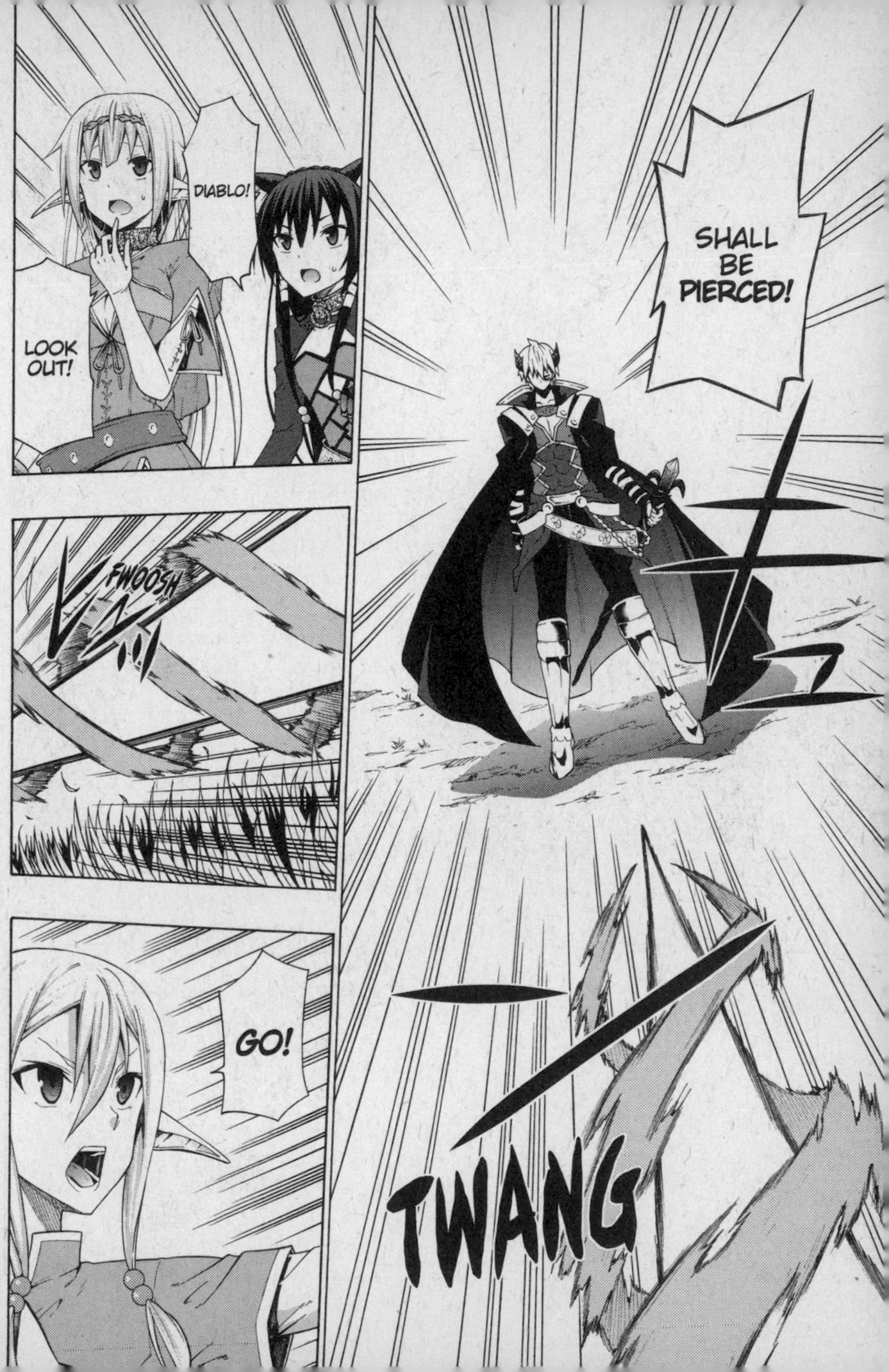
SHALL BE PIERCED!
TWANG
DIABLO!
LOOK OUT!
FWOOSH
GO!

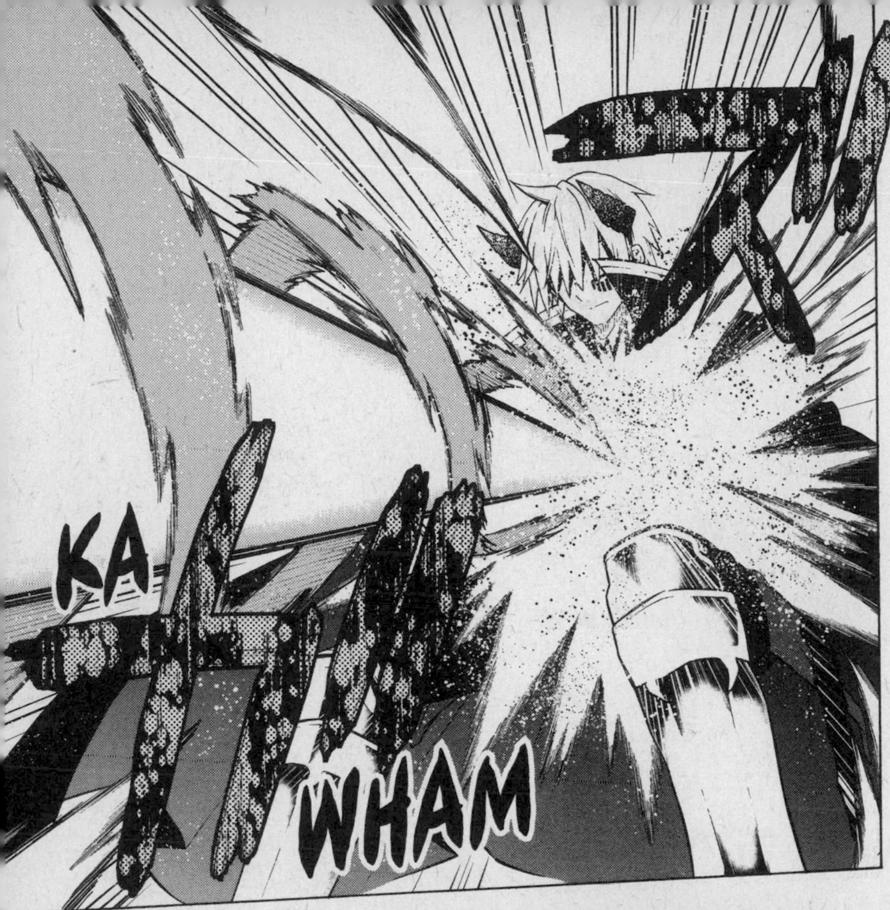
KA
WHAM
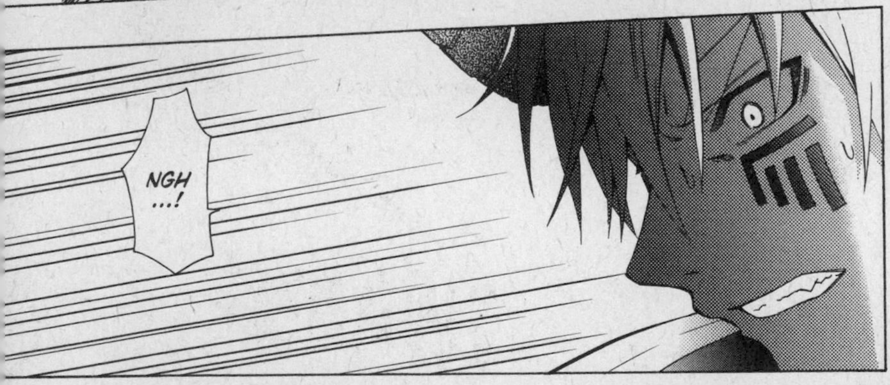
NGH ...!

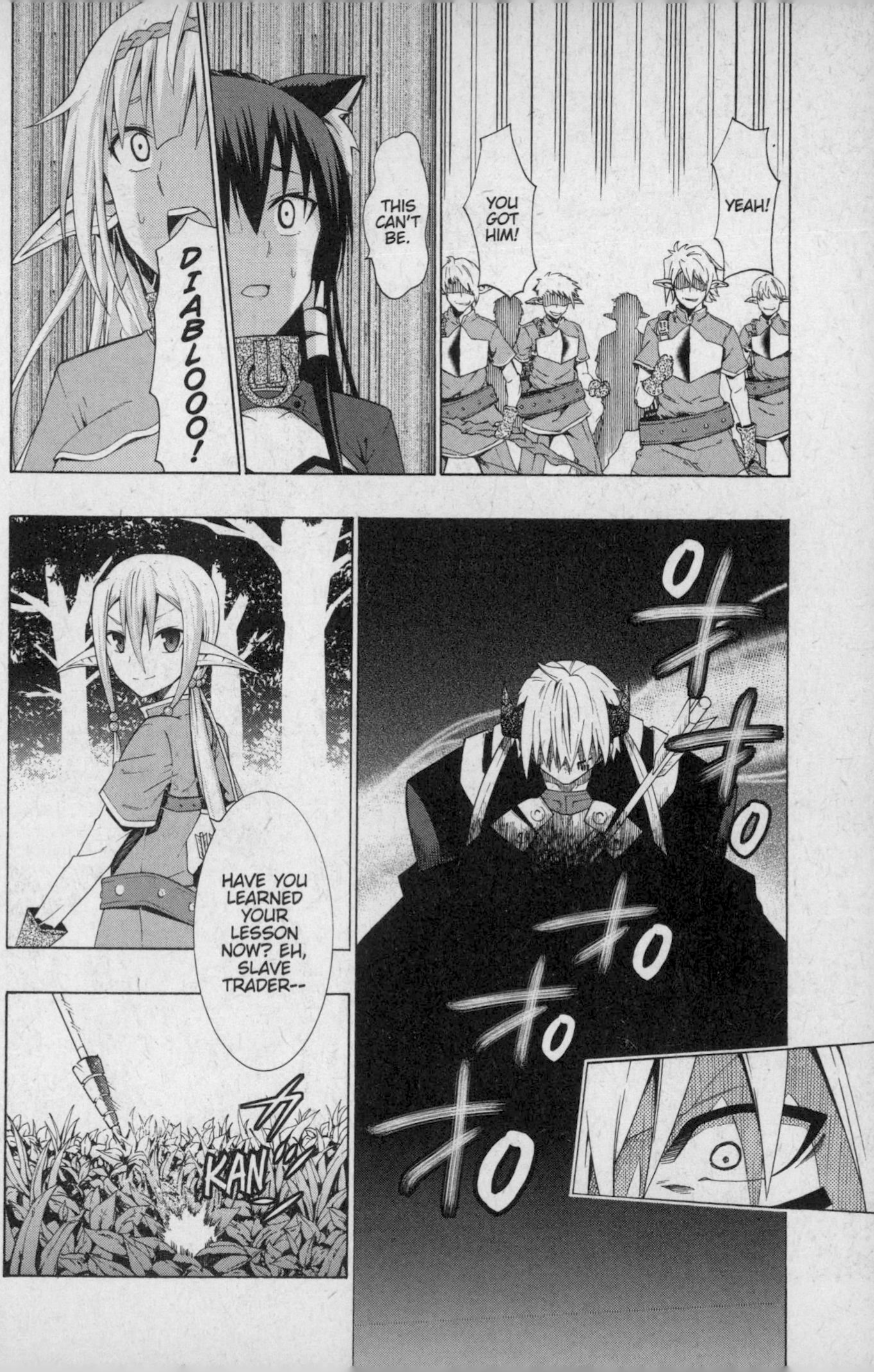
YEAH!
YOU GOT HIM!
THIS CAN'T BE.
DIABLOOO!
HAVE YOU LEARNED YOUR LESSON NOW? EH, SLAVE TRADER--
KAN

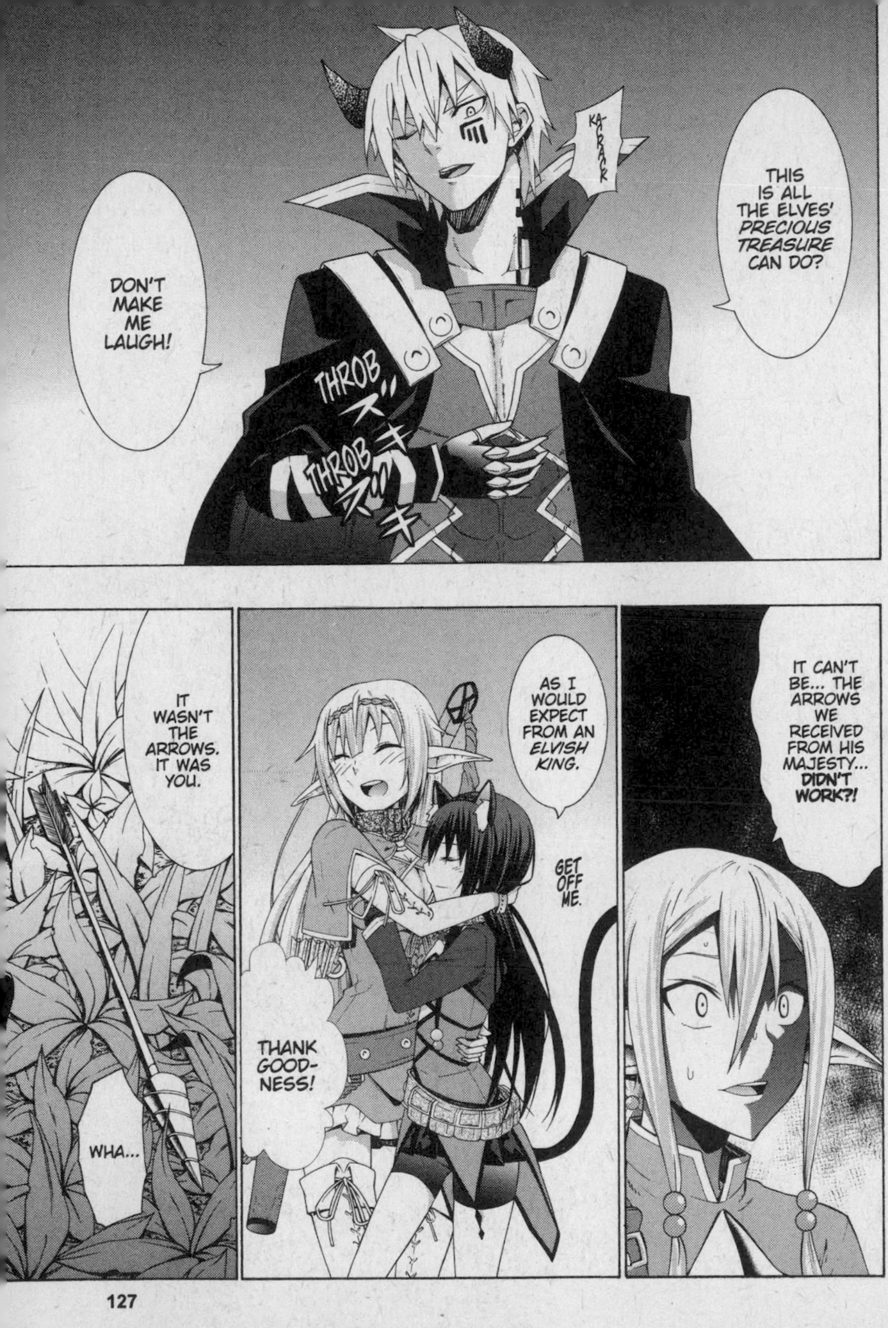
THIS IS ALL THE ELVES' *PRECIOUS TREASURE* CAN DO?
KA-CRACK
DON'T MAKE ME LAUGH!
THROB THROB
IT CAN'T BE... THE ARROWS WE RECEIVED FROM HIS MAJESTY... **DIDN'T WORK?!**
AS I WOULD EXPECT FROM AN *ELVISH KING.*
GET OFF ME.
THANK GOOD-NESS!
IT WASN'T THE ARROWS. IT WAS YOU.
WHA...

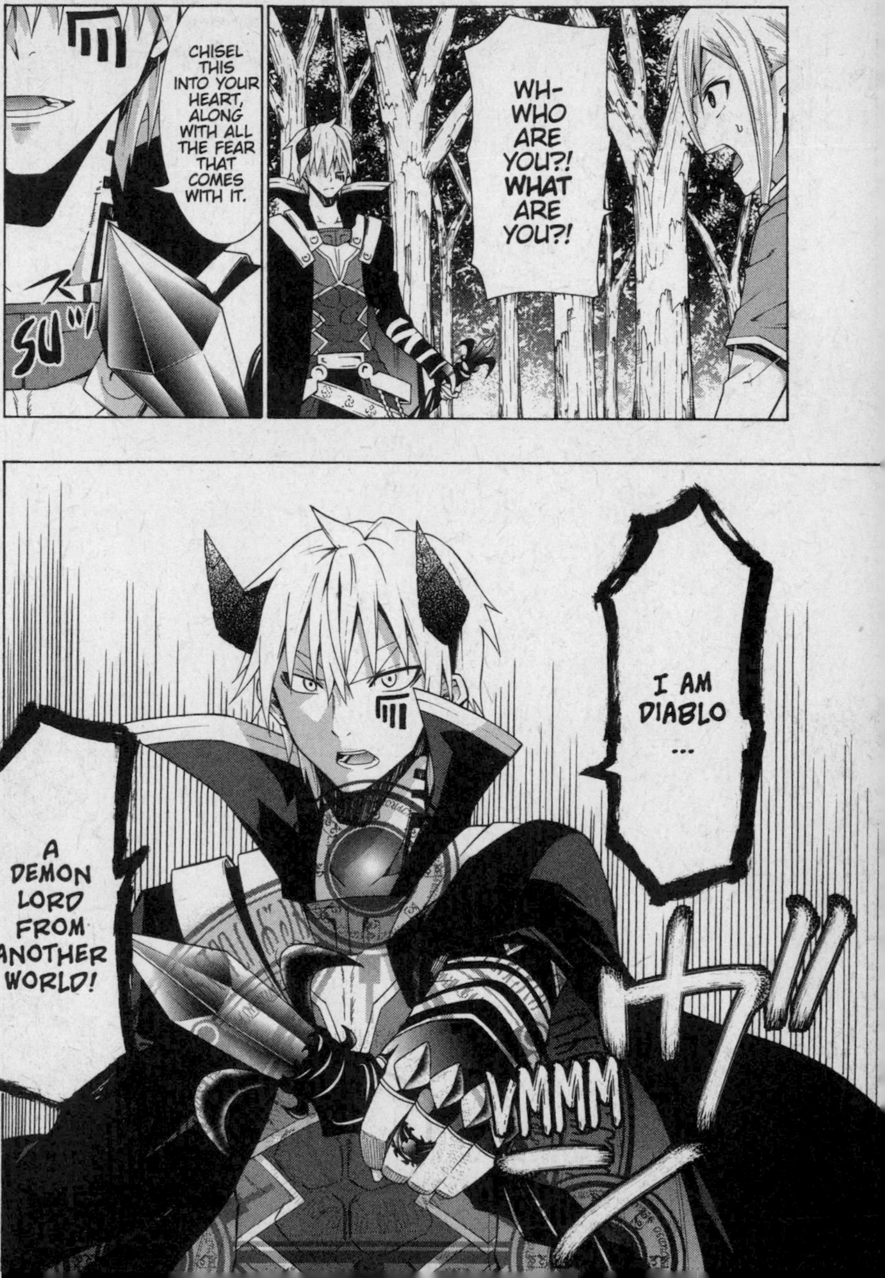
WH- WHO ARE YOU?! WHAT ARE YOU?!
CHISEL THIS INTO YOUR HEART, ALONG WITH ALL THE FEAR THAT COMES WITH IT.
SU
I AM DIABLO ...
A DEMON LORD FROM ANOTHER WORLD!
VMMM

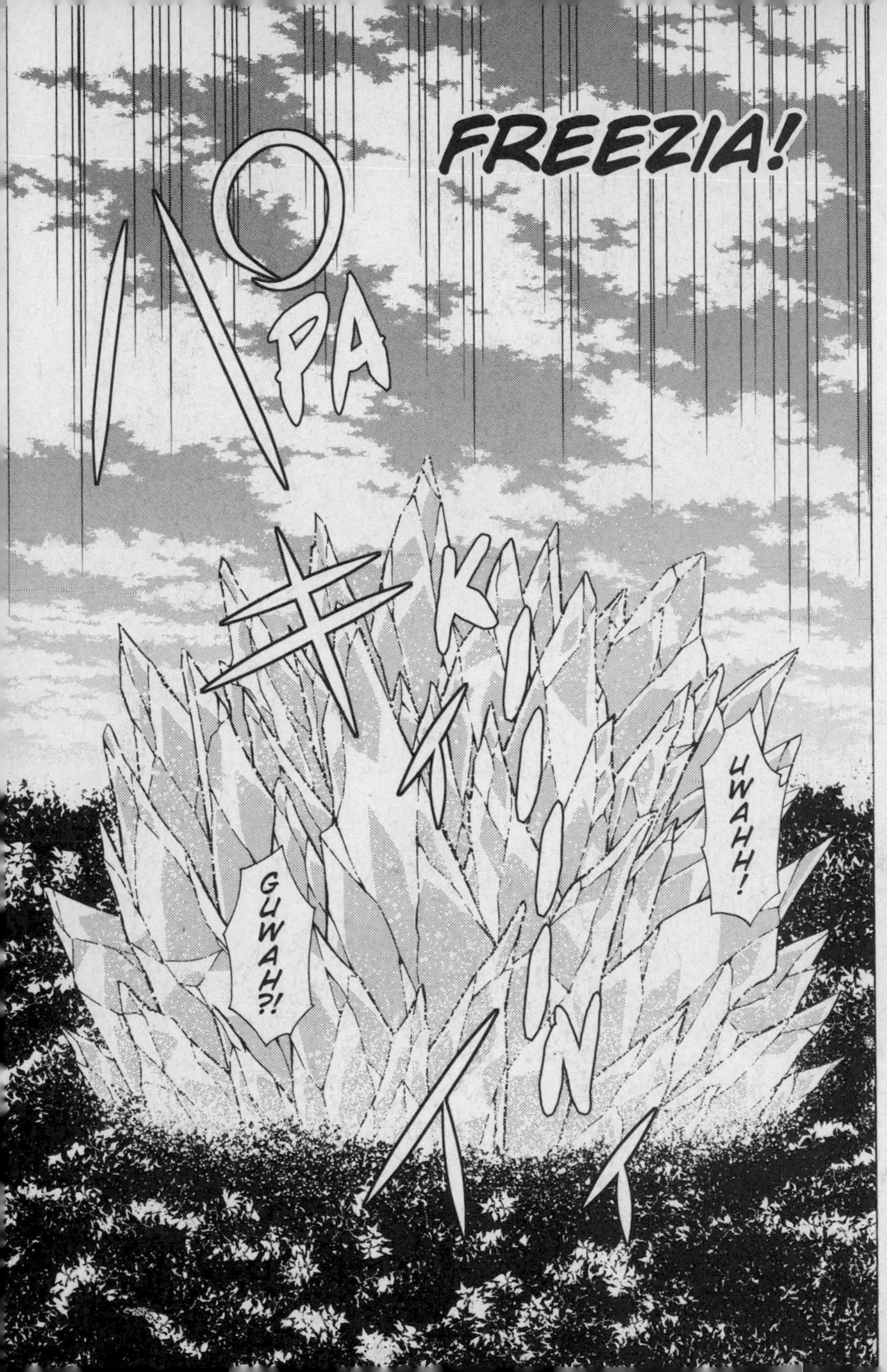
FREEZIA!
PA
KIIIIIN
UWAHH!
GUWAH?!

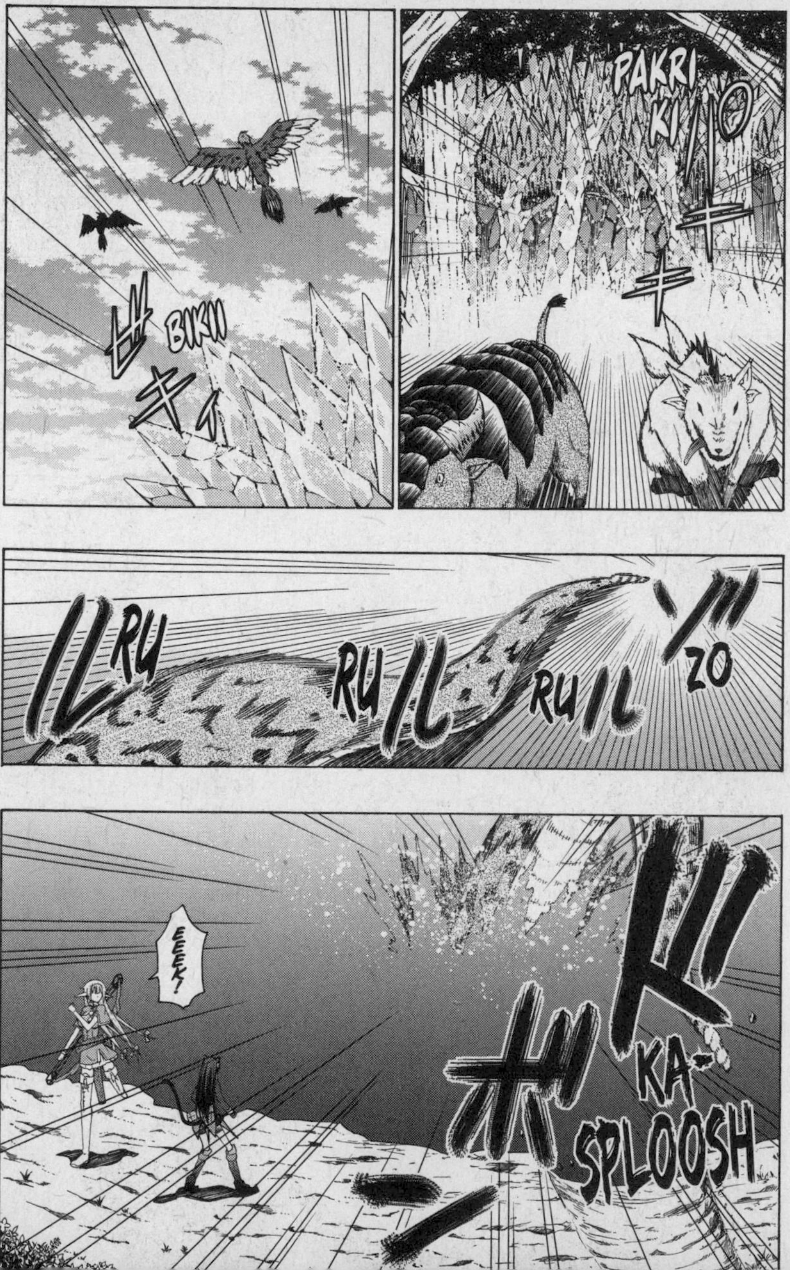
PAKRI KI
BIKII
RU
RU
RU
ZO
EEEEK!
KA-SPLOOSH

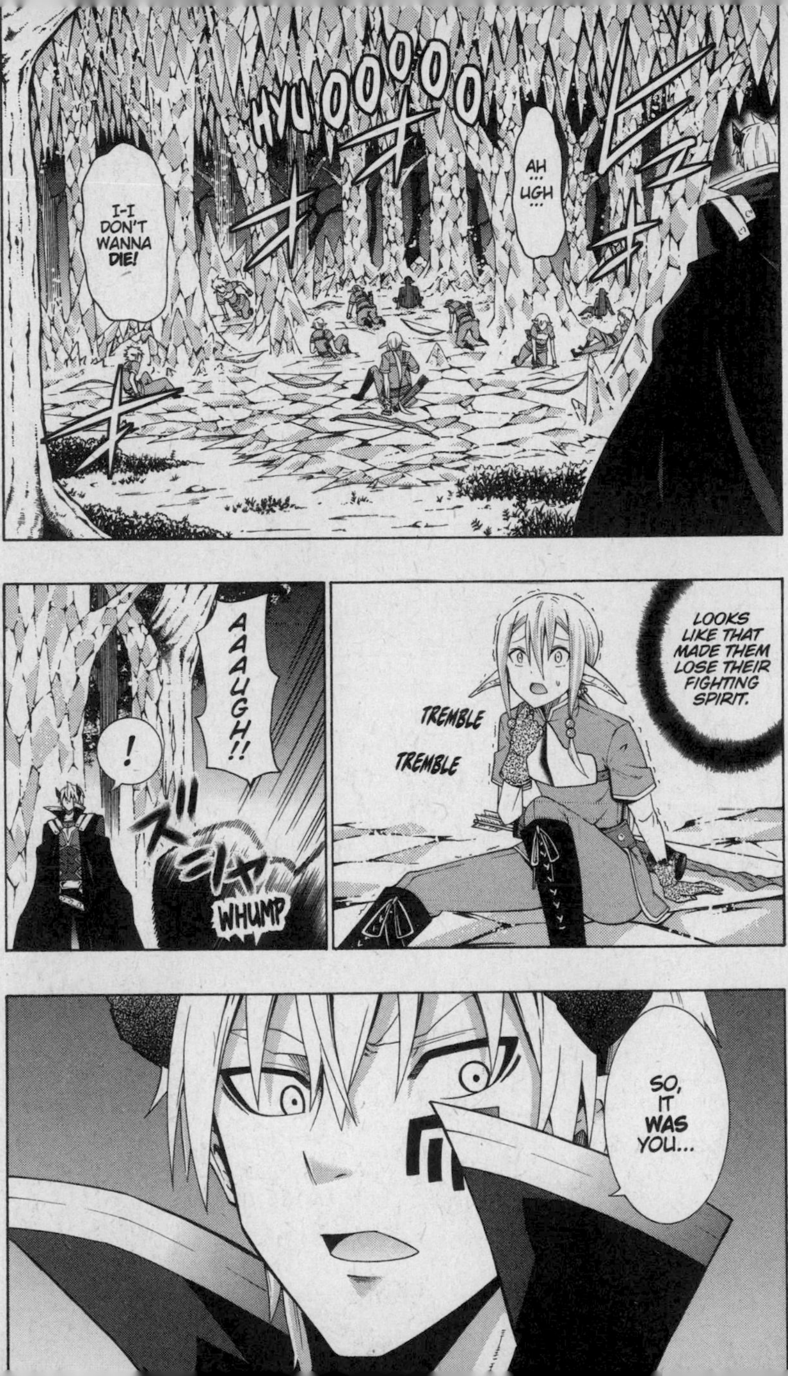
HYUOOOOO
AH... UGH...
I-I DON'T WANNA DIE!
LOOKS LIKE THAT MADE THEM LOSE THEIR FIGHTING SPIRIT.
TREMBLE
TREMBLE
AAAUGH!!
!
WHUMP
SO, IT WAS YOU...

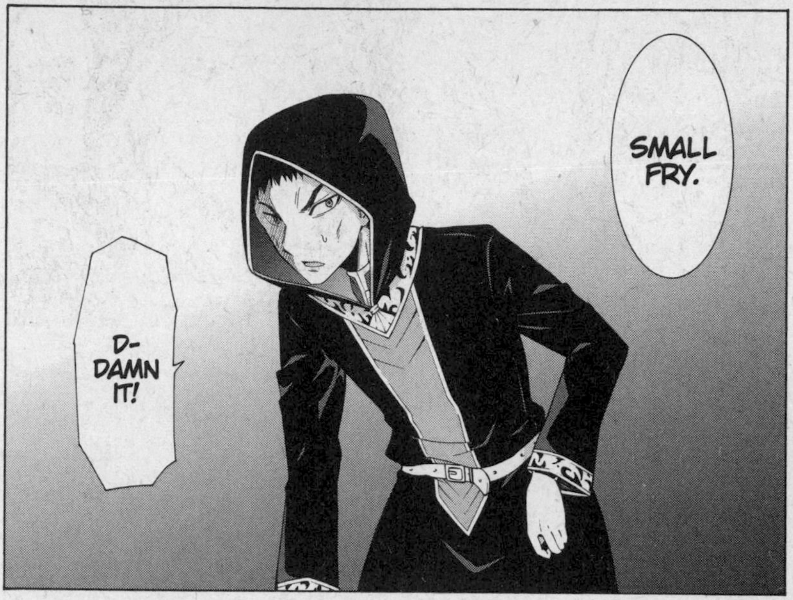
SMALL FRY.
D-DAMN IT!

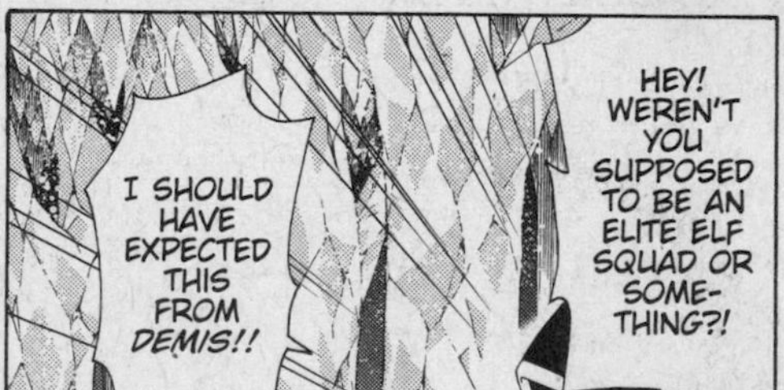
HEY! WEREN'T YOU SUPPOSED TO BE AN ELITE ELF SQUAD OR SOME-THING?!
I SHOULD HAVE EXPECTED THIS FROM *DEMIS*!!

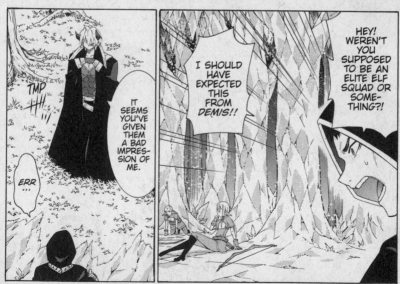

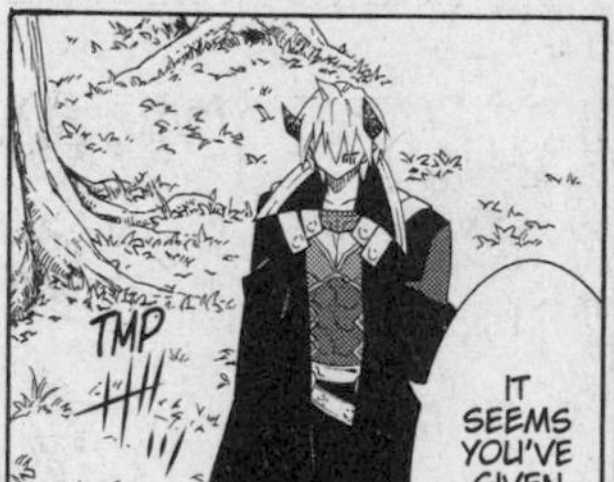
IT SEEMS YOU'VE GIVEN THEM A BAD IMPRES-SION OF ME.
TMP
ERR...

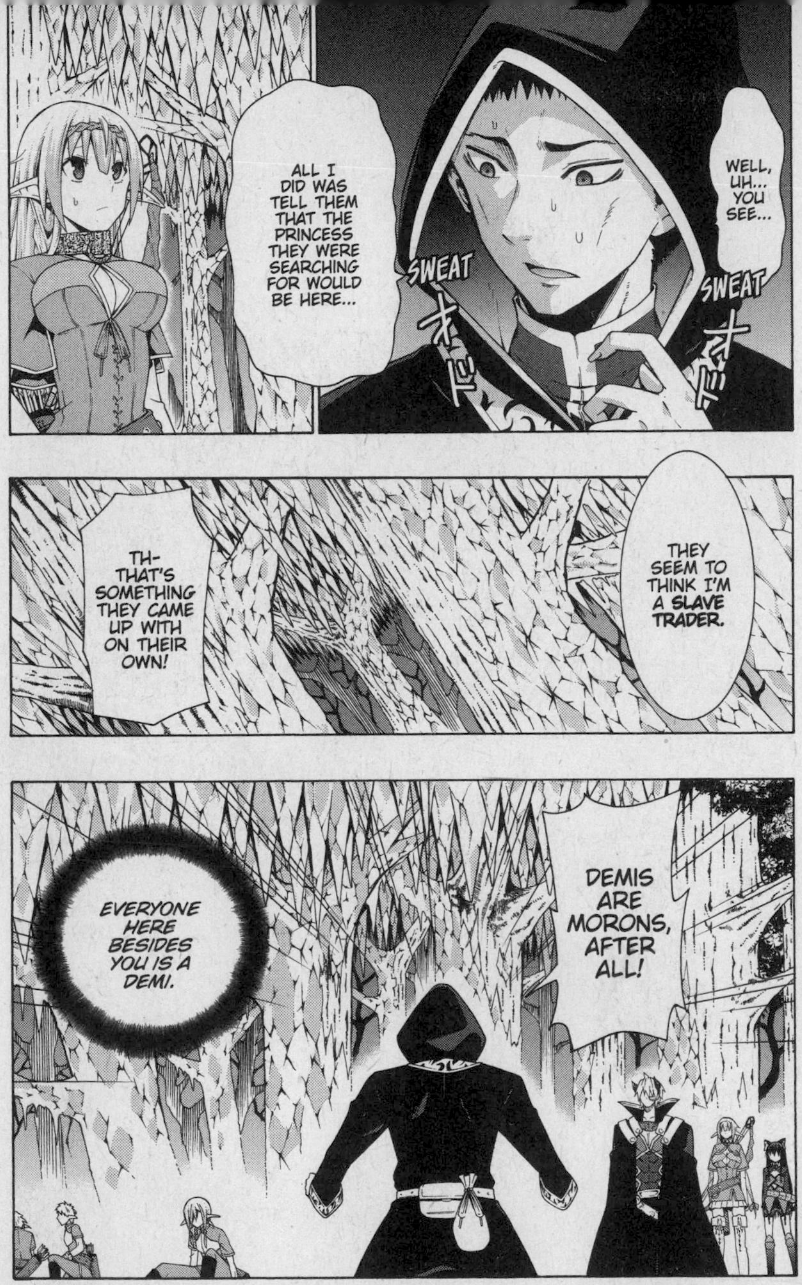
WELL, UH... YOU SEE...
SWEAT
SWEAT
ALL I DID WAS TELL THEM THAT THE PRINCESS THEY WERE SEARCHING FOR WOULD BE HERE...
THEY SEEM TO THINK I'M A SLAVE TRADER.
TH-THAT'S SOMETHING THEY CAME UP WITH ON THEIR OWN!
DEMIS ARE MORONS, AFTER ALL!
EVERYONE HERE BESIDES YOU IS A DEMI.

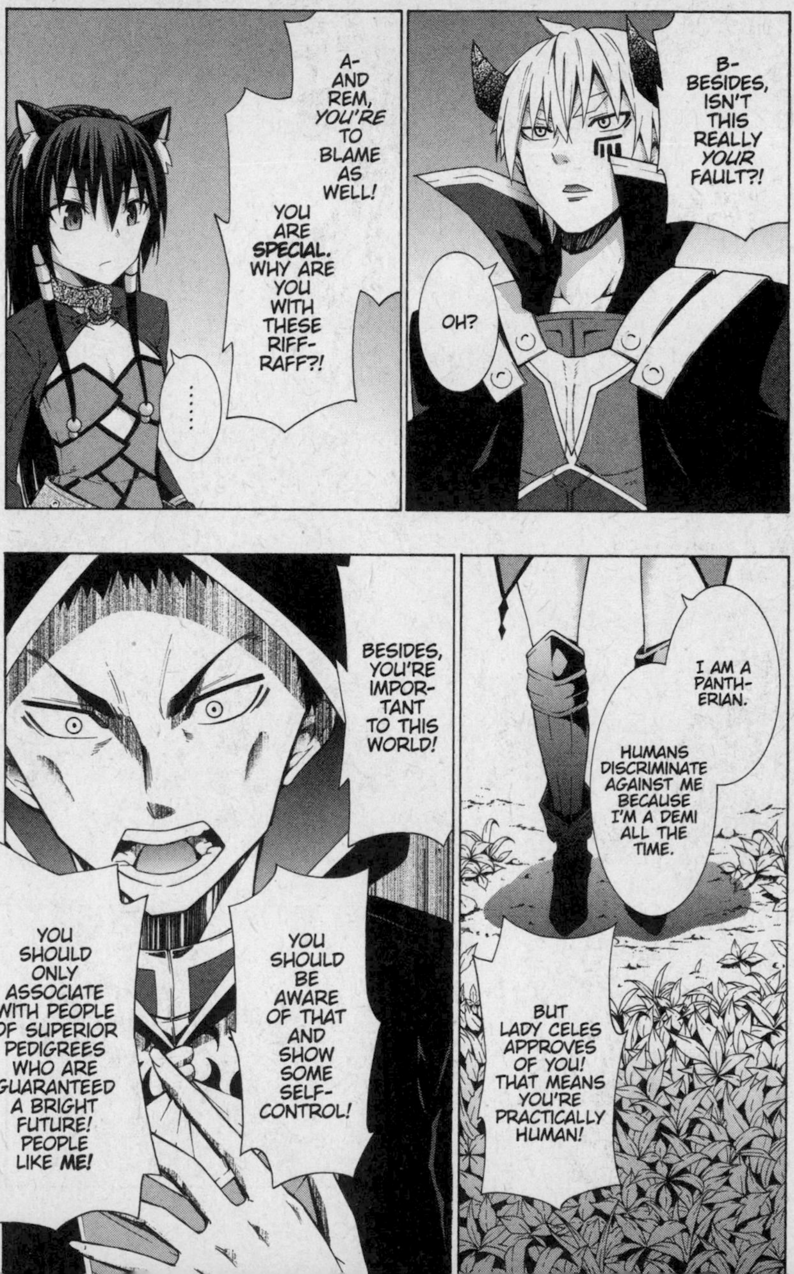
B- BESIDES, ISN'T THIS REALLY YOUR FAULT?!
OH?
A- AND REM, YOU'RE TO BLAME AS WELL!
YOU ARE SPECIAL. WHY ARE YOU WITH THESE RIFF-RAFF?!
......
I AM A PANTH-ERIAN.
HUMANS DISCRIMINATE AGAINST ME BECAUSE I'M A DEMI ALL THE TIME.
BUT LADY CELES APPROVES OF YOU! THAT MEANS YOU'RE PRACTICALLY HUMAN!
BESIDES, YOU'RE IMPOR-TANT TO THIS WORLD!
YOU SHOULD BE AWARE OF THAT AND SHOW SOME SELF-CONTROL!
YOU SHOULD ONLY ASSOCIATE WITH PEOPLE OF SUPERIOR PEDIGREES WHO ARE GUARANTEED A BRIGHT FUTURE! PEOPLE LIKE ME!

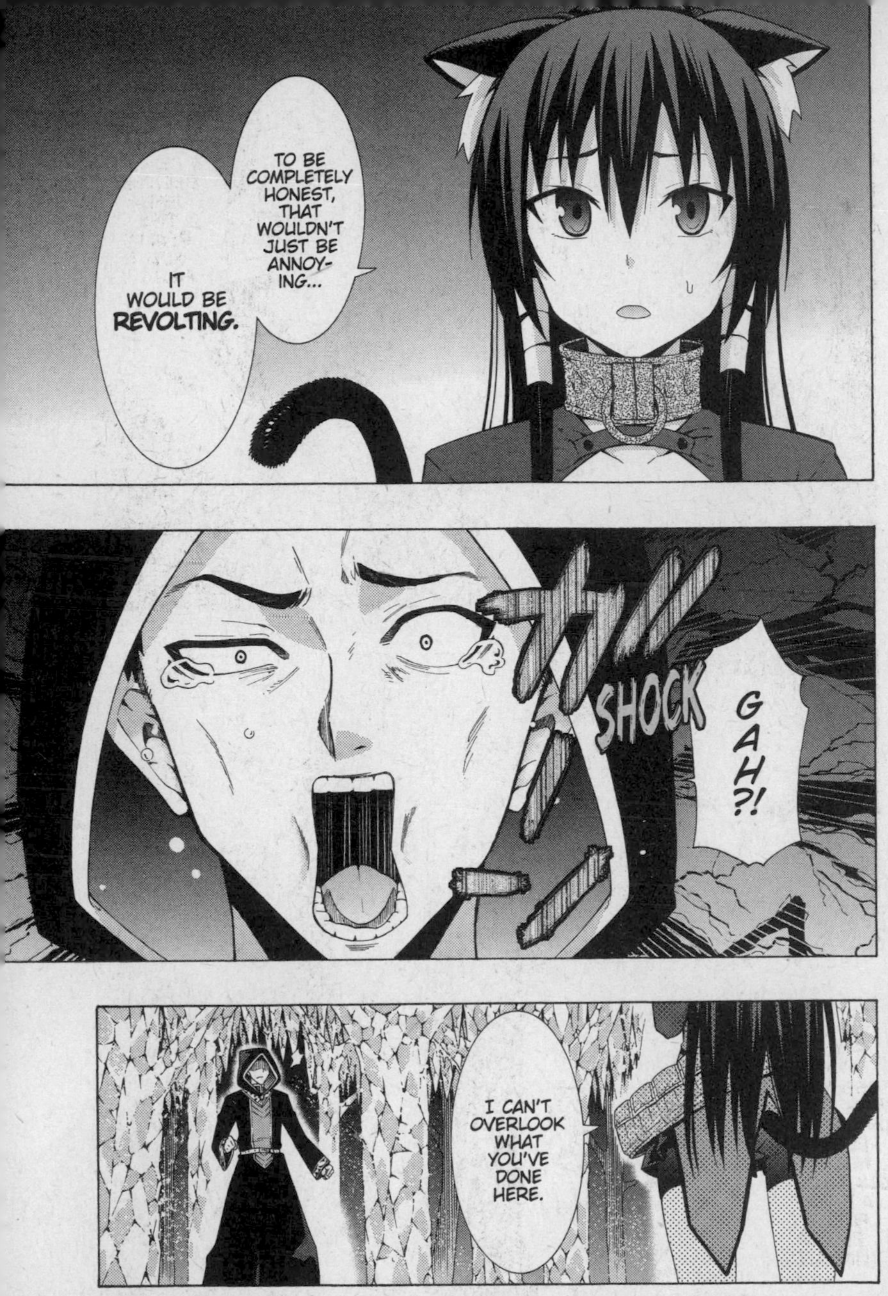
TO BE COMPLETELY HONEST, THAT WOULDN'T JUST BE ANNOY-ING...
IT WOULD BE REVOLTING.
SHOCK
GAH?!
I CAN'T OVERLOOK WHAT YOU'VE DONE HERE.

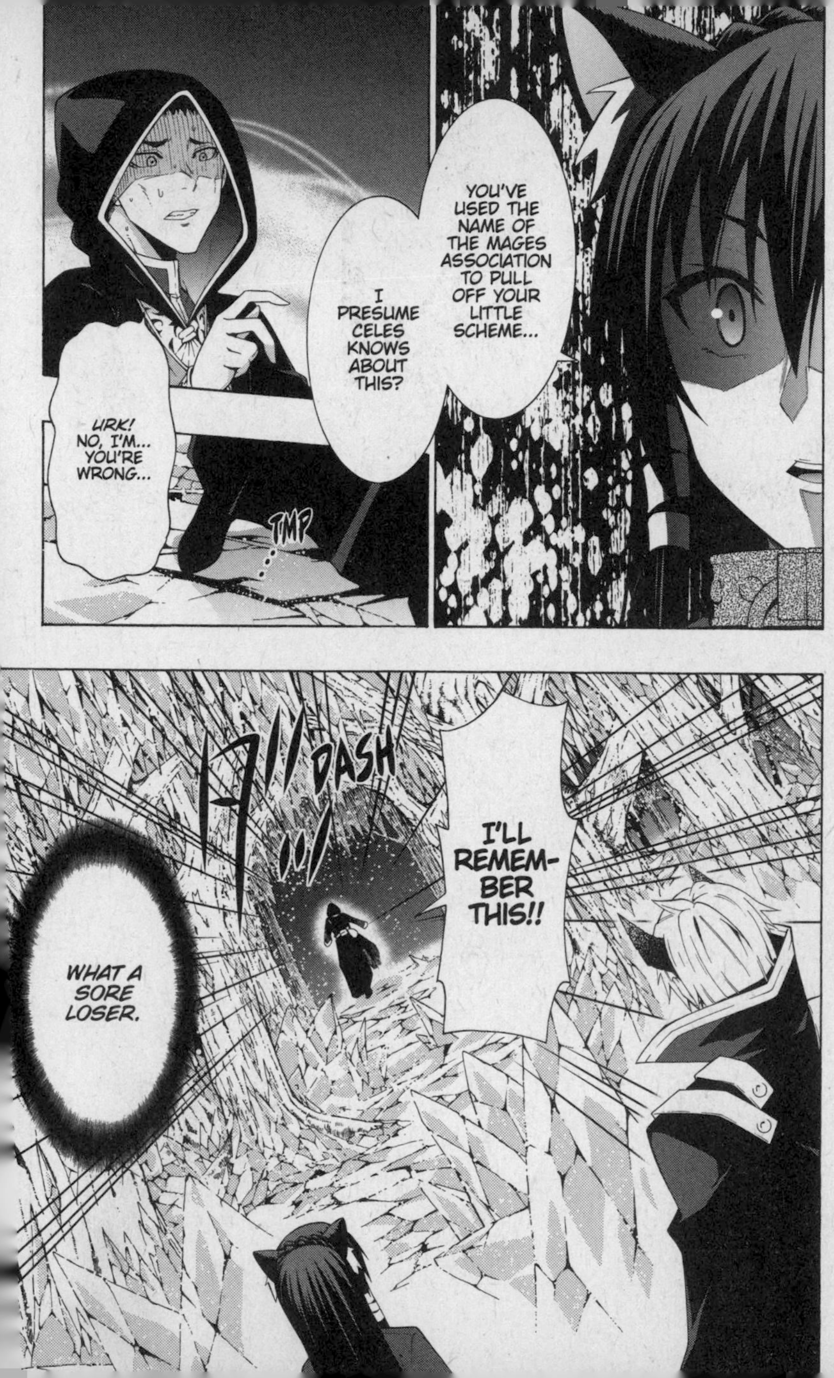
YOU'VE USED THE NAME OF THE MAGES ASSOCIATION TO PULL OFF YOUR LITTLE SCHEME...
I PRESUME CELES KNOWS ABOUT THIS?
URK! NO, I'M... YOU'RE WRONG...
TMP
I'LL REMEMBER THIS!!
DASH
WHAT A SORE LOSER.

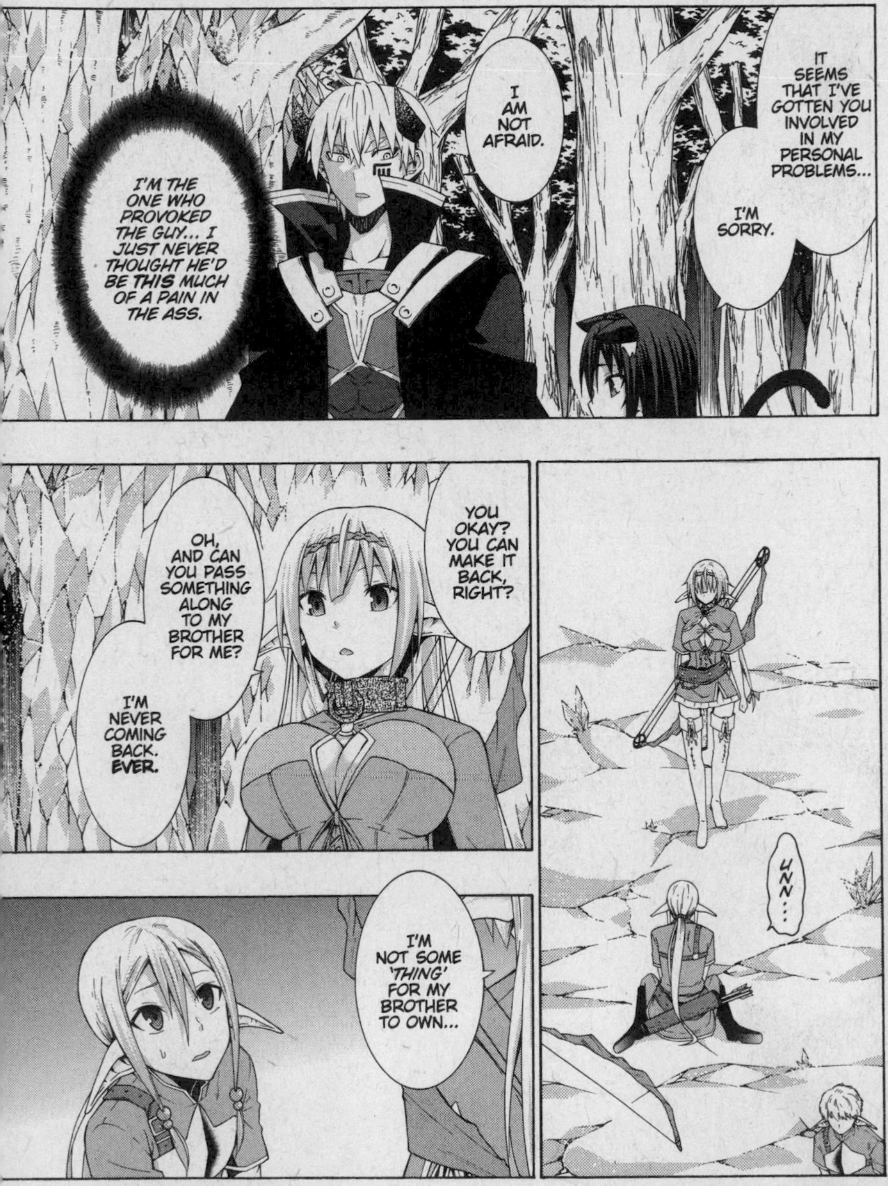
IT SEEMS THAT I'VE GOTTEN YOU INVOLVED IN MY PERSONAL PROBLEMS...
I'M SORRY.
I AM NOT AFRAID.
I'M THE ONE WHO PROVOKED THE GUY... I JUST NEVER THOUGHT HE'D BE **THIS** MUCH OF A PAIN IN THE ASS.
UNN...
YOU OKAY? YOU CAN MAKE IT BACK, RIGHT?
OH, AND CAN YOU PASS SOMETHING ALONG TO MY BROTHER FOR ME?
I'M NEVER COMING BACK. **EVER.**
I'M NOT SOME *'THING'* FOR MY BROTHER TO OWN...

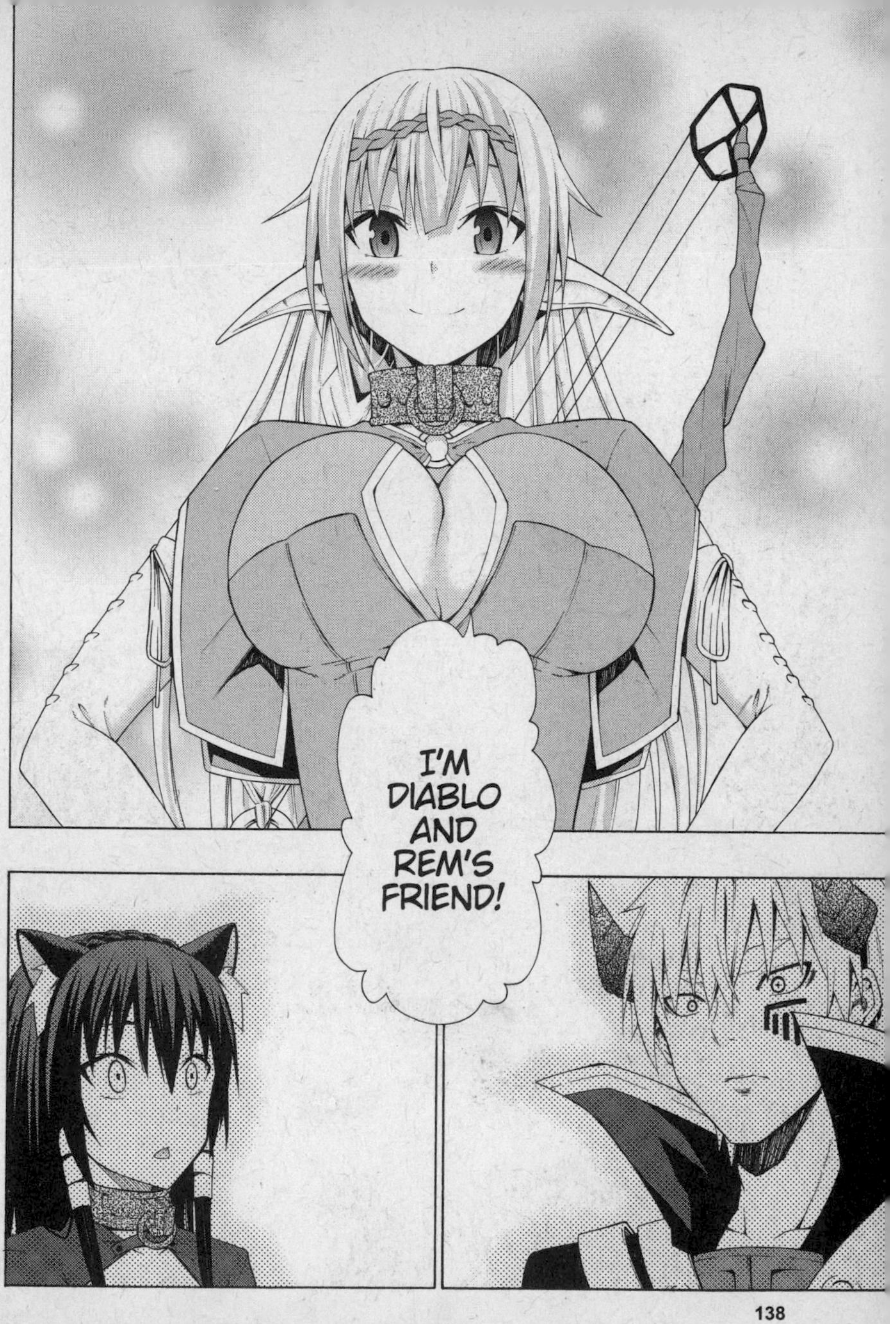
I'M DIABLO AND REM'S FRIEND!

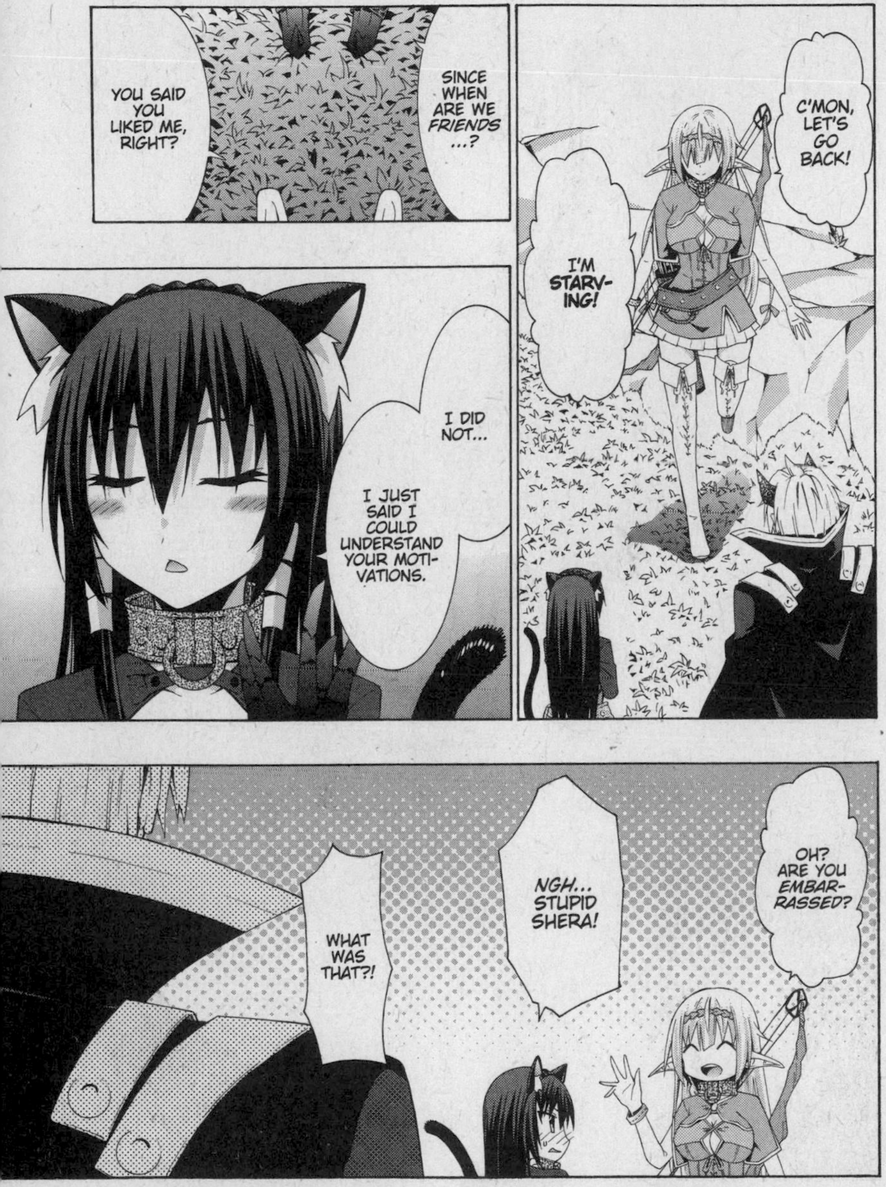
SINCE WHEN ARE WE *FRIENDS* ...?
YOU SAID YOU LIKED ME, RIGHT?
I DID NOT...
I JUST SAID I COULD UNDERSTAND YOUR MOTIVATIONS.
C'MON, LET'S GO BACK!
I'M STARVING!
OH? ARE YOU EMBARRASSED?
NGH... STUPID SHERA!
WHAT WAS THAT?!

I'M...
HER...
FRIEND...?

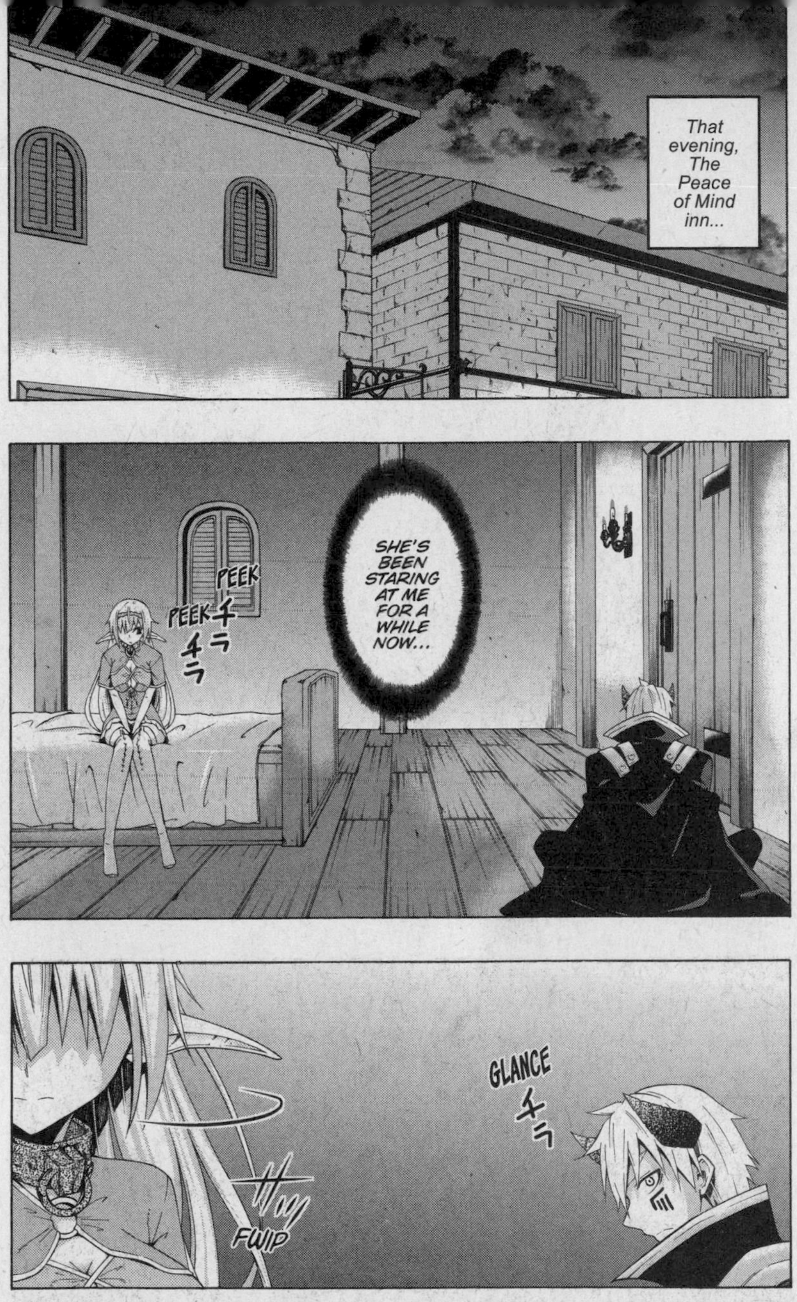
That evening, The Peace of Mind inn...
SHE'S BEEN STARING AT ME FOR A WHILE NOW...
PEEK
チラ
PEEK
チラ
GLANCE
チラ
FWIP

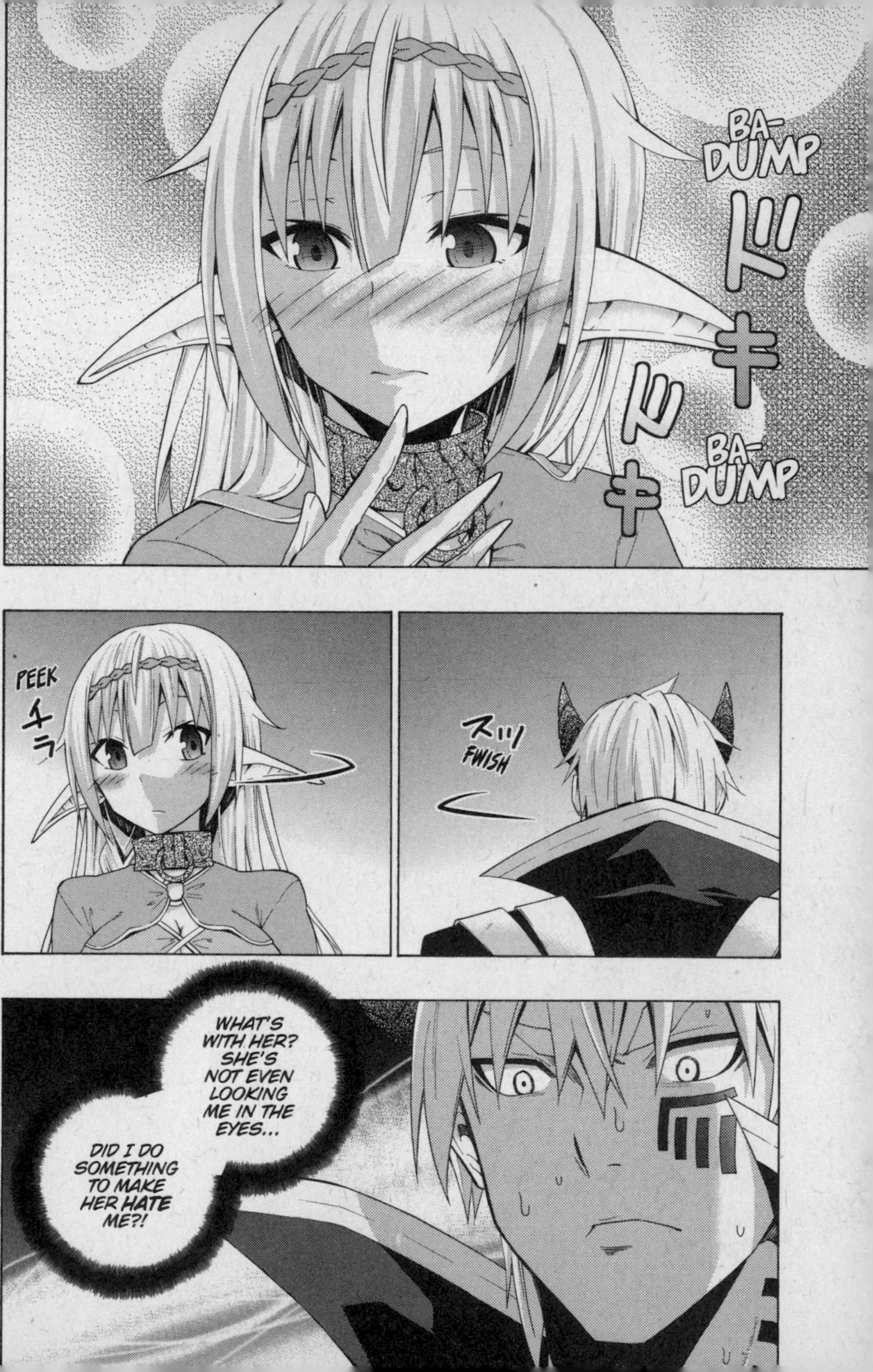
BA-DUMP
BA-DUMP
スッ
FWISH
PEEK
チラ
WHAT'S WITH HER? SHE'S NOT EVEN LOOKING ME IN THE EYES...
DID I DO SOMETHING TO MAKE HER HATE ME?!

HOW NOT
TO SUMMON A
DEMON LORD

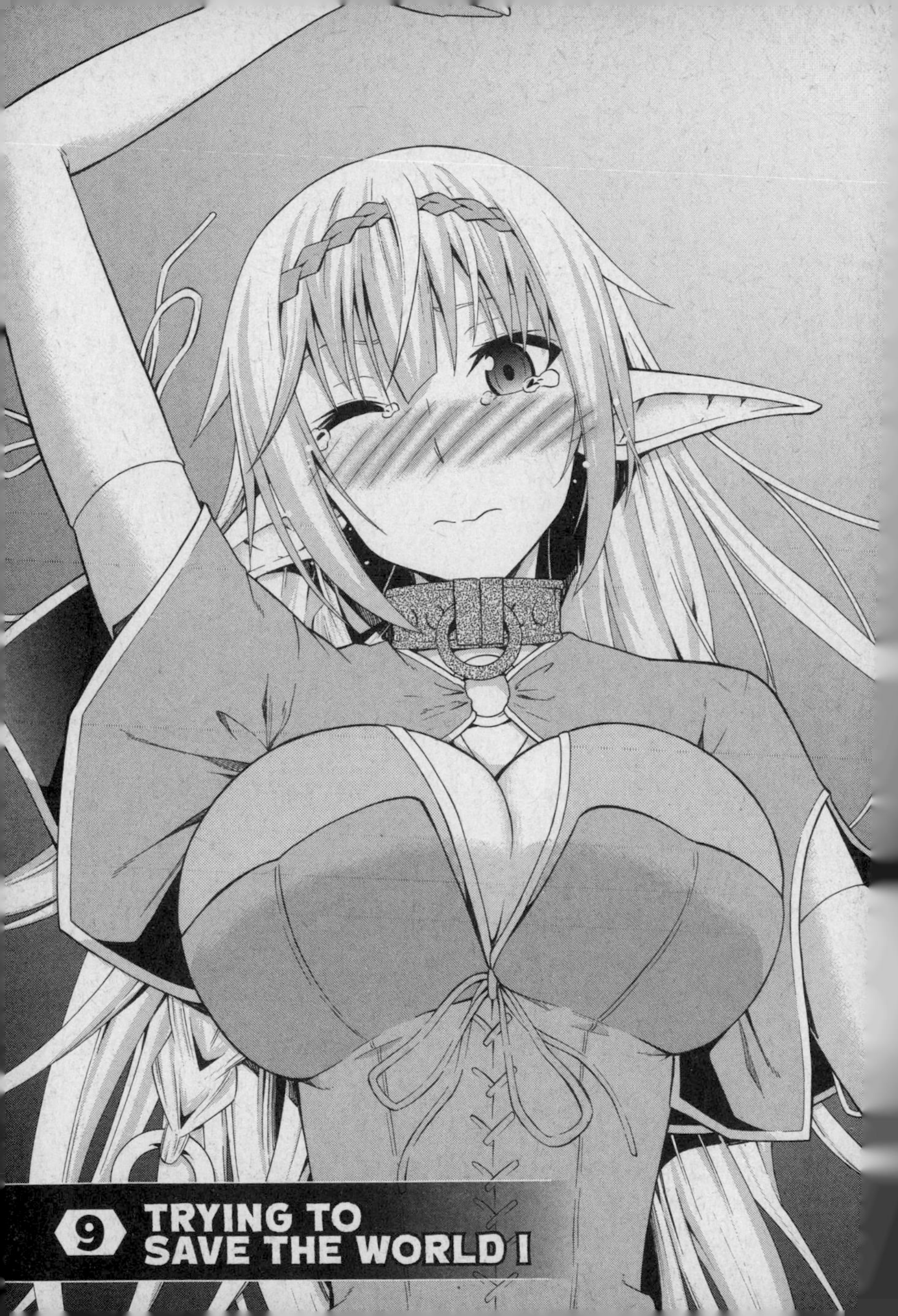
9
TRYING TO
SAVE THE WORLD I

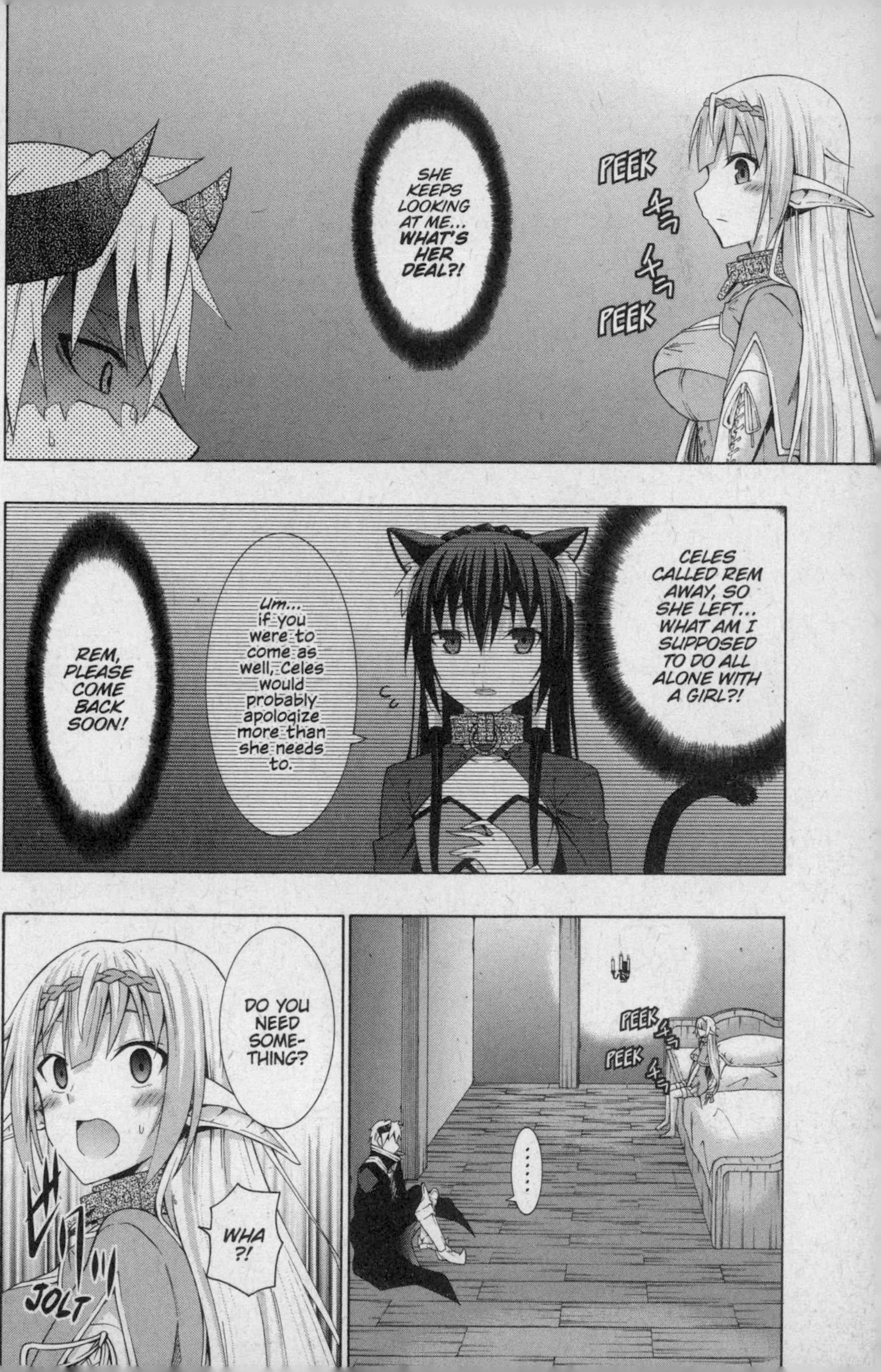
PEEK
PEEK
SHE KEEPS LOOKING AT ME... WHAT'S HER DEAL?!
CELES CALLED REM AWAY, SO SHE LEFT... WHAT AM I SUPPOSED TO DO ALL ALONE WITH A GIRL?!
Um... if you were to come as well, Celes would probably apologize more than she needs to.
REM, PLEASE COME BACK SOON!
PEEK
PEEK
......
DO YOU NEED SOME-THING?
WHA?!
JOLT

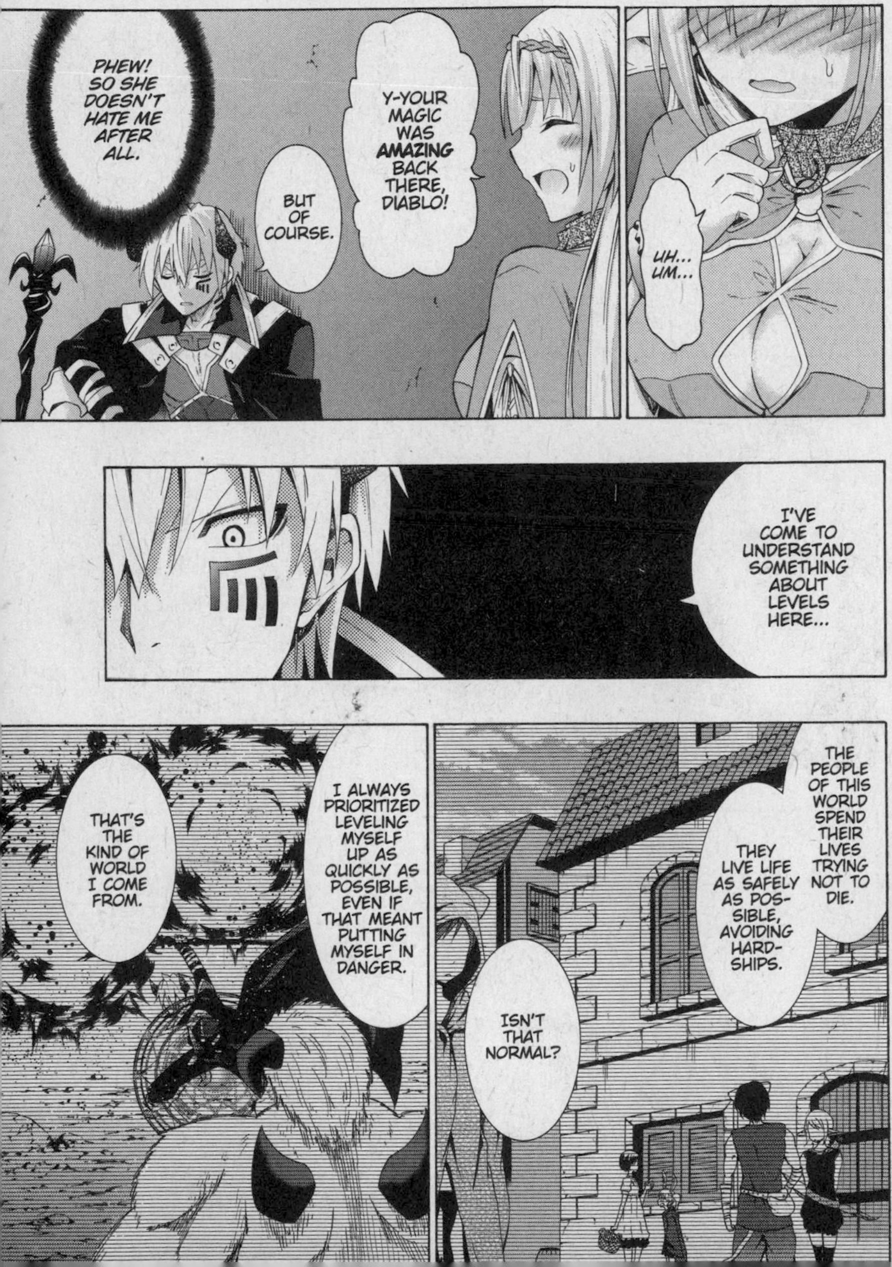
UH... UM...
Y-YOUR MAGIC WAS AMAZING BACK THERE, DIABLO!
BUT OF COURSE.
PHEW! SO SHE DOESN'T HATE ME AFTER ALL.
I'VE COME TO UNDERSTAND SOMETHING ABOUT LEVELS HERE...
THE PEOPLE OF THIS WORLD SPEND THEIR LIVES TRYING NOT TO DIE.
THEY LIVE LIFE AS SAFELY AS POSSIBLE, AVOIDING HARDSHIPS.
ISN'T THAT NORMAL?
I ALWAYS PRIORITIZED LEVELING MYSELF UP AS QUICKLY AS POSSIBLE, EVEN IF THAT MEANT PUTTING MYSELF IN DANGER.
THAT'S THE KIND OF WORLD I COME FROM.

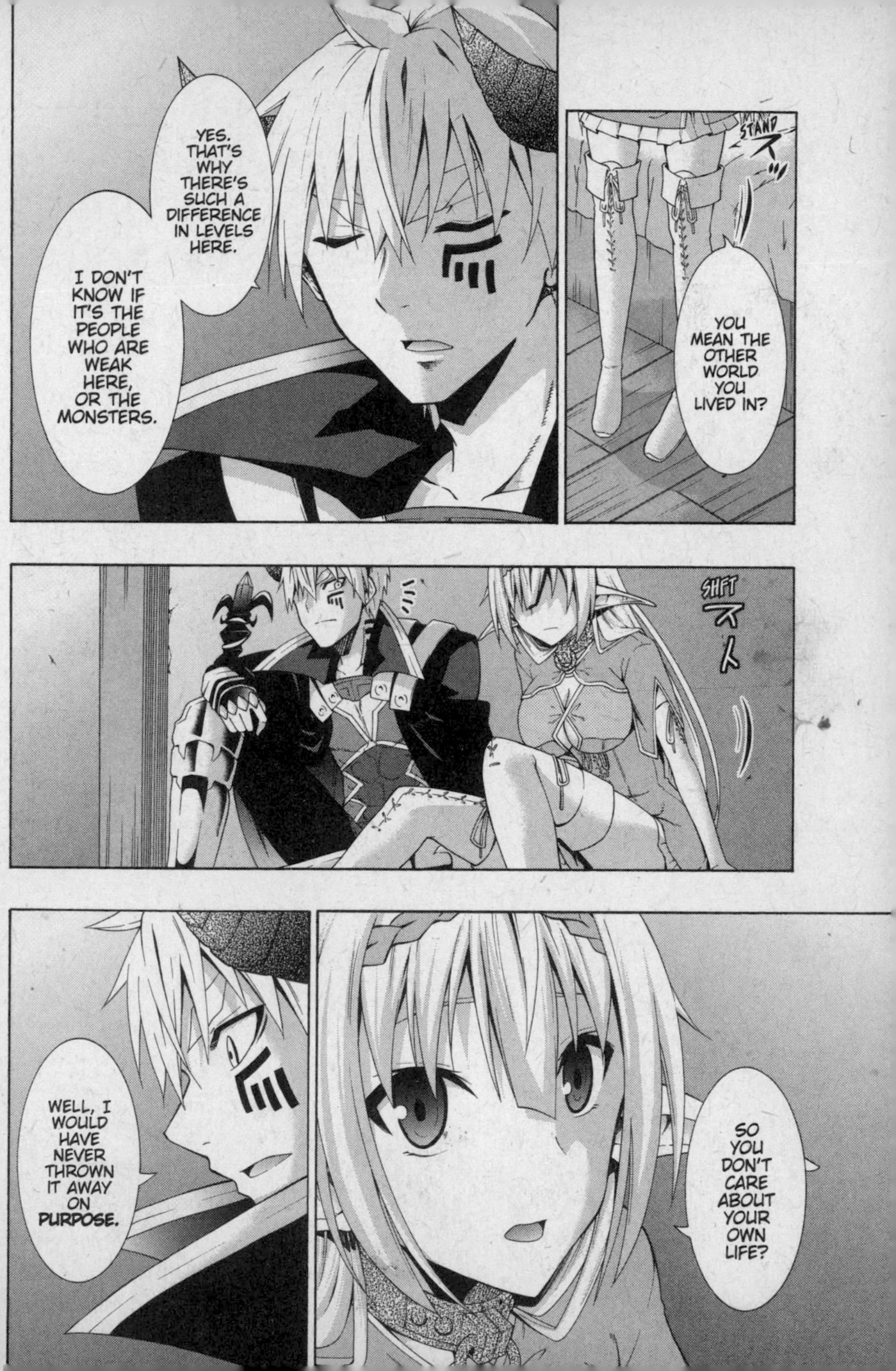
STAND
YOU MEAN THE OTHER WORLD YOU LIVED IN?
YES. THAT'S WHY THERE'S SUCH A DIFFERENCE IN LEVELS HERE.
I DON'T KNOW IF IT'S THE PEOPLE WHO ARE WEAK HERE, OR THE MONSTERS.
SHFT
SO YOU DON'T CARE ABOUT YOUR OWN LIFE?
WELL, I WOULD HAVE NEVER THROWN IT AWAY ON PURPOSE.

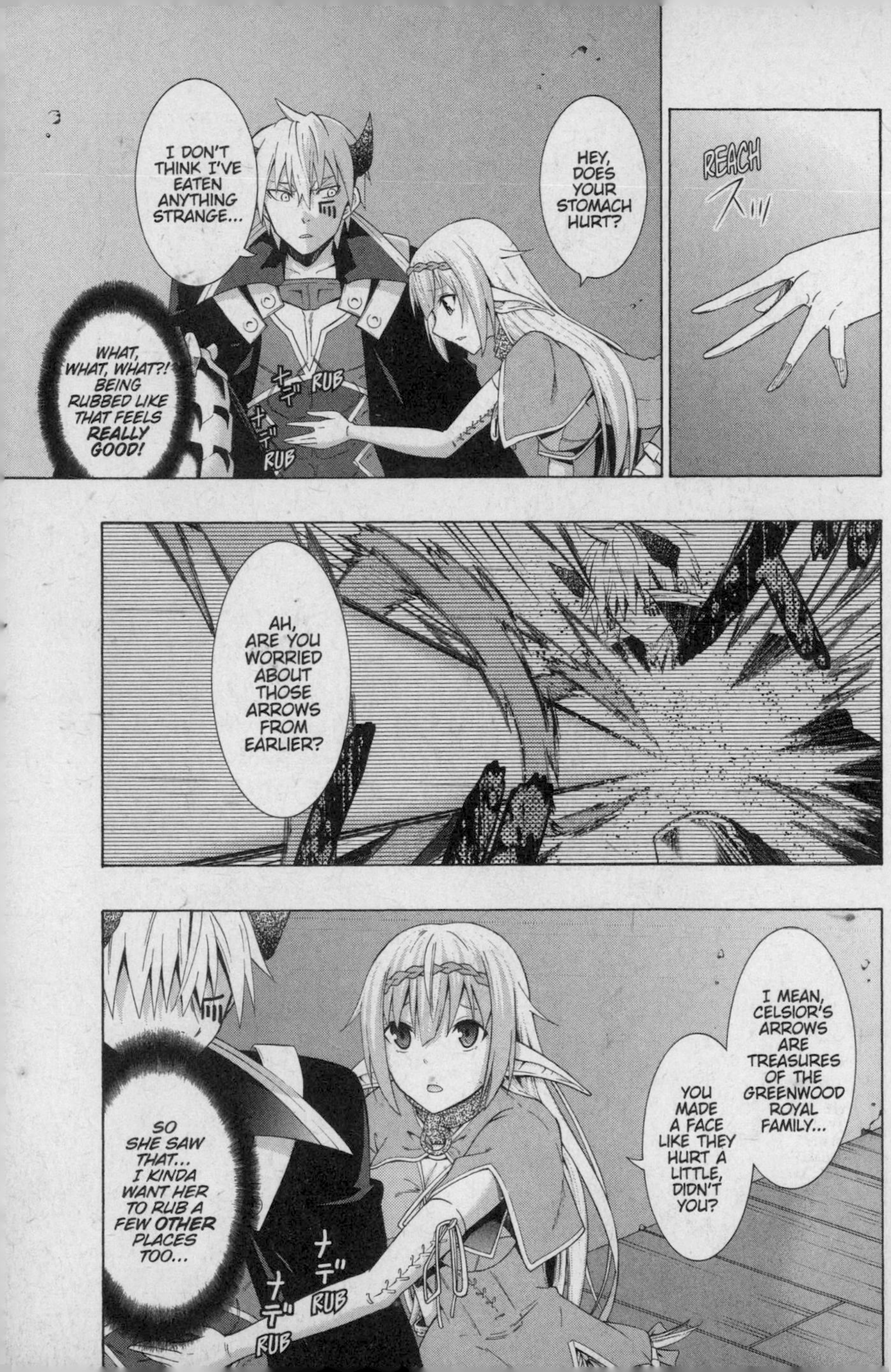
REACH
HEY, DOES YOUR STOMACH HURT?
I DON'T THINK I'VE EATEN ANYTHING STRANGE...
RUB
RUB
WHAT, WHAT, WHAT?! BEING RUBBED LIKE THAT FEELS REALLY GOOD!
AH, ARE YOU WORRIED ABOUT THOSE ARROWS FROM EARLIER?
I MEAN, CELSIOR'S ARROWS ARE TREASURES OF THE GREENWOOD ROYAL FAMILY...
YOU MADE A FACE LIKE THEY HURT A LITTLE, DIDN'T YOU?
SO SHE SAW THAT... I KINDA WANT HER TO RUB A FEW OTHER PLACES TOO...
RUB
RUB

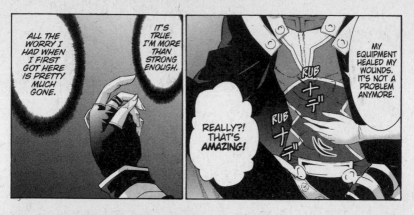

MY EQUIPMENT HEALED MY WOUNDS. IT'S NOT A PROBLEM ANYMORE.
RUB ナデ
RUB ナデ
REALLY?! THAT'S AMAZING!
IT'S TRUE. I'M MORE THAN STRONG ENOUGH.
ALL THE WORRY I HAD WHEN I FIRST GOT HERE IS PRETTY MUCH GONE.
......
HEY, DIABLO...
WHAT?
ARE YOU... GOING TO CHOOSE REM AFTER ALL?
WHAT DO YOU MEAN?

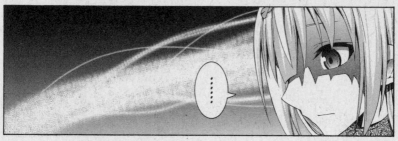

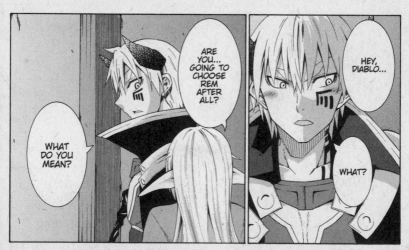

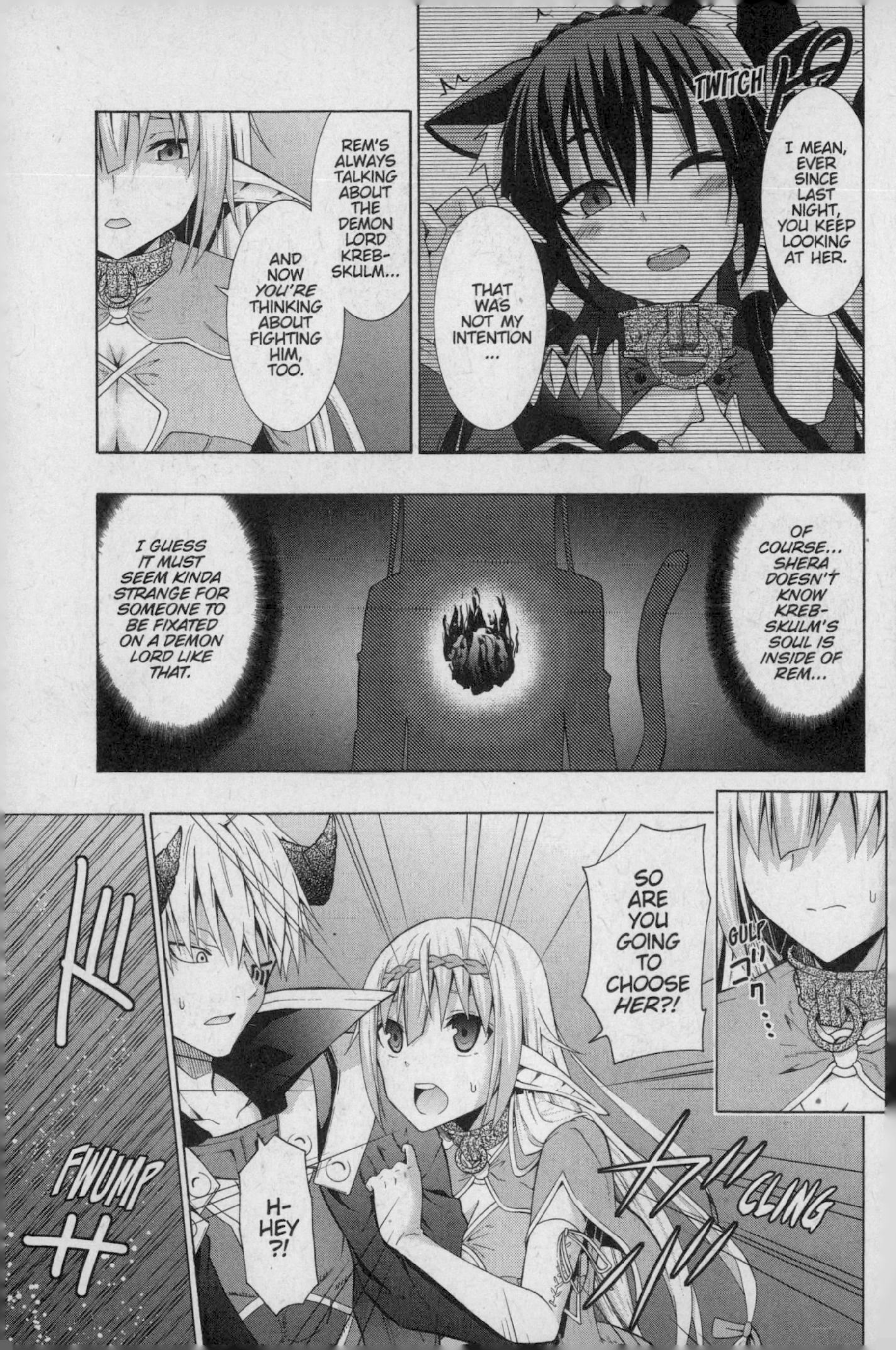
TWITCH
I MEAN, EVER SINCE LAST NIGHT, YOU KEEP LOOKING AT HER.
THAT WAS NOT MY INTENTION ...
REM'S ALWAYS TALKING ABOUT THE DEMON LORD KREBSKULM...
AND NOW YOU'RE THINKING ABOUT FIGHTING HIM, TOO.
OF COURSE... SHERA DOESN'T KNOW KREBSKULM'S SOUL IS INSIDE OF REM...
I GUESS IT MUST SEEM KINDA STRANGE FOR SOMEONE TO BE FIXATED ON A DEMON LORD LIKE THAT.
GULP
SO ARE YOU GOING TO CHOOSE HER?!
CLING
FWUMP
H-HEY ?!

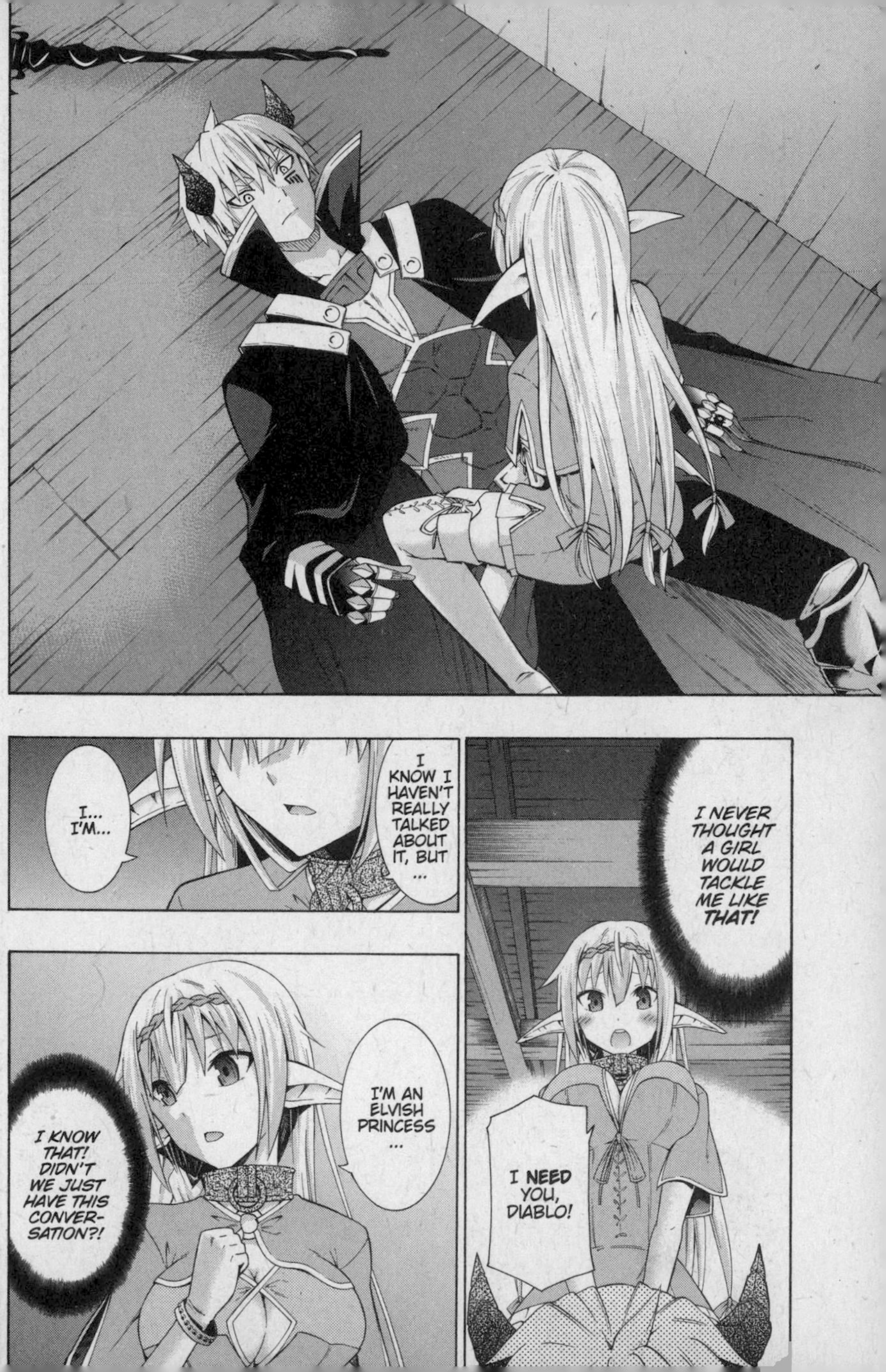
I NEVER THOUGHT A GIRL WOULD TACKLE ME LIKE THAT!
I NEED YOU, DIABLO!
I KNOW I HAVEN'T REALLY TALKED ABOUT IT, BUT ...
I... I'M...
I'M AN ELVISH PRINCESS ...
I KNOW THAT! DIDN'T WE JUST HAVE THIS CONVER-SATION?!

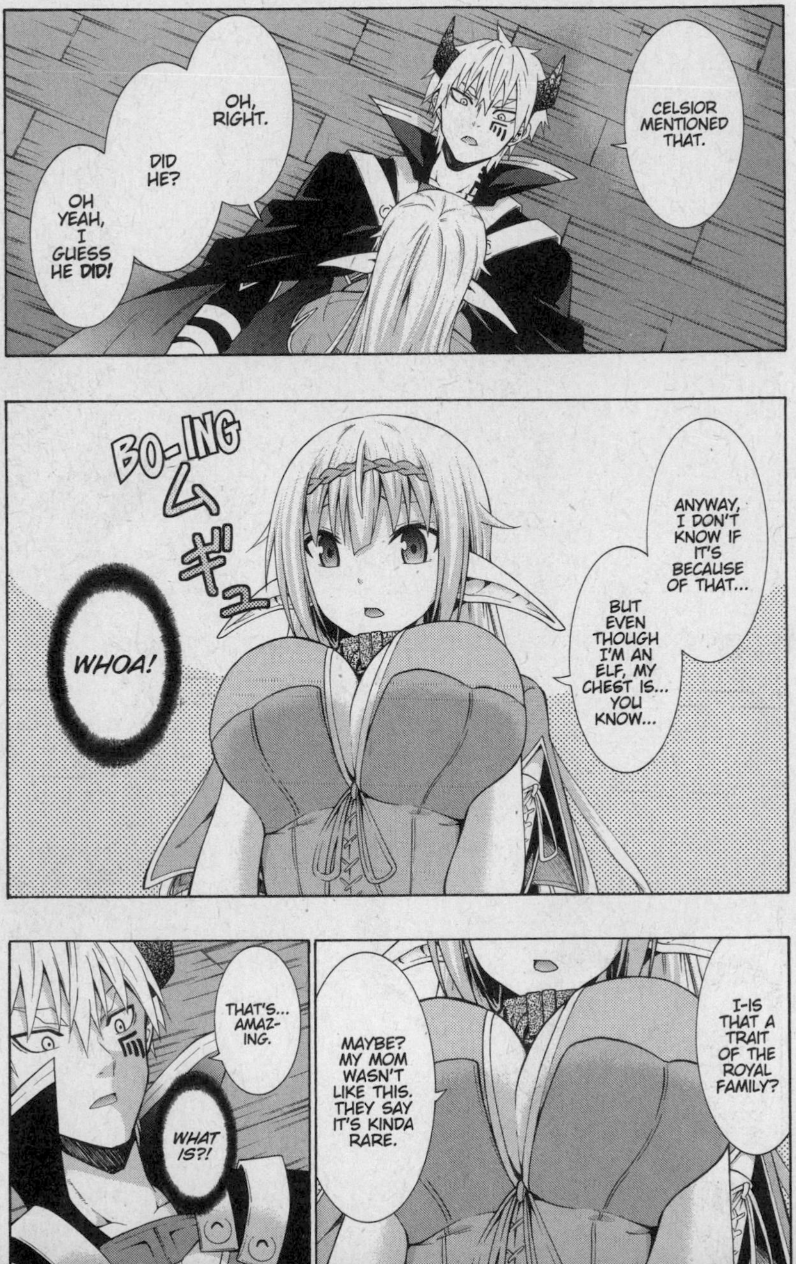
CELSIOR MENTIONED THAT.
OH, RIGHT.
DID HE?
OH YEAH, I GUESS HE DID!
BO-ING
ムギュ
ANYWAY, I DON'T KNOW IF IT'S BECAUSE OF THAT...
BUT EVEN THOUGH I'M AN ELF, MY CHEST IS... YOU KNOW...
WHOA!
I-IS THAT A TRAIT OF THE ROYAL FAMILY?
MAYBE? MY MOM WASN'T LIKE THIS. THEY SAY IT'S KINDA RARE.
THAT'S... AMAZ-ING.
WHAT IS?!

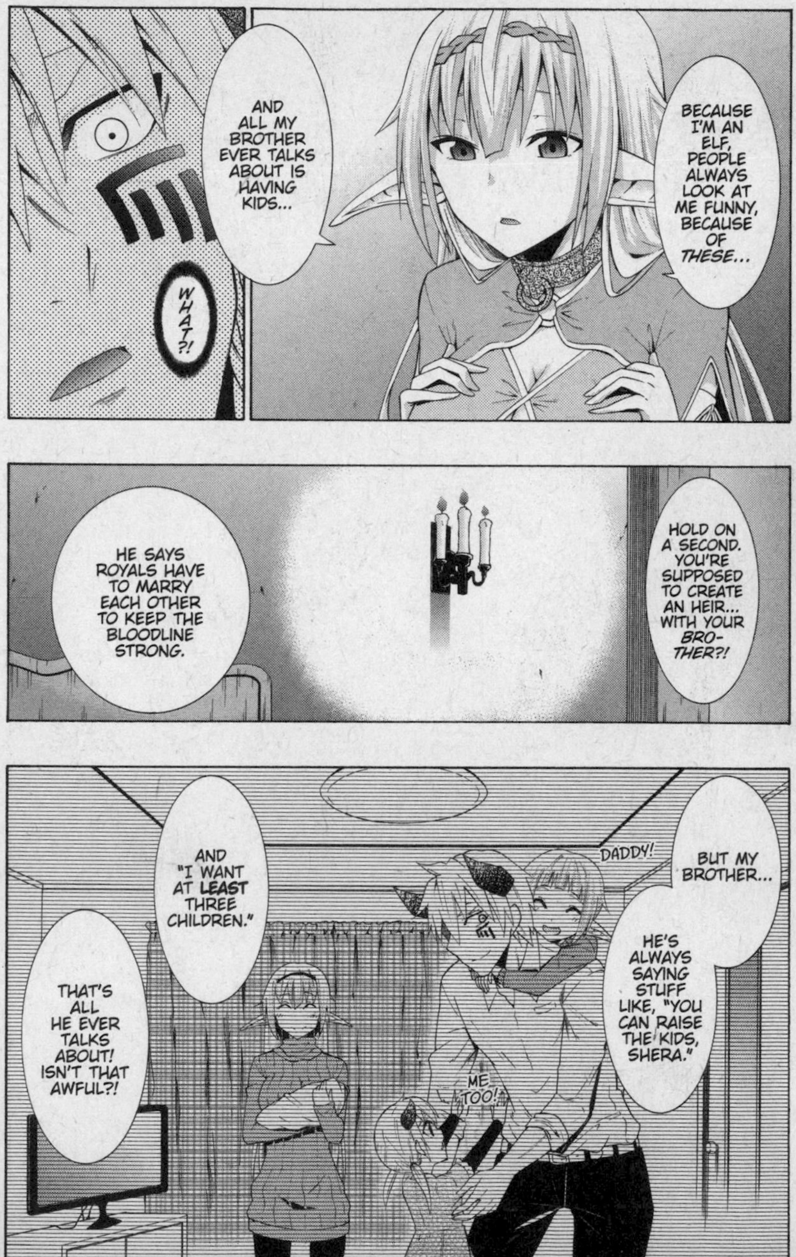
BECAUSE I'M AN ELF, PEOPLE ALWAYS LOOK AT ME FUNNY, BECAUSE OF *THESE*...
AND ALL MY BROTHER EVER TALKS ABOUT IS HAVING KIDS...
WHAT?!
HOLD ON A SECOND. YOU'RE SUPPOSED TO CREATE AN HEIR... WITH YOUR *BRO-THER*?!
HE SAYS ROYALS HAVE TO MARRY EACH OTHER TO KEEP THE BLOODLINE STRONG.
BUT MY BROTHER...
DADDY!
HE'S ALWAYS SAYING STUFF LIKE, "YOU CAN RAISE THE KIDS, SHERA."
AND "I WANT AT **LEAST** THREE CHILDREN."
ME TOO!
THAT'S ALL HE EVER TALKS ABOUT! ISN'T THAT AWFUL?!

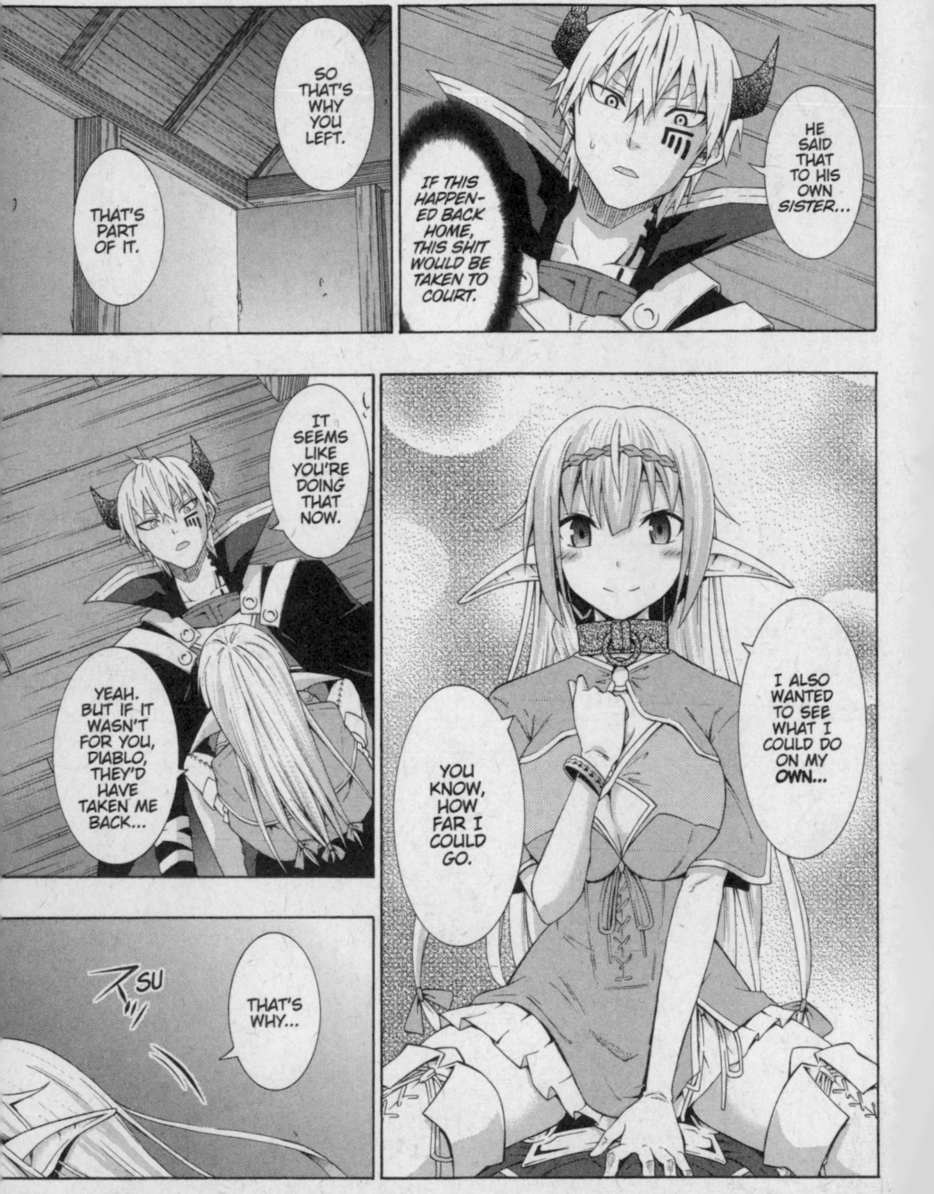
HE SAID THAT TO HIS OWN SISTER...
IF THIS HAPPENED BACK HOME, THIS SHIT WOULD BE TAKEN TO COURT.
SO THAT'S WHY YOU LEFT.
THAT'S PART OF IT.
I ALSO WANTED TO SEE WHAT I COULD DO ON MY OWN...
YOU KNOW, HOW FAR I COULD GO.
IT SEEMS LIKE YOU'RE DOING THAT NOW.
YEAH. BUT IF IT WASN'T FOR YOU, DIABLO, THEY'D HAVE TAKEN ME BACK...
THAT'S WHY...
SU

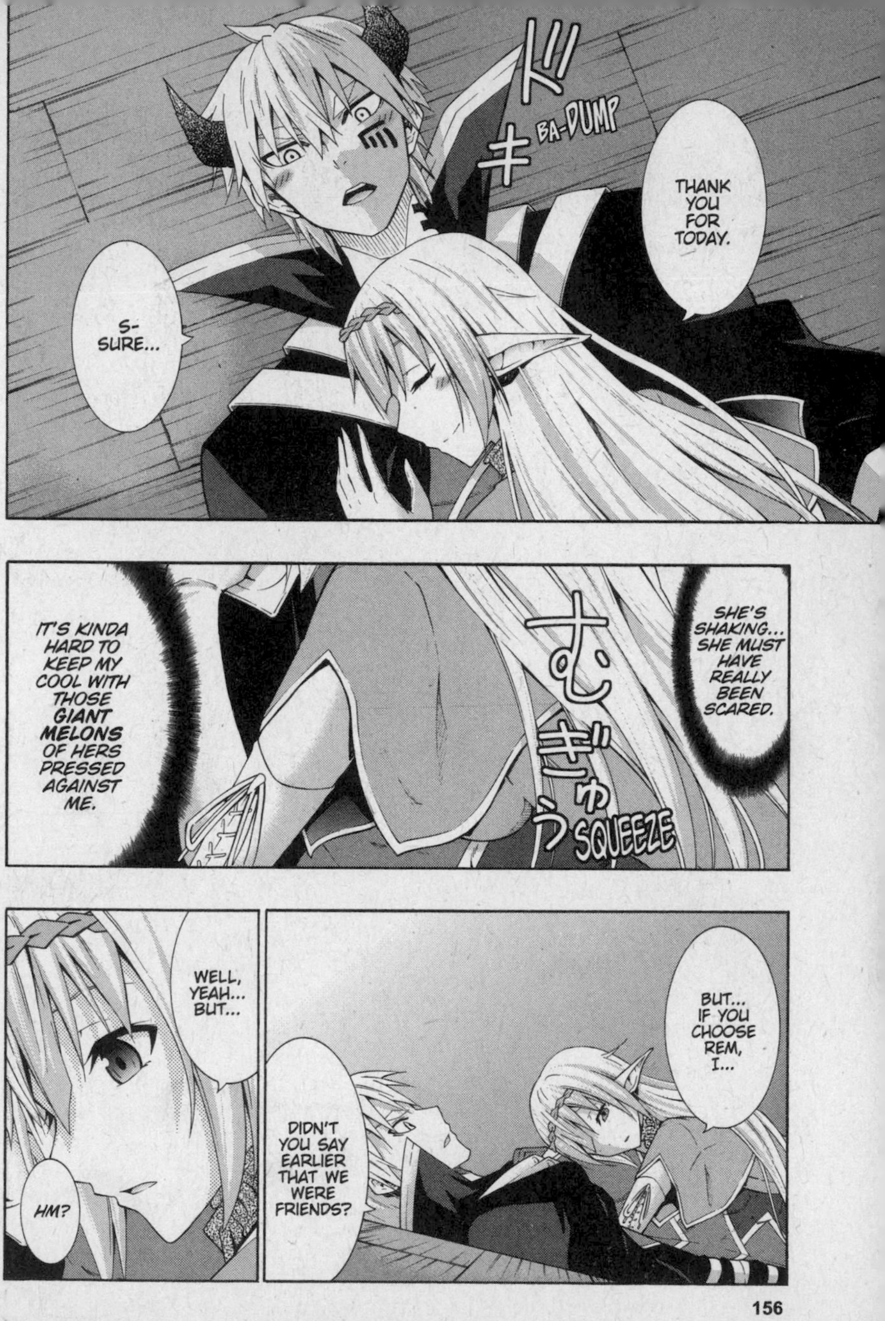
ドキ
BA-DUMP
THANK YOU FOR TODAY.
S-SURE...
SHE'S SHAKING... SHE MUST HAVE REALLY BEEN SCARED.
むぎゅう
SQUEEZE
IT'S KINDA HARD TO KEEP MY COOL WITH THOSE GIANT MELONS OF HERS PRESSED AGAINST ME.
BUT... IF YOU CHOOSE REM, I...
DIDN'T YOU SAY EARLIER THAT WE WERE FRIENDS?
WELL, YEAH... BUT...
HM?

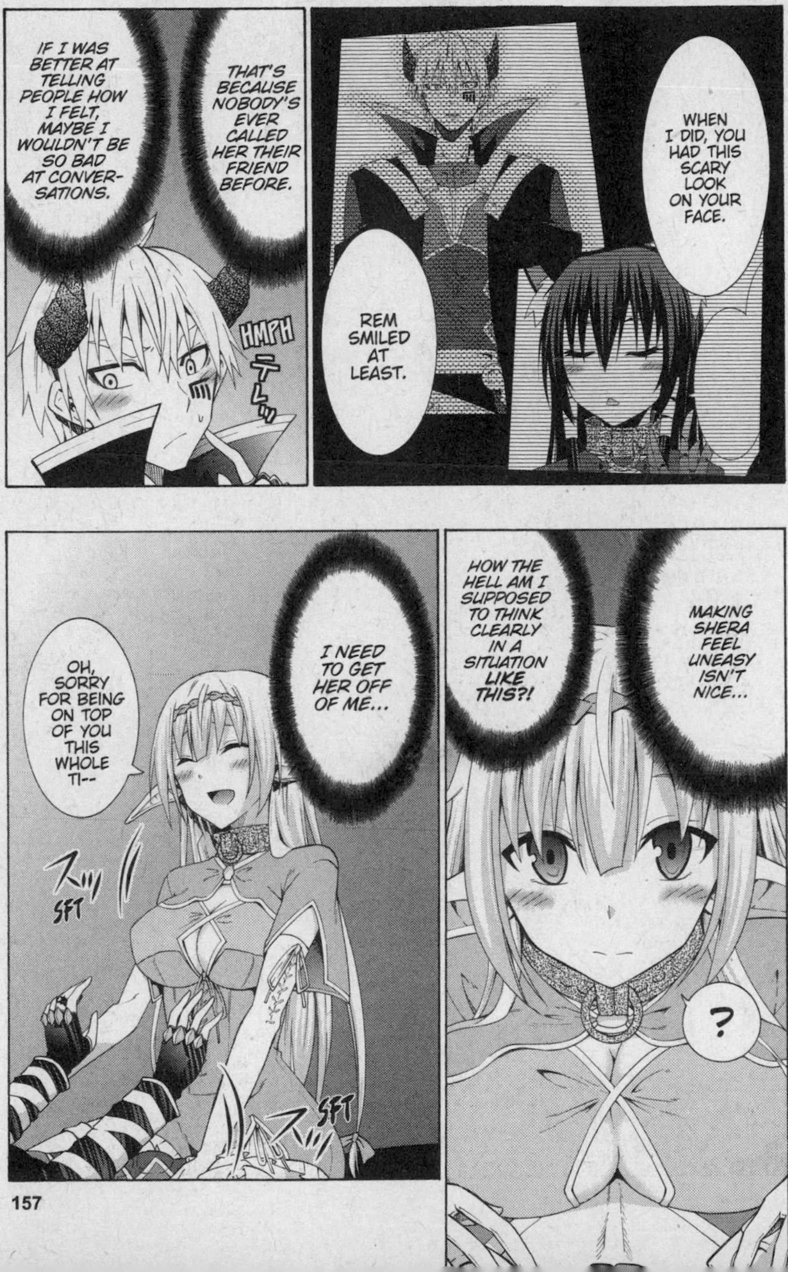
WHEN I DID, YOU HAD THIS SCARY LOOK ON YOUR FACE.
REM SMILED AT LEAST.
THAT'S BECAUSE NOBODY'S EVER CALLED HER THEIR FRIEND BEFORE.
IF I WAS BETTER AT TELLING PEOPLE HOW I FELT, MAYBE I WOULDN'T BE SO BAD AT CONVERSATIONS.
HMPH
テレッ
MAKING SHERA FEEL UNEASY ISN'T NICE...
HOW THE HELL AM I SUPPOSED TO THINK CLEARLY IN A SITUATION LIKE THIS?!
?
I NEED TO GET HER OFF OF ME...
OH, SORRY FOR BEING ON TOP OF YOU THIS WHOLE TI--
スッ
SFT
スッ
SFT

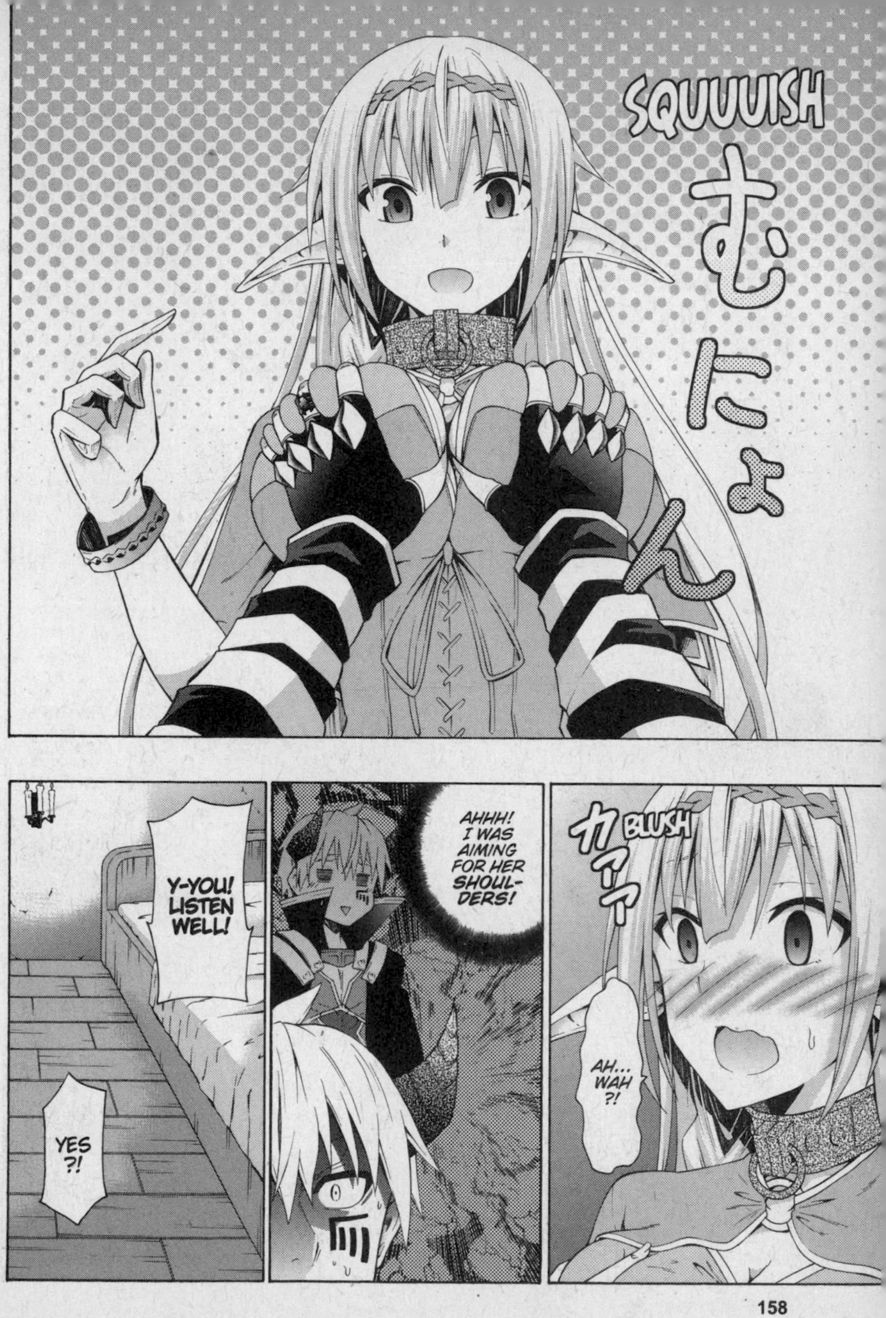
SQUUUISH
むにょん
カァァ
BLUSH
AH... WAH?!
AHHH! I WAS AIMING FOR HER SHOUL-DERS!
Y-YOU! LISTEN WELL!
YES?!

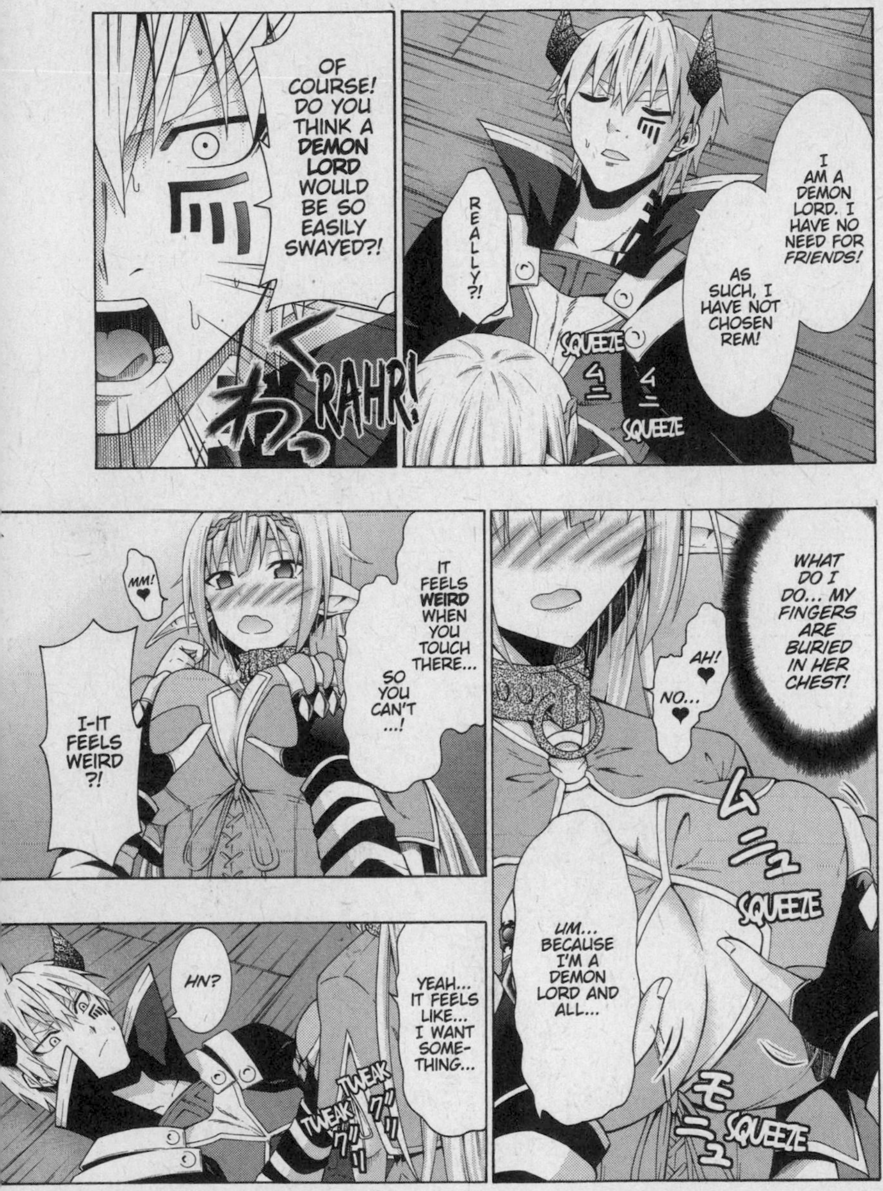
I AM A DEMON LORD. I HAVE NO NEED FOR FRIENDS!
AS SUCH, I HAVE NOT CHOSEN REM!
SQUEEZE
SQUEEZE
REALLY?!
OF COURSE! DO YOU THINK A DEMON LORD WOULD BE SO EASILY SWAYED?!
RAHR!
WHAT DO I DO... MY FINGERS ARE BURIED IN HER CHEST!
AH! ♥
NO... ♥
SQUEEZE
UM... BECAUSE I'M A DEMON LORD AND ALL...
SQUEEZE
MM! ♥
IT FEELS WEIRD WHEN YOU TOUCH THERE...
SO YOU CAN'T ...!
I-IT FEELS WEIRD ?!
YEAH... IT FEELS LIKE... I WANT SOME-THING...
HN?
TWEAK
TWEAK

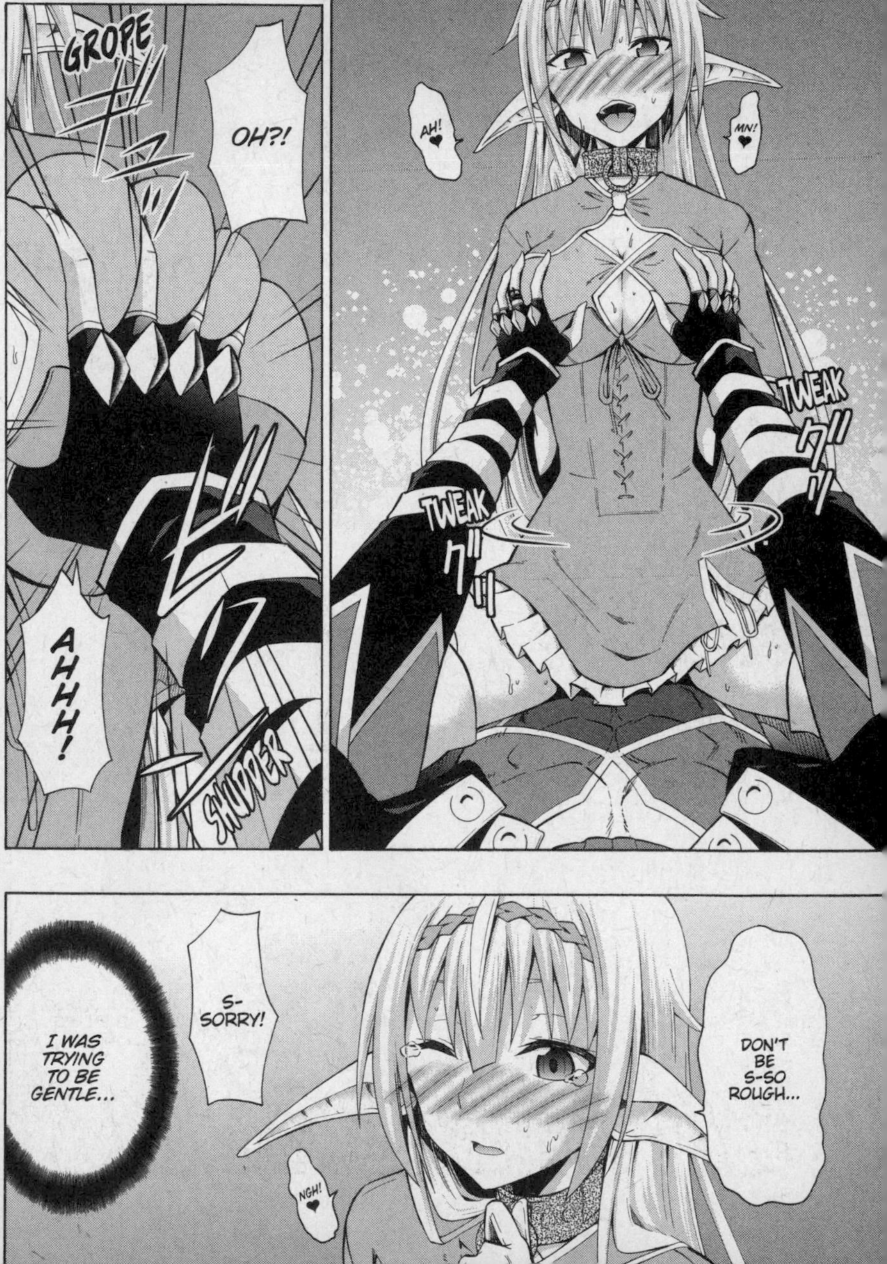
MN! ♥
AH! ♥
TWEAK
TWEAK
GROPE
OH?!
AHHH!
SHUDDER
DON'T BE S-SO ROUGH...
NGH! ♥
S- SORRY!
I WAS TRYING TO BE GENTLE...

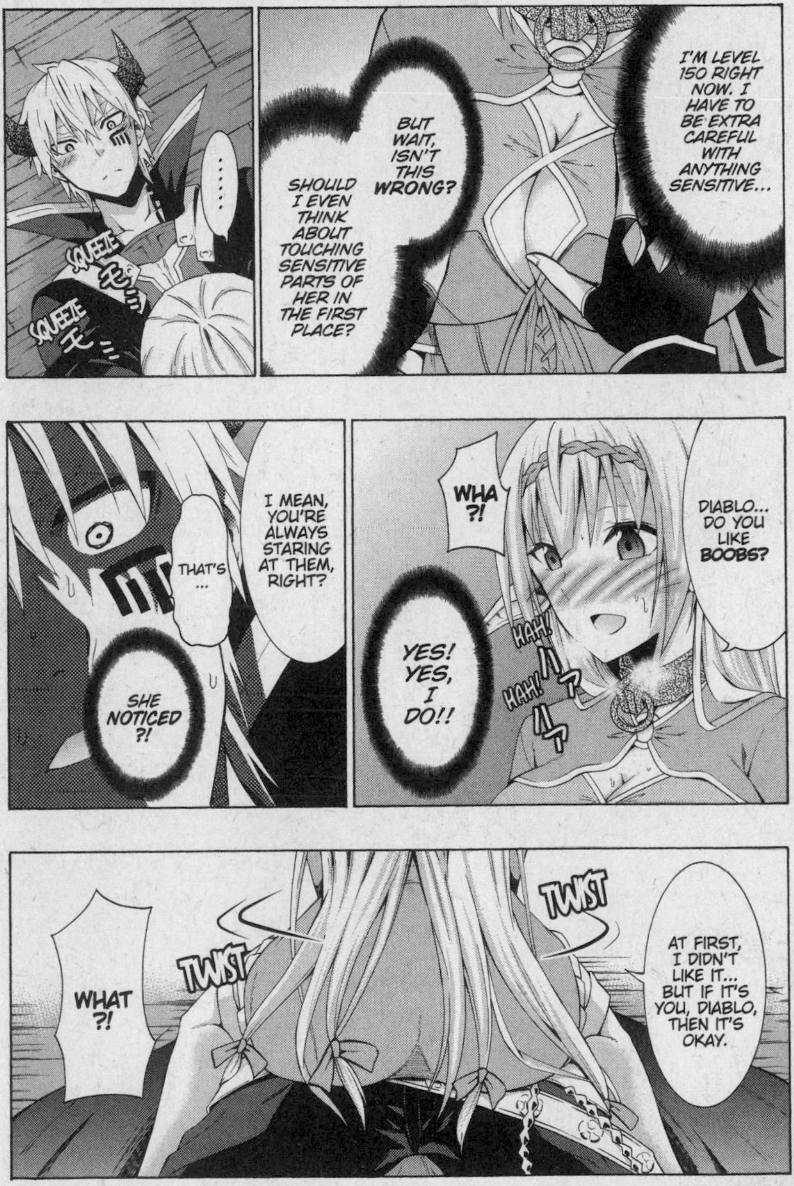
I'M LEVEL 150 RIGHT NOW. I HAVE TO BE EXTRA CAREFUL WITH ANYTHING SENSITIVE...
BUT WAIT, ISN'T THIS WRONG?
SHOULD I EVEN THINK ABOUT TOUCHING SENSITIVE PARTS OF HER IN THE FIRST PLACE?
......
SQUEEZE
SQUEEZE
DIABLO... DO YOU LIKE BOOBS?
WHA ?!
YES! YES, I DO!!
HAH!
HAH!
I MEAN, YOU'RE ALWAYS STARING AT THEM, RIGHT?
THAT'S ...
SHE NOTICED ?!
AT FIRST, I DIDN'T LIKE IT... BUT IF IT'S YOU, DIABLO, THEN IT'S OKAY.
TWIST
TWIST
WHAT ?!

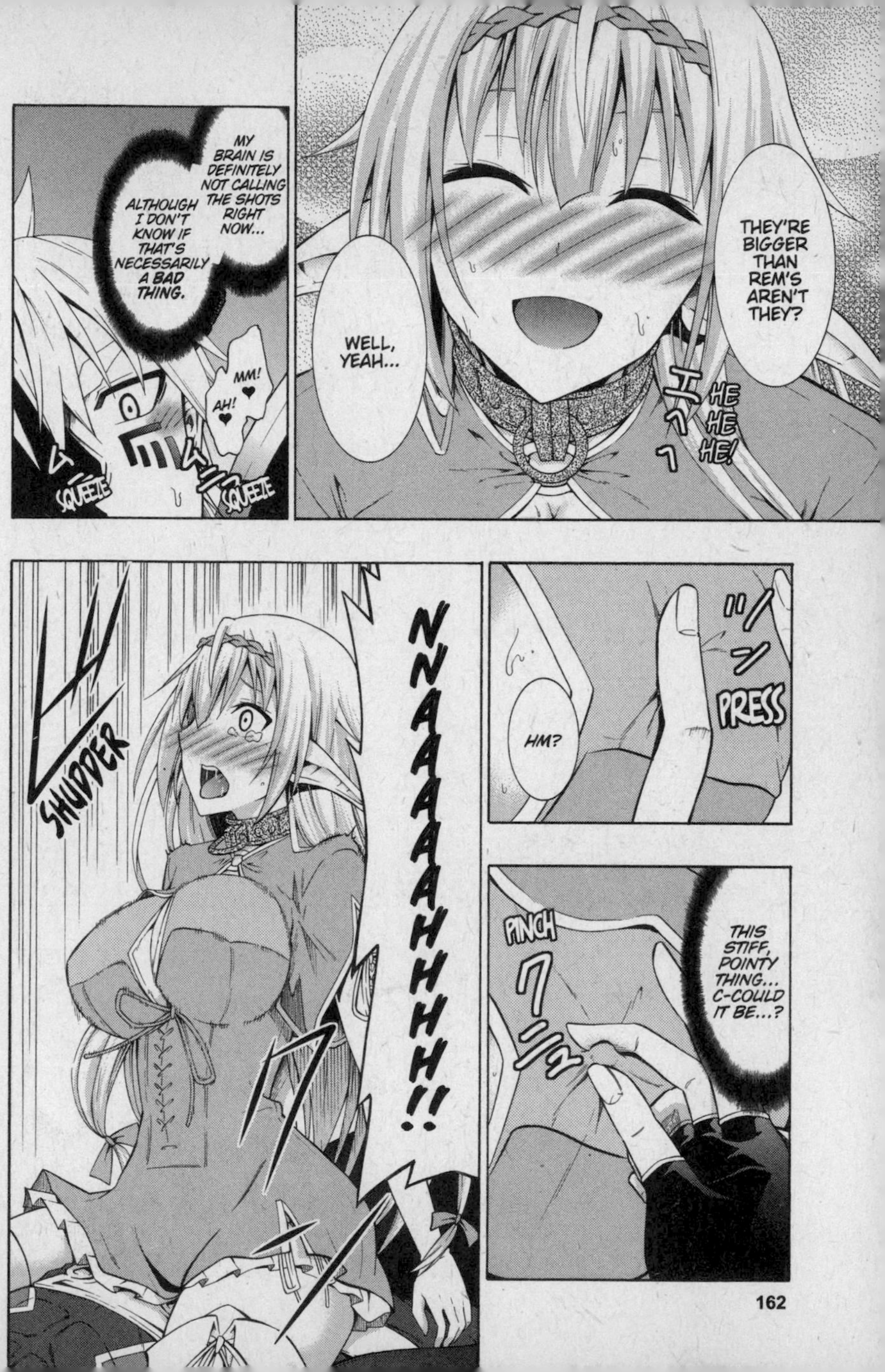
THEY'RE BIGGER THAN REM'S AREN'T THEY?
HE HE HE!
WELL, YEAH...
MY BRAIN IS DEFINITELY NOT CALLING THE SHOTS RIGHT NOW...
ALTHOUGH I DON'T KNOW IF THAT'S NECESSARILY A BAD THING.
MM!
AH!
SQUEEZE
SQUEEZE
PRESS
HM?
THIS STIFF, POINTY THING... C-COULD IT BE...?
PINCH
NNAAAAAAAAHHHHHH!!
SHUDDER

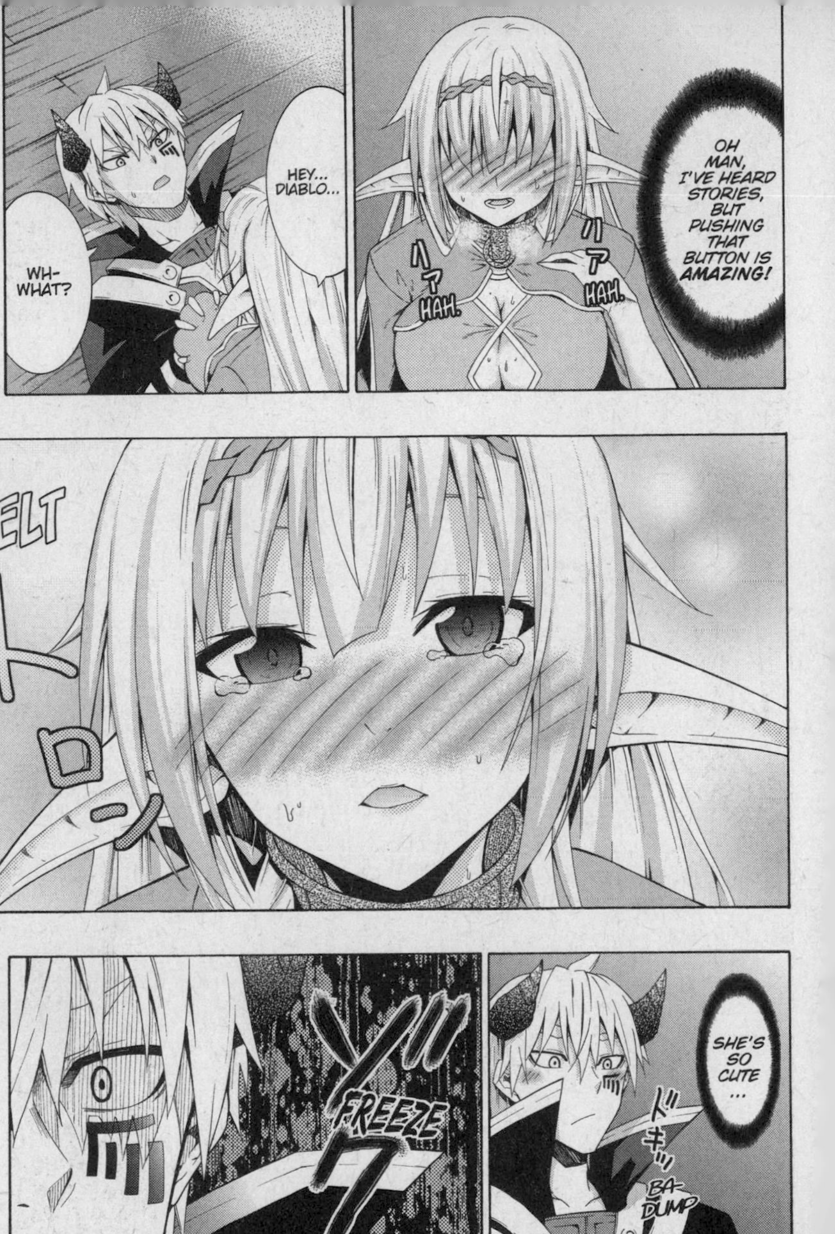
OH MAN, I'VE HEARD STORIES, BUT PUSHING THAT BUTTON IS **AMAZING!**
ハア
HAH.
ハア
HAH.
HEY... DIABLO...
WH- WHAT?
MELT
トロー
SHE'S SO CUTE ...
ドキッ
BA-DUMP
ゾクッ
FREEZE

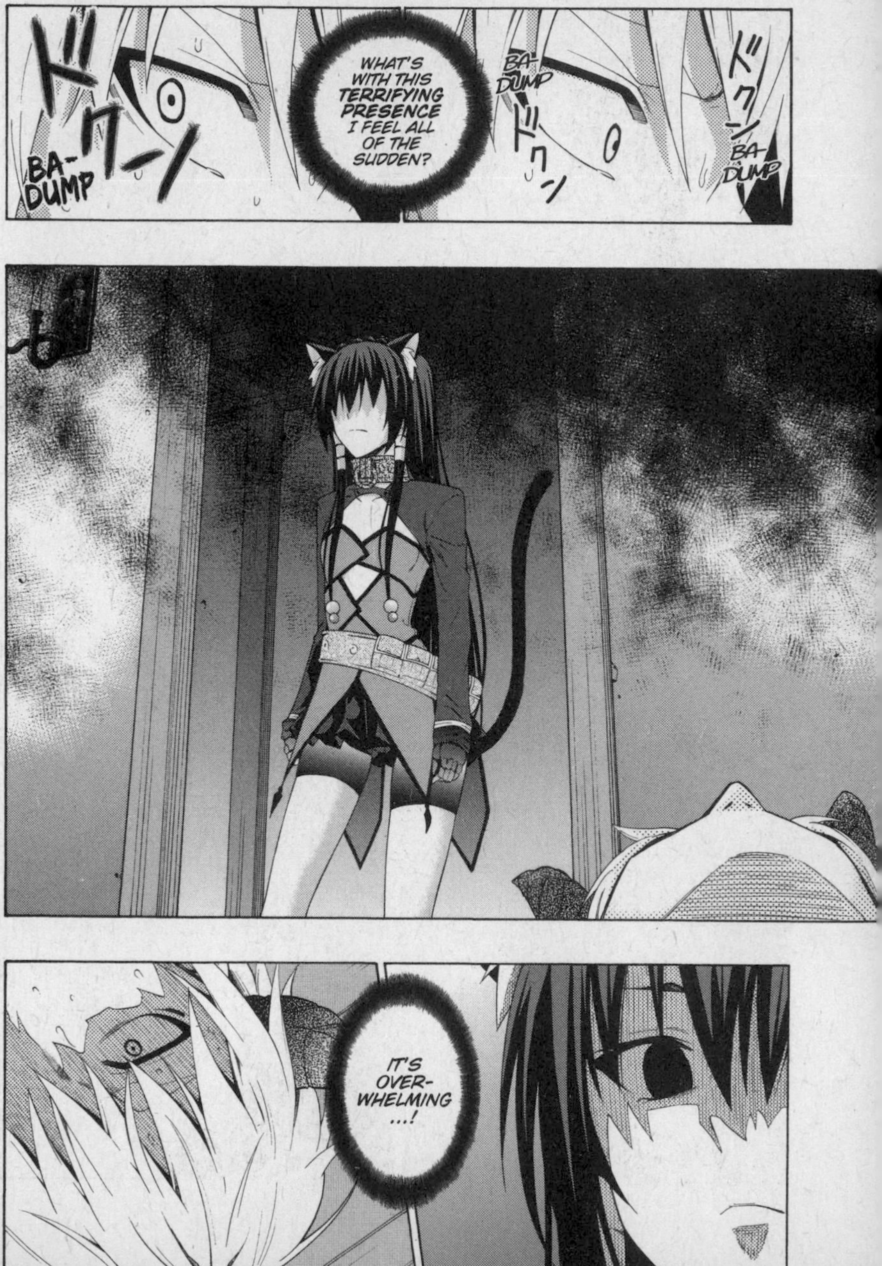
BA-DUMP
BA-DUMP
WHAT'S WITH THIS TERRIFYING PRESENCE I FEEL ALL OF THE SUDDEN?
BA-DUMP
IT'S OVER-WHELMING ...!

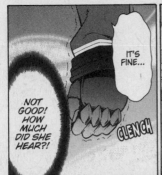

OH, IT'S REM~!
SQUISH
SQUISH
IT'S FINE...
CLENCH
NOT GOOD! HOW MUCH DID SHE HEAR?!
AFTER ALL...
I'M SMALL, RIGHT?!
SHE HEARD THAT MUCH?!
AFTERWARD THERE WAS MUCH APOLOGIZING.
SORRY...
I SAID I WAS SORRY, REM!

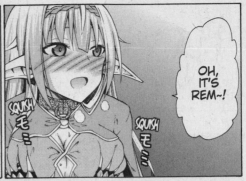

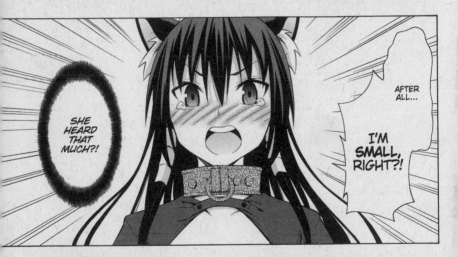

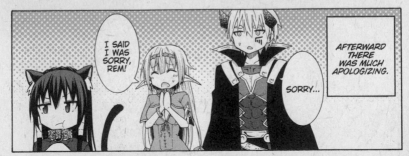

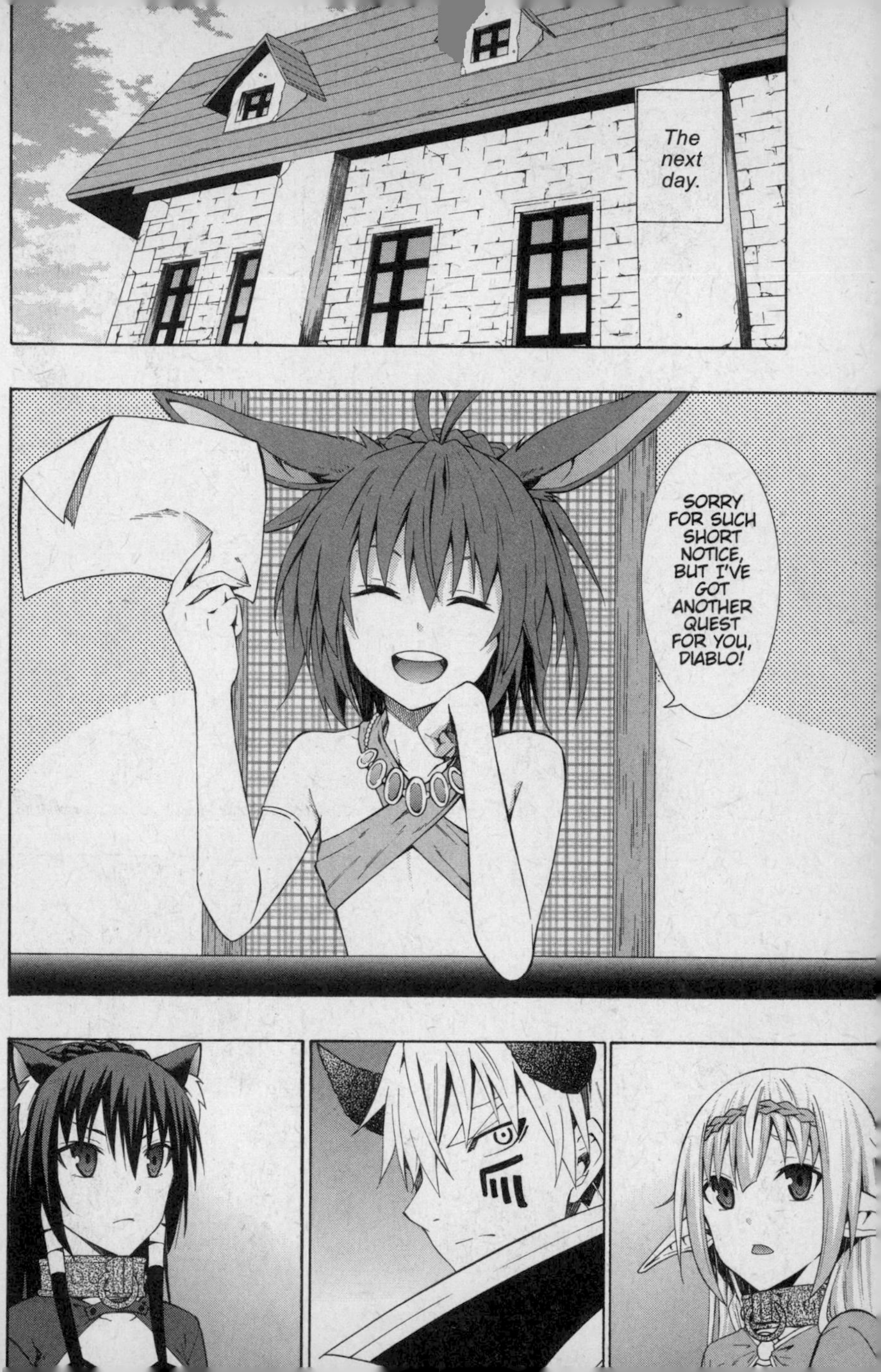
The next day.
SORRY FOR SUCH SHORT NOTICE, BUT I'VE GOT ANOTHER QUEST FOR YOU, DIABLO!

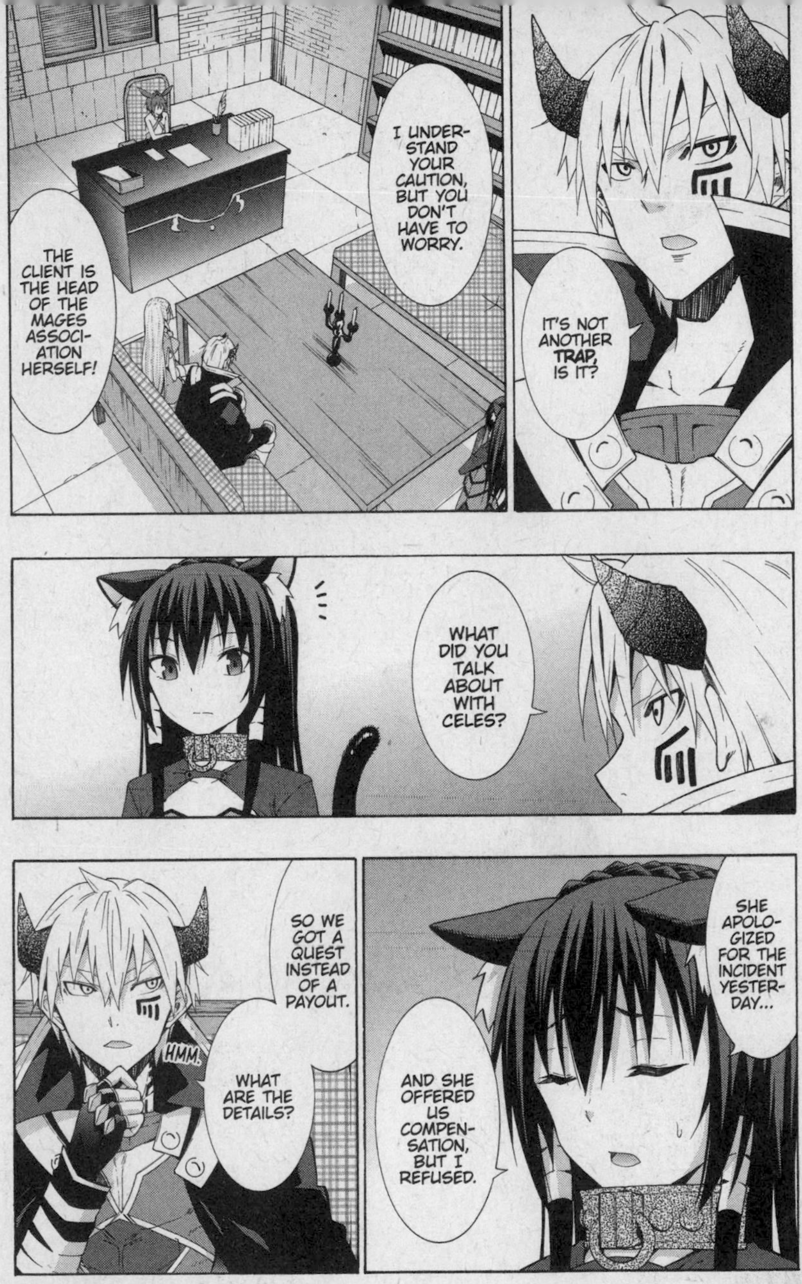
IT'S NOT ANOTHER TRAP, IS IT?
I UNDERSTAND YOUR CAUTION, BUT YOU DON'T HAVE TO WORRY.
THE CLIENT IS THE HEAD OF THE MAGES ASSOCIATION HERSELF!
WHAT DID YOU TALK ABOUT WITH CELES?
SHE APOLOGIZED FOR THE INCIDENT YESTERDAY...
AND SHE OFFERED US COMPENSATION, BUT I REFUSED.
SO WE GOT A QUEST INSTEAD OF A PAYOUT.
HMM.
WHAT ARE THE DETAILS?

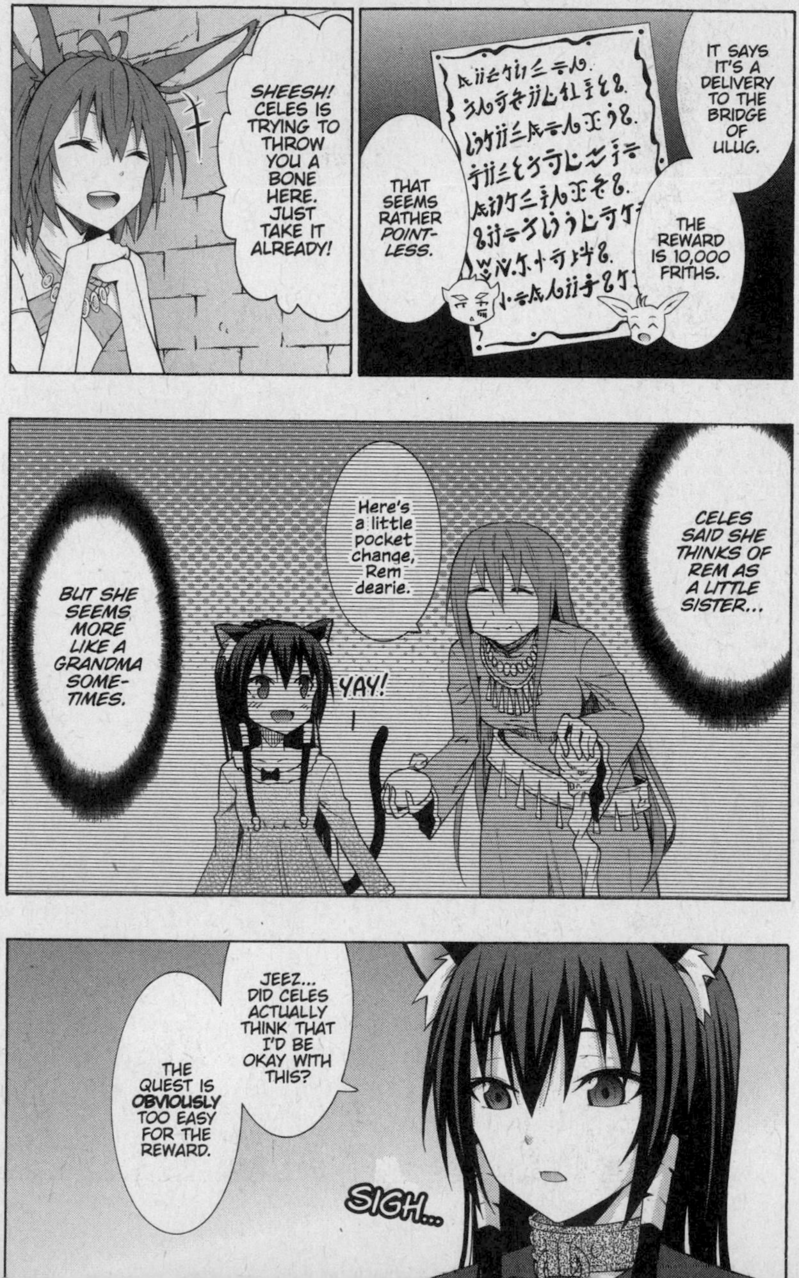
IT SAYS IT'S A DELIVERY TO THE BRIDGE OF ULUG.
THE REWARD IS 10,000 FRITHS.
THAT SEEMS RATHER POINTLESS.
SHEESH! CELES IS TRYING TO THROW YOU A BONE HERE. JUST TAKE IT ALREADY!
CELES SAID SHE THINKS OF REM AS A LITTLE SISTER...
Here's a little pocket change, Rem dearie.
YAY!
BUT SHE SEEMS MORE LIKE A GRANDMA SOME-TIMES.
JEEZ... DID CELES ACTUALLY THINK THAT I'D BE OKAY WITH THIS?
THE QUEST IS OBVIOUSLY TOO EASY FOR THE REWARD.
SIGH...

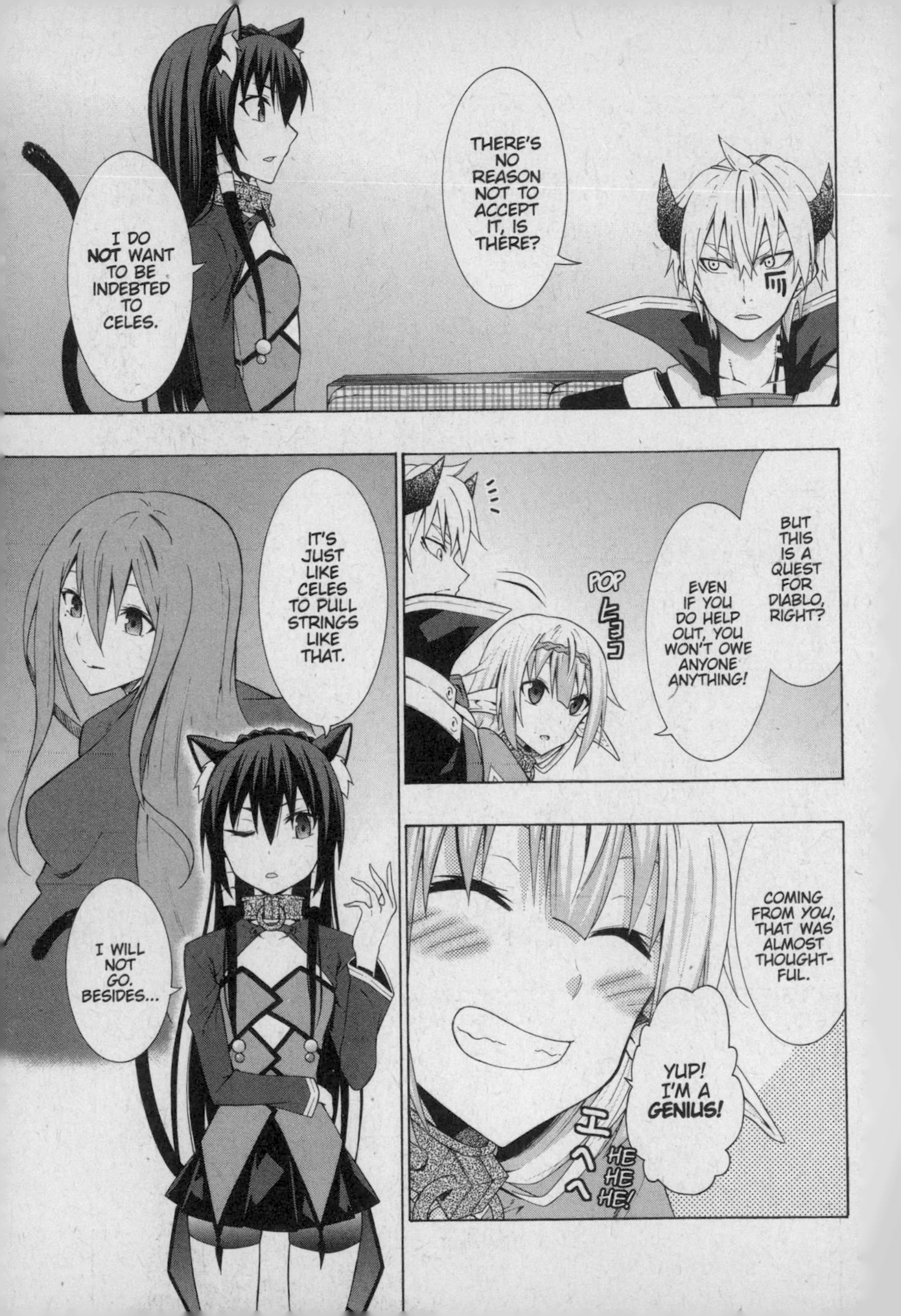
THERE'S NO REASON NOT TO ACCEPT IT, IS THERE?
I DO NOT WANT TO BE INDEBTED TO CELES.
BUT THIS IS A QUEST FOR DIABLO, RIGHT?
EVEN IF YOU DO HELP OUT, YOU WON'T OWE ANYONE ANYTHING!
POP
ヒョコ
COMING FROM YOU, THAT WAS ALMOST THOUGHT-FUL.
YUP! I'M A GENIUS!
エヘヘ
HE HE HE!
IT'S JUST LIKE CELES TO PULL STRINGS LIKE THAT.
I WILL NOT GO. BESIDES...

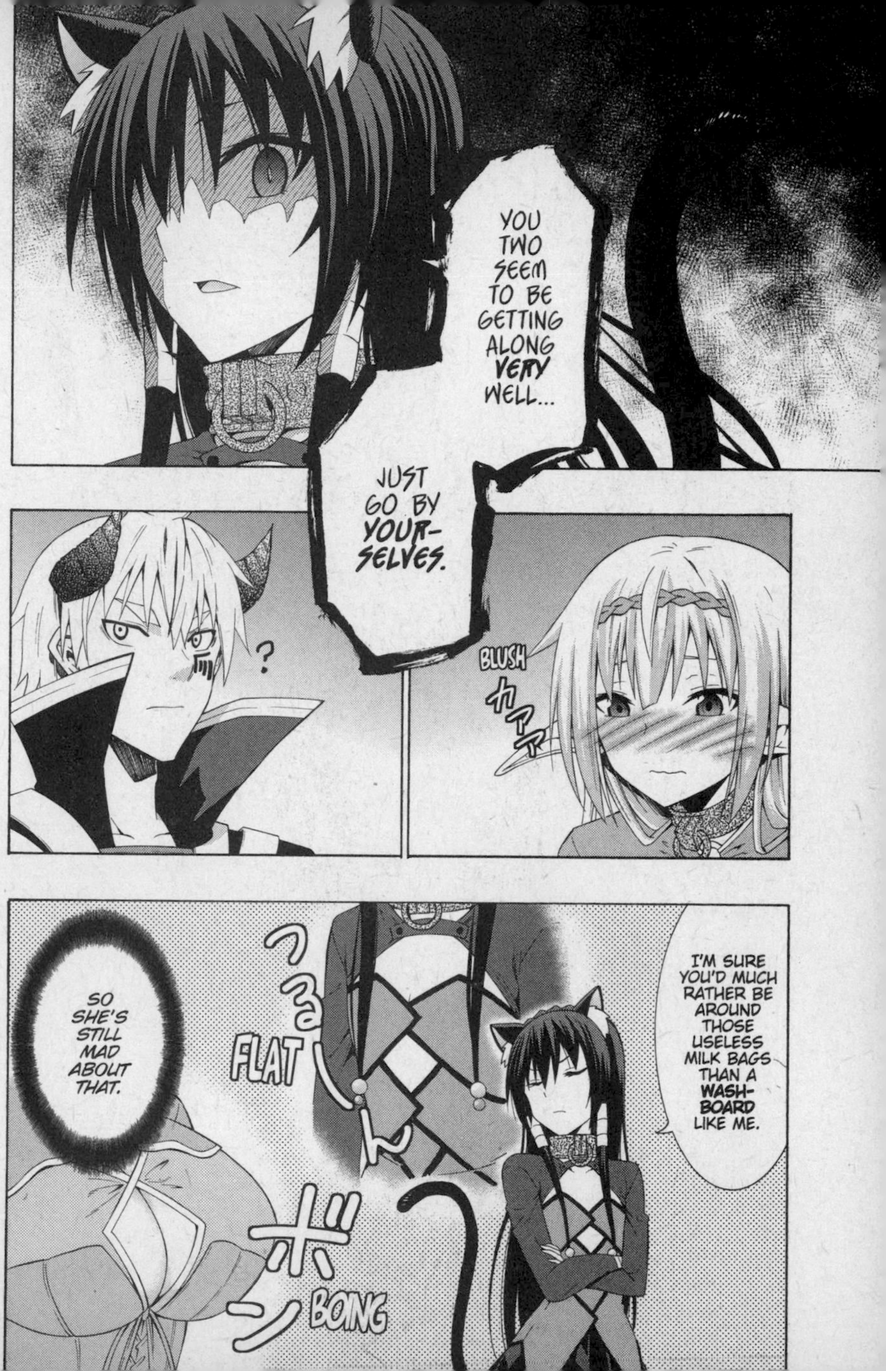
YOU TWO SEEM TO BE GETTING ALONG VERY WELL...
JUST GO BY YOUR-SELVES.
BLUSH
カァァ
?
I'M SURE YOU'D MUCH RATHER BE AROUND THOSE USELESS MILK BAGS THAN A WASH-BOARD LIKE ME.
つるーん
FLAT
ボヨーン
BOING
SO SHE'S STILL MAD ABOUT THAT.

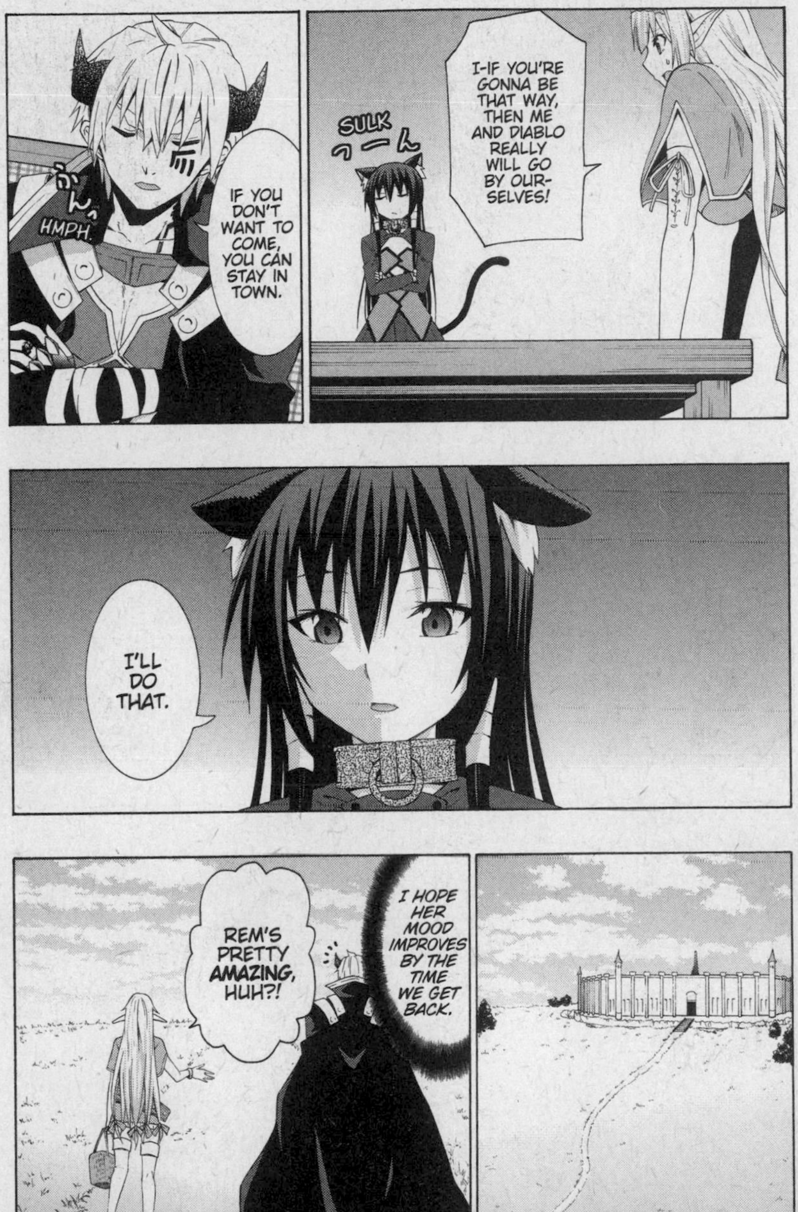
I-IF YOU'RE GONNA BE THAT WAY, THEN ME AND DIABLO REALLY WILL GO BY OURSELVES!
SULK
つーん
IF YOU DON'T WANT TO COME, YOU CAN STAY IN TOWN.
HMPH.
I'LL DO THAT.
REM'S PRETTY AMAZING, HUH?!
I HOPE HER MOOD IMPROVES BY THE TIME WE GET BACK.

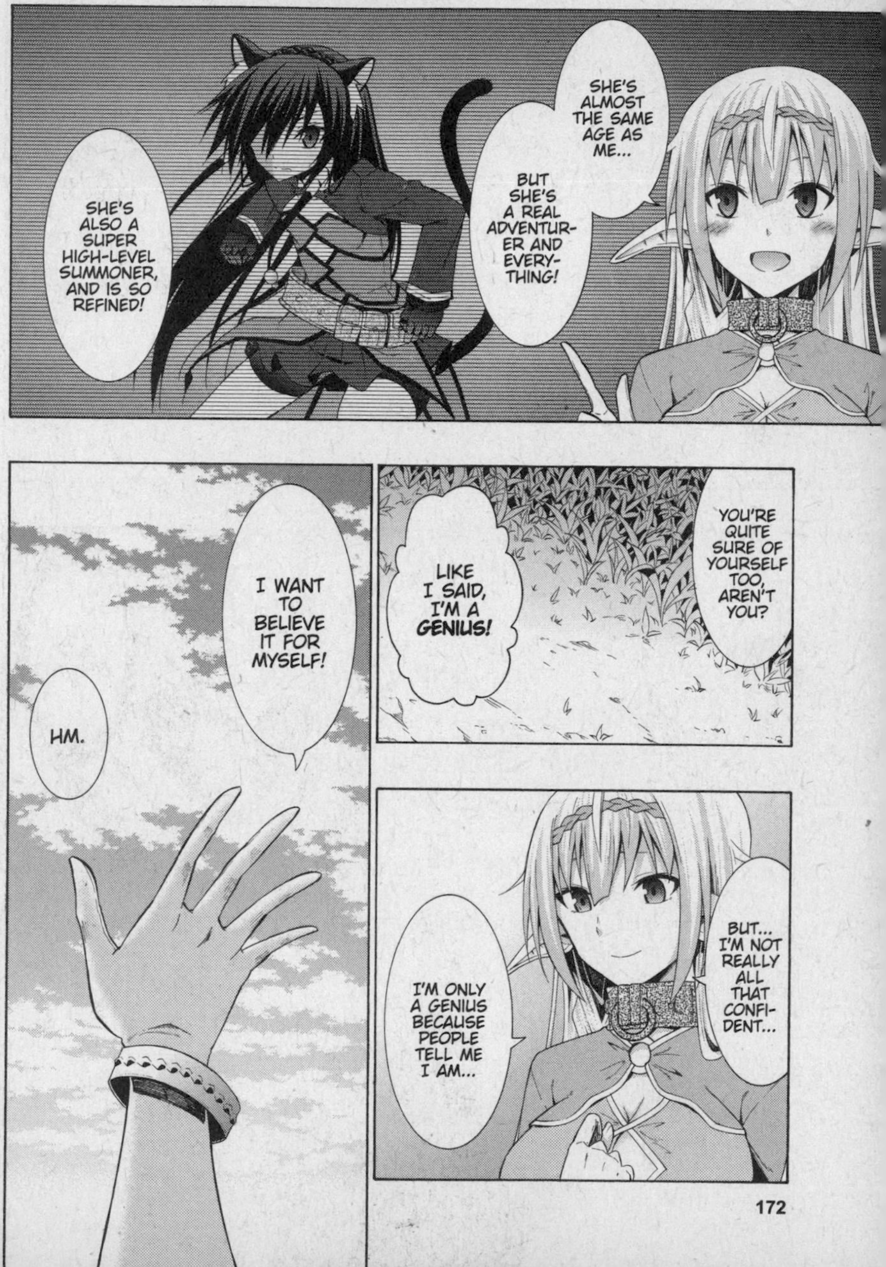
SHE'S ALMOST THE SAME AGE AS ME...
BUT SHE'S A REAL ADVENTURER AND EVERYTHING!
SHE'S ALSO A SUPER HIGH-LEVEL SUMMONER, AND IS SO REFINED!
YOU'RE QUITE SURE OF YOURSELF TOO, AREN'T YOU?
LIKE I SAID, I'M A GENIUS!
BUT... I'M NOT REALLY ALL THAT CONFIDENT...
I'M ONLY A GENIUS BECAUSE PEOPLE TELL ME I AM...
I WANT TO BELIEVE IT FOR MYSELF!
HM.

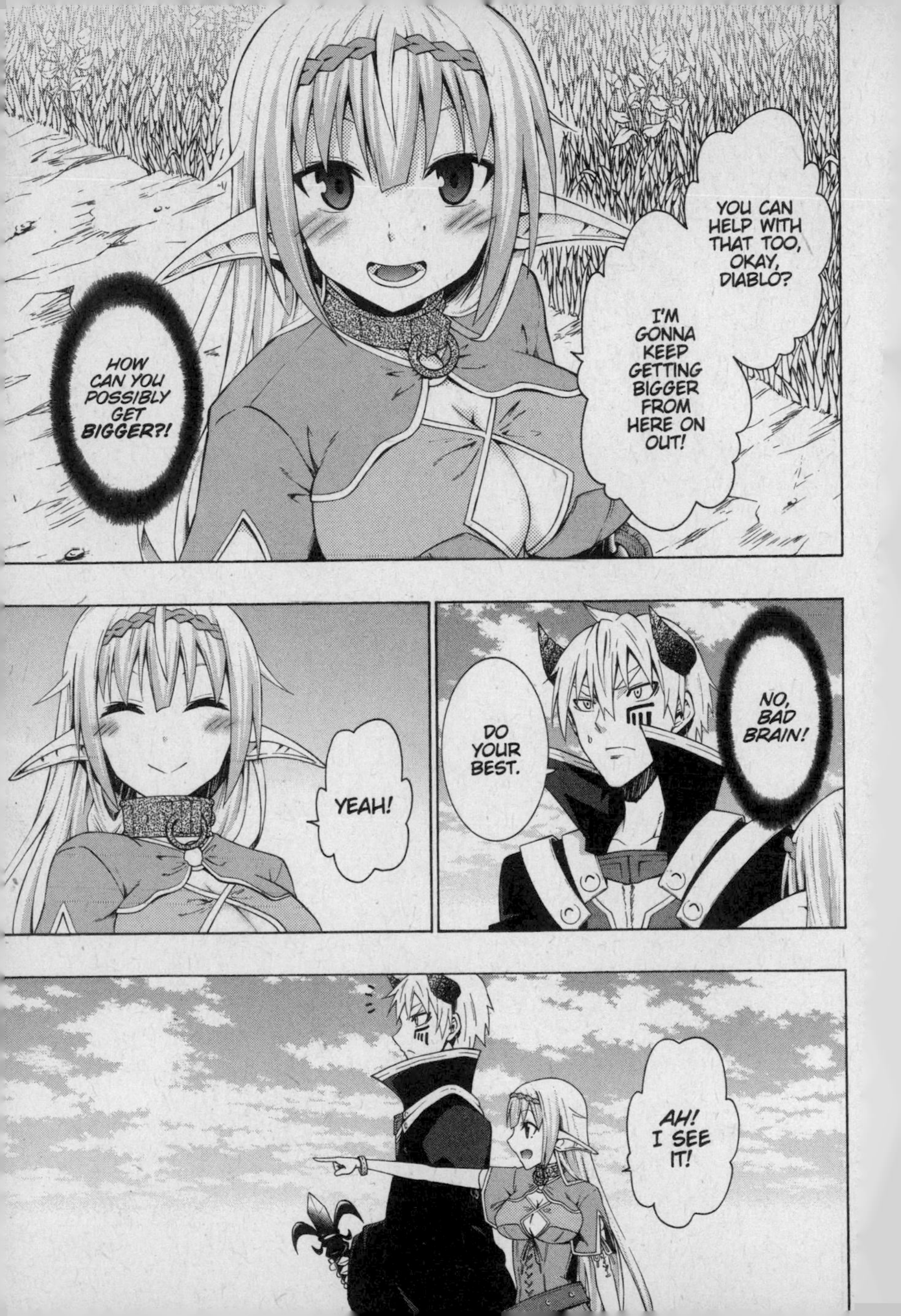
YOU CAN HELP WITH THAT TOO, OKAY, DIABLO?
I'M GONNA KEEP GETTING BIGGER FROM HERE ON OUT!
HOW CAN YOU POSSIBLY GET BIGGER?!
NO, BAD BRAIN!
DO YOUR BEST.
YEAH!
AH! I SEE IT!

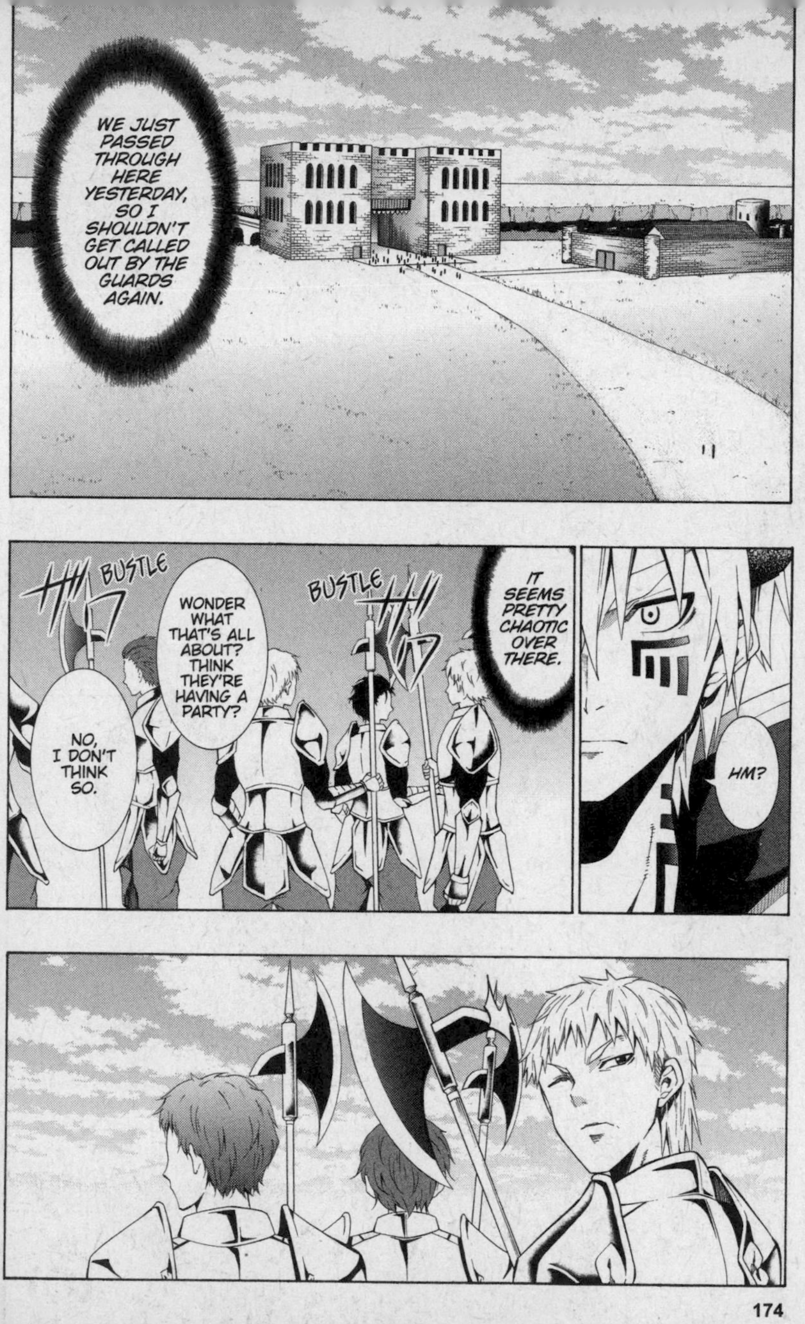
WE JUST PASSED THROUGH HERE YESTERDAY, SO I SHOULDN'T GET CALLED OUT BY THE GUARDS AGAIN.
HM?
IT SEEMS PRETTY CHAOTIC OVER THERE.
BUSTLE
WONDER WHAT THAT'S ALL ABOUT? THINK THEY'RE HAVING A PARTY?
BUSTLE
NO, I DON'T THINK SO.

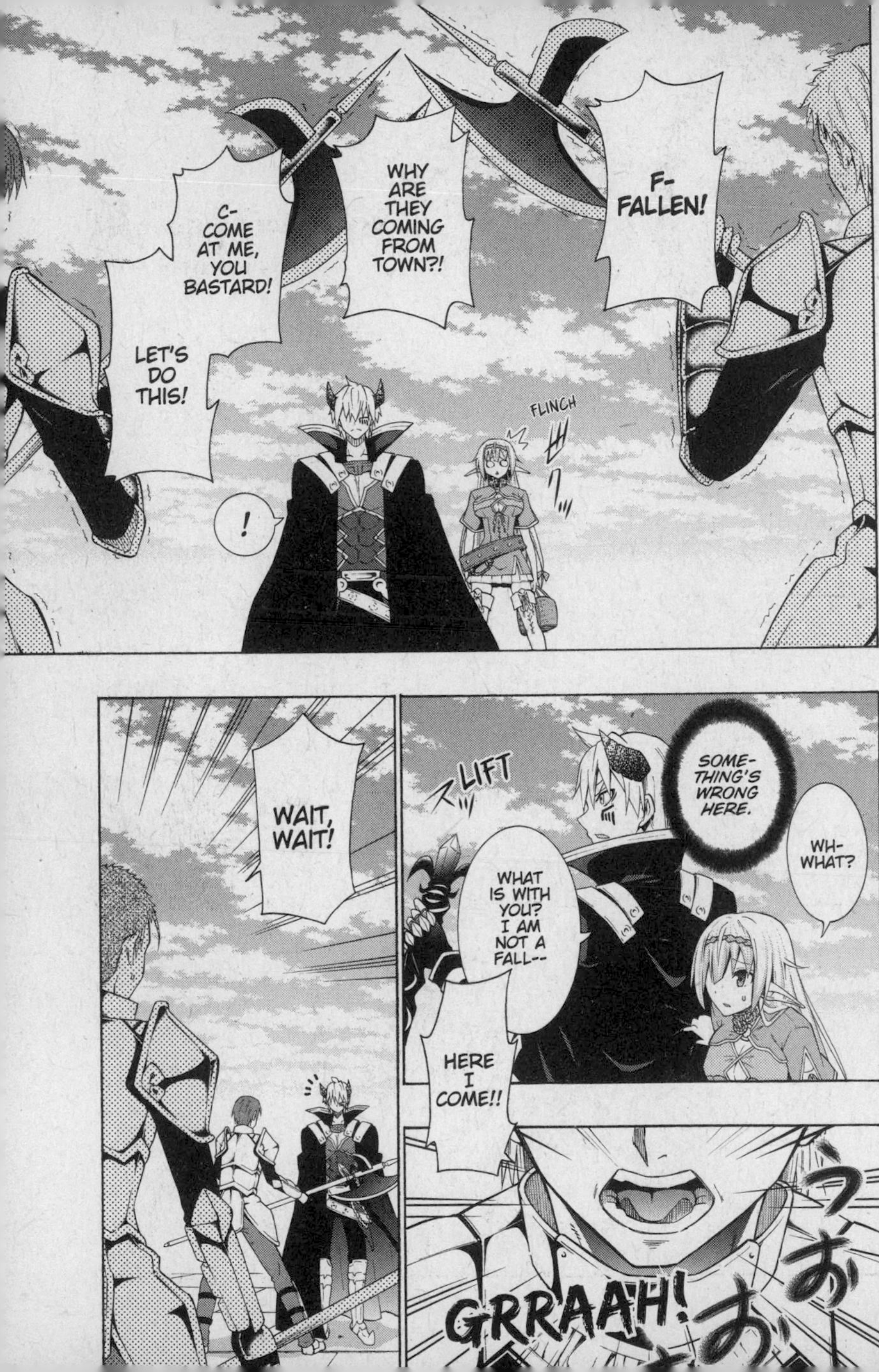
F-FALLEN!
WHY ARE THEY COMING FROM TOWN?!
C-COME AT ME, YOU BASTARD!
LET'S DO THIS!
FLINCH
!
LIFT
SOMETHING'S WRONG HERE.
WH-WHAT?
WHAT IS WITH YOU? I AM NOT A FALL--
GRRAAH!
HERE I COME!!
WAIT, WAIT!

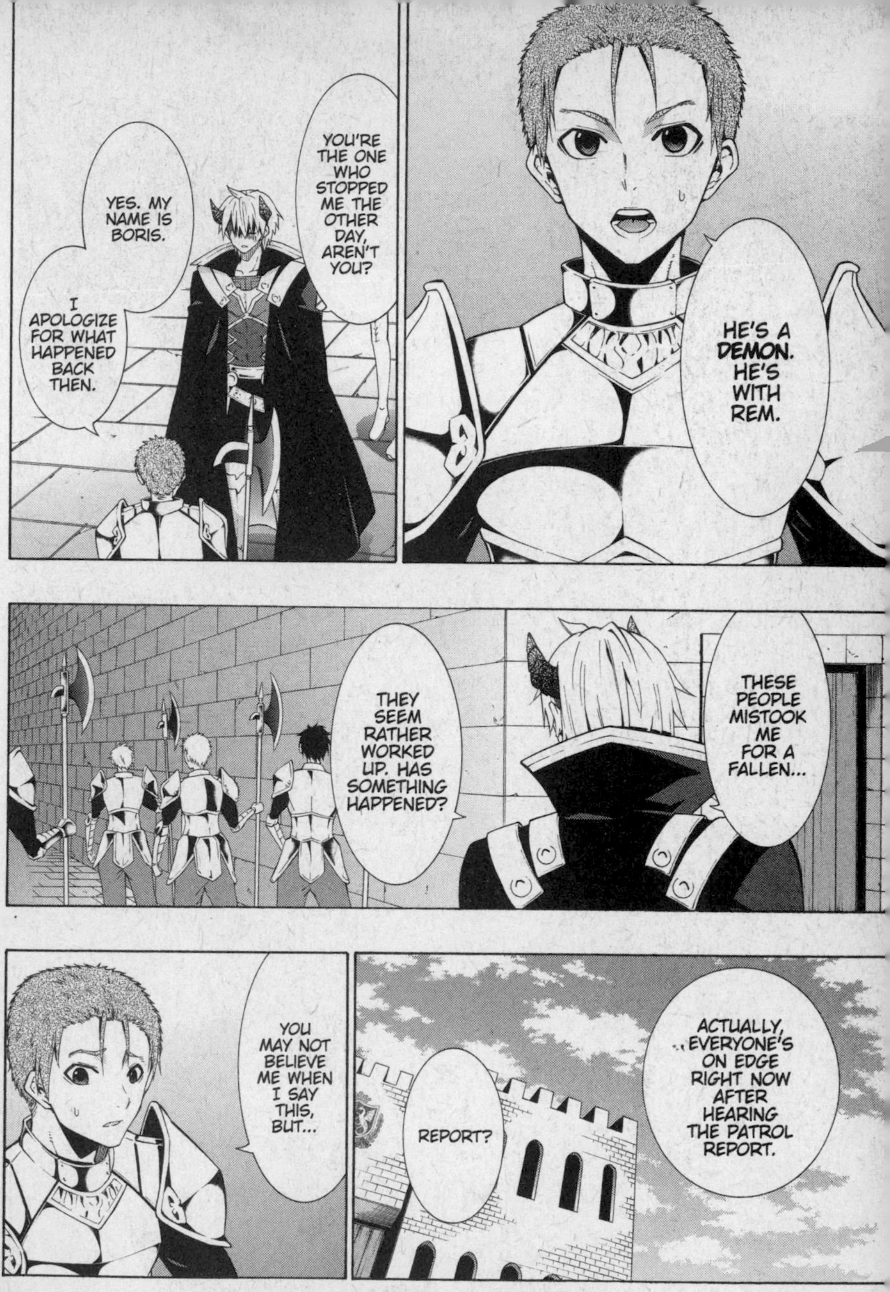
HE'S A DEMON. HE'S WITH REM.
YOU'RE THE ONE WHO STOPPED ME THE OTHER DAY, AREN'T YOU?
YES. MY NAME IS BORIS.
I APOLOGIZE FOR WHAT HAPPENED BACK THEN.
THESE PEOPLE MISTOOK ME FOR A FALLEN...
THEY SEEM RATHER WORKED UP. HAS SOMETHING HAPPENED?
ACTUALLY, EVERYONE'S ON EDGE RIGHT NOW AFTER HEARING THE PATROL REPORT.
REPORT?
YOU MAY NOT BELIEVE ME WHEN I SAY THIS, BUT...

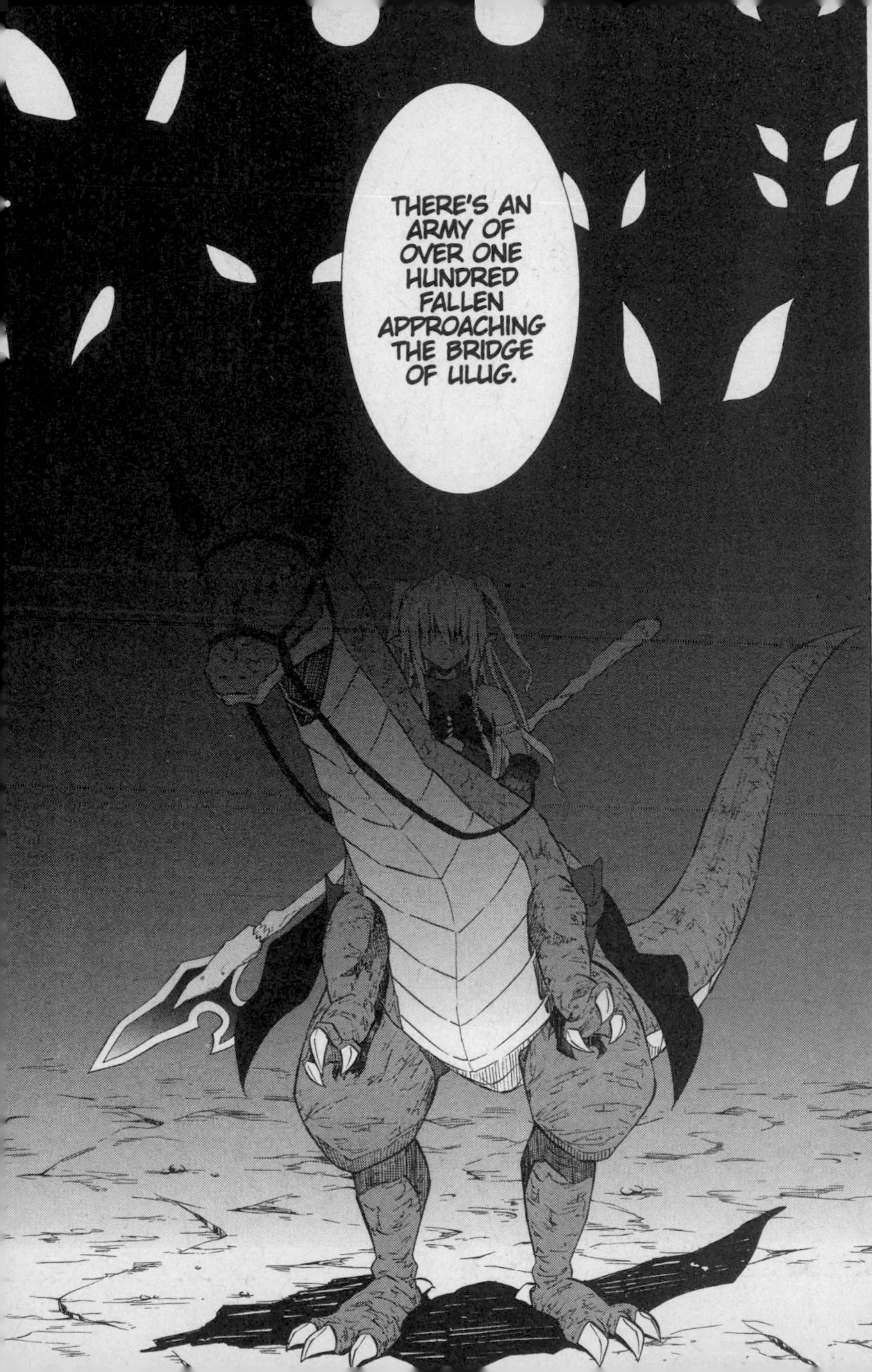
THERE'S AN ARMY OF OVER ONE HUNDRED FALLEN APPROACHING THE BRIDGE OF ULUG.

HOW NOT
TO SUMMON A
DEMON LORD

to be continued...

SPECIAL THANKS FOR VOLUME 2

YUKIYA MURASAKI

TAKAHIRO TSURUSAKI

ASSISTANTS:

YOSHITSUGU OHARA
TAKUYA NISHIDA
DAIKI HARAGUCHI
YUU TAKIGAWA
AKARI MATSUURA
CHITOSE SAKURA
NAGISA

THANK YOU FOR READING!

IT'S A TRAP?

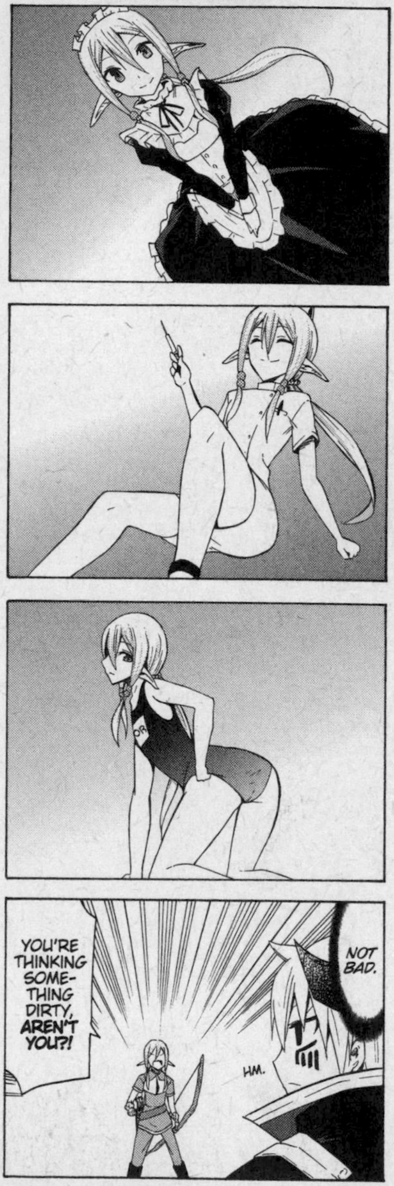
NOT BAD.
YOU'RE THINKING SOME-THING DIRTY, AREN'T YOU?!
HM.

THE MAID SAW IT

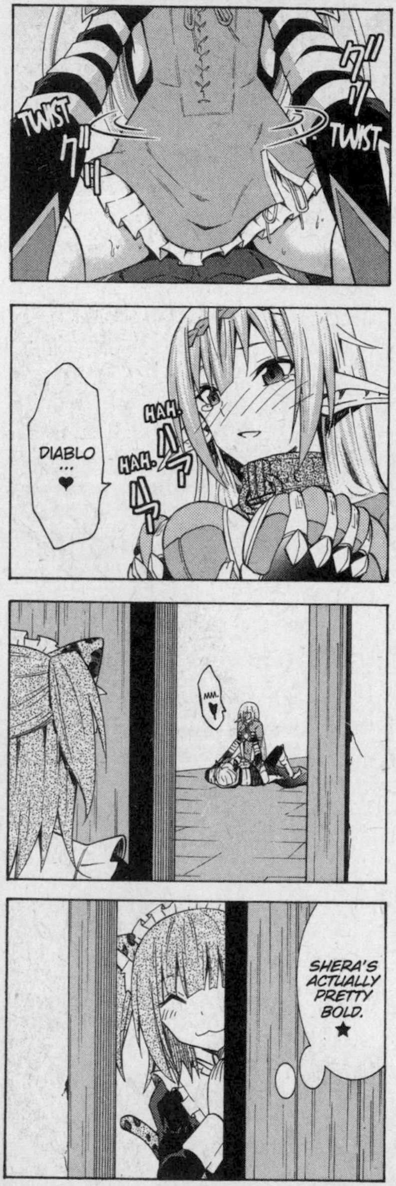
グッ
TWIST
TWIST
グッ
HAH. ハァ
HAH. ハァ
DIABLO... ♥
MM. ♥
SHERA'S ACTUALLY PRETTY BOLD. ★

A SECRET

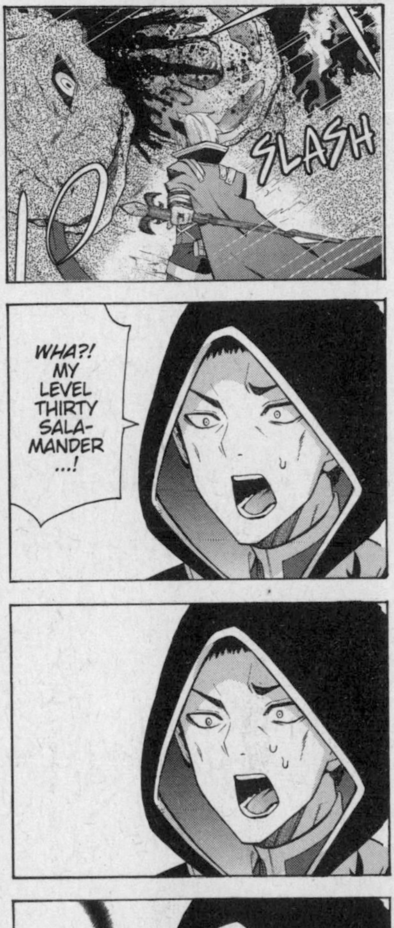
SLASH
WHA?! MY LEVEL THIRTY SALA-MANDER ...!
OH CRAP... I PEED A LITTLE...

THE DAILY TRAINING ROUTINE

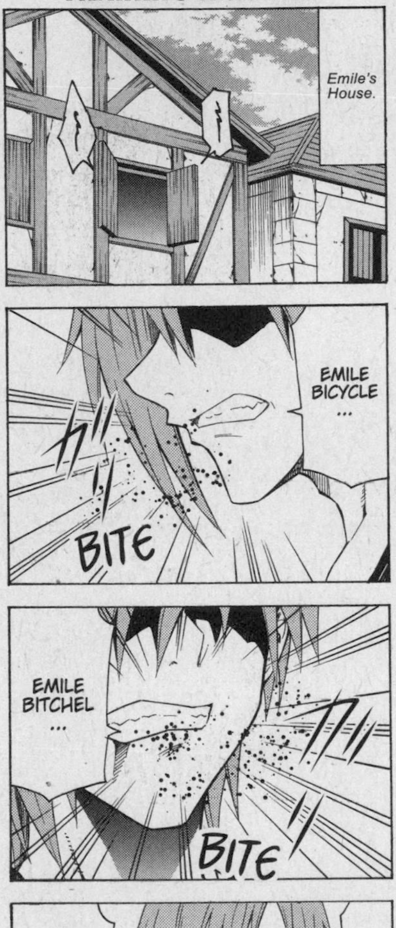
Emile's House.
EMILE BICYCLE ...
BITE
EMILE BITCHEL ...
BITE
NGH ...
FOR THE SAKE OF ALL WOMEN, I CAN'T LOSE HERE!

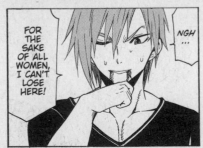

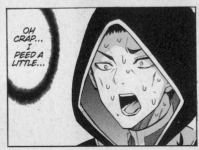

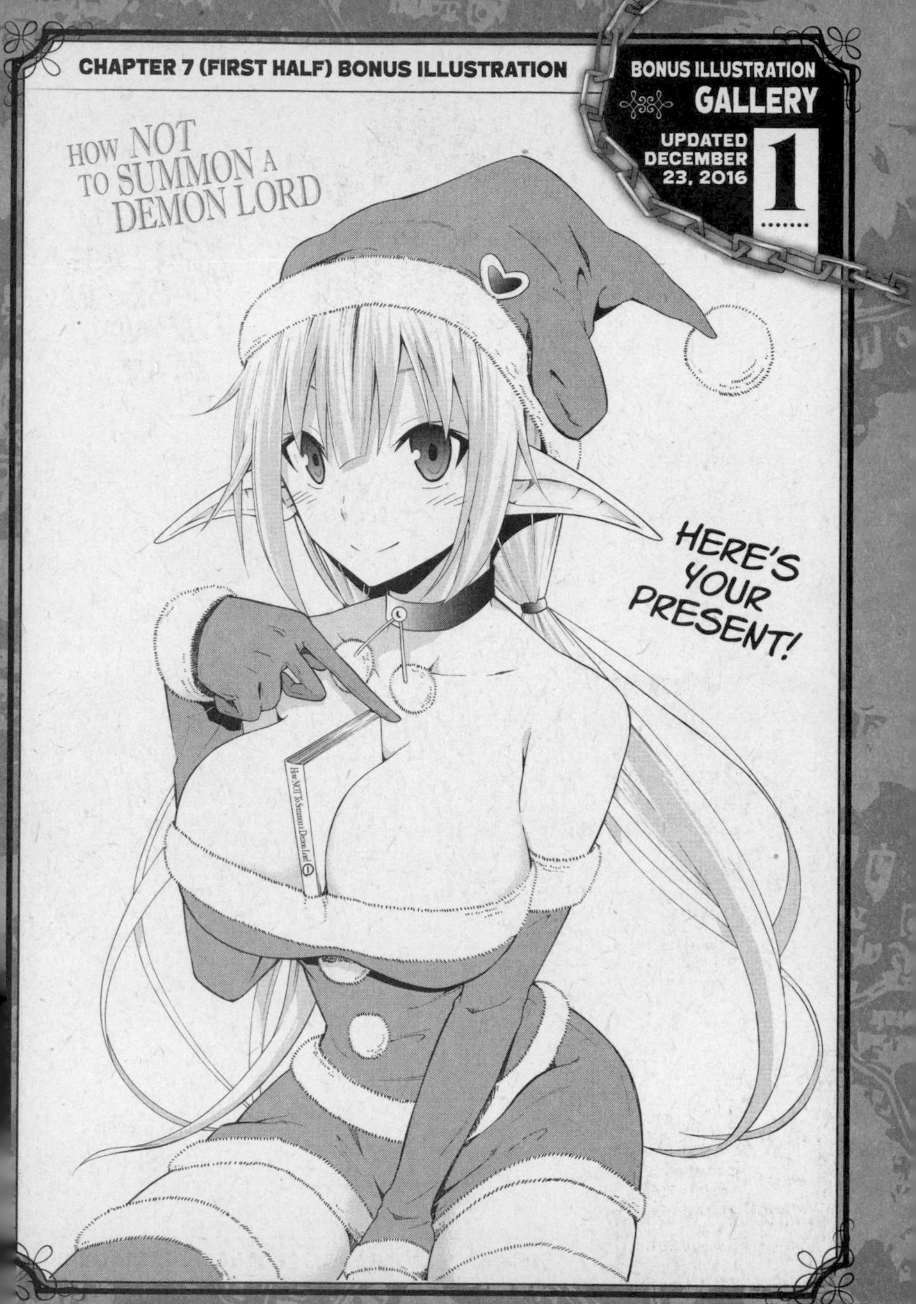
CHAPTER 7 (FIRST HALF) BONUS ILLUSTRATION
BONUS ILLUSTRATION GALLERY
UPDATED DECEMBER 23, 2016
1
HOW NOT TO SUMMON A DEMON LORD
HERE'S YOUR PRESENT!

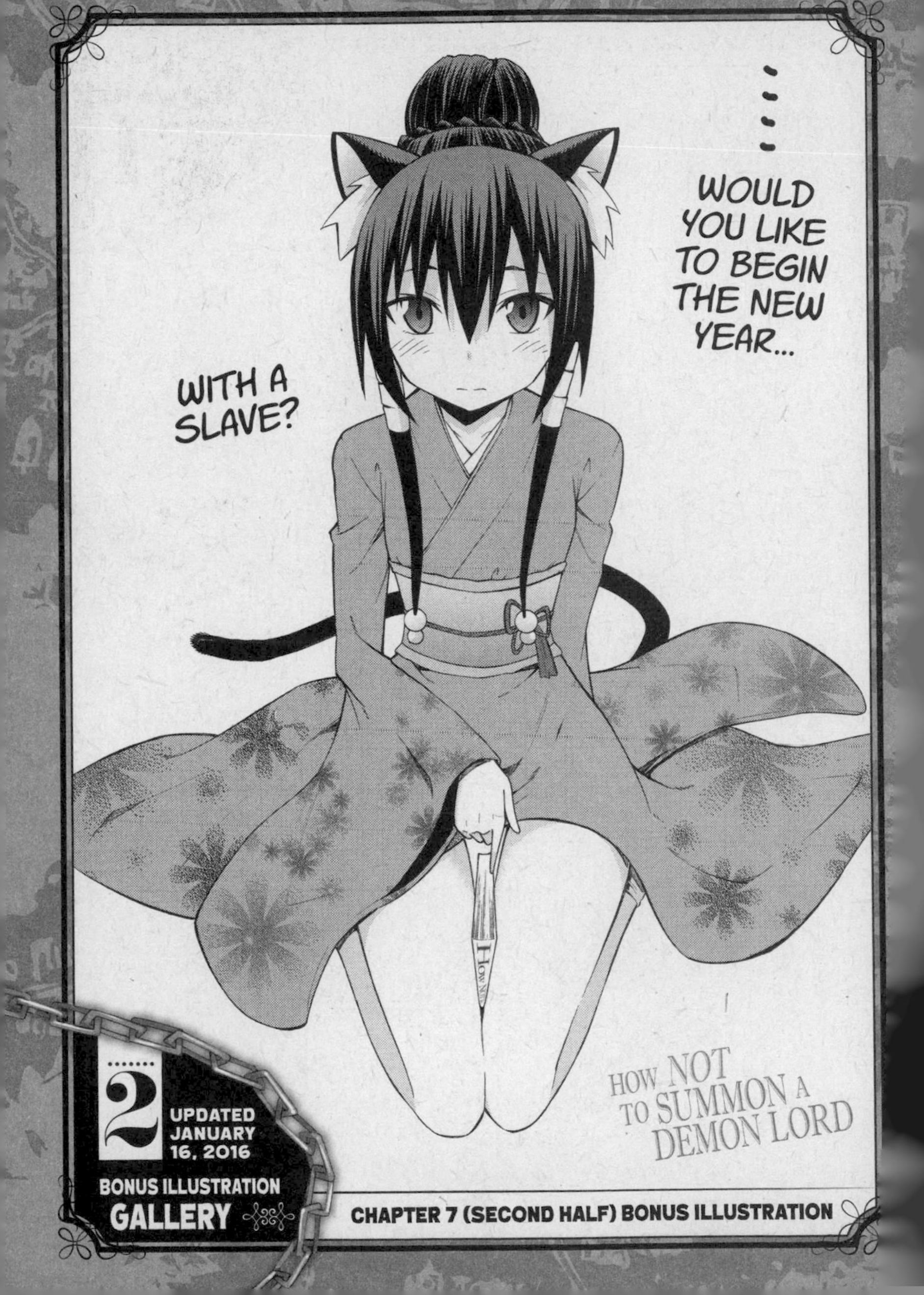
...
WOULD YOU LIKE TO BEGIN THE NEW YEAR...
WITH A SLAVE?
HOW NOT TO SUMMON A DEMON LORD
2
UPDATED JANUARY 16, 2016
BONUS ILLUSTRATION GALLERY
CHAPTER 7 (SECOND HALF) BONUS ILLUSTRATION

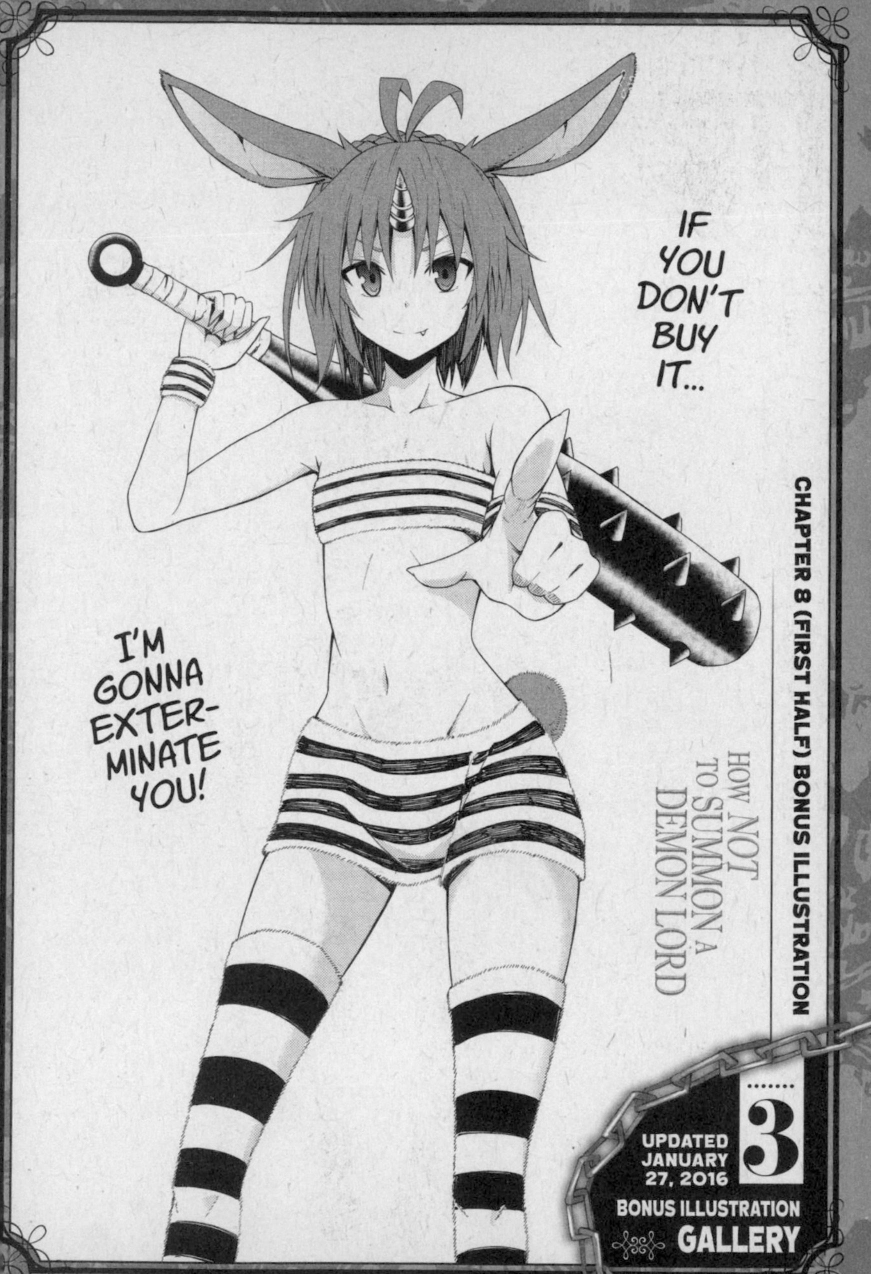

IF YOU DON'T BUY IT...
I'M GONNA EXTER-MINATE YOU!
CHAPTER 8 (FIRST HALF) BONUS ILLUSTRATION
HOW NOT TO SUMMON A DEMON LORD
3
UPDATED JANUARY 27, 2016
BONUS ILLUSTRATION GALLERY

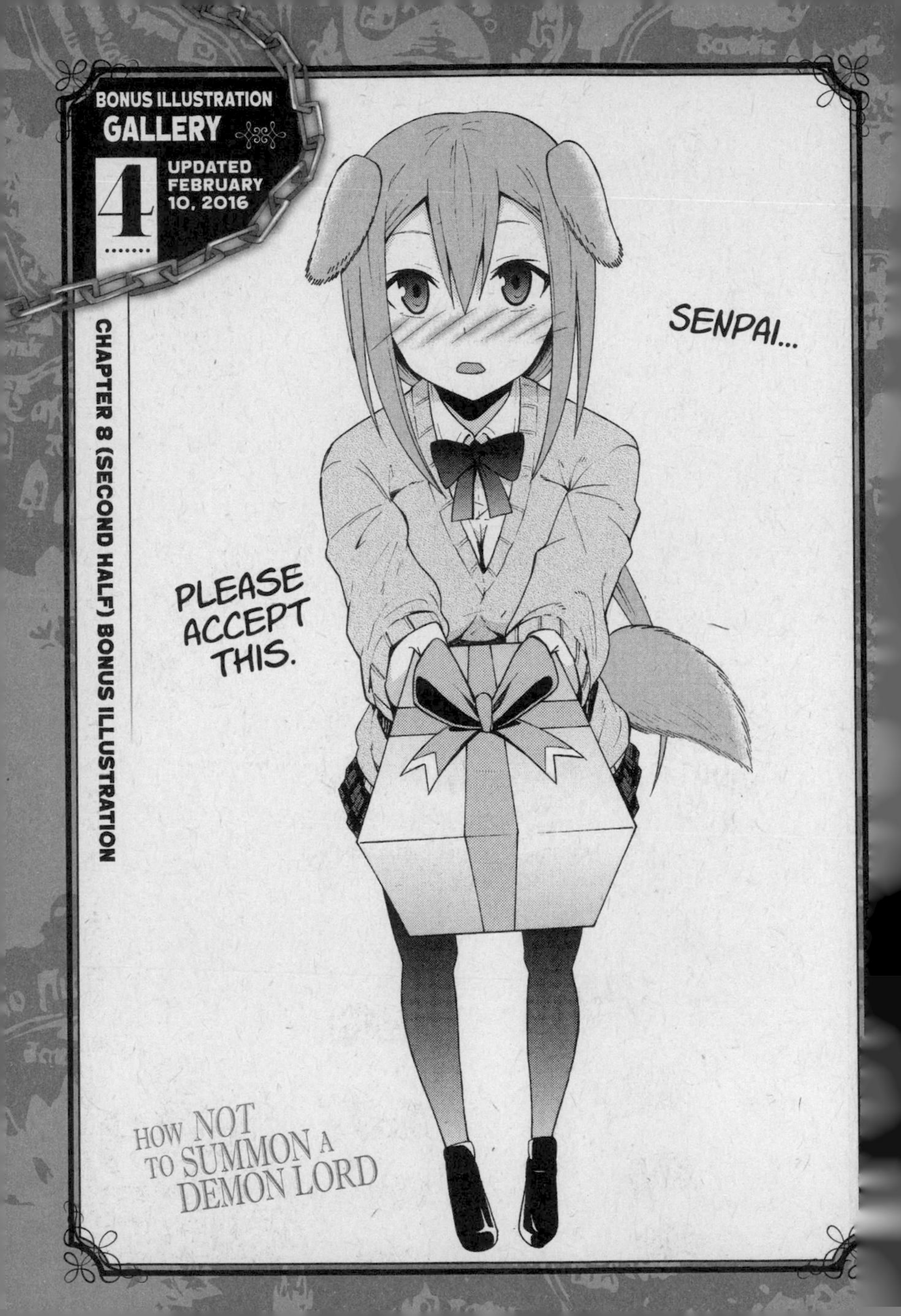
BONUS ILLUSTRATION
GALLERY
4
UPDATED FEBRUARY 10, 2016
CHAPTER 8 (SECOND HALF) BONUS ILLUSTRATION
SENPAI...
PLEASE ACCEPT THIS.
HOW NOT TO SUMMON A DEMON LORD

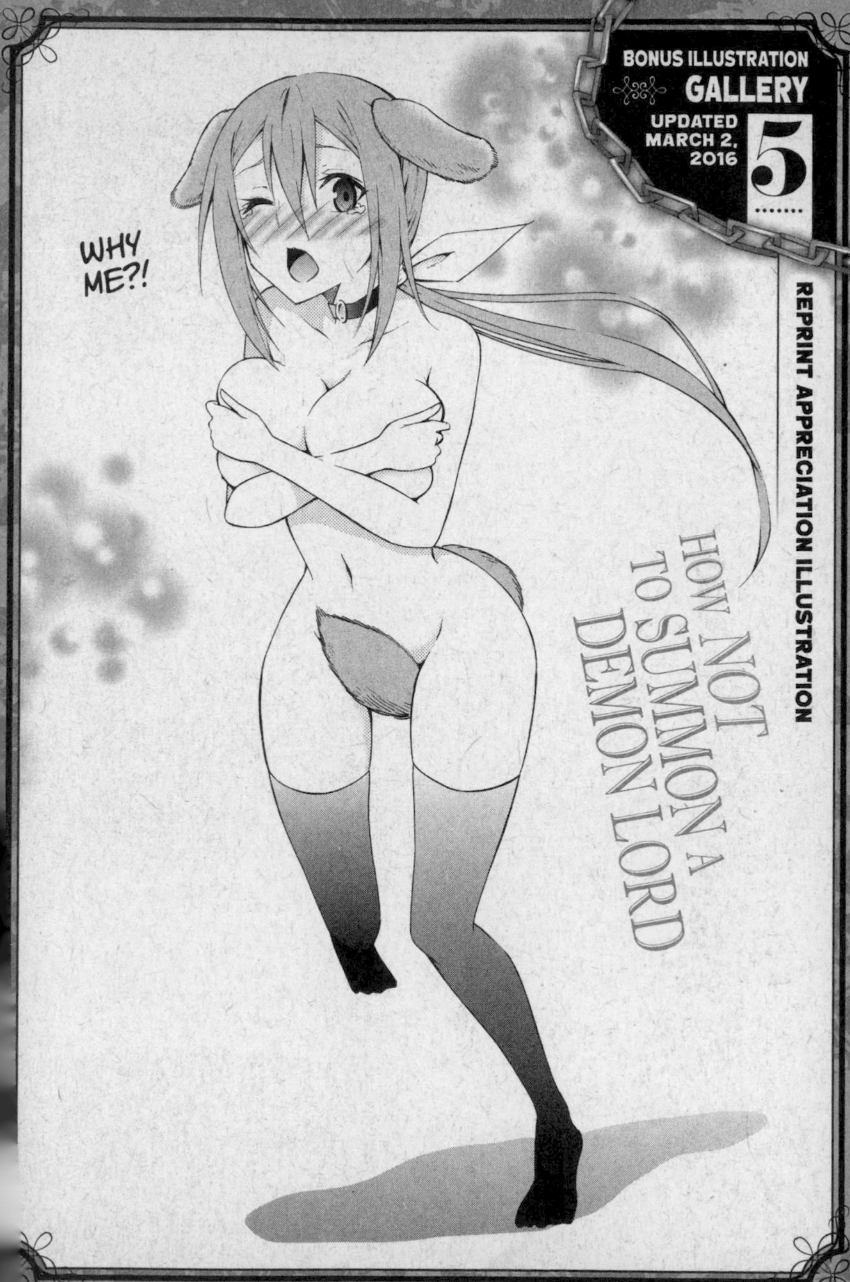
BONUS ILLUSTRATION GALLERY
UPDATED MARCH 2, 2016
5
REPRINT APPRECIATION ILLUSTRATION
HOW NOT TO SUMMON A DEMON LORD
WHY ME?!

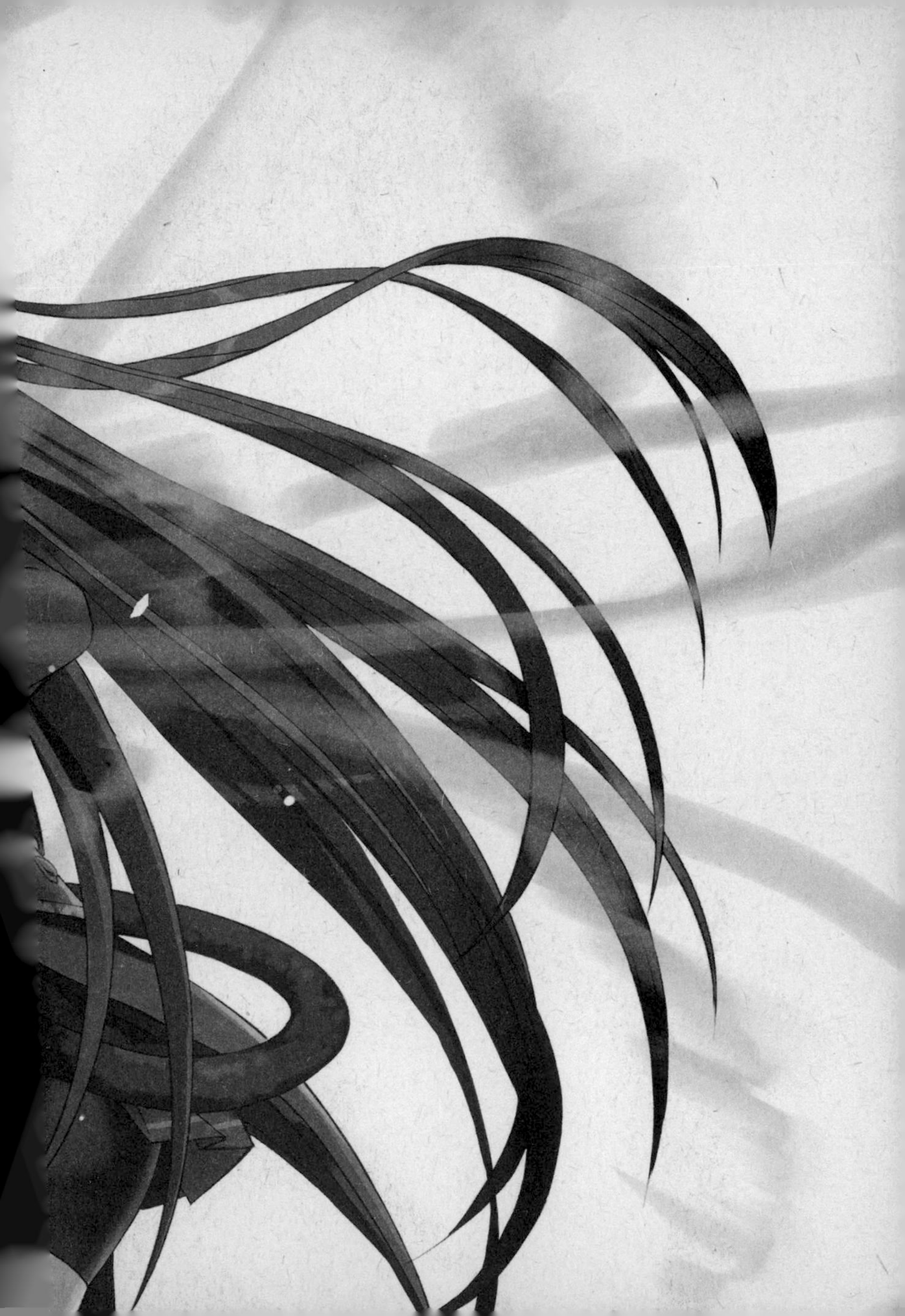

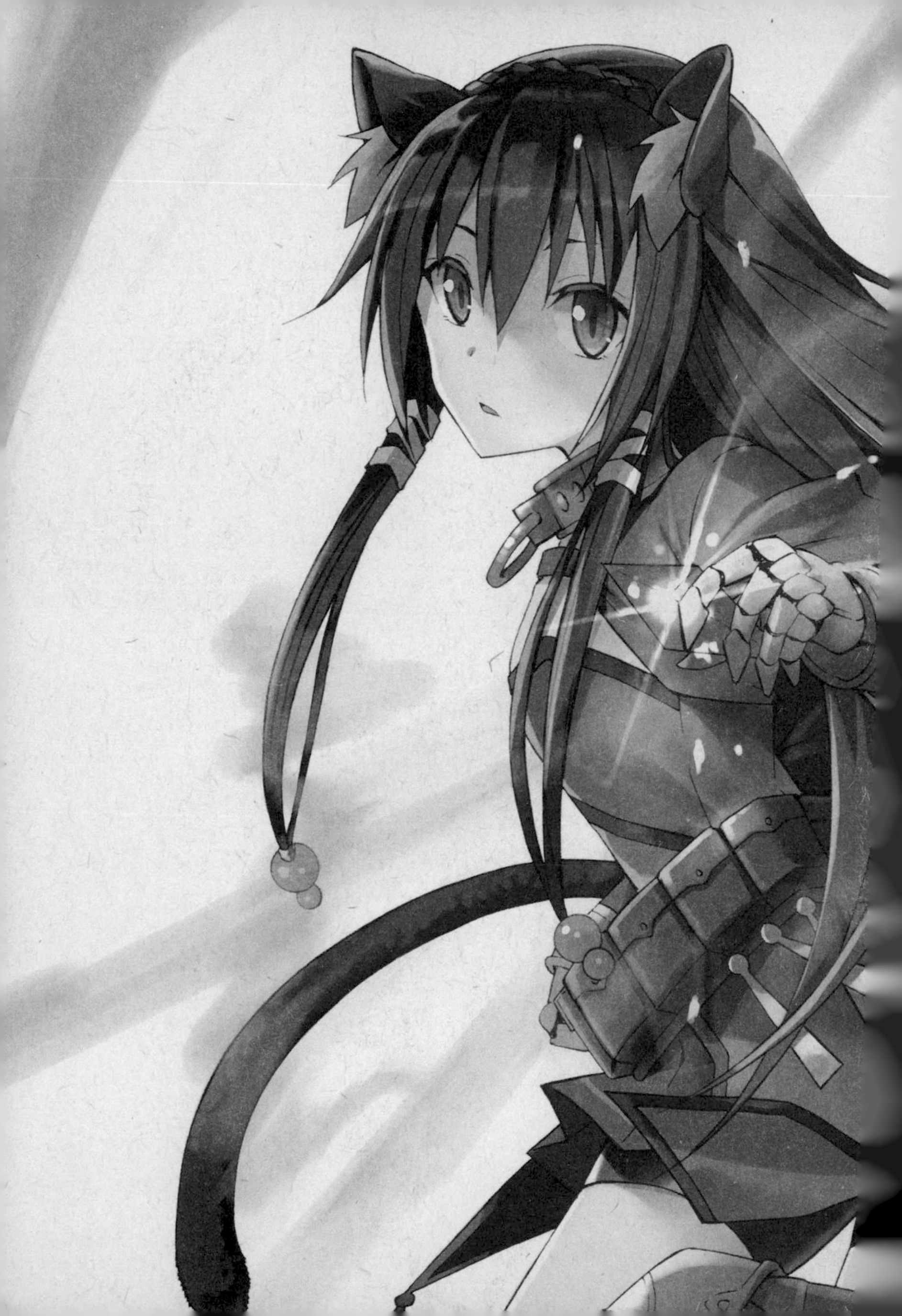